C+H

Brougham

THE GRAND CAMOUFLAGE

The Grand
CAMOUFLAGE

*The Spanish Civil War
and Revolution, 1936—39*

by

BURNETT BOLLOTEN

INTRODUCTION BY H. R. TREVOR-ROPER

FREDERICK A. PRAEGER, *Publishers*
New York • Washington • London

FREDERICK A. PRAEGER, *Publishers*
111 Fourth Avenue, New York, N.Y. 10003, U.S.A.
77-79 Charlotte Street, London W.1, England

Published in the United States of America in 1961
by Frederick A. Praeger, Inc., Publishers

Second printing, 1968

© 1961 by Burnett Bolloten
Introduction © 1968 by Frederick A. Praeger, Inc.

Library of Congress Catalog Card Number: 67-29697

Printed in the United States of America

TO GLADYS
WHOSE UNREMITTING LABOURS
AND SELF-SACRIFICE MADE
THIS BOOK POSSIBLE

Contents

Contents

PART IV

FROM THE REVOLUTIONARY MILITIA TO A REGULAR ARMY

PART V

THE COMMUNIST TRIUMPH

Photographs of the principal persons mentioned in the text appear, in alphabetical order, between pages 162 and 163. Some have been reproduced from newspapers, when these were the only available source.

Foreword

THIS volume is the product of many years of incessant and exhaustive research. To those persons who expected an earlier completion I should like to offer a few words of explanation. More than twenty years ago I set to work to reconstruct from limited materials and a limited knowledge of the subject, acquired as a United Press correspondent in Spain, some of the principal political events of the Spanish Civil War and Revolution; but no sooner had I begun than I realized that the information at my disposal was not in keeping with the complexity and magnitude of the subject, so I undertook the work of investigation on a scale commensurate with the need. From that time on more than one hundred thousand newspapers and periodicals, approximately two thousand five hundred books and pamphlets, and hundreds of unpublished documents were consulted. This massive documentation was not available in any one institution or in any one country, but had to be secured, sometimes under difficult circumstances, from a dozen different countries: from Spain, Great Britain, France, Germany, Italy, the United States, and Mexico, as well as from half a dozen other Latin American republics, where thousands of Spaniards took refuge after the Civil War. In the course of many years of unremitting research and inquiry considerably more than twenty thousand letters were written and received, and a very large number of interviews were obtained from persons who had played a role in the Civil War and Revolution. Often enough many years went by before a particular publication could be located or a particular fact could be verified to my satisfaction.

I therefore feel that I am entitled to the indulgence of those friends and acquaintances who looked forward year after year, seemingly in vain, to the publication of this volume. I can hardly be criticized for not being able to estimate how long it would take to complete; for there was no gauge by which I could measure the length of time required to collect the necessary materials, comb and re-comb sources of information for fresh evidence in a thousand different places, read and re-read, digest and assimilate, sift and combine this vast store of materials.

Only an infinitesimal portion of the documentation amassed since I first started collecting materials at the outbreak of the Spanish Civil War could be pressed into the compass of a readable volume, and the same is true of the testimony furnished by individuals with whom I was in personal or written communication for many years. But this does not imply that their information did not serve a most useful purpose, and I should like them to know that it broadened and deepened my knowledge and made it possible for me to check the reliability of materials actually incorporated.

In preparing this volume I have allowed myself to be guided solely by a desire to reveal the truth. I have endeavoured by the most diligent research, by the most conscientious selection of materials, and, what was still more exacting, by a rigorous control of my own emotions and convictions, to maintain the highest possible standards of scrupulosity and objectivity, and regret that in so doing I have had to ignore the political susceptibilities of friends and acquaintances who provided me so generously with personal testimony and documentary material. Had I acted otherwise, I should have been guilty of conduct unworthy of an historian; for, in the words of Cervantes, historians should be "exact, truthful, and impartial, and should not allow themselves either through self-interest, fear, rancour, or sympathy to deviate from the path of truth."

Because of the highly controversial nature of the subject dealt with in this volume, because memories are short, and because there is a tendency to falsify and distort even the most elementary fact connected with the Spanish Civil War and Revolution, I have been forced to substantiate almost every important point in my exposition. Hence the footnotes. The reader, of course, is not compelled to go through them all, but were he to ignore them entirely he would miss much valuable and fascinating material, which for stylistic reasons could not be embodied in the text.

And now I should like to express my gratitude to all those persons, institutions, publishers, and journals listed alphabetically on pp. 337-9, which have greatly assisted or at least facilitated the preparation of this volume. Considerations of space do not permit a detailed account of the manner in which each made a contribution, such as furnishing me with testimony, searching for or collecting, giving, loaning, or microfilming materials, helping me to make valuable contacts, authorizing me (when permission was necessary) to quote from publications, giving me the benefit of their knowledge and experience, and rendering many other services for which I am sincerely grateful. *None of them, however, bears the slightest responsibility for any conclusions expressed or implied in this volume.*

But more than to anyone else I owe special gratitude to my former wife, Gladys Bolloten. Her devoted assistance, encouragement, sympathy, enthusiasm, good judgment, suggestions, and hard work for nearly fifteen years helped to make this book what it is.

BURNETT BOLLOTEN

Santa Clara, California, 1960

Introduction to the Second Printing

by H. R. Trevor-Roper

MR. Burnett Bolloten's book, *The Grand Camouflage*, is, I believe, one of the few permanently valuable works on the Spanish Civil War. It deals with a limited aspect of that war, over a limited period. But it is a crucial aspect, and a crucial period; and by concentrating on it a wide and meticulous research, Mr. Bolloten has shed new light on the whole history of the war. In order to see what he has done, it is necessary to look at his work in its context: that is, in its relation not only to the external facts, but also to the myths which took such deep root at the time and which still condition public attitudes toward Spain.

For the Spanish Civil War of 1936–39 was, at the time, far more than a local or even a political struggle. It engaged the interests and passions of the world—and engaged them so fiercely that its real character was often totally disguised. Whatever the immediate origins of the war, which were anyway rarely understood or even considered outside Spain, it soon became an international problem and an ideological issue, like the war in Vietnam today, and its international, ideological character soon buried its domestic significance as a purely Spanish struggle, and prevented its proper understanding. Liberal men outside Spain, preoccupied by the threat of fascism, saw the Civil War as a local dress rehearsal for the coming international struggle, the first skirmish in the imminent Armageddon between dictatorship and democracy. They saw General Franco as a fascist leader, the puppet of Hitler and Mussolini, the destroyer of Spanish democracy; and they saw the Spanish Republic, which he was seeking to overthrow, as the legitimate, liberal, democratic government of Spain, the natural ally of "the West" in its struggle against the new tyranny of fascism. This seemed reasonable enough. The legitimacy of the Republic could hardly be denied; General Franco's "crusade" was unquestionably a rebellion. If the liberalism of the Republic could be questioned, that was only

I

(we all said) because it was temporarily suspended. It was disciplined by the overriding necessities of war.

And these necessities, it had to be admitted, were aggravated by the hypocrisy of "the West." While Hitler and Mussolini supplied Franco with money, arms, and men, "the West" stood aside. It preached non-intervention, and it did not intervene. But, meanwhile, the "Non-intervention Committee" in London did nothing to prevent massive intervention by Germany and Italy. Thus the legitimate Spanish government was in danger of destruction. While its natural allies held the ring and declined to help it, its domestic enemies drew on the support of the European enemies of freedom. Hitler's battleship shelled Almería and his Stukas bombed Guérnica. Mussolini's submarines sank the supply ships of the Republic and his "volunteers" were routed at Guadalajara. What wonder if, in such circumstances, the imperiled government should accept the help of Communist Russia—the only power that was willing to face reality and defy the hypocrisy of "non-intervention"? Besides, at that time, Russia was the friend of the West. Within Russia, those might be the years of terror, of Stalin's great purges. Abroad, they were the years of the Popular Front against fascism. Even British conservatives welcomed the support of "Communists" in Spain—as they would in Europe after 1941. The International Brigades, organized by Russia, were seen by many as the first model of a grand coalition against fascism. As an English writer said at the time, "a handful of Communists" might prove to be the last defenders of the British Empire.

I confess that at that time, being of that generation, I myself accepted this view. It was a view based not necessarily on ideology, but on a general outlook on European politics. As such it may conceivably have been right, or at least justified; for who could have foreseen, and dared to venture all upon the narrow margins of General Franco's decisions in the coming war? But, intellectually, as an interpretation, it suffered from one great defect. Proceeding from general premises— from ideological loyalties or international considerations—it took little notice of the purely Spanish facts. The foreign champions of Largo Caballero and Negrín, like the foreign champions of Franco, saw Spain from afar, as the distant theater of ideological war. They failed to see it from within, as the laboratory of civil war. Too often they imported their judgments, already half-formed, from outside.

To me, the great illumination came when I read that wonderful work, Gerald Brenan's *The Spanish Labyrinth,* first published in 1943. Here, for the first time, the Spanish Civil War was placed in its own context: not horizontally, against the background of contemporary Europe—where Spain has seldom fitted—but, as it were, vertically, against the background of Spanish history. After reading that great work, it was impossible to see General Franco merely as a Spanish agent of "international fascism," or the Republic as the Spanish version of Western liberal democracy. Whatever their external relations and dependencies, whatever temporary colors they might find it convenient to borrow from Europe, both now appeared as authentic Spanish forces, nourished out of the complex Spanish past, and inexplicable if they were detached from it. Mr. Brenan has since explained to me why he wrote that book. Living in Spain, he saw the English liberal and radical intelligentsia coming to Spain, inspired by generous European traditions, to offer their support, military or literary, to the beleaguered Republic; and he was amazed, even indignant, at their utter ignorance of the true native character of the struggle. That the supporters of the Right should be wrong, he conceded, was natural. That was to be expected. But the illusions of the Left, the men of liberal reason, his natural allies, exasperated him; and in his exasperation, he set out to explain the background to the struggle. Explaining, he transformed it so that—to those who have read this book or studied Spanish history— it could never seem the same.

The Spanish Civil War, then, must be seen as a Spanish war, rising out of Spanish conditions; and Spanish conditions are not, and never have been, the same as European conditions. Whoever wishes to study that war objectively must free his mind of cis-Pyrenean generalizations. In doing so, he may find himself a heretic among the rival conformities of his native world, but he will see more clearly than those—like Hitler, Mussolini, and Stalin—who sought to impose on that obstinate peninsula an intelligible pattern from outside.

Such a heretic is Mr. Bolloten. He too has seen the Spanish Civil War in its Spanish context. A journalist working for the United Press, he happened to be on vacation in Barcelona in the summer of 1936, and on the outbreak of the Civil War he was sent, first to the Aragon front, then to Valencia, whither the government of Largo Caballero moved in November. While in Spain he began to collect material. At first he contemplated a book on a specific subject: the

vindication of Colonel José Villalba, who was made the scapegoat for
the Republican loss of Málaga in February, 1937. Afterwards he
widened his aim. He proposed to himself a more general history of
the Civil War. He remained in Spain for two years, reporting and
collecting. Then, in 1938, he emigrated to Mexico and began the long
work of study, interpretation, and re-interpretation that makes the
difference between journalism and history.

The study was formidable. In his apartment in Mexico City Mr.
Bolloten amassed more than 100,000 periodicals, 2,500 books and
pamphlets, and hundreds of unpublished documents. He questioned
the exiled Republican politicians who had fled, after their defeat, to
this citadel of the Spanish-speaking Left. After 1945, he returned to
Europe to supplement his material by visits to Spanish and other
libraries, and returned with 120,000 microfilm exposures to continue
his task of recollecting emotion in tranquillity. He planned, at this
time, to write a detailed history, in three volumes, of the politics of
the Spanish Republic at war.

There is no need to emphasize the depth and extent of Mr. Bolloten's study. It is clear from his book, and even his sharpest critics
have acknowledged it. More interesting to us is the re-interpretation
which it forced upon him. When he left Spain he was, he says, "profoundly influenced by official propaganda, from which only time and
diligent research could free me." He took his time and was diligent in
research; and as he studied, he found himself, as every good historian
does—it is one of the pleasurable excitements of his work—gradually
modifying the views originally based on personal involvement.

Time and research had other effects, too. Financial pressure—he was
obliged to sell his unique collection of documents to American libraries
and universities in order to continue his work—was accompanied by
failure of health. By 1950, although his material was complete, he
decided to abandon, or it least to suspend, his more ambitious projects
and to content himself with the publication of one volume out of
three, covering one year out of the three years of civil war. This one
volume, however, was to be self-contained, held together by the unity
of its theme and its own internal logic. It was to cover the period from
the outbreak of civil war in July, 1936, to the fall of Francisco Largo
Caballero in May, 1937. In a true and detailed history of this one year,
he would show the decisive phase in the transformation of the Republi-

can government from a true Popular Front to a liberal façade for the Russian-controlled faction of the Spanish Communist Party.

The fact of this change has, of course, been stated before. Particular aspects of it, or details in it, have been described. But the descriptions have often been confused with propaganda, or have been personal and impressionistic, and the details have been divorced from general explanation. By his massive documentation, which no critical reader will regard as otiose, Mr. Bolloten has established the course of events in detail, and clearly. In so doing he has shocked the venerable orthodoxy of the European Left without giving—if he is properly read—any comfort to the Spanish Right. His service is not to any political party but to history.

For what Mr. Bolloten shows is, first of all, the discontinuity between the Republic at peace and the Republic at war. At the time it was customary to believe that the Republican government which resisted Franco and his foreign allies was still the same government which the other powers had recognized: a liberal democracy of the Popular Front, which had been returned to power in the valid elections of February, 1936. In fact, Mr. Bolloten shows, this was hardly so. Convenient though it was to preserve the outward appearance of such continuity, the Popular Front, and with it liberal democracy in Spain, had effectively collapsed at the first attack by the armed forces of the Right. Militarily it might take Franco three years to destroy his enemies, but politically he destroyed them at once. The liberal regime as such had never been strong. It had always been at the mercy of organized parties. In July, 1936, it simply distintegrated, and the war which followed was not, strictly speaking, a war between Franco and the liberal Republic, but a war between Franco and the successors of that Republic, who continued to use its forms. This was a necessity to them, since only thus could they claim the benefits of legitimacy and legality—benefits of which, it must be added, the Non-Intervention Committee in London nevertheless largely deprived them.

Once this fact is admitted, we have to ask a further question. Who were the successors of the Republic? As the Spanish state dissolved in dust and ashes, revolutionary committees everywhere seized and exercised local and often arbitrary power. These committees were dominated either by left-wing Socialists or by Anarchists; and in the moment of their power, and the areas of their rule, they carried out a

long-envisaged revolution, so thoroughgoing that they believed it
would be final. It was not merely a *jacquerie,* a rising of the poor
against the rich. It was a social revolution in depth. Freed at last from
all the coercive powers of the state—for army, civil guards, and police
had deserted the Republic and gone over to the rebels—the Anarchist
committees set out to realize the old utopian dream of messianic, puri-
tan, anticlerical, rural Spain. They collectivized factories and services,
small businesses and agriculture. They set up Libertarian communes.
They abolished money and religion. They declared that the millennium
had come. To it they would win universal adherence, not by force but
by persuasion of the Elect. Nevertheless, force was useful too. As Mr.
Bolloten says, there was no central dictatorship, but there was "in
countless localities . . . a multiplicity of parochial dictatorships . . . in
naked form."

   The Anarchist revolution of 1936 has been described before, but
seldom, I think, as vividly as by Mr. Bolloten. His description of it,
amply documented from direct, local sources, is one of the most fascinating parts of his book. But it is, in effect, only the introduction. For
that revolution, while it effectively dissolved the old Republic, contributed nothing to the immediate task of resisting the rebellion of
Franco. The Anarchist revolution was not, in itself, a force of resistance.
It had come into being not in order to fight, but for its own sake. It
had exploited the weakness of government in order to set up a new
form of society. Left to itself, between the hostility of other classes and
the arms of the nationalists, it would probably have collapsed. If Franco
were to be resisted—and resistance was demanded not only by all
supporters of the now shattered Popular Front but by all those foreign-
ers who feared the conquest of Spain for international fascism—some
other force must emerge which could either reanimate the Republic
or, behind its continuing legal forms, create a new political force, capable of fighting, even of victory.

   That force proved to be the Communist Party. The Spanish Communist Party was negligible in strength in 1936. Spain has never
accepted Communism, or indeed fascism, or any ideology that has
taken firm root in Europe. The European ideas which it has embraced
have been the rejected heresies of Europe—or, if orthodoxies, orthodoxies radically transformed by their passage over the Pyrenees. Not
Marx but Bakunin is the prophet of Spanish radicalism. And so, in

1936, while the Anarchists were able to make a revolution, the Spanish Communists were too weak even to think of conspiracy. At most they had 40,000 members, represented by 16 deputies in the Cortes. Nevertheless, within a year, the Communist Party was the effective master of the Republican government. By the end of the war, General Franco was really fighting not against the Popular Front but against a Communist dictatorship.

How did the Communists, from so slender a basis, achieve this rapid triumph? To this question Mr. Bolloten offers a detailed answer. He shows how the Russian government, conscious of its own weakness in international affairs and of the weakness of the Communist Party in Spain, set itself a double task. First, it must outwardly defend the shattered Spanish Republic as a legal, democratic government. This was a real necessity. Stalin's immediate fear was of Germany, and the defeat of fascism in Spain was more important to him than the victory of Communism. To have supported the Spanish Communist Party openly would have been suicidal; so feeble a party was not in itself worth supporting, and open support of such a faction would destroy both the Popular Front in France and the hope of concerted opposition to Germany in Europe, including Spain. Therefore the Spanish Communist Party, on orders from Moscow, denied its Marxist doctrines. To the astonishment of doctrinal purists it presented itself as the party of conservatism on the Republican side, the champion of the bourgeoisie and the small landlords whom the Anarchists had affronted by their expropriations. By these means it did not, indeed, win Britain and France from their policy of non-intervention, but it did vastly increase its own following in the country. It became the political leader of the peasant farmers and the urban middle class, and by these additions its membership jumped in a few months to a quarter of a million.

But while the Communist Party thus presented itself as a party of bourgeois conservatism in the country, it did not forget its ultimate aims at the center of politics. Mr. Bolloten describes, in fascinating detail, the political in-fighting whereby the Spanish Communists, exploiting their position as the channel for Russian aid, set out, "under cover of a democratic superstructure," to capture power in the state. He shows how they turned the Republican police into "a mere arm of the Soviet police," how they outmaneuvered the Anarchists, settled accounts with the most dangerous of their rivals, whether Trotskyist or Anarchist, captured control of the army, and finally closed in on the center of power. The removal of Largo Caballero as Prime Minister, and his replacement by Negrín, was a crucial stage in the process whereby the Republic became the political instrument of Stalin. It is a process which has since become classical. The conservative beginnings have been shown in Russian dealings with wartime resistance movements in Nazi-dominated Europe and "anticolonial" resistance movements since. The political takeover is familiar from the postwar history of Eastern Europe.

Such is Mr. Bolloten's story. He has called it *The Grand Camouflage.* The title refers to the contrast between the public professions of the Russian government—its overt defense, not of Communism but of the "bourgeois" liberal Republic—and its secret purpose: the conversion of the Anarchist revolution of 1936 into a Communist government of Spain. How deliberate this purpose was from the beginning may perhaps be questioned. Certainly the Spanish Republic—even a "Western," liberal, "bourgeois" republic—was of more value to Russia in 1936 than a "fascist" dictatorship, patronized and perhaps controlled by Nazi Germany. It is possible that the process which Mr. Bolloten describes owes more to the inner momentum of events than to a systematic plan. But however originated, the double policy of public conservatism and secret communization set a precedent which has been applied consistently ever since.

I have described Mr. Bolloten as a heretic. He is a heretic because his work supports the orthodoxy neither of the Left nor of the Right, neither of the Spanish Republicans and their supporters nor of General Franco and his supporters. The former do not like to be told that the Republic had already collapsed by July, 1936, and that the government which appeared to be a liberal regime thereafter was in fact, within a year, the façade of a Stalinist organization. The latter, though they may welcome some of his conclusions, can hardly relish the evidence by which they are reached, for Mr. Bolloten entirely disposes of the official Spanish doctrine of the Communist threat in 1936 and the "national crusade" against it. Perhaps it is for these reasons that his book has had, since he completed it, so curious a history.

He completed it in 1952, but it was not published till 1961. This was not, as a jaundiced Republican critic has suggested, because Mr.

Bolloten, in those years, was changing his political allegiance. It was, quite simply, because no publisher would accept it. Over eight years it was offered to numerous American publishers, including five university presses. All turned it down. When it finally appeared in England and in the United States in 1961, it fell almost unnoticed from the press. Why it was thus disliked by publishers, or publishers' readers, and disdained by critics is to me a mystery. Perhaps they are right about its merits and I am wrong; but I am glad to find that, if so, I am wrong in the best company. Or can it be that there is a more subtle reason: that the Anglo-American literary establishment is still stuck in the fashionable postures of the 1930's, which Mr. Bolloten implicitly undermines? I confess that I cannot altogether exclude this possibility, at least as a hypothesis. Such things have happened before. I recall that another heretic, George Orwell, encountered similar difficulties when he sought, in 1945, to reopen a question which the voice of liberal orthodoxy had declared closed.* And time has vindicated him.

Even more curious has been the fate of Mr. Bolloten's book in General Franco's Spain. Scarcely had *The Grand Camouflage* been published in England when a Spanish publisher in Barcelona, without consulting the author, put out a Spanish translation, prefaced by a laudatory introduction by Sr. Manuel Fraga Iribarne, then director of the Institute of Political Studies at Madrid, and soon to be General Franco's Minister of Information. Mr. Bolloten at once repudiated this Spanish version. He pointed out that it was unscholarly in method (Spanish texts having been retranslated from the English), that serious omissions had been made in the interest of official propaganda, and that Sr. Fraga Iribarne's introduction necessarily damaged the impartiality of the book.† We can therefore ignore it. But the fact remains that the supporters of General Franco have found comfort in this book, although it undermines their mythology, just as his adversaries have disliked it,

---

* George Orwell, "The Prevention of Literature" (*Polemic* 2, London, 1946; reprinted in his *Shooting an Elephant and Other Essays,* [London: Secker & Warburg; New York: Harcourt Brace, 1950]). See also, for the controversy engendered by this essay, Randall Swingler, "The Right to Free Expression" (annotated by George Orwell), in *Polemic* 5, September–October, 1946.

† Mr. Bolloten's repudiation applies only to the Spanish edition of 1961. While these lines were being written, the Spanish publisher has issued a new translation of the book, in which all of Mr. Bolloten's objections have been met. This new version, *El Gran Engaño* (Barcelona: Caralt, 1967), is authorized by Mr. Bolloten.

although it supports the claims of the Popular Front to have been the legitimate government of Spain.* This, on the face of it, seems paradoxical and requires explanation.

The explanation given by Mr. Bolloten's critics is simple, even naïve. While admitting that the book is "the most pro-Republican book yet to be openly published in Franco's Spain," they conclude that what is welcomed there is not its "meticulous pro-Republican research" but its "pro-Franco conclusion"; and they find, between research and conclusion, so striking a difference that "one might almost doubt whether the two parts are the work of the same man." Indeed, some of them, we are told, have so far rationalized these doubts as to suppose that Mr. Bolloten is dead and that it is his heirs or executors who have attached their "pro-Franco" conclusions to his "pro-Republican research."† This supposition at least, they think, would "save the phenomena"—that is, save the obsolete categories of thoughts in which they are bound.

But why should we save such categories? Nothing so illustrates the obsessive character of the Spanish Civil War, and the fixity of the loyalties which it engendered, as this habit of defining and judging historical work as "pro-Republican" or "pro-Franco." History itself is not "pro-" or "anti-" anyone or anything; these moral or political qualifications merely illustrate the position from which it has sometimes been viewed, and such views are necessarily distorted. The true historian does not dig himself into such positions. He does not use such terms. He studies the facts and leaves those who will to take from his study such comfort or discomfort as they like. If any conclusion is to be drawn from the discomfort of Mr. Bolloten's critics, it is simply this: that history eludes the patterns which they have sought to impose upon it. Between 1936 and 1937, Mr. Bolloten suggests, the objective

---

* To give one instance out of many, Mr. Bolloten refutes the nationalist claim that the Russian government had planned to set up a Communist regime in Spain before the outbreak of the Civil War, and implicitly rejects as forgeries the documents on which this claim was based. Even Mr. Hugh Thomas, whose book *The Spanish Civil War* appeared simultaneously with Mr. Bolloten's book in 1961, accepted these documents as genuine—although he has since, as he says, "seen the light" (see *The Spanish Civil War* [Harmondsworth, Middlesex and Baltimore, Md.: Penguin Books, 1965], p. 150 n.). In this instance the "pro-Franco" work of Mr. Bolloten is more "Republican" than the "pro-Republican" work of Mr. Thomas.

† See Herbert R. Southworth, *Le mythe de la croisade de Franco* (Paris: Maspero, 1964), pp. 245–52.

situation in Spain changed. If we like, we may express it by saying that Franco's foreign-backed rebellion against the legitimate, elected government of Spain precipitated, both in Spain and within that government, a series of significant changes, and that these changes, aided by external events—the neutrality of Britain and France, the intervention of Russia—ended by creating the situation by which that revolt falsely claimed to have been justified. This change may be disconcerting to those who have adopted rigid loyalties based upon the balance of political virtue at a given moment, but by documenting it Mr. Bolloten has shown that history is not rigid; it moves.

Perhaps, now, the historians will move too. If so, this book may claim to have given them a salutary push. Good books operate slowly; they create the mental climate in which they are appreciated. I am glad that *The Grand Camouflage,* in spite of its initial neglect in the liberal world and its compromising acceptance in Spain, is now being reprinted. Time may modify its thesis but will not, I think, devalue it as a classic in the analytical historiography of the Spanish Civil War.

IMPORTANT

All data used in the preparation of this volume can be found in newspapers, periodicals, books, pamphlets, documents, and clippings held by one or more of the following United States and European libraries unless otherwise stated in the bibliography.[1]

Biblioteca Universitaria de Barcelona, Barcelona.

Bibliothèque Nationale, Paris.

British Museum Newspaper Library, London.

Harvard College Library, Cambridge, Mass.

Hemeroteca Municipal de Madrid, Madrid.

The Hoover Institute and Library on War, Revolution, and Peace, Stanford University, Calif. (See Burnett and Gladys Bolloten Collection on the Spanish Civil War, especially microfilm section, and Vols. 1–10 of *The Grand Camouflage* materials.)

The Library of Congress, Washington, D.C.

The New York Public Library, New York.

University of Michigan Library, Ann Arbor, Mich. (See Labadie Collection.)

The place of publication of all newspapers and periodicals cited in this volume is given in the bibliography. However, to simplify identification, this information is also given in the footnotes in the following instances: (1) When a journal, published by refugees after the Spanish Civil War (April, 1939), has the same title as a newspaper or periodical published in Spain during the Civil War; (2) When two journals, published outside Spain during or after the Civil War, bear the same name.

[1] The precise location of all documents, whether originals or copies, is given in the bibliography.

PART I

THE SPANISH REVOLUTION

I

The Grand Camouflage

ALTHOUGH the outbreak of the Spanish Civil War in July, 1936, was followed by a far-reaching social revolution in the anti-Franco camp—more profound in some respects than the Bolshevik Revolution in its early stages—millions of discerning people outside Spain were kept in ignorance, not only of its depth and range, but even of its existence, by virtue of a policy of duplicity and dissimulation of which there is no parallel in history.

Foremost in practising this deception upon the world, and in misrepresenting in Spain itself the character of the revolution, were the Communists, who, although but an exiguous minority when the Civil War began, used so effectually the manifold opportunities which that very upheaval presented that before the close of the conflict in 1939 they became, behind a democratic frontispiece, the ruling force in the left camp.

The overthrow in May, 1937, of the government of Francisco Largo Caballero, who was the most influential and popular of the left-wing leaders at the outbreak of the Civil War, marked the Communists' greatest triumph in their rise to power. What was the secret of their success? And why did they attempt to screen from the outside world and to misrepresent in Spain itself the revolution that had swept the country? The answer lies within these pages.

2

The Brewing Upheaval

THE fissures that gave rise to the Spanish Civil War in July, 1936, were not of sudden growth. They had been steadily developing over the course of years, albeit at an increasing tempo since the fall of the Monarchy and the proclamation of the Republic in 1931, and more especially since the victory of the Popular Front in the February, 1936, elections.

In the months that lay between the February elections and the Civil War, the Republic had experienced, both in town and country, a series of labour disturbances without precedent in its history, disturbances that were largely a reaction to the policy of the right-wing governments that had ruled Spain from December, 1933. In that period, not only had the laws fixing wages and conditions of employment been revoked, modified, or allowed to lapse,[1] but much of the other work of the Republic had been undone. "The Labour Courts," testifies Salvador de Madariaga, a conservative Republican, "assumed a different political complexion, and their awards were as injurious to the workers as they had previously been to the employers. Simultaneously, the Institute of Agrarian Reform was deprived of funds. Viewed from the standpoint of the countryside and in terms of practical experience, of the bread on the peasant's table, these changes were disastrous. There were many, too many, landowners who had learned nothing and forgotten nothing and who behaved themselves in such an inhuman and outrageous fashion towards their working folk—perhaps out of revenge for the insults and injuries suffered during the period of left rule—that the situation became worse not only in a material but also in a moral sense. The wages of the land workers again fell to a starvation level; the guarantee of employment vanished, and the hope of receiving land disappeared altogether."[2]

[1] See *Le contrat de travail dans la république espagnole*, p. 18.
[2] *España*, p. 513.

". . . Since the advent of the Republic," stated the right-wing Republican paper *El Sol*, "we have been oscillating dangerously between two extremes, especially in the countryside. During the first two years [1931–3] agriculture was burdened with a ridiculous working day, and the wave of idleness and indiscipline through which it passed ended by ruining it. The farm labourers received high wages and worked as little as possible. . . . During the second two years [1933–5] we fell into the other extreme. Within a few months wages declined sharply from ten and twelve pesetas a day to four, three, and even two.[3] Property took revenge on labour, and did not realize that it was piling up fuel for the social bonfire of the near future. At the same time, many landlords who had been forced on government orders to reduce rents devoted themselves to evicting tenant farmers. . . . These errors prepared the triumph of the Popular Front, a triumph that was due less to the real strength of the Left, considerable though it was, than to the lack of political understanding of the Right."[4]

And José María Gil Robles, War Minister during the second year of right-wing rule, avowed after his term of office had ended: ". . . there were many [employers and landowners], who, as soon as the Right came to power, revealed a suicidal egoism by lowering wages, raising rents, trying to carry out unjust evictions, and forgetting the unfortunate experiences of the years 1931 to 1933. As a result, in many provinces the Left increased its votes among the small cultivators and the agricultural workers, who would have remained with us had a just policy been followed."[5]

It was largely for the above-mentioned reasons that the victory of the

[3] It is worth adducing here the following passage from a speech by José Antonio Primo de Rivera, the Falangist (fascist) leader, in the Spanish legislature, on July 23, 1935: ". . . life in the Spanish countryside is absolutely intolerable. . . . Yesterday I was in the province of Seville. In that province there is a village called Vadolatosa, where the women leave their homes at three in the morning to gather chick-peas. They end their work at noon, after a nine-hour day, which cannot be prolonged for technical reasons. And for this labour these women receive one peseta."—As reprinted in José Antonio Primo de Rivera, *Discursos frente al parlamento*, p. 224. Referring to a decree promulgated in 1934, rescinding whatever laws the Republic has passed regarding hours of work, wages, and location of labour in the rural areas, a left-wing historian writes: "Wages fell by fifty per cent and there were places where the peasants did not even work for wages, but for maintenance, that is, for a dish of *gazpacho* and a crust of bread."—A. Ramos Oliveira, *Politics, Economics and Men of Modern Spain, 1808–1946*, p. 493.

[4] June 9, 1936.

[5] Interview given to *El Debate*, published on March 6, 1936.

Popular Front in February, 1936, was followed by a grave crisis in the countryside, a crisis that found expression not only in the strikes of land workers for higher wages and shorter hours—to which employers often replied by allowing the corn to burn or rot in the fields⁶—but in the rebellious mood of landless peasants who had grown impatient of the Agrarian Reform Law of the Republic and of what they regarded as dilatoriness on the part of government officials in the matter of land distribution. "Time is passing and the land remains in the hands of the caciques," wrote a local peasant leader. "Disappointment is once again setting in and we are on the same road as that of 1931. Is the Popular Front government going to destroy the illusions of the peasants? Are the peasants ready to see their hopes evaporate yet again? No. They want land, and those whose job it is to let them have it must not be surprised, should they fail to quicken their pace, if the peasants seize what the government does not give them and what they need so badly."⁷

In many villages patience was already at an end, and the peasants

⁶ Two versions of this aspect of the agrarian crisis, which complement rather than contradict each other, were given by the Republican press: "Every day," said the right-wing Republican *El Sol* (June 14, 1936), "we receive letters telling us the same thing. The harvest is less than the average, but the labourers, without worrying about it, demand ridiculous conditions for reaping and threshing. In some villages, these conditions are such that the tenant farmers, landowners, small peasant proprietors and *colonos* [peasants settled on the land under the Agrarian Reform Law]—and the latter more than the former—affirm that they will have to let the grain rot or burn, because if they were to accede to the imperious and menacing demands of the unions they would have to sell every bushel at a price that would scandalize the purchasers. . . .

"Not only powerful landowners and comfortable absentee landlords cultivate the Spanish soil. There are hundreds of thousands of small proprietors and *colonos* for whom an equitable solution of the present agricultural strikes is a question of life and death."

On the other hand, the left-wing Republican *La Libertad* stated (June 26, 1936): ". . . in the countryside . . . there clearly exists a definite aim on the part of reactionary elements to boycott the régime, to drive the peasant masses to desperation and place the government in a very difficult position. Otherwise, how can it be explained that there are entire provinces where employers intend leaving the harvest in the fields . . . , using it exclusively as fodder, whereas it would be far more profitable to pay the wages they should pay and gather the crop? How too can cases like that of Almendralejo be explained, where the employers swore not to offer a single day's work, threatening to kill any proprietor who did?"

⁷ *El Obrero de la Tierra*, May 30, 1936. This paper was the organ of the Socialist Federation of Land Workers. For editorials protesting against the procrastination of the government, see issues of March 28, April 11, 25, 1936.

refused to wait until the government, composed entirely of liberal Republicans, might satisfy their needs. "[The peasant leaders]," wrote a Communist, "calculate that the agrarian law plans fifty thousand settlements a year, which means that it will take twenty years to settle a million peasants and more than a century to give land to all. Realizing this, the peasants just occupy the land."[8]

"The peasants of Cenicientos in the province of Madrid," reported the organ of the Socialist Federation of Land Workers, "have occupied in a body the pasture land called 'Encinar de la Parra,' covering an area of 1,317 hectares, and have begun to work it. When the occupation was completed, they sent the following letter to the Minister of Agriculture:

" 'In our village there is an extensive pasture land capable of cultivation, which in the past was actually cultivated, but which today is used for shooting and grazing. Our repeated requests to lease the land from the owner, who, together with two or three other landowners, possesses almost the entire municipal area—at one time communal property—have been in vain. As our hands and ploughs were idle and our children hungry, we had no course but to occupy the land. This we have done. With our labour it will yield what it did not yield before; our misery will end and the national wealth will increase. In doing this, we do not believe that we have prejudiced anyone, and the only thing we ask of Your Excellency is that you legalize this situation and grant us credits so that we can perform our labours in peace.' "[9]

And an article in a Communist paper ran:

"The agricultural workers of a small village near Madrid showed the way by taking over the land for themselves. Two weeks later the farm labourers of ninety villages in the province of Salamanca did the same thing. A few days afterwards this example was followed by the peasants of several villages in Toledo province;[10] and at daybreak on March 25, eighty thousand peasants of the provinces of Cáceres and Badajoz occupied the land and began to cultivate it. The revolutionary action of [these] peasants caused absolute panic in government circles. . . .

". . . [But] instead of using force the government was obliged to

[8] Paul Nizan in the *International Press Correspondence*, August 1, 1936. Although published in August, this article was written before the outbreak of the Civil War.

[9] *El Obrero de la Tierra*, March 7, 1936.

[10] On March 17 the left-wing Republican newspaper *La Libertad* published the following telegram from Manasalbas in Toledo province: "Two thousand hungry peasants of this locality have just seized the estate 'El Robledo' which [Count] Romanones appropriated to himself twenty years ago without giving anything to the people."

send a large contingent of experts and officials from the Institute of Agrarian Reform in order to give an appearance of legality to the seizure of the land."[11]

If the unrest in the countryside was a source of acute disquietude to the government no less so were the labour disputes in the urban centres.

From the end of May until the outbreak of the Civil War, the Republic had been convulsed by strikes affecting almost every trade and every province. The columns of the press abounded with reports of strikes in progress, of old strikes settled, of new strikes declared, and of others threatened; of partial strikes and general strikes, of sit-down strikes, and sympathetic strikes.[12] There were strikes not only for higher wages, shorter hours, and paid holidays, but for the enforcement of the decree of February 29, compelling employers to reinstate and indemnify all workmen who had been discharged on political grounds after January 1, 1934.[13]

[11] César Falcón in *La Correspondance Internationale*, May 9, 1936. See also Pedro Checa, *ibid.*; E. Varga, *ibid.*, June 4, 1936; the Spanish refugee periodical, *El Socialista* (Algiers), October 16, 1944; *The Times*, April 15, 1936 (Madrid correspondent); Gerald Brenan, *The Spanish Labyrinth*, p. 312; José María Capo, *España desnuda*, pp. 87–9; Horsfall Carter in *The Listener*, April 29, 1936; José Plá, *Historia de la segunda república española*, IV, 356–7; Ramos Oliveira, *Politics, Economics and Men of Modern Spain, 1808–1946*, p. 539. The work by Capo acquires greater authority from the commendatory preface by Marcelino Domingo, Minister of Education in the government formed after the February, 1936, elections.

[12] Within the limits of this brief account, it is impossible to do more than give a rough idea of the magnitude of the strike wave; even to enumerate all the strikes would require many pages. The general picture given here is based on reports in the following Spanish newspapers: *El Adelanto*, Salamanca, *La Batalla*, Barcelona, *Claridad*, Madrid, *El Día Gráfico*, Barcelona, *Diario de Burgos*, Burgos, *La Libertad*, Madrid, *Mundo Obrero*, Madrid, *El Noticiero*, Saragossa, *Política*, Madrid, *El Socialista*, Madrid, *El Sol*, Madrid, *Solidaridad Obrera*, Barcelona, *Unión*, Seville.

[13] *Gaceta de Madrid*, March 1, 1936. This measure was promised in Section I of the Popular Front programme (*La Libertad*, January 16, 1936), and was particularly resented by employers. See, for example, the manifesto signed by their various associations, *El Sol*, March 1, 1936, and the report of Sir Auckland Geddes, Chairman of the British-owned Rio Tinto Company, to the shareholders in April, 1936: "We have had men pushed back on to our pay roll for whom we have no economic work," he said, "and within the last few days we have had an irritating stoppage, the result of demands for compensation for what amounts to accusations of wrongful dismissals of men who were in fact in prison for taking part in the revolutionary movement in October, 1934, and to whom naturally we did not pay wages while they were in jail."—*Rio Tinto Company Limited*, Report of the Transactions at the Sixty-third Ordinary General Meeting, p. 7.

One of the most serious of these stoppages was the Madrid building strike, which was prolonged for weeks not only by the adamantine attitude of the Anarchosyndicalist workers,[14] many of whom were jailed and whose headquarters the government closed in a sterile attempt to end the stoppage, but also by the intransigence of the building contractors themselves, who refused to accept the government's award, and whose "rebelliousness," to quote from a statement issued by their National Association after the outbreak of the Civil War, "contributed so much to the preparation of a favourable atmosphere for the crusade to reconquer immortal Spain."[15]

A powerful psychological factor contributing to the prevailing turbulence was undoubtedly the memory of the repression that followed the left-wing insurrection in the Asturias in October, 1934. That repression, writes a conservative Republican, a one-time Cortes deputy and an uncompromising opponent of the Left, was savage and pitiless in its methods. "The accused were tortured in the jails; prisoners were executed without trial in the courtyards of the barracks, and eyes were closed to the persecutions and atrocities committed by the police during those sixteen months. Officially, there were only three executions. What clemency! But there were thousands of prisoners and hundreds of dead, tortured, and mutilated. Execrable cruelty! There we have the tragic balance-sheet of a repression which, had it been severe yet legal, clean and just in its methods, would have caused far less harm to the country."[16]

As a result of the revengeful feelings that the repression engendered, as a result of the animosity between workers and employers in the towns and rural areas, and, finally, as a result of the rooted antagonism between the parties of the Left and Right the spring and early summer following the February, 1936, elections passed in a continual commotion, a commotion heightened by provocations and retaliations on both sides. Even the arrest of hundreds of members of Primo de Rivera's fascist party, the *Falange Española*, which was in some measure responsible for the ferment, did nothing to calm the situation, and the State of Alarm that had been proclaimed on the morrow of the elections was prolonged month after month at the expense of civil liberties. Day after day, and week after week, there occurred fresh scenes of violence and effervescence: mass meetings and demonstrations, arson and destruction, the closing of party and trade union headquarters,

[14] Members of the Anarchist-oriented trade unions.
[15] *ABC*, Seville, January 20, 1937.
[16] Clara Campoamor, *La révolution espagnole vue par une républicaine*, pp. 71–2.

seizures and attempted seizures of property, rioting and bloody clashes with the police, and assassinations and counter-assassinations, culminating in the slaying of the Monarchist leader, Calvo Sotelo, as a reprisal for the murder of Lieutenant José Castillo, a left-wing member of the Republican Assault Guard.[17] "Everyone in his senses knew," writes a Republican army officer, "that Spain, far from being a happy and blissful country, was living on a volcano."[18]

It was in this turmoil that the military revolt against the Republic supported by a large section of the police corps, by landowning Monarchists, by the powers of finance and business, by a large part of the Catholic clergy, by Falangists, and other forces of the Right, broke out in Spanish Morocco on July 17, 1936, initiating the Civil War.

This is not to suggest that the leaders of the revolt waited for the turmoil to reach its peak before planning their *coup d'état*. In point of fact, according to the testimony of one historian in General Franco's camp, the principal directives for a rising were prepared at the end of February, 1936, shortly after the elections, "should circumstances make it necessary, as was easily imagined at the time."[19] Moreover, the same historian reveals that the idea of a rebellion had been stirring in the

[17] In preparing this summary of events, the newspapers mentioned in note 12 of this chapter have been consulted. Owing to the press censorship countless incidents were not published, but a sufficiently reliable, though necessarily one-sided and therefore incomplete, chronological record is given for part of the period by the right-wing historian, Plá, *Historia de la segunda república española*, IV, 290–300, 311–23, 341–56, 375–83, 411–22. For a left-wing account of the acts of violence during this period, see Ramos Oliveira, *Politics, Economics and Men of Modern Spain, 1808–1946*, pp. 540–1, 546–7. Referring to the press censorship, Frank E. Manuel (*The Politics of Modern Spain*, p. 168) testifies: "Government censorship tried to suppress the news of strikes and assassinations because the ministers feared the contagion of violence. Copy for daily newspapers had to be rushed to the official press bureau for examination; the deleted sections appeared as blank space or with broken type. The Paris *Temps*, arriving a few days late in Madrid, was often more informative than the newspapers of the Spanish capital. Only when one gathered a batch of provincial papers and turned to the pages entitled *Social Conflicts* could one fully realize the scope of labour discontent for which there were no official statistics."

[18] Martín Blázquez, *I Helped to Build an Army*, p. 67.

[19] Felipe Bertrán Güell, *Preparación y desarrollo del alzamiento nacional*, p. 116. The official (Franco) history of the rising, *Historia de la cruzada española*, II, p. 467, reveals that a meeting of generals was held early in March "to prepare a defensive action should a situation of very grave danger for the country arise, as was feared by the course of events." See also, Manuel Goded, *Un "faccioso" cien por cien*, p. 26. The author of this work, the son of General Goded, who was the leader of the revolt in the Balearic Islands and in Barcelona, says that before the elections he was present with his father at several conspiratorial meetings.

minds of military and political leaders ever since General Sanjurjo's abortive revolt against the Republic in August, 1932.[20] But while it is true that anti-Republican leaders had considered the idea of an uprising ever since Sanjurjo's insurrection and that the latter, according to his biographer, had been urging, in order to forestall a possible victory of the Popular Front, that a *coup d'état* be carried out just before the February elections,[21] it is no less true that the electoral triumph of the left coalition increased the resolve of right-wing leaders to transmute their designs into practice. The landed proprietors knew that the measures adopted by the Right since December, 1933, to undo the agrarian reform of the first years of the Republic would be repealed.[22] The employers of labour knew that the laws fixing wages and conditions of work, which had been rescinded or allowed to lapse, would now be revived.[23] The Church knew that the anti-clerical provisions of the Constitution, which had been disregarded, would once more be enforced.[24] The Army officers knew that their grievances against the

[20] *Ibid.*, pp. 99–100. In a speech on November 22, 1937, Antonio Goicoechea, leader of *Renovación Española*, the party of Alfonso Monarchists, declared that in March, 1934, he and other right-wing parties had "planned a *coup d'état* backed by an insurrection of the army." He also said that he and other Spanish Monarchists had visited Italy in order to secure the support of the Italian Government in the event civil war should break out in Spain."—As reported in the *Manchester Guardian*, December 4, 1937. See also reproduction of documents in the handwriting of Goicoechea, recording his interview with Mussolini on March 31, 1934, in *How Mussolini Provoked the Spanish Civil War*, pp. 6–9.

[21] Julio Romano, *Sanjurjo*, p. 188. It is worth recording that Sanjurjo was leader-designate of the military rebellion in July, 1936, but lost his life at the outbreak of the war when flying from Portugal to Spain, his place later being taken by General Franco.

[22] The abrogation of two of these measures was promised in Section III of the Popular Front programme (*La Libertad;* January 16, 1936), namely, the law providing for the return of their estates to landowners implicated in the Sanjurjo rising (*Gaceta de Madrid*, April 25, 1934), and the Law of Leases (*ibid.*, March 24, 1935). According to *Política del frente popular en agricultura*, p. 14, the latter resulted in the expulsion of eighty thousand tenant farmers during the first two months. See also *Claridad*, October 5, 26, 1935; *Democracia*, November 22, 1935; *La reforma agraria en España*, pp. 40–1.

[23] Section VII of the Popular Front programme (*La Libertad*, January 16, 1936) stated that labour legislation would be restored "in all the purity of its principles."

[24] Referring to the situation after the formation of the first right-wing government in December, 1933, the conservative Republican, Salvador de Madariaga, writes: "The Jesuits went on teaching; Azaña's plans for the substitution of lay for religious education in new institutions were shelved, and a law was passed granting the priests two-thirds of their salaries for the year 1934

military reforms of the Republic would not now be redressed,[25] and, finally, they all knew that, although the liberal government formed after the elections wished to remain within the framework of the Popular Front programme,[26] broad sections of the working class and peasantry were determined to go beyond it, and that the course of events, to judge from the revolutionary fervour that had gripped the country, could only be reversed by force, or, as one book favourable to the military rising expressed it, by "a surgical operation."[27]

Viewed from this angle of social antagonisms, the Civil War was strictly Spanish in its origin. No foreign intervention was necessary to ignite the tinder of social enmity, although it is true that foreign powers used the war for their own purposes. Weeks before the outbreak of the military revolt, weeks before the first foreign aeroplane or tank reached Spain, the country was ripe for a conflagration. It needed only the failure of the revolt in some of the main cities—a failure that ruined all possibility of the decisive initial victory planned by the insurgents[28]— to precipitate a far-reaching social revolution. Instead of protecting the propertied classes from the incursions of the Left, the revolt, to use the phrase of Federica Montseny, a leader of the FAI, the formidable Iberian Anarchist Federation,[29] "hastened the revolution we all desired, but which no one had expected so soon."[30]

She was speaking of course for the powerful Anarchist-oriented trade union federation, the CNT,[31] over which the FAI exercised a

---

as a gracious act of the Republic, politically wise, perhaps, but of doubtful fidelity to the Constitution."—*España*, p. 512. See also E. Allison Peers, *The Spanish Tragedy*, pp. 145–6. Section VIII of the Popular Front programme (*La Libertad*, January 16, 1936) declared that "the Republic must regard the educational system as the indefeasible function of the state." After the outbreak of the Civil War, the Minister of Education published a decree directing local authorities to take possession, in the name of the state, of all religious schools.— *Gaceta de Madrid*, July 28, 1936.

[25] For a balanced account of these grievances by a Republican officer, see Coronel Jesús Pérez Salas, *Guerra en España*, pp. 22, 47–53, 85.

[26] Manuel Azaña, speaking in the Cortes as Prime Minister before his elevation to the Presidency, stated, according to *La Libertad* (April 4, 1936), that his government would fulfil the Popular Front programme "without removing a period or a comma, and without adding a period or a comma."

[27] M. Liébana y G. Orizana, *El movimiento nacional*, p. 5.

[28] That the military leaders believed that after declaring martial law everything would be plain sailing is confirmed by Juan Antonio Ansaldo (*¿Para qué . . . ?*, p. 120), who helped in the preparation of the insurrection.

[29] *Federación Anarquista Ibérica*.

[30] Speech reported by *Solidaridad Obrera*, December 22, 1936.

[31] *Confederación Nacional del Trabajo*, or National Confederation of Labour.

directing influence, not for the substantial body of moderate opinion
represented in the Popular Front coalition. Certainly a revolution was
not desired by Manuel Azaña, the President of the Republic; nor was
it desired by his intimate associate, Santiago Casares Quiroga, the
Premier and War Minister, who, in an attempt to maintain a balancing
position between the Left and Right, in accordance with the policy of
Azaña, had recoiled from any step that might have disturbed the
already precarious social equilibrium,[32] and who, after the outbreak of
the rebellion in Spanish Morocco on July 17, had refused to arm the
working-class organizations in Madrid lest the power of state pass into
their hands.[33] Nor was a revolution any the more desired by Manuel

[32] It is worth recording that he had ignored the warnings of Republican
officers regarding the conspiratorial activities in the Army (see, for example,
General Nuñez de Prado's complaints, as quoted by Diego Martínez Barrio in
Hoy, April 13, 1940, and Comandante Aberri, ibid., July 29, 1939), and had
taken no action against right-wing Army leaders, undoubtedly from fear of
precipitating the military coup—a coup which, according to a reliable authority
(Pérez Salas, Guerra en España, p. 79), he knew was in preparation. The same
apprehension had guided the policy of Manuel Azaña as Prime Minister before
his elevation to the Presidency in May, 1936. In reply to attacks upon the Army
leaders, his War Minister had issued a communiqué on March 18, saying in
part: "Certain rumours, which would appear to be circulating insistently
concerning the state of mind of officers and non-commissioned officers, have
come to the knowledge of the Minister of War. These rumours, which, of
course, can be described as false and without foundation, tend indubitably to
maintain public disquiet, sow animosities against the military, and undermine,
if not destroy, discipline, which is the fundamental basis of the Army. The
Minister of War has the honour of making public that all the officers and non-
commissioned officers of the Spanish Army maintain themselves within the
limits of the strictest discipline, disposed at any moment to fulfil their duties
scrupulously and—needless to say—to obey the orders of the legally constituted
government."—El Sol, March 19, 1936. It is noteworthy that according to
Indalecio Prieto, the moderate Socialist leader, Azaña turned a deaf ear to every
warning regarding the approaching military insurrection.—Palabras al viento,
pp. 279–81.
   Julián Zugazagoitia, director before the war of the moderate Socialist organ,
El Socialista, recounts that on his commenting in the paper upon certain
subversive military activities, of which he had been informed by military
friends, Manuel Azaña personally reprimanded him on the ground that such
comments did more harm than good. The truth of the matter was, he adds,
that Azaña was annoyed at that time, not with the military, "who were carefully concealing their designs through the exercise of a perfect discipline," but
with the voters "who had ensured the victory of the Popular Front, and who
were provoking a fabulous number of strikes and disturbances in the sphere of
public order."—Historia de la guerra en España, pp. 5–6.
[33] For his denying arms, see Zugazagoitia, Historia de la guerra en España, pp. 39–41.

Azaña's and Casares Quiroga's Left Republican Party, *Izquierda Republicana*, whose membership was mainly recruited from the civil service, liberal professions, small landowners and tenant farmers, and from small traders and manufacturers. Nor was it desired by Diego Martínez Barrio, Speaker of the Cortes and Vice-President of the Republic, whose party, the Republican Union, *Unión Republicana*, formed the most moderate section of the Popular Front coalition, and had, together with Azaña's party, declared its opposition, in the Popular Front programme itself, to working-class control of production as well as to the nationalization of the land and its free distribution to the peasants.[34] Nor, indeed, was a revolution desired by Indalecio Prieto, the leader of the moderate or centre faction of the Socialist Party, who, in distinction from the numerically stronger left-wing Socialists led by Francisco Largo Caballero, the secretary of the powerful trade union federation, the UGT,[35] had pursued a policy of restraint in the months preceding the rebellion,[36] and had denounced the strikes and disorders that had racked the country.[37]

Manuel Azaña, like Casares Quiroga, like Martínez Barrio, and like Indalecio Prieto, was a man of temperate views who sought to hold Spain on a middle course. "I wish to govern within the law without dangerous experiments," he had told a foreign correspondent, when Prime Minister after the February elections,[38] and in the Cortes he had condemned the acts of violence and the seizures of property that were

---

[34] *La Libertad*, January 16, 1936. In the matter of agriculture, the programme promised: reduction of rents and taxes, suppression of usury, increase of agricultural credits, revaluation of agricultural produce, stimulation of exports, irrigation and afforestation, settlement of families on the land, and the repeal of the two measures mentioned in n. 22, p. 25, above.

[35] *Unión General de Trabajadores*, or General Union of Workers.

[36] "Two positions, equally disinterested and honest," writes Julián Zugazagoitia, himself a moderate Socialist, "confronted each other in the Socialist Party: the majority, led by Largo Caballero, which regarded the coalition with the Republicans as a thing of the past and advocated the formation of a united working-class front with a view to the total exercise of power . . .; the minority personified by Prieto, which took into account the realities of the Spanish scene, and which considered, in view of the fact that the conservative parties were fighting resolutely, that any dissociation from the Republic and the Republicans would be extremely dangerous."—*Historia de la guerra en España*, p. 4; see also Gabriel Morón, *Política de ayer y política de mañana*, p. 25.

[37] See his speeches, reported in *El Socialista*, May 2, 1936; *La Libertad*, May 26, 1936.

[38] Interview reported in *La Libertad*, February 21, 1936.

embarrassing his government.[39] True, he wished for substantial reforms within the framework of the Republican Constitution, but not for a deluge that would submerge that Constitution. It was for this reason that after the revolt had broken out in Spanish Morocco on July 17 and was spreading to the peninsula, President Azaña still hoped for a solution that would save the Republic from being ground between the upper and nether millstones of the Right and Left. On the evening of July 18, in a last-minute endeavour to prevent the country from plunging into civil war and revolution, he had the government of Casares Quiroga resign,[40] and entrusted Martínez Barrio—whose party, the Republican Union, it will be remembered, constituted the most moderate segment of the Popular Front coalition—with the formation of a new Cabinet of a somewhat conservative hue in the expectation that this might encourage the insurgent Army leaders to negotiate.

"I have accepted this task," Martínez Barrio declared over the radio, "for two essential reasons: to spare my country the horrors of civil war and to protect the Constitution and the institutions of the Republic."[41] There was no time to lose if he was to achieve his purpose. Every minute was increasing the danger to the Republic as garrison after garrison rose in revolt, and as the left-wing organizations mobilized their members and demanded arms with ever more insistence in order to combat the military insurrection. Already in Madrid the working class, which had secured five thousand rifles in contravention of Casares Quiroga's orders,[42] was taking police functions into its own hands.

[39] Speech, *ibid.*, April 4, 1936. According to the right-wing Republican paper, *El Sol* (March 28, 1936), political commentators noted that Azaña's government was being subjected every day to greater pressure from the extreme Left, which not only demanded, and obtained, the fulfilment of the basic points of the Popular Front programme, but on many occasions hastened to carry out measures whose execution was being delayed. "This tactic," the paper remarked, "is in conflict with the sobriety of the Prime Minister. No one doubts this, but what can he do at the present time?"

[40] Indalecio Prieto in *Correo de Asturias*, May 1, 1943.

[41] His announcement was not published at the time, but is quoted by Martínez Barrio himself in *Hoy*, April 20, 1940.

[42] They had been handed out by Lieutenant-Colonel Rodrigo Gil, chief of the Artillery Park, and political associate for many years of Largo Caballero, the left-wing Socialist leader of the UGT. This information was given to the author by Margarita Nelken, left Socialist deputy at the time of the events, who was sent to the Artillery Park by the *Casa del Pueblo*, headquarters of the UGT. For corroborative testimony, see General José Asensio in *Nuestra España*, November, 1936, and Martin Blázquez, *I Helped to Build an Army*, p. 112. The version given by Lázaro Somoza Silva in his biography of General José Miaja *El General Miaja*, pp. 124-5) to the effect that the General, who was military

"Groups of armed workers were patrolling the streets and beginning to hold up automobiles," Martínez Barrio recalls. "Not a single soldier could be seen and, what is still more surprising, not a single guardian of public order. The absence of the coercive organs of the state was manifest. . . ."[43] And a Communist testifies: "At the stroke of midnight, all the exits from the *Puerta del Sol*, the approaches to the barracks, the working-class headquarters, the workers' districts, and the entrances to the city are being watched. The armed workers control motor traffic. Automobiles and tramcars are carefully searched. Flying patrols race through the different suburbs, carrying orders and inspecting sentry posts."[44]

Caught between the military rebellion and the counter-action of the Left, Martínez Barrio was confronted by a double peril. To parry the danger, he would not only have to withhold the distribution of arms for which workers were clamouring outside the Ministry of the Interior—a point around which his talks with prospective members of his Cabinet centred[45]—but above all he would have to dissuade the

---

commander of Madrid at the time, ordered the distribution not only lacks confirmation but conflicts with his presence a few hours later in Martínez Barrio's government, which, as will be seen, was committed to the withholding of arms. In fact, when Nuñez Maza, then Technical Secretary in the General Direction of Aviation, asked Miaja to give arms to the *Casa del Pueblo*, the General refused to do so, according to reliable information given to the author by Ignacio Hidalgo de Cisneros, second-in-command at that time of the General Direction of Aviation, under General Nuñez de Prado.

[43] *Hoy*, April 20, 1940.

[44] César Falcón, *Madrid*, p. 60.

[45] Felipe Sánchez Román, who became a member of Martínez Barrio's government and who was the leader of the National Republican Party, which had refused to join the Popular Front, told the author, when interviewed after the Civil War, that, on arriving at the Presidential Palace where he had been called by President Azaña before the formation of the new government, he was advised of what was described as a "serious development," namely, the appearance of workers demanding arms outside the Ministry of the Interior. Martínez Barrio, he said, was already there and had been insisting that arms be withheld. Asked by Barrio for his opinion, Sánchez Román replied that if arms were distributed it would be "ineffective militarily and pregnant with inconceivable dangers politically." See Clara Campoamor, *La révolution espagnole vue par une républicaine*, pp. 42, 133, n. 1, who confirms and supports Barrio's opposition to the distribution of arms. Clara Campoamor was a Radical Party deputy until 1934 and mixed in Madrid political circles at the time of the rising (*ibid.*, p. ii). Barrio himself relates (*Hoy*, April 20, 1940) that at a meeting of the Casares Quiroga government at 6 p.m. on Saturday (July 18), attended by Indalecio Prieto, the moderate Socialist, and by Largo Caballero, the left-wing Socialist,

military leaders from their drastic course. With this end in view he held
telephone conversations with various garrisons, in an attempt, according to his own testimony, to secure the adhesion of Army leaders who
were still undecided and to deflect from their purpose those who had
already revolted.[46] Of these conversations, the most important was
held with General Mola in Pamplona, who, it was later learned, was in
charge of the rebel plans on the peninsula.[47] But it was in vain that
Barrio strove to obtain the General's support. "If you and I were to
reach a compromise," Mola replied, "we should betray our ideals as
well as our men. We should both deserve to be lynched."[48] In spite of
this response Martínez Barrio proceeded with the formation of what
he later called his government of conciliation.[49] If it possessed a dis-
tinctly moderate complexion, it did so not so much from the presence
of five members of the Republican Union, all known for their comparatively conservative views, as from the inclusion of three members
of the National Republican Party, which had declined to adhere to the
Popular Front programme.[50]

---

everyone with the exception of himself remained silent in response to Caballero's "resolute opinion" that arms should be distributed, his own answer being
that the people should be urged "to rally round the legitimate organs of government." It is noteworthy that Indalecio Prieto, in an article commenting on
Martínez Barrio's narration of the governmental crisis, neither confirms nor
denies the assertion that he was among those who remained silent when
Caballero proposed that arms be distributed.—*Correo de Asturias*, May 1, 1943.

[46] *Hoy*, April 27, 1940.

[47] See, for example, Felipe Bertrán Güell, *Caudillo, profetas y soldados*, p. 202.

[48] Quoted by Bertrán Güell, *Preparación y desarrollo del alzamiento nacional*,
p. 76, and by Joaquín Pérez Madrigal, *Augurios, estallido y episodios de la guerra
civil*, p. 168, both supporters of the military rising. A different version of this
part of the conversation is given by Martínez Barrio (*Hoy*, April 27, 1940),
who says that Mola replied to his question, "Do you realize the extent of your
responsibility?" with the following words: "Yes, but I cannot go back on my
decision. I am under the orders of my General, Don Francisco Franco, and I
have a duty towards the valiant Navarrese who have placed themselves under
my command. If I wanted to act differently they would kill me. Obviously, it
is not death that frightens me, but the ineffectiveness of this new move and my
own conviction. It is late, too late." The *Pensamiento Navarro*, published in
Pamplona, Mola's headquarters, stated in its issue of July 19, 1936, which
appeared a few hours after the conversation, that Barrio had offered Mola the
Ministry of War. See also Ino Bernard, *Mola, mártir de España*, p. 77, and José
María Iribarren, *Mola*, p. 107, who both confirm this offer. However, it is not
mentioned by Barrio.

[49] *Hoy*, April, 27, 1940.

[50] The complete list of names, as given in the *Gaceta de Madrid*, July 19, 1936,
is as follows: Diego Martínez Barrio, Manuel Blasco Garzón, Antonio Lara,

But the new government was ill-fated from the outset, for the control of events had already passed into the hands of men intent on a final reckoning between the Right and Left.

For nearly two days the plans of the insurgent Army leaders had been unfolding. Following their seizure of Spanish Morocco on Friday, July 17, they had risen in Seville on Saturday at 3 p.m., in Cadiz at 4 p.m., in Malaga at 5 p.m., in Cordova at 6 p.m., in Valladolid on Sunday at 12.30 a.m., and in Burgos at 2 a.m. In two of these provincial capitals, Burgos and Valladolid, not only the Civil Guard, the gendarmerie created by the Monarchy, but also the Assault Guard, the police force created by the Republic, had joined the rebellion.[51] Even as

Plácido Alvarez Buylla, Bernardo Giner de los Rios, Felipe Sánchez Román, Justino Azcárate, Ramón Feced, Enrique Ramos, Augusto Barcia, Marcelino Domingo, José Giral, Juan Lluhí y Vallescá, and José Miaja. In his account of the governmental crisis, Martínez Barrio states (*Hoy*, April 20, 1940) that he invited Indalecio Prieto to join his Cabinet, but that the Executive Committee of the Socialist Party, which was controlled by the moderate wing, decided against participation (see also Marcelino Domingo, *España ante el mundo*, p. 231), although it offered its "determined and loyal support." This offer of support is inferentially confirmed by Julián Zugazagoitia, director of *El Socialista*, organ of the Executive Committee, who states that when the director of another newspaper asked him what the attitude of his own paper would be towards the new government in view of the fact that Martínez Barrio would deny arms, as Casares Quiroga had done, he replied: "I shall confine myself to giving the news of the crisis and its solution. I do not think we should make any violent comment. We should do more harm than good. From now on, and as long as the war lasts, *El Socialista* will be an organ that adheres scrupulously to the government unless the party should decide otherwise."—*Historia de la guerra en España*, p. 45.

[51] In Burgos, according to the *Diario de Burgos*, July 20, 1936, "the Assault and Civil Guards adhered to the movement from the first moment." See also M. Liébana y G. Orizana, *El movimiento nacional*, p. 175. In Valladolid, according to the *Norte de Castilla*, July 19, 1936, published in that city, the Assault and Civil Guards "joined the movement unanimously." See also Francisco J. de Raymundo, *Cómo se inició el glorioso movimiento nacional en Valladolid*, p. 19. However, in Seville, Cadiz, and Malaga, likewise according to insurgent sources, the Assault Guards, with few exceptions, supported the Popular Front. See, for example, Manuel Sánchez del Arco, *El sur de España en la reconquista de Madrid*, p. 24; Guzmán de Alfarache, *¡18 de Julio!*, pp. 68, 92; Angel Gollonet y José Morales, *Sangre y fuego, Malaga*, pp. 24–5. In Cordova, on the other hand, there was only slight opposition to the rising on the part of the Assault Guards. See, for example, Liébana y Orizana, *El movimiento nacional*, pp. 144–5. It should be noted that the Assault Guard, although created by the Republic in order to defend itself against the Left and the Right, comprised many individuals hostile to the régime who had entered the corps when the latter was under the control of Muñoz Grande during the period of right-wing rule prior to the

Martínez Barrio was announcing to the press about 5 a.m. the composition of his government,[52] events were moving faster than his words. In Saragossa, where Assault Guards had been carrying out arrests in trade union and left-wing party headquarters shortly after midnight,[53] the troops under General Cabanellas had just declared martial law, and, in Huesca, General Gregorio de Benito had also risen, seconded by a small garrison of Assault and Civil Guards. In Barcelona, the insurgents were leaving their barracks to occupy strategic points, and in the south a force of Moorish troops that would play a decisive role in securing Cadiz for the rebel cause was nearing that vital port. Moreover, General Franco was flying from the Canary Islands to Spanish Morocco to assume command of the Moors and Foreign Legionaries, and at 7 a.m. would reach his destination.

If Martínez Barrio's government was rejected by the Right, it was also rejected by the Left. In working-class circles alarm and indignation were extreme when the list of the new Cabinet became known,[54] for not a little distrust was attached to some of the ministers' names.[55] Even inside the middle-class Left Republican Party there was marked hostility, despite the presence of four of its members in the government. "In the headquarters of the Left Republicans," writes Marcelino Domingo, the President of the party, representing its right wing, and

---

electoral victory of the Popular Front.—See, for example, Zugazagoitia, *Historia de la guerra en España*, p. 131. These persons do not appear to have been removed after the elections; for, according to the official (Franco) history of the military rebellion, *Historia de la cruzada española*, IV, p. 381, adversaries of the Republican régime abounded in the corps. And it adds: "Lieutenant-Colonel Agustín Muñoz Grande, who until the advent of the Popular Front had been commander of this corps, maintains contact with many of its officers, and is therefore aware of the excellent disposition of hundreds of guards to participate in a coup against the government."

[52] Time given by Barrio in *Hoy*, April 27, 1940.

[53] *El Noticiero*, July 23, 1936.

[54] See Martínez Barrio in *Hoy*, April 27, 1940.

[55] See n. 50 above for names of ministers. *Claridad*, organ of the left Socialists, once said of Felipe Sánchez Román (January 18, 1936) that, while being a "Republican of unquestionable sincerity," he was "one of the most reactionary figures discovered by the new [Republican] régime," and of Antonio Lara, another member of the government, it wrote (October 12, 1935) that he was a "low political trickster." As for Martínez Barrio, the Anarchosyndicalist *Solidaridad Obrera* stated a few months before the outbreak of the Civil War (April 2, 1936) that he possessed intimate friends among the Andalusian landowners and that he had frequently been seen in the lobbies of the Cortes "conversing amicably with the fiercest enemies of the working class."

a minister in the new Cabinet, "many colleagues of mine, on hearing of the formation of the government, destroyed their membership cards with shameful anger without stopping to consider that my participation at least should have been a reason for respect as well as a guarantee for them. Their understanding of duty and of the sacrifices that duty imposes was different from mine."[56] In the streets the atmosphere became tense with excitement, as members of the left-wing organizations voiced their opposition. "Large demonstrations are formed spontaneously," wrote an eye-witness. "They move towards the Ministry of the Interior and towards the Ministry of War like an avalanche. The people shout, 'Traitors, cowards!' Impromptu speakers harangue the masses, 'They have sold us out! We must begin by shooting them first.' "[57]

Faced by this storm of popular indignation and disappointed in his hopes of a peaceful settlement with the insurgent Army leaders, Martínez Barrio could do no other than resign. "Only Prieto made a last attempt to dissuade me," he writes. "But it was a vain attempt, shattered by my attitude. Within a few minutes the political demonstration had brought about the ruin of my government. It was senseless to ask me to combat the military rebellion with mere shadows, stripped of authority, and ludicrously retaining the name of ministers."[58]

[56] *España ante el mundo*, p. 233. According to Julián Zugazagoitia (*Historia de la guerra en España*, p. 45), Isaac Abeytua, the director of *Política*, organ of the Left Republican Party, was strongly opposed to the government.

[57] Eduardo de Guzmán, *Madrid, rojo y negro*, p. 37. See also Martínez Barrio in *Hoy*, April 27, 1940; Manuel Blasco Garzón (a member of Barrio's government) in *España Republicana*, November 6, 1947; Arturo Barea, *The Forging of a Rebel*, p. 510.

[58] *Hoy*, April 27, 1940. It is worthy of notice that Sánchez Román, a member of the government, confirmed, when interviewed by the author, that Prieto urged Martínez Barrio to remain in office, contending that the street demonstrations did not warrant his resignation.

3

The Revolution

REBUFFED by the Left and by the Right, Martínez Barrio's government of conciliation passed into oblivion even before the names of its members appeared in that morning's official gazette. All thought of compromise with the insurgent generals had to be abandoned and a new government was formed, which, in order to combat the rebellion, decided that it must accede to the demands of the working-class organizations for the distribution of arms. "When I took charge of the Government of the Republic . . . ," testifies its Premier, "I had to consider that the only way of combating the military rising was to hand to the people the few arms we had at our disposal."[1] But it was a government in name only, swept along helplessly by the tide, a government that presided not over the preservation of the Republican régime but over its rapid dissolution under the double impact of military rebellion and social revolution.

Such was the government of liberal Republicans formed by José Giral, confidant of Manuel Azaña, the President of the Republic.[2]

In town after town and province after province the state shivered

---

[1] José Giral in *La Vanguardia*, July 19, 1938. See also his speech reported in *La Voz Valenciana*, March 10, 1937. "Lacking the means of throttling the insurrection," declared Salvador Quemades, leader of the Left Republican Party (speech reported in *Política*, November 2, 1938), "the government had to yield the way to the political and trade union organizations—the people—so that they could grapple with the rebel movement."

[2] Its composition, as given in the *Gaceta de Madrid*, July 20, 1936, was as follows: José Giral (Premiership), Augusto Barcia (Foreign Affairs), Manuel Blasco Garzón (Justice), Luis Castelló (War), Enrique Ramos Ramos (Finance), Sebastián Pozas (Interior), Francisco Barnés (Education), Juan Lluhí (Labour, Health, and Supplies), Mariano Ruiz Funes (Agriculture), Plácido Alvarez Buylla (Industry and Commerce), and Bernardo Giner de los Rios (Communications and Merchant Marine). On July 21, 1936, Antonio Velao was made Minister of Public Works, *ibid.*, July 22, 1936, and on August 6, Juan Hernández Sarabia succeeded Luis Castelló in the Ministry of War, *ibid.*, August 7, 1936.

into fragments as rebellious garrisons joined the insurrectionary movement or met with defeat at the hands of armed workers and forces
loyal to the government.[3] "Of 15,000 [Army] officers," writes Julio
Alvarez del Vayo, Foreign Minister at a later period, "barely 500
remained in the service of the Republic . . .; practically nothing
remained from the old army which could be put to any use."[4] The
Civil Guard, the constabulary created by the Monarchy and preserved
by the Republic as a rampart of the state, also crumbled,[5] and only a
few thousand of its members continued under the tenuous authority
of the government;[6] the secret police likewise dissolved, most of its
agents siding with the insurrection.[7] Even the power of the Assault
Guards, the police corps created in the early days of the Republic as a
buttress for the new régime, was shattered as a result of widespread
defections to the rebel cause[8] and of the assumption, in those places

[3] A detailed account of the attitude and fate of the garrisons in the various
provinces is given in the *Historia de la cruzada española*.

[4] *Freedom's Battle*, p. 122. See also Colonel Segismundo Casado in the
National Review, July, 1939; Pérez Salas, *Guerra en España*, p. 259.

[5] As in the case of the military garrisons, a full account of the attitude of the
Civil Guard in the different provinces can be found in the *Historia de la cruzada
española*. See also Liébana y Orizana, *El movimiento nacional*.

[6] Of a pre-war total of thirty-four thousand men (Madariaga, *España*, p. 602),
the corps comprised only fifteen thousand members in November, 1936
(according to an article in *Mundo Obrero*, November 3, 1936), but this was after
its reorganization as the National Republican Guard (*Gaceta de Madrid*, August
31, 1936) and the subsequent addition of thousands of new recruits. It is doubtful
whether the number of guards in the entire left camp at the inception of the
war, subject to the orders of the government, totalled more than five or six
thousand, and even this figure was substantially diminished by later desertions
en masse.—See, for example, the account by Captain Reparaz of his escape
together with a large body of Civil Guards from Jaen in Capitán Reparaz y
Tregallo de Souza, *Desde el cuartel de Miaja, al santuario de la virgen de la cabeza*;
report in *Solidaridad Obrera*, February 18, 1937, of the attempt by forty Civil
Guards to join General Franco's forces, and Zugazagoitia, *Historia de la guerra en
España*, p. 103.

[7] This corps, according to information given to the author by José Muñoz
López, top-ranking official in the SIM (Military Investigation Service) in the
later part of the war, ceased to function entirely at the outbreak of the rebellion
and had to be re-created, only three hundred of its three thousand members
remaining loyal to the government.

[8] Some of the provincial capitals where the Assault Guards supported the
rising were Burgos, Huesca, Saragossa, Valladolid (see pp. 32–3, above),
Cáceres, Granada, León, Logroño, Pamplona, Salamanca (Liébana y Orizana,
El movimiento nacional, pp. 209–10, 154, 201–2, 192, 216, 193 respectively),
Oviedo (Oscar Pérez Solis, *Sitio y defensa de Oviedo*, p. 24; G. Carrascal, *Asturias*,
p. 52), and Teruel (*Historia de la cruzada española*, IV, p. 238).

where the revolt had foundered, of police functions by armed militia units improvised by the left-wing organizations.[9]

"The State collapsed and the Republic was left without an army, without a police force, and with its administrative machinery decimated by desertions and sabotage," writes Alvarez del Vayo.[10] "From the Army leaders and the magistrates on the Supreme Tribunal down to the customs officials, we were obliged to replace the majority of the personnel who until July 18, 1936, had been in charge of the machinery of the Republican State. In the Foreign Ministry alone ninety per cent of the former diplomatic corps had deserted."[11] In the words of a Communist leader, "the whole state apparatus was destroyed and state power lay in the street";[12] indeed, so complete was the collapse that, to quote a Republican jurist, only "the dust of the state, the ashes of the state" remained.[13]

The control of ports and frontiers, a vital element of state power, formerly exercised by the *carabineros*, or customs officials and guards, was undertaken by workmen's committees or by local bodies under the authority of the labour unions and left-wing parties. "The government could do absolutely nothing," recalled Juan Negrín, when Premier in a later Cabinet, "because neither our frontiers nor our ports were in its hands. They were in the hands of individuals, of local, district, or provincial bodies, and naturally the government could not makes its authority felt."[14] In the Navy, according to its Commissar

[9] For frank accounts of the absolute impotence of the remnants of the government police corps in the first days of the war, see speech by the Socialist politician Angel Galarza (*La Correspondencia de Valencia*, August 5, 1937), who became Minister of the Interior in September, 1936, speech by Juan García Oliver, the Anarchist leader, who was made Minister of Justice in November, 1936, *Fragua Social*, June 1, 1937. See also Jesús de Galíndez (a friend of the Republic), *Los vascos en el Madrid sitiado*, pp. 15–19, and the preamble to the Minister of the Interior's decree of December 26, 1936, *Gaceta de la República*, December 27, 1936.

[10] *Freedom's Battle*, p. 261.

[11] *Ibid.*, p. 224.

[12] Dolores Ibarruri, *Speeches and Articles, 1936–1938*, p. 214.

[13] Angel Ossorio y Gallardo, *Vida y sacrificio de Companys*, p. 179; see also *ibid.*, p. 169. Should further corroborative testimony from the Republican camp on the collapse of the state still be needed, see Manuel Azaña, *Madrid* (speech of November 13, 1937), pp. 7–8; *Política*, July 16, 1938 (editorial); *La Correspondencia de Valencia*, August 5, 1937 (speech by Angel Galarza); *El Poble Català*, February 2, 1940 (article by Major Josep Guarner).

[14] Speech reported by *El Día Gráfico*, December 2, 1937. "The control of the frontier [at Ripoll]," reported a Communist daily, "is strictly maintained by workers and customs officials, who take their orders only from the working-

General during the Civil War, seventy per cent of the officers were killed by their men, and authority was exercised by sailors' committees.[15] The functions of municipalities and other local governing bodies in the left camp were also assumed by committees in which the Socialist and Anarchist-oriented labour unions were the ruling force.[16] ". . . these organs of the revolution," declared an Anarchosyndicalist leader a few weeks after the outbreak of the Civil War, ". . . have resulted in the disappearance of government delegates in all the provinces we control, because they had no option but to obey the decisions of the committees. . . . The local organs of administration of the old bourgeois régime have become mere skeletons, because their life force has been replaced by the revolutionary vitality of the workers' unions."[17] The courts of law were supplanted by revolutionary tri-

class organizations."—*Treball*, July 22, 1936. See *La Humanitat*, August 6, 1936, for the control of the entire Catalan French border from Bausén to Port-Bou by the working-class militia. "In the customs room at Port-Bou," wrote an eye-witness, "there is no sign of the revolution that agitated all of us in Paris. The customs officials are still in their old uniforms and they go about their tasks listlessly as though something has shorn them even of this power. A door opens into the passport room. Here is the explanation for everything. At various points in the room, members of the anti-fascist militia stand guard. They wear blue overalls over which an ammunition belt is thrown. They are armed to the teeth with pistols and rifles. Behind a long table sit three workers with pistols at their sides. They are examining passports and credentials."—M. Sterling in *Modern Monthly*, December, 1936. See also Walter Duranty in the *New York Times*, September 17, 1936; R. Louzon in *La Révolution Prolétarienne*, August 10, 1936; Alvarez del Vayo, *Freedom's Battle*, p. 164; H. E. Kaminski, *Ceux de Barçelone*, p. 11; John Langdon-Davies, *Behind the Spanish Barricades*, pp. 90–1; Pérez Salas, *Guerra en España*, p. 122.

[15] Bruno Alonso, *La flota republicana y la guerra civil de España*, p. 25. "The group of officers that survived the acts of violence," writes a moderate Socialist, who was later Minister of the Interior, "was dependent on committees elected by the sailors, who did exactly as they pleased."—Zugazagoitia, *Historia de la guerra en España*, p. 157.

[16] An exception must be made of the Basque provinces, where events took a less revolutionary course. See Manuel de Irujo, *La guerra civil en Euzkadi antes del estatuto*, pp. 23–5, 45–6, 50–2, 64–5, and report to the central government by José Antonio Aguirre, Premier of the autonomous Basque government, pp. 2–4, 7–8, 10–11, 13–15, 17–18, 22.

[17] Juan López, speech published in *CNT*, September 21, 1936. See also his article in *Cultura Proletaria*, January 8, 1938, and speech reported in *Fragua Social*, May 29, 1937. "The committees," ran an article in a left-wing Socialist review (*Spartacus*, September–October, 1938), "were the germ of proletarian power. All revolutionary segments were represented in them. . . . In the villages they assumed control of political and economic life. In the towns . . . they took into their hands the direction of all activities." "In the atmosphere

bunals, which dispensed justice in their own way.[18] Judges, magistrates, and district attorneys were relieved of office, some were imprisoned and others executed,[19] while judicial records were burnt in many places.[20] Penitentiaries and jails were invaded, their records destroyed, their inmates liberated.[21] Hundreds of churches and convents were burned or put to secular uses.[22] Thousands of members of the clergy and

---

charged with electricity and powder . . . that followed immediately on July 19," wrote Rafael Tasis y Marca, Director General of Prisons in Catalonia, "the municipalities [in the Catalan provinces] became lifeless, colourless. . . . The rubber stamps of the committees replaced . . . the signatures of the mayors."— *La revolución en los ayuntamientos*, pp. 16–17. "There is not a single place," said an Anarchosyndicalist paper, with reference to the province of Tarragona, "where a local anti-fascist militia committee has not been set up. These committees control the entire life of the community."—*Boletín de Información*, CNT-FAI, as given in *El Día Gráfico*, August 16, 1936. "The centre of gravity of the war and of politics," writes A. Ramos Oliveira, a Socialist, "was the street. Power was in the hands of the people, the parties, the committees."— *Politics, Economics and Men of Modern Spain, 1808–1946*, p. 595. See also speeches by the Socialist politician, Angel Galarza, who became Minister of the Interior in September, 1936 (*La Correspondencia de Valencia,* February 2, 1937; August 5, 1937), and R. Louzon in *La Révolution Prolétarienne*, August 10, 1936.

[18] "Everybody created his own justice and administered it himself," declared García Oliver, a leading Anarchist who became Minister of Justice in November, 1936. "Some used to call this 'bumping a person off,' but I maintain that it was justice administered directly by the people in the complete absence of the regular judicial bodies."—Speech reported in *Fragua Social*, June 1, 1937. In Madrid, according to Arturo Barea, a Socialist, each of the branches and groups of the trade unions and political parties set up "its own police, its own prison, its own executioners, and a special place for its executions."—*The Forging of a Rebel*, p. 536; see also pp. 545–7. For an account by a Republican Cortes deputy of the collapse of the administration of justice in the region of Catalonia, see Mariano Rubió y Tudurí, *La justicia en Cataluña*, p. 13.

[19] See, for example, Francisco Lacruz, *El alzamiento, la revolución y el terror en Barcelona*, p. 159, for such incidents in Barcelona.

[20] For the burning of judicial records in Barcelona and Castellon respectively, see Rubió y Tudurí, *La justicia en Cataluña*, p. 13, and *Datos complementarios para la historia de España*, p. 237.

[21] . . . the jails were opened to release friendly political prisoners, and the common-law criminals who came out with them acted on their own account," writes a supporter of the Republic.—Galíndez, *Los vascos en el Madrid sitiado*, p. 10. For the freeing of the convicts from the San Miguel de los Reyes Penitentiary, see p. 328, below; also Julián Gorkin, *Canibales Políticos*, p. 120, for the release of prisoners from the Model Prison, Madrid.

[22] See, for example, the memorandum presented to the Largo Caballero government by Manuel de Irujo, Basque Nationalist Minister, as reproduced in A. de Lizarra, *Los vascos y la república española*, pp. 200–4. "Catholic dens no longer exist," declared the Anarchosyndicalist organ, *Solidaridad Obrera* (August

religious orders as well as of the propertied classes were killed,[23] but others, escaping arrest or summary execution, fled abroad in foreign warships or took refuge in embassies and legations in Madrid.[24] "... We have confirmed something we only knew in theory," wrote a leading Anarchist in the welter of these events, "namely, that the revolution, in which uncontrolled and uncontrollable forces operate imperiously, is blind and destructive, grandiose, and cruel; that once the first step has been taken and the first dyke broken, the people pour

---

15, 1936). "The torches of the people have reduced them to ashes." "The oppressed people," said an article in an Anarchist youth paper (*Ruta*, November 14, 1936), ". . . put to the torch whatever dens of obscurantism and deception they found in their path. Churches, convents, centres of reaction, whatever smacked of incense and darkness, were fuel for the flames." "For the revolution to be a fact," ran an Anarchist youth manifesto (*Tierra y Libertad*, August 13, 1936), "we must demolish the three pillars of reaction: the Church, the Army, and capitalism. The Church has already been brought to account. The temples have been fuel for the flames and the ecclesiastical crows who were unable to escape have been taken care of by the people." In the province of Tarragona, reported *Solidaridad Obrera* (July 29, 1936), "the churches in all the villages have been fuel for the flames. Only those buildings that could be used for the benefit of the people have been kept, but not those that were a serious danger after burning. Many churches have been converted into communal warehouses as well as into garages for the anti-fascist militia." For confirmatory testimony by non-Anarchist, but pro-Republican sources, on the destruction of ecclesiastical property, see Ramos Oliveira, *Politics, Economics and Men of Modern Spain, 1808–1946*, p. 571; story by Lawrence Fernsworth in *Nothing but Danger*, pp. 13–47.

[23] For confirmation by a pro-Republican source of the killing of thousands of members of the priesthood and religious orders, see memorandum presented to the Largo Caballero government by Manuel de Irujo, Basque Nationalist minister, as reproduced in Lizarra, *Los vascos y la república española*, pp. 200–4. In his memorandum Irujo also stated that in the Basque provinces nobody attacked the Church or interfered with religious worship, because, in contrast to the rest of the left camp, the clergy in those provinces sympathized with democratic and Republican institutions.

[24] The number of refugees in foreign missions in Madrid has been variously estimated. Norman J. Padelford (*International Law and Diplomacy in the Spanish Civil Strife*, p. 157) says that it was calculated to be in excess of five thousand. Aurelio Nuñez Morgada, Chilean Ambassador and dean of the diplomatic corps in Madrid, affirms that it exceeded fifteen thousand (*Los sucesos de España vistos por un diplomático*, p. 338), and Alvarez del Vayo, *Freedom's Battle*, p. 240, who as Foreign Minister conducted the negotiations for the evacuation of the refugees, gives it as twenty thousand. This figure is more likely considering that the Norwegian Legation alone, which was among the least important of the missions extending asylum to political refugees, housed nine hundred, according to Felix Schlayer (Norwegian Chargé d'Affaires), *Diplomat in Roten Madrid*, p. 59.

like a torrent through the breach, and that it is impossible to dam the flood. How much is wrecked in the heat of the struggle and in the blind fury of the storm! Men are as we have always known them, neither better nor worse. . . . They reveal their vices and their virtues, and while from the hearts of rogues there springs a latent honesty, from the depths of honest men there emerges a brutish appetite—a thirst for extermination, a desire for blood—that seemed inconceivable before."[25]

"The revolution," wrote President Azaña some time later, "commenced under a Republican government that neither wished to support it nor could support it. The excesses began to unfold them-

[25] Federica Montseny in *La Revista Blanca*, July 30, 1936. "We do not wish to deny," avows a prominent Anarchist in the region of Catalonia, "that the 19th of July brought with it an overflowing of passions and abuses, a natural phenomenon of the transfer of power from the hands of the privileged to the hands of the people. It is possible that our victory resulted in the death by violence of four or five thousand inhabitants of Catalonia who were listed as rightists and were linked to political or ecclesiastical reaction. But this shedding of blood is the inevitable consequence of a revolution, which, in spite of all barriers, sweeps on like a flood and devastates everything in its path, until it gradually loses its momentum."—Diego Abad de Santillán, *La revolución y la guerra en España*, p. 176. "Blood, a great deal of innocent blood was shed on both sides . . . ," writes a Basque Nationalist, a Republican and Catholic. "But the most radical difference as far as the Republican zone was concerned—which does not justify, but at least explains, the excesses—lies in the very fact of the [military] insurrection. The Army, almost the entire secret police, the administration of justice, whatever police forces there were, whose duty it was to maintain order, revolted, leaving the legal government defenceless. The latter was compelled to arm the people, the jails were opened to release friendly political prisoners and the common-law criminals who came out with them acted on their own account. Furthermore, with the stirring up of the lower depths of society, the malefactors that exist in every city, in every nation, came to the surface, and found an easy field for their work. In normal times, the police would have kept them under control, but the very insurrection deprived the government of coercive forces and helped the criminals to secure arms. Is it surprising that during the first few days of the revolt these uncontrolled elements did as they pleased? At the same time the extreme left-wing organizations dispensed justice in a rude and elementary fashion, the justice of men who had suffered and had been moulded in an atmosphere of hatred. All this does not justify the crimes committed in the Republican zone, but it readily explains them.

"What cannot be explained, and even less justified, are the crimes, much greater in number and in sadism, that were committed in the fascist zone where an army and a police force existed, where the people were not armed and the common-law prisoners remained in jail. Yet those crimes were committed precisely by that army, by that police force, by those educated young gentlemen who lacked for nothing and who boasted of their Catholicism."—Galíndez, *Los vascos en el Madrid sitiado*, pp. 9–10.

selves before the astonished eyes of the ministers. Faced by the revolution the government had the choice either of upholding it or suppressing it. But even less than uphold it could the government suppress it. It is doubtful whether it had forces enough for this. I am sure it did not. Even so, their use would have kindled another civil war."[26]

Shorn of the repressive organs of the state, the government of José Giral possessed the nominal power, but not the power itself,[27] for this was split into countless fragments, and scattered in a thousand towns and villages among the revolutionary committees that had instituted control over post and telegraph offices,[28] radio stations,[29] and telephone exchanges,[30] organized police squads and tribunals, highway and frontier patrols, transport and supply services, and created militia units for the battle fronts. In short, nowhere in Spain did the Cabinet of José Giral exercise any real authority.[31]

The economic changes that followed the military insurrection were no less dramatic than the political.

In those provinces where the revolt had failed the workers of the two trade union federations, the Socialist UGT and the Anarchosyndicalist CNT,[32] took into their hands a vast portion of the economy.[33]

[26] *La velada de Benicarló*, p. 96. This book is in the form of a dialogue. Garcés, a former minister, who makes the above statement, expresses ideas commonly attributed to Manuel Azaña.

[27] The same, of course, is true of the Government of the Generalitat in the semi-autonomous region of Catalonia, which, in the words of Angel Ossorio, the Republican jurist (*Vida y sacrificio de Companys*, p. 172), had become a "purely nominal organ," the real power in the region having been assumed by the Central Anti-Fascist Militia Committee.

[28] Confirmation of this was given to the author by several trade union leaders.

[29] Barea, *The Forging of a Rebel*, p. 660.

[30] See, for example, *Boletín de Información*, CNT–FAI, August 25, 1936; *Solidaridad Obrera*, July 31, 1938.

[31] If evidence in support of this be needed from prominent adherents of the anti-Franco camp, see, for example, Prieto, *Palabras al viento*, p. 281, and his article in *Correo de Asturias*, August 15, 1942; Zugazagoitia, *Historia de la guerra en España*, p. 47, Alvarez del Vayo, *Freedom's Battle*, p. 262; Falcón, *Madrid*, p. 122; Pérez Salas, *Guerra en España*, p. 113; Major Josep Guarner in *El Poble Català*, February 2, 1940.

[32] *Unión General de Trabajadores* and *Confederación Nacional del Trabajo* respectively.

[33] Proof of this is not lacking even from Communist sources. "Are the big industrialists who rose against the people still owners of the factories?" asked José Díaz, general secretary of the Communist Party (speech, May 9, 1937, reprinted in Díaz, *Tres años de lucha*, pp. 350–66). "No, they have disappeared

Landed properties were seized; some were collectivized, others were divided among the peasants,[34] and notarial archives as well as registers of property were burnt in countless towns and villages.[35] Railways, tramcars and buses, taxicabs and shipping, electric light and power companies, gasworks and waterworks, engineering and automobile

and the factories . . . are in the hands of the workers, controlled by the unions." "Today," declared Antonio Sesé, secretary of the Communist-controlled Catalan section of the UGT (*Treball*, April 9, 1937), "the workers have the factories, the workers have the banks, the workers have the land, and the workers have the arms." See also Antonio Mije (member of the Politbureau), *Por una potente industria de guerra*, p. 3; Federico Melchor (member of the Executive Committee of the Communist-run Unified Socialist Youth Federation), *Organicemos la producción*, p. 4; and Michael Koltzov (leading Soviet journalist and Stalin's personal agent in Spain) in *Pravda*, September 26, 1936, who stated that according to a rough estimate the number of industrial and commercial enterprises taken over by the workers' unions and by the state amounted to approximately eighteen thousand, two thousand five hundred of which were located in Madrid and three thousand in Barcelona.

[34] "In every province [in the anti-Franco camp]," affirmed José Díaz, Communist Party general secretary, "big landowners no longer exist."—Report to the Central Committee in March, 1937, reprinted in Díaz, *Tres años de lucha*, pp. 288–339. Hundreds of the seizures made by the agricultural workers' unions affiliated with the UGT and CNT were subsequently registered with the Institute of Agrarian Reform, a department of the Ministry of Agriculture, which issued frequent reports listing confiscated properties. From the wording of these reports it might appear to the uninformed that the estates had been sequestered by the Institute and then turned over to the agricultural workers' unions, but the fact is that, with very few exceptions, the Institute merely recorded the expropriations. "I can affirm," writes Rafael Morayta Nuñez, Secretary General of the Institute during the first months of the revolution, "and this everyone knows, that it was not the government that handed the land to the peasants. The latter did not wait for a governmental decision, but appropriated the estates and cultivable lands themselves."—*Tribuna*, October, 1948. ". . . an overwhelming majority of all the larger estates [in the province of Ciudad Real] have been expropriated and collectivized by their hands," wrote Franz Borkenau (*The Spanish Cockpit*, p. 148), "and the business of the [Institute of Agrarian Reform] in the whole matter has only been to give a legal *placet*." Nevertheless, the unions saw an advantage in registering their confiscations with the Institute of Agrarian Reform, for this tended to legalize their action and rendered the sequestered estates eligible for technical and economic assistance from the Institute. For some of the latter's reports listing confiscated properties, see *Claridad*, October 12, 14, 1936; *CNT*, August 15, 18, 19, 1936; *Mundo Obrero*, August 8, 1936; *Política*, August 11, 14, 23, 27, 28, 30, September 1, 16, 17, 23–5, 27, October 10, 15, 28, 1936; *El Socialista*, August 26, September 29, 1936. For data on the collectivization of landed property, see n. 1, p. 48, below.

[35] This destruction of the registers of property is acknowledged in the

assembly plants, mines and cement works, textile mills and paper factories, electrical and chemical concerns, glass bottle factories and perfumeries, food-processing plants and breweries, as well as a host of other enterprises, were confiscated or controlled by workmen's committees, either term possessing for the owners almost equal significance in practice.[36] Motion-picture theatres and legitimate theatres, newspapers and printing shops, department stores and hotels, *de luxe* restaurants and bars, were likewise sequestered or controlled as were the headquarters of business and professional associations and thousands of dwellings owned by the upper classes.[37]

But the economic changes in town and country, as will be seen in the ensuing chapters, were not confined to the property of the wealthy strata of society. With the collapse of the state all barriers had fallen away, and it was too enticing a moment for the revolutionary masses not to attempt to remould the entire economy to their heart's desire.

---

preamble of a decree published in the *Gaceta de la República*, October 22, 1937. See also speech by the Under-Secretary of Finance, Jerónimo Bugeda, as reported in *El Día Gráfico*, February 9, 1937; article by Federica Montseny in *Tierra y Libertad*, October 29, 1936; report of the Committee of War of the Iron Column, *Nosotros*, February 16, 1937; *Solidaridad Obrera*, August 13, 1936 (article on Pina).

[36] A good example of a controlled enterprise is the following: in the region of Catalonia the telephone system belonging to the *Compañía Telefónica Nacional de España*, a subsidiary of the International Telephone and Telegraph Corporation, was placed under the control of a joint CNT–UGT committee, with the consequence—according to the testimony of the Anarchosyndicalists themselves, who were the dominant influence on that body—that the management was left with practically no other function but that of keeping an account of income and expenses, and was powerless to withdraw funds without the committee's consent.—*Boletín de Información*, CNT–FAI, August 25, 1936. Another good example is that of the hydro-electric enterprise, *Riegos y Fuerzas del Ebro*, a subsidiary of the Barcelona Traction, Light and Power Company, which was also controlled by a joint CNT–UGT committee. This committee took charge of the company's installations, its banking accounts, and other assets, with the result that the management, according to an official report, was unable to "exercise effective control over its business and its finances."—Statement issued by the Barcelona Traction, Light and Power Company, Limited, on September 3, 1936; see also statement issued on November 16, 1936.

[37] On the question of the confiscation and control of property by the unions and also by the left-wing parties a great deal could be written based on left sources alone. But considerations of space do not permit more than a brief reference to some of these sources under each of the following heads:

RAILROADS. "The boards of directors disappeared," said one trade union report, "and works councils were formed in which the working-class organizations were directly represented."—*CNT*, October 2, 1936. This control of the railroads by the working-class organizations is confirmed in the preamble of a government decree published in the *Gaceta de Madrid*, August 16, 1936. See also *Avant*, July 26, 1936; *La Batalla*, August 18, 1936; *Boletín de Información*, CNT–FAI, August 26, 1936; *CNT*, October 5, 1936; *Cultura Proletaria*, June 15, 1940 (article by Gaston Leval); *El Día Gráfico*, September 24, 1936; *Fragua Social*, April 7, 1937; *Solidaridad Obrera*, August 11, 19, 1936; *La Vanguardia*, October 14, 1936; *Collectivizations. L'oeuvre constructive de la révolution espagnole*, pp. 49–55; *De julio a julio* (article by Juan de Arroyo), pp. 165–8.

OTHER SECTIONS OF THE TRANSPORT INDUSTRY. According to Victor Zaragoza, secretary of the National Committee of the CNT National Transport Federation, when interviewed by the author, every important transport enterprise was appropriated by the labour unions. This of course excludes the Basque provinces, where there were comparatively few changes in the economic field (see, for example, G. L. Steer, *The Tree of Gernika*, p. 73). For the confiscation of some of the most important transport enterprises in Barcelona, Madrid, and Valencia, see *Boletín de Información*, CNT–FAI, August 7, 1936, also article reproduced from this paper in *El Día Gráfico*, August 18, 1936; *CNT*, August 7, 10, 1936; *La Noche*, August 6, 1936; *Nosotros*, July 8, 19, 1937; *Política*, August 8, 1936; *Solidaridad Obrera*, August 1, 4, October 13, November 19, December 17, 1936; *Tierra y Libertad*, May 1, 1937; *La Vanguardia*, October 8, 1936; *Collectivizations. L'oeuvre constructive de le révolution espagnole*, pp. 58–9.

PUBLIC UTILITIES. According to Mariano Cardona Rosell, a member of the National Committee of the CNT, every public utility enterprise in the left camp was taken over by the CNT and UGT (letter to author). Some of the most important were: *Compañía Catalana de Gas y Electricidad, Compañía Hidroeléctrica Española, Compañía Madrileña de Gas, Cooperativa Electra, Electra Valenciana, Eléctrica Santillana, Empresa Concesionaria de las Aguas Subterráneas del Río Llobregat, Gas Lebon, Riegos y Fuerzas del Ebro, Saltos del Duero, Sociedad Anónima de Fuerzas Eléctricas, Sociedad General de Aguas de Barcelona, Unión Eléctrica Madrileña.* For details on some of these enterprises, see *La Batalla*, August 2, 23, 1936; *Boletín de Información*, CNT–FAI, July 27, 1937; *CNT*, August 31, 1936; *Luz y Fuerza*, January, 1938; *Nosotros*, July 3, 1937; *Solidaridad Obrera*, August 13, 15, 1936, January 10, 1937.

MANUFACTURING, MINING, AND BANKING ENTERPRISES. See *Acracia*, October 24, 1936; *La Batalla*, September 22, 1936; *Boletín de Información*, CNT–FAI, August 7, September 30, 1936, also articles reproduced from this paper in *El Día Gráfico*, August 5, 6, 14, 25, 1936; *Claridad*, March 1, 1937 (speech by Vicente Uribe); *CNT*, September 23, October 5–7, 1936; *CNT* (Paris), December 26, 1947, December 3, 1948, November 20, 1949; *CNT–FAI–AIT Informationsdienst*, August 15, 1936; *La Correspondencia de Valencia*, March 2, August 14, 1937; *Cultura Proletaria*, November 25, 1939; *El Día Gráfico*, December 6, 1936; *Diario Oficial de la Generalitat de Catalunya*, October 28, 1936 (see preamble of the collectivization decree); *Documentos Históricos de España*, July, 1938; *L'Espagne Antifasciste*, No. 8 (no date), November 21, 1936 (article by Christian Couderc); *España Libre*, Toulouse, September 18, 1949; *Fragua Social*, as given in *Tierra y Libertad*, February 13, 1937; *El Mercantil Valenciano*, August 30, 1936, May 11, 1937 (statement by Belarmino Tomás); *Mundo Obrero*, August 20, 1936; *Nosotros*, July 6, 14, 1937, also article reproduced from this paper in *Boletín de Información*, CNT–FAI, June 16, 1937; *La Révolution Prolétarienne*, September 25, 1936 (article by Jean Leunois); *El Socialista*, August 27, 1937; *Solidaridad Obrera*, August 7, 18, 22, September 4, 16, 19, 25, 29, 30, October 21, 23, November 18–21, December 2, 5, 11, 15, 17, 19, 1936; January 21, 28, April 1, 24, June 30, August 15 (article by Cardona Rosell), October 23, 1937; *Solidaridad Obrera*, Paris, July 16, 1949; *Spanish Revolution*, September 5, 1936, August 6, 1937; *Tierra y Libertad*, January 30, March 27, July 24, October 9, 16, 30, November 13, 1937; *Treball*, December 6 (speech by Angel Estivill), 13, 1936; *La Vanguardia*, April 21, 1938 (interview with Vidal Rosell). See also p. 42, n. 33, above; Kaminski, *Ceux de Barcelone*, pp. 223–7; Gaston Leval, *Social Reconstruction in Spain*, pp. 6–7, 10, 22–3, 32; Peter Merin, *Spain between Death and Birth*, pp. 233–5; *Collectivisations. L'oeuvre constructive de la révolution espagnole*, pp. 161, 170, 184, 189, 198, 201, 209. According to reliable information given to the author by Antonio Villanueva, secretary at one time of the CNT metal workers' union of Valencia, the following firms were taken over by his union: *Brunet, Davis, Mateu, Sanz, Torras* and *Unión Naval de Levante*.

URBAN REAL ESTATE. See, for example, *La Batalla*, September 23, 1936; *Boletín de Información*, CNT–FAI, August 29, September 26, November 7, 1936; *CNT*, August 10, 1936; *El Día Gráfico*, July 24, August 29, 1936; *Mundo Obrero*, July 31, 1936; *Política*, July 23–4, 31, August 1, 19, 1936; *Solidaridad Obrera*, November 19–20, December 2, 5, 17, 19, 1936, January 20, 1937, June 5, 1938; *Tierra y Libertad*, January 23, 1937 (article by Gaston Leval); decree of the Minister of Finance, published in the *Gaceta de Madrid*, September 29, 1936, which confirms the appropriation of urban real estate by trade union and political organizations; also statement to the press by the Minister of Finance, *El Pueblo*, December 24, 1936; Vicente Saenz, *España en sus gloriosas jornadas de julio y agosto de 1936*, p. 18; Lazarillo de Tormes (Benigno Bejarano), *España, cuña de la libertad*, p. 67.

MOTION-PICTURE THEATRES AND LEGITIMATE THEATRES. See *La Batalla*, August 9, 1936; *Claridad*, August 17, 1936; *CNT–AIT–FAI Informationsdienst*, August 15, 1936; *La Humanitat*, September 12, 1936; *Solidaridad Obrera*, August 15, November 19, 1936; *Tiempos Nuevos*, December 1, 1936 (article by A. Souchy); *Ultima Hora*, August 6, 1936; *La Veu de Catalunya*, October 29, 1936; R. Louzon, *La contrarrevolución en España*, p. 34.

HOTELS, RESTAURANTS, BARS, AND DEPARTMENT STORES. See *Acracia*, October 24, 1936; *La Batalla*, February 27, 1937; *Boletín de Información*, CNT–FAI, as given in *El Día Gráfico*, August 21, November 25, 1936; *CNT*, October 7, 1936; *El Día Gráfico*, July 24, 1936; *Pravda*, September 26, 1936 (article by Michael Koltzov); *Mundo Obrero*, October 2, 1936; *Política*, August 15, 1936; *Solidaridad Obrera*, November 1, 1936; *Spanish Revolution*, August 6, 1937; *Tierra y Libertad*, October 30, 1937; *Umbral*, No. 14, as given in *Documentos Históricos de España*, March, 1938; *La Vanguardia*, November 24, 1937; Abad de Santillan, *Por qué perdimos la guerra*, p. 80; Leval, *Social Reconstruction in Spain*, p. 32; Louzon, *La contrarrevolución en España*, p. 34; *Collectivisations. L'oeuvre constructive de la révolution espagnole*, p. 27.

NEWSPAPERS AND PRINTING SHOPS. See *CNT*, July 24, September 1, October 7, 1936; *El Día Gráfico*, July 28, 1936; *Mundo Obrero*, July 21, 23, August 27, 1936; *Treball*, July 25, 1936.

For the intervention by the Ministry of Industry in industrial concerns in Madrid, see the *Gaceta de Madrid*, July 27, 1936; also *CNT*, August 3, 1936; *Mundo Obrero*, August 1, 1936; *Política*, August 18, 1936. It should be observed that the immense majority of these firms had previously been taken over by the trade unions. For an example of this, see Michael Koltzov in *Pravda*, September 26, 1936.

4

The Revolution
Hits the Small Bourgeoisie

TO the dismay of thousands of handicraftsmen, small manufacturers, and tradesmen, their premises and their equipment were expropriated by the labour unions of the Anarchosyndicalist CNT, and often enough by the somewhat less radical unions of the Socialist UGT.[1]

In Madrid, for instance, the unions not only took over the premises and equipment of shoemakers, cabinet-makers, and other small-scale producers, but collectivized all the beauty parlours and barber shops, establishing the same wages for the former owners as for their employees.[2] In Valencia, a city of over three hundred and fifty thousand inhabitants, nearly all plants, both large and small, were sequestered by the CNT and UGT,[3] while in the region of Catalonia, where the Anarchosyndicalists were in almost unchecked ascendancy during the first months of the revolution,[4] collectivization in many towns was carried out so thoroughly that it embraced not only the large factories

[1] These confiscations, to be sure, were often carried out without the approval of the national leaders of the UGT. For criticisms by Pascual Tomás, its vice-secretary, of the confiscation of small property by local UGT unions, see *La Correspondencia de Valencia*, December 21, 1936; *Adelante*, February 13, 1937; *Spartacus*, July–August, 1938.

[2] See *Claridad*, August 27, 1936; *CNT*, October 7, 1936.

[3] See speech by the local Communist Party trade union secretary, reported in *Frente Rojo*, March 30, 1937. In a letter to the author, Antonio Villanueva, a member of the Valencia CNT, stated that the premises and equipment of nearly all the printers, cabinet-makers, tailors, dressmakers, barbers, beauticians, bootmakers, and other leather goods producers were taken over by the unions of that city. For the collectivization of the bakeries, confectioneries, hotels, cafés, and bars in Valencia, see *Nosotros*, November 27, December 3, 1937.

[4] The revolutionary developments in this region, although touched on occasionally, lie beyond the purview of this volume.

but the least important branches of handicraft.[5] The collectivization movement also infringed upon another preserve of the middle classes. In Barcelona, the capital of Catalonia, with a population of nearly one million two hundred thousand, the Anarchosyndicalist workers collectivized the wholesale business in eggs and fish,[6] and set up a control committee in the slaughter house, from which they excluded all intermediaries;[7] they also collectivized the principal market for fruit and vegetables and suppressed all dealers and commission agents as such, permitting them, however, to join the collective as wage earners.[8] The milk trade in Barcelona was likewise collectivized. The Anarchosyndicalists eliminated as unhygienic over forty pasteurizing plants, pasteurized all the milk in the remaining nine, and proceeded to displace all dealers by establishing their own dairies.[9] Many of the retailers entered the collective, but some refused to do so: "They asked for a much higher wage than that paid to the workers . . . , claiming that they could not manage on the one allotted to them."[10] In Granollers, one of the principal market towns of Catalonia and a hive of middlemen before the war, all intermediaries were suppressed or crowded out of the channels of trade, the peasants having no alternative but to dispose of their produce through local supply committees set up by the CNT.[11] And this was the case in countless other localities all over the left camp.[12] In the region of Valencia, the centre of the great orange industry, to take yet another example of the invasion by the unions of the field of private trade, the CNT set up an organization for purchasing, packing, and exporting the orange crop, with a network of 270 committees in different towns and villages, elbowing out of this important trade several thousand middlemen.[13] In short, the labour unions impinged upon the interests of the middle classes in almost every field. Retailers

---

[5] See the Anarchosyndicalist organ, *Solidaridad Obrera*, December 19, 1936; also speech by Federico Melchor, a Communist, as reprinted in Melchor, *Organicemos la producción*, pp. 4–5.

[6] *Solidaridad Obrera*, December 3, 4, 1936.

[7] *Ibid.*, December 29, 1936.

[8] *Ibid.*, October 7, 1936.

[9] See account in *Tierra y Libertad*, August 21, 1937.

[10] *Ibid.*

[11] *Solidaridad Obrera*, December 15, 1936.

[12] See, for example, *CNT*, August 10, 1936 (Madrid province); *Tierra y Libertad*, January 23, 1937 (Carcagente); *Orientaciones Nuevas*, February 6, 1937 (Montmeló).

[13] See articles on the CLUEA in *Fragua Social*, January 31, 1937; *Nosotros*, April 19, 1937. Although the UGT was represented on the CLUEA, the CNT was the dominant influence.

and wholesalers, hotel, café and bar owners, opticians and doctors, barbers and bakers, shoemakers and cabinet-makers, dressmakers and tailors, brickmakers and building contractors, to cite but a few examples, were caught up relentlessly by the collectivization movement in numberless towns and villages.[14]

If some members of the middle classes accommodated themselves to their new situation as workers instead of employers in their former businesses, in the mute hope that the revolutionary fever would quickly burn itself out and that their property would be restored, they were soon to be disappointed; for, after the first few weeks of wide-spread and unco-ordinated seizures, some of the unions began a systematic reorganization of entire trades, closing down hundreds of small plants and concentrating production in those with the best equipment. "Those small employers of labour who are a little enlight-ened," declared *Solidaridad Obrera*, the principal Anarchosyndicalist organ in Spain, "will easily understand that the system of producing goods in small plants is not efficient. Divided effort holds back produc-tion. Operating a tiny workshop with handicraft methods is not the same as operating a large plant that utilizes all the advances of tech-nology. If our aim is to do away with the contingencies and insecurities of the capitalist régime, then we must direct production in a way that ensures the well-being of society."[15] In accordance with this outlook, the CNT workers, sweeping along with them those of the UGT,

[14] For examples not already given in this chapter, the reader is referred to the following publications: *Acracia*, October 24, 1936, November 17, December 3, 1937; *La Batalla*, October 3, 1936; *Boletín de Información*, CNT–FAI, Septem-ber 14, 17, 23, October 8, November 7, 1936; *CNT*, August 10, September 19, 23, October 7, 8, 16, 1936; *Cultura Proletaria*, January 8, 1938; *El Día Gráfico*, September 4, November 25, 1936; *España Libre*, Toulouse, September 18, 1949 (article by A. Costales); *Ideas*, January 7, 1937; *Nosotros*, February 15, November 15, 1937; *El Noticiero Universal*, September 11, 1936; *La Nouvelle Espagne Antifasciste*, December 2, 1937; *Orientaciones Nuevas*, January 30, February 6, 1937; *La Révolution Prolétarienne*, June 25, 1937 (article by R. Louzon); *Solidaridad Obrera*, August 13, September 24, November 18, 19, 20, 22, December 2, 5, 11, 15, 17, 19, 25, 27, 1936; January 20, April 23, June 30, August 3 (article by Mariano Cardona Rosell), 1937; *Solidaridad Obrera*, Paris, February 10, 1951 (article by Gaston Leval); *Tierra y Libertad*, January 23 (article by Gaston Leval), February 27, April 17, December 25, 1937; January 15, 1938; *Umbral*, July 24, 1937; Gaston Leval, *L'indispensable révolution*, p. 192, and pamphlet by the same author entitled *Social Reconstruction in Spain*, pp. 10–11; *Collectivisations. L'oeuvre constructive de la révolution espagnole*, pp. 27, 187, 204–5. See also pp. 60–9, below, on Libertarian (Anarchist) Communism, especially n. 15, p. 61.

[15] February 4, 1937.

closed down more than seventy foundries in the region of Catalonia, and concentrated their equipment and personnel in twenty-four.[16] "In these," a spokesman for the socialized industry declared, "we rectified the defects [in the foundries] of those small employers who did not concern themselves with technical matters and whose plants were centres of tuberculosis."[17] In Barcelona, the CNT Woodworkers' Union —which had already set up control committees in every shop and factory and used the former employers as technical managers at the standard wage for workers[18]—reorganized the entire industry by closing down hundreds of small workshops and concentrating production in the largest plants.[19] In the same city the CNT carried out equally radical changes in the tanning trade, seventy-one plants being reduced to forty,[20] while in the glass industry, one hundred plants and warehouses were cut down to thirty.[21] Still more drastic was the CNT's reorganization of the barber shops and beauty parlours in Barcelona; 905 were closed, and their personnel and equipment were concentrated in 212 of the largest establishments, the dispossessed owners being given the same rights and duties as their former employees.[22] A similar reorganization, or socialization, as it was called, was effected in the dressmaking, tailoring, metal, and leather goods trades in Valencia,[23] in the shoemaking industry of Sitges,[24] the metal and textile industries of Alcoy,[25] the lumber trade of Cuenca,[26] the brickmaking industry of Granollers,[27] the tanning trade of Vich,[28] the baking industry of

[16] *Solidaridad Obrera*, September 1, 1937; see also *Las Noticias*, July 1, 1937.

[17] *Solidaridad Obrera*, September 1, 1937.

[18] *Ibid.*, October 2, 1937.

[19] *Ibid.*, December 24, 1936; see also *Boletín de Información*, CNT–FAI, December 25, 1936; Aristide Lapeyre, *Le probleme espagnole*, pp. 22–3.

[20] *Boletín de Información*, CNT–FAI, April 10, 1937; see also *CNT*, Paris, July 17, 1949.

[21] *Tierra y Libertad*, January 23, 1937; see also *Solidaridad Obrera*, January 20, 1937.

[22] *Ibid.*, November 23, 1938; *Ultima Hora*, September 28, 1936; Lapeyre, *Le problème espagnol*, p. 22; *Collectivisation. L'oeuvre constructive de la révolution espagnole*, pp. 139–47.

[23] For this information I am indebted to Antonio Villanueva, a member of the Valencia CNT. For details of the collectivized clothing industry in that city, see *Nosotros*, October 21, 1937.

[24] *Solidaridad Obrera*, October 20, 1936.

[25] *CNT*, September 23, 1936; Leval, *L'indispensable révolution*, pp. 192–3; see also *Social Reconstruction in Spain*, p. 23, by the same author.

[26] Leval, *Social Reconstruction in Spain*, p. 32.

[27] *Boletín de Información*, CNT–FAI, August 18, 1937.

[28] *Ibid.*, January 15, 1937.

Barcelona,[29] and the cabinet-makers' trade of Madrid,[30] and of Carcagente,[31] to give only a few examples. "In all the towns and villages of Catalonia, Aragon, the Levante, and Castile," writes one observer who had travelled widely in these regions, "the small plants where work was carried on badly under uneconomic and unhygienic conditions were closed down as rapidly as possible. The machinery was gathered together in several workshops, sometimes in a single workshop. In this way, the regulation of production was simplified and co-ordination of effort was more effective."[32]

It is no wonder then that in the first shock of these revolutionary events the small-scale producers and businessmen looked on themselves as ruined; for even when the Anarchosyndicalists respected the small man's property there were some among them who made it clear that this was only a temporary indulgence while the war lasted. "Once this war has ended and the battle against fascism has been won," warned a prominent Anarchosyndicalist in Valencia, "we shall suppress every form of small property and in the way it suits us. We shall intensify collectivization and socialization, and make them complete."[33] To be sure, the Anarchosyndicalists claimed that the "accommodating and intelligent behaviour of the workers captured the sympathy of many small businessmen and manufacturers who had no objection whatever to socializing their businesses and becoming workers with the same rights and duties as the others,"[34] but only in the most exceptional cases did members of the small bourgeoisie welcome the revolutionary changes,[35] and the good will they showed could not afford a real index of what they felt in their hearts. The working class was armed; it was

[29] *Ibid.*, September 17, 1936; *Dialética*, February, 1938; José Peirats, *La CNT en la revolución española*, pp. 174–5.

[30] According to Mariano Cardona Rosell, member of the National Committee of the CNT, in a letter to the author.

[31] See *Tierra y Libertad*, January 23, 1937 (article by Gaston Leval).

[32] Leval, *L'indispensable révolution*, p. 192. See also *Social Reconstruction in Spain*, p. 11, by the same author.

[33] Speech by Tomás Cano Ruiz at the closing session of the November, 1936, Congress of the Valencia CNT, quoted, *Fragua Social*, November 17, 1936.

[34] *Solidaridad Obrera*, April 7, 1937. See also *ibid.*, October 4, 1936; February 4, 1937.

[35] The opposition of countless small businessmen to the collectivization movement in Catalonia was frankly admitted in an official report of the CNT; see report of the *Junta del Control del Comité Económico*, as given in *Memoria del congreso extraordinario de la confederación regional del trabajo de Cataluña celebrado en Barcelona los días 25 de febrero al 3 de marzo de 1937*, pp. 363–5.

virtual master of the situation, and the small bourgeoisie had no course but to defer to the will of events.

Nevertheless, the more radical workers did not rely entirely upon force or the threat of force to achieve their ends. Sometimes they tried persuasion: "You small shopkeepers who know nothing of social questions . . . ," ran an appeal issued by the Food Section of the Shop Assistants' Union of Barcelona, "are about to be absorbed by developments that will completely transform the present social structure into one more just and more noble, in which the exploitation of man by man will be a thing of the past.

"The grovelling existence you have led until now, devoted exclusively to a business at which you work twelve to fourteen hours a day in order to sell four wretched cabbages, two kilos of rice and three litres of oil, must end. . . .

". . . This Food Section calls upon you to educate yourselves every day with the help of our union, located on the mezzanine of 12, Plaza de Macià, where, as a result of continual contact with our comrades, you will succeed in freeing yourselves socially and morally from the prejudices that have dominated you until today."[36]

But the middle classes had not schemed and saved for years, they had not struggled to survive the competition of the larger concerns in order to see their hopes of independence ruined in a day. If they had expected anything from the revolution, it was freedom from competition and a greater share of the social wealth, not expropriation and a worker's wage. Even before the collectivization movement had struck them with its full force, a profound disquietude had diffused itself among them, and it was in vain that the Anarchosyndicalists had tried to allay their fears by painting the future in attractive colours. "News that the small bourgeoisie is deeply alarmed has reached our ears," said *Solidaridad Obrera* in the second month of the revolution. "We were under the impression that the anxiety of the first few days had evaporated, but the uneasiness of the shopkeeper, the businessman, the small manufacturer, the artisan, and small peasant holder persists. They lack confidence in the leadership of the proletariat. . . .

"The small bourgeoisie will lose nothing by the disappearance of capitalism. It must not doubt that it will profit many times over. For example, take the daily anxiety of the majority of the shopkeepers and small manufacturers over the payment of bills, rents, and taxes. . . .

". . . When private property and freedom to trade in other people's goods have disappeared, we shall have saved from a nightmare many

[36] *Solidaridad Obrera*, September 9, 1936.

shopkeepers who live under the constant threat of eviction and distraint. . . .

"The small bourgeoisie must not worry. It must draw closer to the proletariat. It can be quite sure that when private property and trade have been abolished a new mode of life will be introduced, a mode of life which will in no way injure those who may feel themselves affected by these social changes.

"The small bourgeoisie should throw off its fears; for once fascism has been crushed, it can look to the future with greater optimism."[37]

[37] August 29, 1936. See also *Solidaridad Obrera*, August 8, September 3, October 8, 1936; statement issued by the Regional Committee of the Catalan CNT and by the Peninsular Committee of the FAI, as given in *El Día Gráfico*, August 26, 1936.

5

The Revolution
in the Countryside

JUST as the artisans, small manufacturers, and small businessmen
were exercised by the collectivization movement, so too were the
peasant owners, tenant farmers, and sharecroppers. While it is true
that rural collectivization was applied at the outset mainly to large
estates on which landless peasants had worked as day labourers before
the revolution—a form of cultivation they spontaneously adopted—
it is no less true that it endangered the individual cultivator, who
apprehended in its rapid growth a mortal danger to himself;[1] for not

[1] For data on some of the agricultural collectives in different parts of the
left camp, the following newspapers and periodicals published during and after
the Civil War may be consulted: *Acracia*, July 19, 1937 (Vallfogona, Castelló
de Farfaña, Bellmunt de Urgel, La Portella, Os de Balaguer), November 16,
17, 29, 30, 1937 (Belvis de Jarama, Alguaire, Serós, Mayals, Rosas de Llobregat),
December 16, 1937 (Palau de Anglesola); *La Batalla*, August 26, 1936 (Raimut);
Boletín de Información, CNT–FAI, September 23, 1936 (Pont de Molins),
October 8, 1936 (Palafrugell, Caldas de Malavella), March 24, 1937 (Cabra del
Campo), August 4, 17, 1937 (Candasnos, Peñarroya de Tastavins), February 11,
1938 (Bujaraloz); *Castilla Libre*, April 16, 1937 (Membrilla), as given in *Docu-
mentos Históricos de España*, November, 1937; *Claridad*, December 14, 1936
(Guadasur), February 16, 1937 (Badajoz); *CNT*, August 10, 17, 1936 (Puente de
Arganda, Belvis del Jarama, Paracuellos de Jarama, Cobena, Villas Viejas),
September 1, 19, 1936 (Navilucillos, Utiel), October 7–9, 1936 (collectives in
the central region and Mestanza and Hellin), June 19, 1937 (Alcalá de Henares);
CNT, Paris, November 5, 12, 1938 (Madrid, García), January 7, 28, 1949
(Hijar, Caspe, Angües, Fraga, Torrente de Cinca, Utrillas, Peñalba, Farlete,
Lécera, Aznara, La Fresnada, Mas de las Matas, Alarcón, Maella), December 25,
1949 (Bot), January 29, 1950 (Cerviá); *CNT*, Toulouse, November 23, 1946
(Tivisa), September 6, 1947 (Hospitalet de Llobregat), December 17, 1950
(Villas Viejas); *Colectivismo*, August 15, 1937 (Infantes), September 15, 1937
(Iniesta), October 15, 1937 (Castuera, Valdepeñas), December 15, 1937 (Ibi),
January–February, 1938 (Marchamalo), March 15, 1936 (Manises), May 1,

only did the collective system of agriculture threaten to drain the rural labour market of wageworkers and to create ruinous competition for him in the sale of farm produce, it also presented a standing threat both to the property of the small owner and to that of the tenant farmer who, having appropriated the land, felt that the revolution had accomplished its mission.

Yet if the individual farmer viewed with dismay the swift and widespread development of collectivized agriculture, the farm workers of the Anarchosyndicalist CNT and the Socialist UGT saw in it, on the contrary, the commencement of a new era. For their part, the Anarchosyndicalists, the classic revolutionaries of Spain and the main promoters of rural collectivization, regarded it as an essential feature

---

1936 (Los Estados de Santo Tomé), June 1, 1938 (Venta del Charco), August 1, 1938 (Rafelguaraf), September 1, 1938 (Villarubia de Santiago), December 1, 1938 (Marchal); *La Correspondencia de Valencia*, October 19, 1937 (Castuera); *Cultura Proletaria*, October 2, 1937 (Peñarroya), January 8, 29, 1938 (Perales de Tajuña, Hospitalet de Llobregat), April 23, 1938 (Valencia province), October 21, 28, November 4, 11, 1939 (Calanda), February 7, 21, 1948 (Farlete, Binéfar, Altamira, Fraga, Alcoriza, Monzón, Híjar, Alcañiz, Caspe), January 28, 1950 (Ballobar); *Cultura y Acción*, August 6, 1937 (Binéfar), May 1, 1937 (Alcañiz) *Documentos Históricos de España*, December, 1938 (Liria); *Fragua Social*, June 17, 1937 (Utiel), August 28, 1937 (Cullera), December 2, 1937 (Gramanet del Besós), February 26, 1938 (Sueca); *Juventud Libre*, October 31, 1936 (Utiel); *Le Libertaire*, July 23, 1948 (the Levante zone); *Mujeres Libres*, July, 1937, (Calanda, Cabeza de Buey Herrera del Castillo y Siruela); *Nosotros*, February 19, 1937 (Simat de Valldigna), June 24, 1937 (Benaguacil), December 1, 1937 (Madrid); *La Nouvelle Espagne Antifasciste*, November 25, 1937 (Balsareny); *Orientaciones Nuevas*, February 6, 1937 (Montmeló); *La Révolution Prolétarienne*, September 10, 1937 (Segorbe); *Solidaridad Obrera*, August 14, 1936 (Bujaraloz), October 6, 1936 (La Figuera), November. 17, 19, 22, 28, 1936 (Valjunquera, Tarrassa, Premiá de Dalt, Martorell), December 5, 11, 19, 27, 1936 (Serdanyola-Ripollet, Villanueva y Geltrú, Sadurni de Noya, Rubi), January 20, 1937 (Amposta), June 26, 30, 1937 (Oliete, Plá de Cabra), November 10, 1937 (Lérida), December 25, 1937 (Caravaca), December 10, 1938 (Vilaboi); *Solidaridad Obrera*, Paris, February 10, 1951 (Tamarite de Litera); *Tierra y Libertad*, August 27, 1936 (Maella), January 16, 1937 (Carcagente, Vallforguna de Balaguer, Pina de Ebro, Palafrugall), February 13, 1937 (Llivia); *Umanità Nova*, January 8, 1950 (Triana); *Umbral*, July 24, 1937 (Amposta); *Vida*, as given in *Solidaridad Obrera*, October 22, 1937 (Beniopa, Oliva, Teresa, Tabernes de Valldigna, Benifairó, Simat). For additional data on rural collectives, see *Timón*, July 1938 (article by Agustín Souchy); Borkenau, *The Spanish Cockpit*, pp. 148–51; Gaston Leval, *Le Communisme*, pp. 60–6; Peirats, *La CNT en la revolución española*, pp. 302–26, 331–53; Agustín Souchy, *Entre los campesinos de Aragón. El comunismo libertario en las comarcas liberadas; Collectivisations. L'oeuvre constructive de la révolution espagnole*; also materials given in n. 15, p. 61, below.

of the revolution. It was one of their prime objectives and held their minds with a powerful fascination. They believed not merely that it would result in an improvement in the standard of living of the peasant by the introduction of scientific agronomy and mechanical equipment;[2] they believed not merely that it would protect him from the hazards of nature and from the abuses of intermediaries and usurers, but that it would uplift him morally. "Those peasants who are endowed with an understanding of the advantages of collectivization or with a clear revolutionary conscience and who have already begun to introduce [collective farming] should endeavour by all convincing means to prod the laggards," said *Tierra y Libertad*, the mouthpiece of the FAI, which organization, as has already been noted, exercised a directing influence over the unions of the CNT. "We cannot consent to small holdings . . . because private property in land always creates a bourgeois mentality, calculating and egotistical, which we wish to uproot for ever. We want to reconstruct Spain materially and morally. Our revolution will be both economic and ethical."[3]

Collective labour, said another publication of the FAI, banishes hate, envy, and egoism, and opens the way for "mutal respect and solidarity, because all those who live collectively treat one another as members of a large family."[4]

Collectivization was also a means of uplifting the peasant intellectually. "The greatest disadvantage of individual farming, which occupies all able-bodied members of the family: the father, the mother, the children,"Abad de Santillán, a leader of the CNT and FAI, contended, "is the excessive amount of labour. . . . There are no fixed hours of work, and the expenditure of physical energy is unlimited. . . . [The] peasant should not sacrifice himself or his children to the point of exaggeration. It is essential that he should have the time and energy to educate himself and his family, so that the light of civilization can illuminate his home.

"Work on collective farms is easier and enables members to read newspapers, magazines, and books, to cultivate their minds and open them to every progressive development."[5]

Similar views were also held by the Socialist UGT,[6] but a still more

[2] See, for example, J. Valero in *Fragua Social*, July 23, 1937.

[3] *Tierra y Libertad*, January 16, 1937.

[4] *Tiempos Nuevos*, September, 1938.

[5] *La revolución y la guerra en España*, pp. 107–8. See also *Solidaridad Obrera*, September 4, 1936; *Frente Libertario*, June 7, 1937.

[6] See, for example, *Colectivismo*, November 15, 1937, "Como trabajan nuestros técnicos"; also statement by a local secretary of the Federation of Land Workers, in *Adelante*, June 16, 1937.

powerful reason for the advocacy of collective farming by the CNT and UGT and for their opposition to the break-up of the large estates lay in their fear that the small landowning peasant might one day become an obstacle and even a threat to the future development of the revolution. "Collectivization," said a local secretary of the powerful Federation of Land Workers, affiliated with the UGT, "is the only means of making headway. We must not even think of parcellation at this stage. The soil is not everywhere the same and some harvests . . . are better than others. If we were to divide up the land we should relapse into that old state of affairs when some hard-working peasants had no food while the lucky ones lived well, and once again we should have masters and servants."[7]

"We Anarchosyndicalists," declared the organ of the youth movement of the CNT and FAI, "believed from the very beginning that individual farming would lead directly to large properties, to the domination of political bosses, to the exploitation of man by man, and finally to the re-establishment of the capitalist system.

"The CNT did not want this to happen and consequently fomented industrial and agricultural collectives."[8]

This fear that a new class of wealthy landed proprietors would eventually rise on the ruins of the old if individual tillage were encouraged was no doubt partly responsible for the determination of the more zealous collectivizers to secure the adherence of the small cultivator, whether willing or forced, to the collective system. It is of course true that the official policy of the CNT, as well as that of the less radical UGT, was, within certain limits, one of respect for the property of the small Republican farmer,[9] but apart from the fact that neither of these

[7] *Adelante*, April 1, 1937. "On no account shall we allow the land, equipment, and livestock to be divided up, because it is our intention to apply collectivization to all expropriated estates so that labour and the product thereof are shared equally among the peasant families."—Notice issued by the Executive Committee of the Federation of Land Workers, published in *El Obrero de la Tierra*, August 30, 1936, as reprinted in *Adelante*, July 21, 1937. However, it is worth recording that in December, 1936, the National Committee of the federation resolved that those of its members who were opposed to the collectivization of the large estates would each receive a proportionate piece of land.—Quoted, *Por la revolución agraria*, p. 8.

[8] *Juventud Libre*, July 3, 1937. See also speech by Juan J. Domenech, *Solidaridad Obrera*, January 7, 1937; report from Barbastro signed by Cosme Sampériz, *ibid.*, September 1, 1936; article by Gaston Leval on Carcagente, *Tierra y Libertad*, January 16, 1937.

[9] See *CNT*, April 5, 1937 (CNT Peasant Congress of Castile); *Fragua Social*, November 15, 1936 (8th Session of the Congress of the Valencia CNT):

organizations permitted him to hold more land than he could cultivate without the aid of hired labour[10] and that in many instances he was unable to dispose freely of his surplus crops, because he was compelled to deliver them to the local committee on the latter's terms,[11] he was often driven under various forms of pressure, as will be shown later in this chapter, to attach himself to the collective system. This was so particularly in those villages where the Anarchosyndicalists were in the ascendant, for whereas the Socialist-led Federation of Land Workers

---

Solidaridad Obrera, September 8, 1936 (Congress of the CNT Peasants' Union of Catalonia); *Adelante*, March 10, 1937 (resolution approved by the provincial congress of the UGT Land Workers of Valencia); *Claridad*, December 16, 1936 (editorial, part of which is quoted on p. 193, below); *La Correspondencia de Valencia*, December 21, 1936 (speech by Pascual Tomás, vice-secretary of the UGT); resolution and manifesto of the Federation of Land Workers, December, 1936, as reprinted in *Por la revolución agraria*, pp. 5–13, 29–33, see also *ibid.*, pp. 38–9. "I consider that voluntary membership should be the fundamental basis of any collective farm," said Ricardo Zabalza, general secretary of the Federation of Land Workers (*Verdad*, January 8, 1937). ". . . I prefer a small, enthusiastic collective, formed by a group of active and honest workers, to a large collective set up by force and composed of peasants without enthusiasm, who would sabotage it until it failed. Voluntary collectivization may seem the longer course, but the example of the small, well-managed collective will attract the entire peasantry, who are profoundly realistic and practical, whereas forced collectivization would end by discrediting socialized agriculture."

[10] See *CNT*, April 5, 1937 (CNT Peasant Congress of Castile); *Cultura y Acción*, February 18, 1937 (Congress of Agricultural Collectives of Aragon); *Fragua Social*, November 15, 1936 (8th Session of the Congress of the Valencia CNT); *Solidaridad Obrera*, September 8, 1936 (Congress of CNT Peasants' Union of Catalonia); *Adelante*, March 10, 1937 (provincial congress of the UGT Land Workers of Valencia); *Claridad*, October 25, 1936 (provincial congress of the UGT Land Workers of Granada); resolution and manifesto of the Federation of Land Workers, December, 1936, as reprinted in *Por la revolución agraria*, pp. 5–13, 29–33.

[11] See, for example, what happened in the village of Guadasur, which was controlled by the UGT and CNT, *Claridad*, December 14, 1936; also resolution approved by the delegates of twenty-one villages controlled by the CNT in Aragon, as given in *Solidaridad Obrera*, August 26, 1936. Of the village of Calanda, Gaston Leval, the well-known foreign Anarchist, wrote: "The individualists were allowed a minimum of freedom. They could possess land, because that is what they desired, but they could not trade with the fruit of their labour. They could not speculate and compete disloyally with the young collective."—*Cultura Proletaria*, November 4, 1939. It is not undeserving of notice that after the formation early in 1937 of the National Peasants' Federation affiliated with the CNT, this organization became, at least theoretically, the sole distributor of the agricultural produce of the individual cultivators and collective farms that came under its jurisdiction.—See *Estatutos de la federación nacional de campesinos*, p. 13.

included in its ranks an appreciable number of smallholders and tenant farmers who had little or no propensity for rural socialization and who had joined the organization because of the protection it had afforded them against caciques, landlords, usurers, and middlemen,[12] the Anarchosyndicalist peasant unions were, at the outbreak of the war, composed almost entirely of labourers and indigent farmers who had been fired by the philosophy of Anarchism and for whom rural collectivization was the foundation stone of the new régime of Anarchist, or Libertarian Communism, as it was called, which they had looked forward to establishing on the morrow of the revolution—a régime "of human brotherhood, which would attempt to solve economic problems without the state and without politics in accordance with the well-known principle, 'from each according to his abilities, to each according to his needs,' "[13] a régime without classes, based on labour unions and self-governing communes, which would be united into a nation-wide confederation, and in which the means of production and distribution would be held in common.[14]

Although no hard and fast rules were observed in establishing Libertarian Communism the procedure was more or less the same everywhere. In each locality where the new régime was instituted a CNT–FAI committee was set up. This committee not only exercised legislative and executive powers, but also administered justice. One of its first acts was to abolish private trade and to collectivize the soil of the rich, and often that of the poor, as well as farm buildings, machinery, livestock, and transport. Except in rare cases, barbers, bakers, carpenters, sandal-makers, doctors, dentists, teachers, blacksmiths, and tailors also came under the collective system. Stocks of food and clothing and other necessities were concentrated in a communal depot

[12] See *Adelante*, April 21, 1937; also article by Ricardo Zabalza, general secretary of the Federation of Land Workers, published in *CNT*, May 26, 1937.

[13] Isaac Puente, *Finalidad de la CNT: el comunismo libertario*, p. 3. See also resolution on Libertarian Communism approved at the Extraordinary Congress of the CNT, as given in *Solidaridad Obrera*, May 12, 1936.

[14] Puente, *Finalidad de la CNT: el comunismo libertario*, pp. 4, 24–6; see also *La Revista Blanca*, January 25, 1937. It is noteworthy that although the majority of CNT–FAI members regarded Libertarian Communism as the final goal of their movement, there were a few "individualist" Anarchists who, while opposed to the employment of hired labour, held that an Anarchist society should not be limited to one particular system of production. "Anarchism," wrote one of the foremost Spanish Libertarians, "must be made up of an infinite variety of systems and of individuals free from all fetters. It must be like an experimental field . . . for all types of human temperament."— Federico Urales, *La anarquía al alcance de todos*, p. 29.

under the control of the local committee, and the church, if not rendered useless by fire, was converted into a storehouse, dining hall, café, workshop, school, garage, or barracks.[15] In many communities money for internal use was abolished, because, in the opinion of Anarchists, "money and power are diabolical philtres, which turn a man into a wolf, into a rabid enemy, instead of into a brother."[16] "Here in Fraga [a small town in Aragon], you can throw banknotes into the street," ran an article in a Libertarian paper, "and no one will take any notice. Rockefeller, if you were to come to Fraga with your entire bank account you would not be able to buy a cup of coffee. Money, your God and your servant, has been abolished here, and the people are happy."[17] In those Libertarian communities where money was sup-

[15] This very brief account was written after consulting the following materials: *Boletín de Información*, CNT–FAI, February 20, 1937 (Tabernes de Valldigna), August 17, 1937 (Peñarroya de Tastavins); *CNT*, October 7, 1936 (Membrilla), May 27, 1937 (Torrevelilla); *CNT*, Paris, December 24, 1948 (Binéfar), November 27, 1949 (Santa Magdalena de Pulpis); *CNT*, Toulouse, August 23, 1947 (Graus), July 22, 1951 (Ballobar); *Cultura y Acción*, March 13, 1937 (Mosqueruela); *L'Espagne Antifasciste*, November 21, 1936 (Alcoy Enguerra, Játiva); *Fragua Social*, April 6, 1937 (Bujaraloz), also article from this paper on Utiel, reproduced in *Boletín de Información*, CNT–FAI, June 19, 1937; *Juventud Libre*, November 14, 1936 (Pedrilla); *Le Libertaire*, July 15, 1937, as given in *Spanish Revolution*, August 6, 1937; *Mar y Tierra*, August 15, 1937 (La Nucia); *Mujeres Libres*, July, 1937 (Calanda); *Nosotros*, February 24, 1937 (Beniopa); *Solidaridad Obrera*, November 13, 19, 27, 1936 (Bujaraloz, Velilla de Ebro, Lécera, Farlete); *Solidaridad Obrera*, Mexico City, May 17, 1947 (Graus); *Solidaridad Obrera*, Paris, February 24, March 10, 1951 (Mas de las Matas), April 7, 14, 21, 1951 (Graus), June 23, 29, 1951 (Alcolea de Cinca), July 7, 14, 1951 (Alcorisa); *Tierra y Libertad*, September 17, 24, 1936 (Maella), January 30, 1937 (Magdalena de Pulpis); *Tierra y Libertad*, Mexico City, January 25, 1947 (Ascó); July 10, 1947 (Ballobar); *Umanità Nova*, December 25, 1950 (Santa Magdalena de Pulpis); Borkenau, *The Spanish Cockpit*, pp.166–7 *Collectivisations. L'oeuvre constructive de la révolution espagnole*, pp. 233–42; José Duque, "La situación de Aragón al comienzo de la guerra," pp. 2–4; José Gabriel, *La vida y la muerte en Aragón*, p. 146; Kaminski, *Ceux de Barcelone*, pp. 118–25; Lapeyre, *Le problème espagnol*, pp. 18–20; Leval, *Social Reconstruction in Spain*, pp. 12–13, 15, 17–18; Peirats, *La CNT en la revolución española*, pp. 319–26; Alardo Prats, *Vanguardia y retaguardia de Aragón*, pp. 84–93; Souchy, *Entre los campesinos de Aragón. El comunismo libertario en las comarcas liberadas.*

[16] Isaac Puente in *Tierra y Libertad*, supplement, August, 1932, as reprinted in Puente, *Propaganda*, p. 101.

[17] *Die Soziale Revolution*, January, 1937, No. 3. "The men and women who stormed the convents [in Barcelona] burned everything they found inside, including money. How well I remember that rugged worker who proudly showed me the corner of a burned thousand peseta bill."—Federica Montseny, "19 de Julio Catalán," *Fragua Social*, July 19, 1937, as reprinted in *De julio a julio*, p. 22.

pressed, wages were paid in coupons, the scale being determined by the size of the family.[18] Locally produced goods, if abundant, such as bread, wine, and olive oil, were distributed freely, while other articles could be obtained by means of coupons at the communal depot. Surplus goods were exchanged with other Anarchist towns and villages, money being used only for transactions with those communities that had not adopted the new system.

Although a complete picture of life in all the Libertarian towns and villages cannot be given here, a good impression can be gleaned from the following descriptions:

In Alcora, according to an eye-witness, money was no longer in circulation. "Everybody can get what he needs. From whom? From the committee, of course. However, it is impossible to provision five thousand persons through a single centre of distribution. Hence, there are stores where, as before, one can satisfy one's requirements, but these are mere centres of distribution. They belong to the entire village and their former owners no longer make a profit. Payment is made not with money but with coupons. Even the barber shaves in exchange for coupons, which are issued by the committee. The principle whereby each inhabitant shall receive goods according to his needs is only imperfectly realized, for it is postulated that everyone has the same needs. . . .

"Every family and every person living alone has received a card. This is punched daily at the place of work; hence no one can avoid working, [for] on the basis of these cards coupons are distributed. But the great flaw in the system is that owing to the lack of any other measure of value, it has once again been necessary to have recourse to money in order to put a value on the labour performed. Everyone— the worker, the businessman, the doctor—receives coupons to the value of five pesetas for each working day. One part of the coupons bears the inscription 'bread,' of which every coupon will purchase a kilo; another part represents a certain sum of money. However, these coupons cannot be regarded as bank bills, as they can be exchanged only for consumers' goods, and this in a limited degree. Even if the amount of these coupons were larger, it would not be possible to acquire means of production and become a capitalist, were it only on the most modest scale, for they can be used solely for the purchase of con-

---

[18] "The characteristic of the majority of CNT collectives is the family wage. Wages are paid according to the needs of the members and not according to the labour performed by each worker."—Agustín Souchy in *Tierra y Libertad*, August 6, 1938.

sumers' goods. All the means of production belong to the community.

"The community is represented by the committee. . . . All the money of Alcora, about 100,000 pesetas, is in its hands. The committee exchanges the products of the community for other goods that are lacking, but what it cannot secure by exchange it purchases. Money, however, is retained only as a makeshift and will be valid so long as other communities have not followed Alcora's example.

"The committee is the paterfamilias. It owns everything; it directs everything; it attends to everything. Every special desire must be submitted to it for consideration; it alone has the final say.

"One may object that the members of the committee are in danger of becoming bureaucrats or even dictators. That possibility has not escaped the attention of the villagers. They have seen to it that the committee shall be renewed at short intervals so that each inhabitant will serve on it for a certain length of time.

"All this has something touching in its naivety. It would be a mistake to criticize it too harshly and to see in it more than an attempt on the part of the peasants to establish Libertarian Communism. Above all, one should not forget that the agricultural labourers and even the small tradesmen of such a community have had until now an extremely low standard of living. . . . Before the revolution a piece of meat was a luxury, and only a few intellectuals have needs that go beyond the bare necessities of life. . . ."[19]

In a conversation between himself and some of the peasants of Alcora, this acute observer goes on to furnish what may be regarded as a typical example of the minute control exercised by the committee of each Libertarian village over the lives of its inhabitants:

" 'What happens if someone wants to go to town for example?'

" 'That's very simple. He goes to the committee and exchanges his coupons for money.'

" 'So he can exchange as many coupons as he likes?'

" 'No, of course not.'

"These good fellows are rather surprised at my difficulty in understanding.

" 'When is he entitled to money, then?'

" 'As often as he needs it. He only has to ask the committee.'

" 'So the committee examines the reasons?'

" 'Of course.'

"I am somewhat alarmed. This regulation, it seems to me, must allow very little freedom under Libertarian Communism, and I try to

[19] Kaminski, *Ceux de Barcelone*, pp. 118–21.

find out on what grounds the committee of Alcora permits travel-ling. . . .

" 'If someone has a girl outside the village, can he get money to pay her a visit?'

"The peasants assure me that he can.

" 'As often as he likes?'

" 'Good heavens, he can go every night from Alcora to see his girl if he wants to.'

" 'But if someone wants to go into town to see a movie, can he also get money?'

" 'Yes.'

" 'As often as he likes?'

"The peasants begin to doubt my common sense.

" 'On holidays, of course, but there is no money for vice.' "[20]

Of the Libertarian village of Castro, another eye-witness writes: "The salient point of the anarchist régime in Castro is the abolition of money. Exchange is suppressed; production has changed very little. . . . The committee took over the estates, and runs them. They have not even been merged, but are worked separately, each by the hands previously employed on its lands. Money wages, of course, have been abolished. It would be incorrect to say that they have been replaced by pay in kind. There is no pay whatever; the inhabitants are fed directly from the village stores.

"Under this system, the provisioning of the village is of the poorest kind; poorer, I should venture to say, than it can possibly have been before, even in the wretched conditions in which the Andalusian *braceros* [farm labourers] are wont to live. The pueblo is fortunate in growing wheat, and not only olives, as many other pueblos of its kind; so there is at any rate bread. Moreover, the village owns large herds of sheep, expropriated with the estates, so there is some meat. And they still have a store of cigarettes. That's all. I tried in vain to get a drink, either of coffee or wine or lemonade. The village bar had been closed as nefarious commerce. I had a look at the stores. They were so low as to foretell approaching starvation. But the inhabitants seemed to be proud of this state of things. They were pleased, as they told us, that coffee drinking had come to an end; they seemed to regard this abolition of useless things as a moral improvement.[21] What few commodities they needed

---

[20] *Ibid.*, pp. 121–2.

[21] It is worth noting that puritanism was a characteristic of the Libertarian movement. Drinking and smoking were nearly always censured. In the Libertarian village of Magdalena de Pulpis, for example, the abolition of alcohol

from outside, mainly clothes, they hoped to get by direct exchange of their surplus in olives. . . . Their hatred of the upper class was far less economic than moral. They did not want to get the good living of those they had expropriated, but to get rid of their luxuries, which to them seemed to be so many vices. Their conception of the new order which was to be brought about was thoroughly ascetic."[22]

In the Anarchist village of Graus, on the other hand, to judge from a Socialist, the standard of living was higher than before the war. "The land, the mills, livestock, business, transport, handicraft workshops, sandalmaking, poultry breeding, and the liberal professions all come under the collective system. The village is an economic unit in the service of the common good. There is work for all. There is well-being for all. Misery and slavery have been driven out. . . .

"A powerful siren regulates the life of the village: the hours of labour, refreshment, and rest. . . .

"Men over sixty years of age are exempted from work. . . . This is one of the first principles of the collective. . . .

"When a collectivist decides to marry, he is given a week's vacation with the usual income, a house is found for him—house property is also collectivized—and he is provided with furniture . . . which he pays off gradually without interest. All the services of the collective are at his disposal. From birth to death he is protected by the collective."[23]

Referring to the village of Membrilla, an Anarchist account records: "On July 22, the big landowners were expropriated, small property was liquidated, and all the land passed into the hands of the commune. The smallholders understood these measures, which freed them from their debts and their worries regarding the payment of wages.

"The local treasury was empty. Among private individuals the sum of thirty thousand pesetas in all was found and seized. All the food, the

---

and tobacco was hailed as a triumph.—*Tierra y Libertad*, January 30, 1937. In the village of Azuara, the collectivists closed the café because they regarded it as a "frivolous institution."—Souchy, *Entre los campesinos de Aragón. El comunismo libertario en las comarcas liberadas,* p. 73. "An Anarchist should not smoke . . . ," the *Revista Blanca* once stated (July 13, 1934). "An Anarchist should never do anything that injures his health, least of all if it costs money." Nor should an Anarchist visit the brothel: "The man who frequents houses of ill fame is not an Anarchist. . . . If an Anarchist is not superior to other men, he cannot call himself an Anarchist. . . . He who buys a kiss puts himself on the level of the woman who sells it. Hence, an Anarchist must not purchase kisses. He should merit them."—*Ibid.,* June 8, 1934.

[22] Borkenau, *The Spanish Cockpit,* pp. 166–7.

[23] Prats, *Vanguardia y retaguardia de Aragón,* pp. 85–93.

clothing, the tools, etc., were distributed equitably among the population. Money was abolished, labour was collectivized, property was taken over by the community and the distribution of consumers' goods was socialized. However, it was not the socialization of wealth but that of poverty. . . .

". . . There is no longer any retail trade. Libertarian Communism reigns. The drugstore is managed by its former owner, whose accounts are controlled by the commune.

". . . Three litres of wine are distributed to every person per week. Rent, electricity, water, medical attention, and medicines are free. The consultation of a specialist outside the commune, if it is necessary, is paid for by the committee. I was seated near the secretary when a woman came in to ask permission to go to Ciudad Real in order to consult a specialist about a stomach ailment. Without bureaucratic dilatoriness she immediately received the cost of her journey."[24]

Far less expeditious was the committee in the Libertarian village of Albalate de Cinca, whose authority to hand out or withhold money gave it autocratic powers. "A woman wanted to go to Lerida to consult a specialist," wrote Agustín Souchy, a prominent foreign Anarcho-syndicalist. "When she arrived [at committee headquarters] it was seven o'clock. . . . Its members work in the fields together with the labour groups, and in their spare time they attend to the affairs of the village as well as of the [CNT] organization.

" 'To obtain money for the journey you must first secure a doctor's certificate,' the president explains.

"This reply did not satisfy the old woman. She complained of rheumatism and tried unsuccessfully to induce the committee to give her the money without a doctor's certificate.

" 'There are some people,' said the president, 'who take advantage of the new possibilities that the collective offers. Many never went to town before. . . . Now that they can travel without cost, they exaggerate a little!'

"Perhaps the explanation of the president was one-sided. The doctor could have given a more objective opinion on the matter."[25]

Describing other aspects of life in the Libertarian villages he visited, Augustín Souchy said of Calaceite: "Here there used to be many small cultivators . . . as well as blacksmiths and carpenters, all of whom had

[24] *Collectivisations. L'oeuvre constructive de la révolution espagnole*, pp. 239–40.

[25] *Entre los campesinos de Aragón. El comunismo libertario en las comarcas liberadas*, p. 92.

their own little workshops, where they laboured in a primitive way without machinery. The collectivist ideal showed them the path to communal labour. Now there is a large smithy in which ten men work; they have modern machinery, a healthy and bright place to produce in. All the carpenters of the village labour together in a big workshop.

". . . The able-bodied [agricultural] workers have been divided into twenty-four labour groups, each group comprising twenty members. According to pre-arranged rules, they till the village lands collectively. Formerly every man worked for himself; today he works for the community. . . .

"The village has two drugstores and a doctor. They belong to the collective, not because they were forced to, but because they wished to. There was trouble with the bakers. They wanted neither to join the collective nor to work under the new conditions, so they left the village. Fresh bakers have not been called in. A temporary solution has been found: the women bake the bread as of old, but the village wants new bakers to come in.

"Once the village was poor; today it is happy. Many people used to go hungry, but now they can eat."[26]

Of Calanda, Souchy wrote:

"What was once the church is now a food warehouse. . . . The new meat market is in the annexe, hygienic and elegant, such as the village has never known. No purchases are made with money. The women receive meat in exchange for coupons without paying anything or rendering any service. They belong to the collective and that is sufficient to entitle them to food. . . .

". . . Collectivists and individualists live peacefully side by side. There are two cafés in the village. One for the individualists, and the other for the collectivists. They can permit themselves the luxury of taking coffee every night. . . .

"A splendid expression of the collective spirit is the communal barber shop, where the service is free. The peasants never used to shave. Now nearly all faces are well groomed. Everyone can have a shave twice a week. . . .

"Wine is served at the rate of five quarts a week. Food is not lacking. . . .

". . . Everything is collectivized with the exception of those small stores whose owners wished to maintain their independence. The drugstore belongs to the collective and so does the doctor, who receives no

[26] *Ibid.*, pp. 84–5.

money.[27] He is provided for like other members of the collective."[28]

In Muniesa, bread, meat, and oil were distributed freely, but in contrast to most Libertarian villages some money was in circulation. 'Every male worker," commented Souchy, "receives a peseta a day; women and girls receive seventy-five *céntimos*; and children under ten, fifty *céntimos*. This money should not be regarded as a wage. It is distributed together with vital necessities so that the population can purchase supplementary goods."[29]

In none of the Anarchist villages, of course, was there any outward sign of religious life.[30] "Catholic mysticism no longer exists," affirmed

[27] With reference to the village of Maella, an article in *Tierra y Libertad* (September 24, 1936) stated: "Money has disappeared. . . . In this village neither doctors nor teachers receive money. With complete unselfishness they have abandoned that ridiculous privilege. Nobody at all receives pay."

[28] *Entre los campesinos de Aragón. El comunismo libertario en las comarcas liberadas*, pp. 45-7.

[29] *Ibid.*, p. 66.

[30] Anti-religious as well as anti-clerical sentiments were deeply rooted in the Spanish working-class movement, particularly among the Anarchists. As far back as 1869, the forerunner of the modern FAI, the *Alianza de la Democracia Socialista*, had declared itself atheist in the first article of its programme, and had called for "the abolition of cults, the substitution of science for faith, and of human justice for divine justice."—Quoted by Abad de Santillán in *Timón*, August, 1938. Moreover, the Russian Anarchist Bakunin, from whom the Spanish Libertarians derived much of their theoretical arsenal, once declared that "the existence of a god is incompatible with the happiness, the dignity, the intelligence, the moral sense, and the liberty of men, because, if in fact there is a god, my intelligence, however great, my will, however strong, are nothing compared with the divine will and intelligence."—Quoted by Abad de Santillán, *La bancarrota del sistema económico y político del capitalismo*, p. 53. And in *God and State*, he affirmed that there were three ways whereby the people could escape from their lot: two imaginary and one real. "The first are the tavern and the church, the debauchery of the body and the debauchery of the mind, the third is the social revolution."—*Bog i gosudarstvo*, p. 16. The attitude of the Spanish Anarchists towards religion had not changed since the days of Bakunin and the Alianza: ". . . Humanity," said an article in *Tierra y Libertad*, shortly before the outbreak of the Civil War (June 5, 1936), "will not enter a new world of justice and liberty so long as it kneels before God and submits humbly to the state." And in the early days of the revolution, *CNT*, the leading Libertarian organ in Madrid, declared editorially (August 5, 1936): "Catholicism must be swept away implacably. We demand not that every church should be destroyed, but that no vestige of religion should remain in any of them and that the black spider of fanaticism should not be allowed to spin the viscous and dusty web in which our moral and material values have until now been caught like flies. In Spain, more than any other country, the Catholic Church has been at the head of every retrograde aim, of every measure

Souchy with reference to the village of Mazaleón. "The priests have disappeared, and the Christian cult has ended. But the peasants did not want to destroy the Gothic building which majestically crowns the mountain. They turned it into a café and an observatory. . . . They broadened the windows of the church and constructed a large balcony where the altar was once located. The view embraces the southern spurs of the Aragonese mountains. It is a place for tranquillity and for reflection. Here the villagers sit on Sundays, taking coffee and enjoying the calm of the evening."[31]

In almost every region of the anti-Franco camp there were ardent spirits who, exhilarated by the initial progress of the collectivist movement in the villages, whether in the virtually all-embracing form of Libertarian Communism or in the restricted form of collectivized agriculture, continued to drive it forward with boiling energy. They had an apostolic belief in the justice and grandeur of their aims and were determined to bring them to fruition wherever they could and without procrastination. "We are in the thick of the revolution," declared one zealous Libertarian, "and we must destroy all the chains that subject us. If we do not break them now, when can we?

"We must carry out a total revolution. Expropriation must also be total. This is not the time for sleeping, but for rebuilding. When our comrades return from the front, what will they say if we have been idle? If the Spanish worker does not carve out his own liberty, the state will return and will reconstruct the authority of the government, destroying little by little the conquests made at the cost of a thousand sacrifices and a thousand acts of heroism.

"The rear should act energetically so that the blood of the Spanish proletariat is not shed in vain. . . . We must carry out our revolution, our own particular revolution, expropriating, expropriating and expropriating the big landlords, as well as those who sabotage our aspirations."[32]

And at a congress of the collective farms of Aragon, one delegate declared that collectivization should be carried out with the maximum intensity, avoiding the example of those villages where it had only been partially realized.[33] This statement exemplified the mood of thousands of fervent proponents of collective farming who were unfettered by

---

taken against the people, of every attack on liberty." See also *Solidaridad Obrera*, August 15, 1936.

[31] *Entre los campesinos de Aragón. El comunismo libertario en las comarcas liberadas*, p. 87–8.

[32] Report from Albalate de Cinca in *Solidaridad Obrera*, August 26, 1936.

[33] *Cultura y Acción*, February 18, 1937.

any fear of alienating those peasant holders and tenant farmers for whom individual cultivation was paramount. They had power in their hands, and paid no heed to the much-reiterated warnings of their leaders, such as the one uttered during the congress of the CNT Peasants' Union of Catalonia, that "to introduce wholesale collectivization would be to invite disaster, because it would clash with the love and affection of the peasants for the land they have obtained at such great sacrifice."[34]

Although CNT-FAI publications cited numerous cases of peasant proprietors and tenant farmers who had adhered voluntarily to the collective system,[35] there can be no doubt that an incomparably larger number doggedly opposed it or accepted it only under extreme duress. This aversion to rural collectivization on the part of smallholders and tenant farmers was on occasions conceded by the Anarchosyndicalists, although they sometimes claimed that they had overcome it. ". . . What we have been up against most," said the general secretary of the CNT Peasants' Federation of Castile, "is the backward mentality of the majority of small owners. Just imagine what it meant for the peasant proprietor, accustomed to his small plot of land, his donkey, his wretched hut, his petty harvest—modest possessions for which he had more affection than for his sons, his wife, and his mother—to have to give up this burden which he has carried with him from time immemorial, and say: 'Take them, comrades. My humble belongings are for everyone. We are all equal. A new life has begun for us.' Yet that is exactly what we have succeeded in getting the Castilian peasant to do. When a child dies in the countryside one no longer hears that heartrending saying once so common: 'Little angels go to heaven.' Under the capitalist system, the peasant used to get furious when his mule or his ass died, but remained quite calm when he lost a child. That was natural. His small property cost him endless sacrifices; not so his child. Often the death of his little children solved his economic problems."[36] Even in Aragon, whose debt-ridden peasants were

[34] Paraphrase by *Solidaridad Obrera*, September 9, 1936, of a passage in a speech by Ramón Porté, delegate for Tarragona province and member of the Regional Committee of the Catalan CNT. He drew attention in this passage to similar warnings by previous speakers.

[35] See, for example, *Castilla Libre*, March 30, 1937; *CNT*, August 10, 1936; *Cultura y Acción*, as given in *Boletín de Información*, CNT-FAI, August 4, 1937; *Nosotros*, June 24, 1937; *Solidaridad Obrera*, December 19, 1936, May 13, 1937; *Tierra y Libertad*, January 16, 1937; *Timón*, July, 1938 (article by Souchy).

[36] *Juventud Libre*, July 10, 1937. See also *ibid.*, November 14, 1936 (article on Pedralba).

strongly affected by the ideas of the CNT and FAI, a factor that gave a powerful spontaneous impetus to collective farming, the Libertarians themselves have occasionally acknowledged the difficulty they encountered when collectivizing the soil. "It has been an arduous and complicated task," said one of them in reference to the village of Lécera. "More correctly, it still is. We want men to convince themselves, by their own experience, of the justice and the advantage of our ideas."[37]

While it is true that rural collectivization in Aragon embraced more than seventy per cent of the population in the area under left-wing control[38] and that many of the region's 450 collectives[39] were largely voluntary, it must be emphasized that this singular development was in some measure due to the presence of militiamen from the neighbouring region of Catalonia, the immense majority of whom were members of the CNT and FAI. It would have been strange had it been otherwise; for after the defeat of the military rising in Barcelona they had left for Aragon not only to prosecute the struggle against General Franco's forces which occupied a substantial part of the region, but to spread the revolution. "... We are waging the war and making the revolution at the same time," declared Buenaventura Durruti, one of the outstanding leaders of the Libertarian movement,[40] himself a commander of a CNT–FAI militia force on the Aragon front. "The revolutionary measures in the rear are not taken merely in Barcelona; they extend from there right up to the firing line. Every village we conquer begins to develop along revolutionary lines."[41] As a conse-

[37] *Solidaridad Obrera*, November 19, 1936. See also article on Calanda in *Mujeres Libres*, July, 1937.

[38] This is the figure given by the Anarchosyndicalist leader, Diego Abad de Santillán, *Por qué perdimos la guerra*, p. 94. It was confirmed to the author by José Duque and José Almudí, the two Communist members of the Defence Council of Aragon, the principal administrative organ in the region during the early months of the revolution. See also Prats (a Socialist), *Vanguardia y retaguardia de Aragón*, p. 81, who says that seventy per cent of the land was collectivized.

[39] Figure given by Prats, *Vanguardia y retaguardia de Aragón*, p. 81.

[40] It is noteworthy that the Anarchists did not refer to the foremost men of their movement as leaders, because this term implied authority and control. Instead, they used the words, "representatives," "delegates," "militants." Still, as these men possessed the qualities of leadership in their ability to guide and influence the members of the CNT and FAI, and, indeed, were leaders by almost every test that distinguishes the leadership of a movement from the rank and file, the author prefers to use this term.

[41] *CNT*, October 6, 1936. "We militiamen must awaken in these persons the spirit that has been numbed by political tyranny," said an article in a CNT newspaper, referring to the villagers of Farlete. "We must direct them along

quence, the fate of the peasant owner and tenant farmer in the communities occupied by the CNT–FAI militia was determined from the outset; for although a meeting of the population was generally held to decide on the establishment of the collective system, the vote was always taken by acclamation, and the presence of armed militiamen never failed to impose respect and fear on all opponents. Even if the peasant proprietor and tenant farmer were not compelled to adhere to the collective system, there were several factors that made life difficult for recalcitrants; for not only were they prevented from employing hired labour and disposing freely of their crops, as has already been seen,[42] but they were often denied all benefits enjoyed by members.[43] In practice, this meant that in the villages where Libertarian Communism had been established they were not allowed to receive the services of the collectivized barber shops, to use the ovens of the communal bakery, the means of transport and agricultural equipment of the collective farms, or to obtain supplies of food from the communal warehouses and collectivized stores. Moreover, the tenant farmer, who had believed himself freed from the payment of rent by the execution or flight of the landowner or of his steward, was often compelled to continue such payment to the village committee.[44] All these factors combined to exert a pressure almost as powerful as the butt of the rifle, and eventually forced the small owners and tenant farmers in many villages to relinquish their land and other possessions

the path of the true life and for that it is not sufficient to make an appearance in the village; we must proceed with the ideological conversion of these simple folk."—*Solidaridad Obrera*, November 27, 1936. Of the village of Bujaraloz, another article in a CNT newspaper stated: ". . . the change is radical. The initiative in carrying it into effect lay with the peasants, and it was confirmed some days later with the arrival of the first column of Catalan volunteers, that of Durruti, which passed through the village on its march towards Saragossa, giving a fresh impulse to the revolutionary atmosphere."—*Fragua Social*, April 6, 1937.

[42] See pp. 58–9, above. In the village of Gelsa, for instance, a proclamation was issued as soon as the revolutionary régime was instituted, stating that "those persons who do not deposit food and clothing of all kinds [in the communal warehouse], but keep them to enrich themselves, will suffer the maximum penalty."—*Solidaridad Obrera*, August 16, 1936.

[43] See resolution approved at the Congress of Agricultural Collectives of Aragon, as given in *Cultura y Acción*, February 18, 1937; also preface by Agustín Souchy to *Collectivisations. L'oeuvre constructive de la révolution espagnole*, p. 20, and *Frente Libertario*, December 25, 1937.

[44] See statement by the Councillor of Agriculture of the Catalan Government *El Día Gráfico*, January 3, 1937; also notice issued by the Peasant Federation of Valencia province, *Verdad*, January 21, 1937.

to the collective farms. As Agustín Souchy, the foreign Anarchosyndicalist, put it:

"Those instances in which the small owners gave up their property for idealistic reasons were few, although not altogether rare. In some cases fear of seizure by force was the reason for relinquishing their land in favour of the collectives.[45] But nearly always the reasons were economic.

"Isolated and left to his fate, the small owner was lost. He had neither means of transport nor machinery. On the other hand, the collectives had economic facilities that he could never afford. Not all the small owners realized this immediately. Many joined the collectives later on when they were convinced, through their own experience, of the advantages they offered."[46]

The fact is, however, that many small owners and tenant farmers were forced to join the collective farms before they had had an opportunity to make up their minds freely. Although there was a tendency in the Libertarian movement to minimize the factor of coercion in the development of collectivized agriculture or even to deny it altogether,[47] it was, on occasions, frankly admitted. "During the first few weeks of the revolution," wrote Higinio Noja Ruiz, a prominent member of the CNT, "the partisans of collectivization acted according to their revolutionary opinions. They respected neither property nor persons. In some villages collectivization was only possible by imposing it on the minority. This necessarily occurs in every revolution. . . . The system, to be sure, is good, and satisfactory work has been done in many places; but it is painful to see antipathies created in other localities owing to a lack of tact on the part of the collectivizers."[48]

---

[45] An interesting example was the collective of Prat de Llobregat. According to an account in *Tierra y Libertad*, the FAI organ, July 2, 1938, it was set up in October, 1936, by one thousand farm labourers, tenant farmers, and peasant owners who had agreed "almost unanimously" to the collective cultivation of the soil. But no sooner had the political situation changed to the disadvantage of the CNT and FAI than the tenant farmers and peasant owners demanded the restoration of their properties, the original collective, according to this account, being reduced to a quarter of its former size.

[46] *Timón*, July, 1938.

[47] See, for example, *Cultura y Acción*, August 6, 1937; *Juventud Libre*, July 10, 1937 (statement by Criado, general secretary of the CNT Peasants' Federation of Castile); *Solidaridad Obrera*, July 11, 1937; also Abad de Santillan, *La revolución y la guerra en España*, p. 103, and Leval, *Social Reconstruction in Spain*, p. 13.

[48] Article in *Estudios*, quoted, Henri Rabasseire, *Espagne: creuset politique*, p. 130. See also *Frente Libertario*, the CNT newspaper, December 25, 1937.

Referring to Catalonia, a rich and productive region, where the mass of peasants were small proprietors and leaseholders, the leading CNT newspaper, *Solidaridad Obrera*, commented: ". . . arbitrary actions have been committed that have produced results contrary to those intended. We know that certain irresponsible elements have frightened the small peasants and that the latter are showing a lack of interest in their daily labours."[49] And writing shortly afterwards with regard to the same region, Juan Peiró, one of the foremost leaders of the CNT, asked: "Does anyone believe . . . that through acts of violence an interest in or a desire for socialization can be awakened in the minds of our peasantry? Or perhaps that by terrorizing it in this fashion it can be won over to the revolutionary spirit prevailing in the towns and cities?

"The gravity of the mischief that is being done compels me to speak clearly. Many revolutionaries from different parts of Catalonia . . . after conquering their respective towns have tried to conquer the countryside, the peasantry. Have they tried to achieve this by informing the peasantry that the hour of its emancipation from the social exploitation to which it has been subjected year after year has arrived? No! Or have they tried to accomplish this by carrying to the countryside, to the consciousness of the peasant, the spirit and the moral standards of the revolution? No, they have not done that either. When they have gone into the countryside, carrying with them the torch of the revolution, the first thing they have done has been to take away from the peasant all means of self-defence, . . . and, having achieved this, they have robbed him even of his shirt.

"If today you should go to different parts of Catalonia to speak to the peasant of revolution, he will tell you that he does not trust you, he will tell you that the standard-bearers of the revolution have already passed through the countryside. In order to liberate it? In order to help it liberate itself? No, they have passed through the countryside in order to rob those who throughout the years and throughout the centuries have been robbed by the very persons who have just been defeated by the revolution."[50]

To compel any person, by whatever means, to enter the collective system was of course contrary to the spirit of Anarchism. Malatesta,

[49] September 10, 1936.

[50] Article in *Llibertat*, September 29, 1936, as reprinted in Peiró, *Perill a la reraguarda*, pp. 102–3; see also *ibid.*, pp. 107–10, 158–9, and Joaquín Ascaso (the Anarchist President of the Defence Council of Aragon, the principal organ of administration in that region during the first year of the Civil War) in *Cultura y Acción*, July 28, 1937.

the Italian Anarchist whose writings had an important influence on the
Spanish Libertarian movement, once stated: "One may prefer communism, or individualism, or collectivism, or any other kind of system
imaginable, and work by propaganda and example for the triumph of
one's ideas, but it is necessary to beware, on pain of inevitable disaster,
of affirming that one's own system is the only one, the infallible one,
good for all men, in all places, and at all times, and that it should be
made to triumph by other means than by persuasion based on the
lessons of experience."[51] And, at another time, he stated: "The revolution has a purpose. It is necessary for destroying the violence of governments and of privileged persons; but a free society cannot be formed
except by free evolution. And over this free evolution, which is
constantly threatened so long as men exist with a thirst for domination
and privilege, the Anarchists must watch."[52] But even this surveillance
implied, in order to be effective, the existence of armed forces, of
elements of authority and coercion. Indeed, in the first social revolution
that occurred after these lines were written—the Spanish Revolution—
the CNT and FAI created armed forces for protecting the collective
system, and used them, moreover, for spreading it. The fact that these
forces were distasteful to some Anarchist leaders only emphasizes the
cleavage between doctrine and practice. If, theoretically, the CNT and
FAI were opposed to the state dictatorship advocated by the Marxists,[53]

[51] *Il Risveglio Anarchico*, November 30, 1929.

[52] *Umanità Nova*, October 14, 1922, as given in Luis Fabbri, *Vida y pensamiento de Malatesta*, p. 220.

[53] Opposition to dictatorship is one of the basic tenets of Anarchist doctrine
as expounded by Bakunin, the great Russian Anarchist, whose influence on the
Spanish Libertarian movement was considerable. Rejecting the Marxist idea
of the dictatorship of the proletariat, he wrote: "The Marxists . . . console
themselves with the belief that this dictatorship will be provisional and short.
They say that its only concern and its only aim will be that of educating and
elevating the people, both economically and politically, and to such a level that
all governments will soon become unnecessary. . . .

"They say that the yoke of state dictatorship is a transitional means indispensable for achieving the complete emancipation of the people: anarchy or
liberty is the objective, the state of dictatorship, the means. Hence, in order to
emancipate the labouring masses, it is first of all necessary to enslave them. . . .

". . . They affirm that only the dictatorship—their own undoubtedly—can
represent the will of the people. But we reply: no dictatorship can have any
other aim than that of its own perpetuation and it cannot produce and develop
among the people who support it anything but slavery. Liberty can be created
only by liberty, that is to say, by the rebellion of the people and by the free
organization of the working masses from below upwards."—*Gosudarstvennost i
anarkhiia* (*State and Anarchy*), pp. 234-5.

they nevertheless established in countless localities, with the aid of vigilance groups and revolutionary tribunals, a multiplicity of parochial dictatorships, which they exercised in a naked form not only against priests and landowners, moneylenders and merchants, but in many cases against small tradesmen and farmers.

PART II

THE RISE OF THE COMMUNISTS

6

Hope for the Middle Classes

FROM what has been said in the foregoing chapters, it is easy to understand the pessimism, bordering on despair, that took possession of a large section of the urban and rural middle classes from the outset of the revolution. Confronted by the brute facts, they found cold comfort in the words of the conservative Republican jurist, Angel Ossorio, that in view of the "immense social revolution" that had taken place "the only thing we members of the middle classes can do is to place ourselves alongside the proletariat."[1] Nor could they take comfort in the promises held out by the revolutionaries of a new and better world once private property and trade had disappeared into the limbo of things past; for the small manufacturers, artisans, tradesmen, peasant proprietors, and tenant farmers, in their immense majority, placed their hopes of a better life, not in the abolition, but in the accumulation of private property. To develop as they wished, they needed freedom of trade, freedom from the competition of the large concerns now collectivized by the labour unions, freedom to produce goods for personal profit, freedom to cultivate as much land as they pleased, and to employ hired labour without restriction. And above all, they needed, in order to defend that freedom, a régime in their own image, based on their own police corps, their own courts of law, and their own army; a régime in which their own power would be unchallenged and undiluted by revolutionary committees. But now all hope of such a régime had gone, and the middle classes had no alternative but to withdraw into the background. They were far too prudent to swim against the tide, and even adapted their attire to suit the changed conditions. "The appearance of Madrid," observed a right-wing Republican, "was incredible: the bourgeoisie giving the clenched-fist salute. . . . Men in overalls and rope sandals, imitating the uniform adopted by the [working-class] militia; women bare-headed;

[1] From a radio address reported in *Solidaridad Obrera*, September 20, 1936.

clothes, old and threadbare; an absolute invasion of ugliness and squalor, more apparent than real, of people who humbly begged permission to remain alive."[2] And referring to Barcelona, a left-wing observer wrote: "The Ramblas lie sloping gradually upwards for more than a mile to the Plaza de Catalunya. From the other end you looked down on an unending harvest of heads. Today there is not a hat, a collar, or a tie to be seen among them; the sartorial symbols of the bourgeoisie are gone, a proletarian freedom has swarmed in along the Calle del Hospital and the Calle del Carmen from the Parallelo. Or, as Puig suggests, the bourgeoisie have disguised themselves for better safety as proletarians by leaving hat, collar, and tie at home."[3]

Short of risking their liberty or their lives in openly opposing the revolution, there was nothing the middle classes could do but to adjust themselves to the new régime in the hope that eventually the tide might change. Certainly they could not look for support to any of the right-wing parties, which until the outbreak of the war had represented their more conservative layers, for they had perished in the flames of the revolution. Nor could they turn to the liberal Republican parties, such as the *Izquierda Republicana*, the *Unión Republicana*, and the Catalan *Esquerra*, the Left Republican Party of Catalonia, the strongest middle-class party in that region, for the majority of the leaders were either accommodating themselves to the radicalism of the situation[4] or were characterized by inertia born of fear, while others, regarding everything as lost, had either left the country or were fleeing to the ports.[5] Even Manuel Azaña, the President of the Republic, only yesterday the

---

[2] Campoamor, *La révolution espagnole vue par une républicaine*, p. 103.

[3] Langdon-Davies, *Behind the Spanish Barricades*, pp. 123–4. See also Louis Fischer, *Men and Politics*, p. 353; Galíndez, *Los vascos en el Madrid sitiado*, p. 22; Frank Jellinek, *The Spanish Civil War*, p. 380; Kaminski, *Ceux de Barcelone*, pp. 30–1; Megan Laird in *The Atlantic Monthly*, November, 1936; E. Puig Mora, *La tragedia roja de Barcelona*, p. 52; *CNT*, May 28, 1937 (article by J. García Pradas); *Solidaridad Obrera*, August 11, 1936 (article by Sixto).

[4] "In twenty-four hours, minds that once appeared averse to change have evolved strikingly," wrote a famous Anarchist within a few days of the revolution. "Displaying a remarkable ability to adapt themselves, men who were spiritually very far removed from us have accepted the new order of things without protest. Nobody is startled today to hear of socialization and the disappearance of private property."—Federica Montseny in *La Revista Blanca*, July 30, 1936.

[5] For criticism of these Republicans by Fernando Valera, a Cortes deputy, and prominent member of *Unión Republicana*, see speech, reported in *El Pueblo*, January 27, 1937. See also article by Juan J. Domenichina, a leading intellectual of *Izquierda Republicana*, in *Hoy*, December 28, 1940.

idol of the liberal segment of the middle classes, was paralysed by pessimism and fear, and had tumbled overnight from his summit of acclaimed leadership. From the very first moment, affirms Angel Ossorio, the Republican jurist, Manuel Azaña felt that the war was lost, and the excesses that had occurred in the early days revolted and demoralized him.[6] True, many of the leaders of the liberal Republican parties would have been capable navigators in calm seas, but they had been helpless in the midst of the storms that had buffeted the Republic before the Civil War and were even more so now in face of the hurricane that had shattered the coercive organs of the state. "The slight resistance we offered to the assaults of other organizations, our silence and our aloofness in face of the daring advances of the audacious led many persons to believe that we no longer existed," declared the President of *Izquierda Republicana*, the Left Republican Party. "They could not understand the noble aim that impelled us to stifle our indignation. The prudence and sense of responsibility that others lacked had to distinguish our behaviour, if the wall of resistance which we had to erect with arms in our hands against the violent onset of the enemy were not to collapse."[7] But floundering in the flood of the revolution, the liberal as well as the conservative members of the middle classes were impressed at the time only by the manifest impotence of their parties and soon began to cast about for an organization that would serve as a breakwater to check the revolutionary tide set in motion by the Anarchist and Socialist labour unions.

They did not have to search for long. Before many weeks had passed the organization that succeeded in focusing upon itself their immediate hopes was the Communist Party.

A relatively unimportant factor in Spanish politics at the outbreak of the Civil War, with only sixteen seats in the Cortes and an officially estimated membership of forty thousand,[8] the Communist Party was soon to mould decisively the course of events in the camp of the anti-Franco forces. Championing the interests of the urban and rural middle classes—a stand few Republicans dared to assume in that atmosphere of revolutionary emotionalism—the Communist Party became within

[6] *Mis Memorias*, p. 226.·

[7] Speech reported in *Política*, December 6, 1938. See also *ibid.*, January 13, 1937. For criticism of the laissez-faire attitude of the Republican parties by a Republican officer, see Pérez Salas, *Guerra en España*, p. 135.

[8] This figure is given by Manuel Delicado, a member of the Central Committee, as the July 18, 1936, membership.—*La Correspondencia Internacional*, July 23, 1939.

a few months the refuge, according to its own figures, of 76,700 peasant proprietors and tenant farmers and of 15,485 members of the urban middle classes.[9] That its influence among these layers went far beyond these aforementioned figures is indubitable, for thousands of members of the intermediate classes in both town and country, without actually becoming adherents of the party, placed themselves under its wing.[10] From the very outset of the revolution, the Communist Party, like the PSUC, the Communist-controlled United Socialist Party of Catalonia,[11] took up the cause of the middle classes who were being dragged into the vortex of the collectivization movement or who were being crippled by the disruption of trade, the lack of financial resources, and by the requisitions carried out by the working-class militia.

"In a capitalist society, the small tradesmen and manufacturers," declared *Mundo Obrero*, the Communist organ in Madrid, "constitute a class that has many things in common with the proletariat. It is of course on the side of the democratic Republic, and it is as much opposed to the big capitalists and captains of powerful fascist enterprises as the workers. This being so it is everybody's duty to respect the property of these small tradesmen and manufacturers.

"We therefore strongly urge the members of our party and the militia in general to demand, and, if need be, to enforce respect for these middle-class citizens, all of whom are workers, and who therefore should not be molested. Their modest interests should not be injured by requisitions and demands that are beyond their meagre resources."[12]

". . . It would be unpardonable," said *Treball*, the Communist organ in Catalonia, "to forget the multitude of small commodity producers and businessmen of our region. Many of them, thinking only of creating what they had believed would be a position of independence for themselves, had succeeded in setting up their own businesses. Then came a change in the situation precipitated by the attempted *coup d'état* of the fascists. The immense majority of small commodity producers and businessmen, who had lived completely on the margin of events,

---

[9] See report to the Central Committee in March, 1937, by José Díaz, general secretary of the party, reprinted in Díaz, *Tres años de lucha*, pp. 288–339. "The Republican middle class," writes a Socialist, "surprised by the moderate tone of Communist propaganda and impressed by the unity and realism which prevailed in this party, flocked in great numbers to join its ranks."—Ramos Oliveira, *Politics, Economics and Men of Modern Spain, 1808–1946*, p. 599.

[10] See, for example, Julio Mateu, general secretary of the Communist-run Peasant Federation of Valencia province, quoted on p. 86, below.

[11] For some information on this party, see pp. 113–14, also n. 37, p. 113, below.

[12] July 27, 1936.

are now more confused than anyone, because they feel that they are being harmed and that they are at an obvious disadvantage in comparison with the wage earners. They declare that nobody is concerned about their fate. They are elements who might tend to favour any reactionary movement, because in their opinion anything would be better than the economic system that is being instituted in our region....[13]

"The distressing situation of many of these people is obvious. They cannot run their workshops and businesses because they have no reserve capital; they have hardly enough to eat, especially the small manufacturers, because the wages they have to pay to the few workers they employ prevent them from attending to their own daily needs. . . .

"A moratorium must be granted to all those people who have placed themselves at the service of the anti-fascist militia, so that they do not have to bear the full weight of the requisitions imposed by the war. A moratorium must be granted and a credit should be opened so that their businesses do not go into liquidation."[14]

As a means of protecting the interests of the urban middle classes in this region the Communists organized eighteen thousand tradesmen, handicraftsmen, and small manufacturers into the *Federación Catalana de Gremios y Entidades de Pequeños Comerciantes e Industriales* (known as the GEPCI),[15] some of whose members were, in the phrase of *Solidaridad Obrera*, the CNT organ, "intransigent employers, ferociously anti-labour," including Gurri, the former President of the Tailoring Trades Association.[16]

[13] This hostility of a large part of the small bourgeoisie to the revolution was acknowledged in an official report of the CNT; see report of the *Junta del Control del Comité Económico*, as given in *Memoria del congreso extraordinario de la confederación regional del trabajo de Cataluña celebrado en Barcelona los días 25 de febrero al 3 de marzo de 1937*, pp. 363–5.

[14] August 8, 1936. For other Communist statements and articles in the first months of the war in defence of the urban middle classes, see *Mundo Obrero*, August 5, 13–15, 20, 31, September 16, 1936; *Treball*, August 17, September 22, December 22 (speech by Sesé), 1936; speeches by Díaz, as reprinted in Díaz, *Tres años de lucha*, pp. 227–34, 247–9, 258–73. The following lines, taken from an article by a former foreign Communist who served in the International Brigades in Spain, are worth quoting: "In Murcia and elsewhere I saw that our placards and leaflets appealed for shopkeepers' membership with the promise of absolute support of private property."—Henry Scott Beattie in *The Canadian Forum*, April, 1938.

[15] This figure is given by Antonio Mije, a member of the Politburo of the Communist Party, *Frente Rojo*, October 21, 1937; see also Miguel Ferrer, secretary-general of the Communist-controlled UGT of Catalonia, in *La Vanguardia*, April 9, 1938.

[16] April 25, 1937.

In the countryside the Communists undertook a spirited defence of the small and medium proprietor and tenant farmer against the collectivizing drive of the rural wage-workers, against the policy of the labour unions prohibiting the farmer from holding more land than he could cultivate with his own hands, and against the practices of revolutionary committees, which requisitioned harvests, interfered with private trade, and collected rents from tenant farmers. While the liberal Republicans were cautious to the point of timidity,[17] the Communists were not backward in profiting from any discontent in the countryside. "In the early days of the military rebellion," wrote Julio Mateu, a member of the Central Committee of the party, in reference to the province of Valencia, "when an endless chain of committees and more committees tried to make a clean sweep of the entire countryside by immediately converting all small proprietors into agricultural workers, by despoiling them of their land and harvests, there was a real danger of setting the peasants against the anti-fascist organizations. The modest agricultural producers, who for a long time had been oppressed by the political bosses and reactionary usurers, were once again maltreated, this time because of lack of understanding on the part of those who should have helped them in their development. The mistake of considering simple Catholic peasants as enemies prompted some organizations to commit such injustices as to collect from the tenant farmers the rents they formerly paid to the land-owners. . . .

"We have passed through moments of real danger, having been within an ace of unleashing a civil war in the rear between the farmers and the agricultural workers. Fortunately this has been averted, although at the cost of bursting our lungs in an intense campaign of political education in the villages aimed at securing respect for small property."[18]

Speaking at a public meeting, Vicente Uribe, a member of the Central Committee of the Communist Party, and Minister of Agriculture from September, 1936, declared:

[17] A consultation of their newspapers offers sufficient proof of this. It is noteworthy that it was not until some months later, when the revolutionary tide was receding, that they ventured to raise their voices. "We are tired of remaining silent," declared Miguel San Andrés, the Left Republican deputy (reported, *Política*, April 19, 1937). "The plundering of the small manufacturer, of the small farmer, and intellectual, of all those people who have been working year after year in order to save a little money can no longer be tolerated. We have seen our interests trampled under foot, and until now we have remained silent."

[18] Article in *Amanecer Rojo*; reprinted in *Verdad*, December 2, 1936.

"The present policy of violence against the peasants has two dangers. The first is that it may estrange those who are on our side, on the anti-fascist side. The other is still more serious: it will endanger the future food supply of Spain. . . . It cannot be tolerated that while at the fronts the soldiers are giving their lives and their blood for the common cause, there are persons far behind the lines who use rifles belonging to the people in order to impose by force ideas that the people do not accept.

"But I tell you, peasants; I tell you, workers of the countryside, that despite the abuses some persons are committing, despite the barbarities they are perpetrating, your obligation is to work the land and extract the utmost from it, because you are protected by the government, by parties and by organizations, and because you have at your side the Communist Party. . . . Even though violence is used, it is your duty as patriots, your duty as Republicans, your duty as anti-fascists to call upon the government, to call upon the Communists, and you can be sure that, in order that you may cultivate the land peacefully, we shall be at your side armed with rifles."[19]

And, speaking a few days later at another meeting, he stated, in reference to the establishment of Libertarian Communism by the Anarchosyndicalists in some of the villages of Valencia province:

"We know that some committees have set up a certain type of régime, a régime in which everyone is subjected to the mercy of their will. We know that they confiscate harvests, and commit other abuses, such as seizing small peasant farms, imposing fines, paying [for goods] with vouchers, in other words, a whole series of irregularities. You know perfectly well that these actions—and listen carefully to this—can never, never have the approval of the government nor even its connivance. . . . We say that the property of the small farmer is sacred and that those who attack or attempt to attack this property must be regarded as enemies of the régime."[20]

It was only natural that the Communists' defence of the interests of peasant owners and tenant farmers should have brought their party a broad wave of adherents. In their campaign they were most successful, of course, in those areas where small and medium-sized farms pre-

---

[19] *Verdad*, December 8, 1936.

[20] *Verdad*, December 1, 1936. For other speeches by Communist leaders in support of the small and middle peasant, see *El Mercantil Valenciano*, January 24, 1937 (Uribe); *Treball*, October 20, 1936 (Comorera), February 7, 1937 (Colomer); Segis Alvarez, *La juventud y los campesinos*; Díaz, *Tres años de lucha*, pp. 227–34, 247–9, 258–73; *El partido comunista por la libertad y la independencia de España* (Pasionaria), pp. 181–91.

dominated. In the rich orange- and rice-growing province of Valencia, for example, where the farmers were prosperous and had supported right-wing organizations before the Civil War, fifty thousand had by March, 1937, according to official figures, joined the Peasant Federation,[21] which the Communist Party had set up for their protection in the first months of the revolution.[22] In addition to providing its members with fertilizers and seed, and securing credits from the Ministry of Agriculture—likewise controlled by the Communists—the Peasant Federation also served as a powerful instrument in checking the rural collectivization promoted by the agricultural workers of the province. That the protection afforded by this organization should have induced many of its members to apply for admission into the Communist Party is understandable. "Such is the sympathy for us in the Valencia countryside," Julio Mateu, general secretary of the federation, affirmed, "that hundreds and thousands of farmers would join our party if we were to let them. These farmers, many of whom believed in God—and still do—and prayed and in private beat their breasts, love our party like a sacred thing. When we tell them that they should not confuse the Peasant Federation with the party, and that even without a membership card it is possible to be a Communist by working for its political line, they are wont to reply, 'The Communist Party is our party.' Comrades, what emotion the peasants display when they utter these words!"[23]

Because the Communist Party gave the urban and rural middle classes a powerful access of life and vigour, it is not surprising that a large part of the copious flow of new members into the party in the months following the revolution came from these classes. It is almost superfluous to say of course that these new recruits were attracted, not by Communist principles, but by the hope of saving something from

[21] Julio Mateu, general secretary of the federation, *La obra de la federación campesina*, p. 7.

[22] "The Communist Party," complained a Socialist, "devotes itself to picking up in the villages the worst remnants of the former *Partido Autonomista*, who were not only reactionary, but also immoral, and organizes these small proprietors into a new peasant union by promising them the possession of their land."—*Claridad*, December 14, 1936. See also article by Santiago Bosca in the left-wing Socialist *Adelante*, as given in *CNT*, May 15, 1937, and letter from the Valencia secretariat of the Federation of Land Workers (Socialist) to the Peasant Federation, published in *Fragua Social*, August 12, 1937. For a strong attack by an Anarchosyndicalist on the well-to-do farmers who entered the Peasant Federation, see *Nosotros*, June 5, 1937.

[23] Mateu, *La obra de la federación campesina*, pp. 9–10.

the ruins of the old social system. Furthermore, in addition to defending their property rights, the Communist Party defined the social overturn, not as a proletarian, but as a bourgeois democratic revolution. Within a few days of the outbreak of the war, Dolores Ibarruri, the woman Communist leader, known as La Pasionaria, declared in the name of the Central Committee:

"The revolution that is taking place in our country is the bourgeois democratic revolution which was achieved over a century ago in other countries, such as France, and we Communists are the front-line fighters in this struggle against the obscurantist forces of the past.

"Cease conjuring up the spectre of Communism, you generals, many times traitors, with the idea of isolating the Spanish people in its magnificent struggle against those who wish to turn Spain into a tragic, backward country, a country in which the military, the clergy, and the political bosses would be the absolute masters of life and property! We Communists are defending a régime of liberty and democracy, and side by side with Republicans, Socialists, and Anarchists we shall prevent Spain from retrogressing, cost what it may. . . .

"It is a lie to speak of chaos; a lie to say that a chaotic situation exists here, as do the reports given out by traitors to the Republic!

"In this historic hour the Communist Party, faithful to its revolutionary principles and respecting the will of the people, places itself at the side of the government which expresses this will, at the side of the Republic, at the side of democracy. . . .

". . . The Government of Spain is a government that emerged from the electoral triumph of February 16, and we support it and we defend it, because it is the legal representative of the people fighting for democracy and liberty. . . .

". . . Long live the struggle of the people against reaction and fascism! Long live the Democratic Republic!"[24]

Thus, from the outset, the Communist Party appeared before the distraught middle classes not only as a defender of property, but as a champion of the Republic and of orderly processes of government. Not that these classes had complete confidence in its good faith, but they were ready to support it so long as it offered them protection and helped to restore to the government the power assumed by revolutionary committees. That their support was shot through with suspicion and fear was natural, for in the past the Communists had pursued an entirely different policy, as will be seen in the ensuing chapter.

[24] *Mundo Obrero*, July 30, 1936.

7

The Popular Front

"OUR task is to win over the majority of the proletariat and to prepare it for the assumption of power . . . ," La Pasionaria had declared towards the end of 1933. "This means that we must bend all our efforts to organize workshop and peasant committees and to create soviets. . . .

". . . The development of the revolutionary movement is extremely favourable to us. We are advancing along the road which has been indicated to us by the Communist International, and which leads to the establishment of a Soviet government in Spain, a government of workers and peasants."[1]

This policy was in strange contrast to that pursued two years later in Spain. The reversal that had subsequently occurred stemmed, of course, from the resolutions adopted at the Seventh World Congress of the Communist International in 1935, introducing the Popular Front policy. At the root of this new policy lay the deterioration in German–Soviet relations since Adolf Hitler's rise to power in January, 1933, and the fear that Germany's revived military strength would ultimately be directed against the U.S.S.R. Suffering from the after-effects of compulsory collectivization, and bending every effort to strengthen her political and military system, the Soviet Union was careful not to offer any provocation that would draw her into permanent estrangement from the Nazi régime.[2] Indeed, *Izvestiya*, the organ of the Soviet

[1] *XIII Plenum IKKI. Stenograficheskii otchet* (Thirteenth Plenum of the Executive Committee of the Communist International; Stenographic Report), p. 531. See also *The Communist International*, December 5, 1934 ("The Struggle against Fascism, the Struggle for Power, for the Workers' and Peasants' Republic in Spain").

[2] "Hitler's bloody suppression of all domestic opposition and his racial persecutions affected diplomatic routine business between Moscow and Berlin as little as it affected similar business between Paris or London and Berlin. Stalin undoubtedly calculated on the strength of the Bismarckian tradition

Government, declared within a few weeks of Hitler's appointment to the Reich Chancellorship that the U.S.S.R. was the only state that had "no hostile sentiments towards Germany, whatever the form and composition of that country's government."[3] But Russia's advances had been coldly received, and at the end of 1933, Molotov, Chairman of the Council of People's Commissars, complained that during the past year the ruling groups in Germany had made a number of attempts to revise relations with the Soviet Union.[4]

With a view to seeking safeguards against the menace of German expansion and to making her influence felt in the chancelleries of Western Europe, the Soviet Union reversed her attitude of hostility towards the League of Nations and joined that body in September of 1934. "On entering the League of Nations," said the Comintern organ, *International Press Correspondence*, "it will be possible for the U.S.S.R. to struggle still more effectively and practically against a counter-revolutionary war on the U.S.S.R."[5] But in spite of this move, uneasiness regarding German intentions continued unabated. ". . . The direct threat of war has increased for the U.S.S.R. . . . ," declared Molotov in January, 1935. "We must not forget that there is now in Europe a ruling party which has proclaimed as its historical task the seizure of territory in the Soviet Union."[6] As a further move to ward off the German threat to her security, Russia concluded a Pact of Mutual Assistance with France on May 2, 1935. However, this treaty

among the German diplomats, a tradition which demanded that the Reich should avoid embroilment with Russia. In the first year of Hitler's Chancellorship he did not utter in public a single word about the events in Germany, though his silence was excruciating to the bewildered followers of the Comintern.

"He broke that silence only at the seventeenth congress of the party, in January, 1934. Even then he refrained from drawing the conclusions from events which had ended so disastrously for the European Left, and he vaguely fostered the illusion that fascism, 'a symptom of capitalist weakness,' would prove short-lived. But he also described the Nazi upheaval as a 'triumph for the idea of revenge in Europe' and remarked that the anti-Russian trend in German policy had been prevailing over the older Bismarckian tradition. Even so, he was at pains to make it clear that Russia desired to remain on the same terms with the Third Reich as she had been with Weimar Germany."—Isaac Deutscher, *Stalin*, p. 415.

[3] March 4, 1933.

[4] Speech at the Fourth Session of the Central Executive Committee of the Soviet Union, as reported by *Izvestiia*, December 29, 1933.

[5] October 12, 1934.

[6] Speech at the Seventh Congress of the U.S.S.R., reported by *Izvestiia*, January 29, 1935.

was favoured by the French mainly in order to remove any links that still remained between the U.S.S.R. and Germany since the Russo-German rapprochement begun at Rapallo in 1922,[7] and to end the opposition of the French Communist Party to the national defence programme;[8] in fact, it was never supplemented by any positive military agreement between the respective general staffs[9] and from the beginning elicited very little enthusiasm even from government circles.[10] Hence, Moscow was fully alive to the possibility that the pact

[7] André Géraud (Pertinax), *The Gravediggers of France*, pp. 244–5, 342–3; Geneviève Tabouis, *Blackmail or War*, p. 90.

[8] Tabouis, *Blackmail or War*, pp. 91–3; Henri de Kerillis, *Français! Voici la guerre*, pp. 111–12; Winston Churchill, *The Gathering Storm*, pp. 134–5. For a well-documented account of the French Communist Party's opposition to the defence programme before the signing of the Franco-Soviet Pact, see Maurice Ceyrat, *La trahison permanente. Parti communiste et politique russe*, pp. 26–41. After the conclusion of the treaty Stalin gave public approval to the programme (see official communiqué as published in *Le Temps*, May 17, 1935), and some time afterwards the French Communist Party executed an about-turn.

[9] Max Beloff, *The Foreign Policy of Soviet Russia 1929–1941*, I, p. 157; Churchill, *The Gathering Storm*, p. 135; Paul Reynaud, *La France a sauvé l'Europe*, I, p. 115 ff. In his book *De la place de la Concorde au cours de l'Intendance*, Fabry, Minister of War at the time of the signing of the Franco-Soviet Pact, reveals that both he and Laval, the Prime Minister, were opposed to the idea of a military convention.—Quoted by Paul Reynaud in his testimony before the Parliamentary Commission of Inquiry set up in 1947 to investigate the events that took place in France between 1933 and 1945 (*Les événements survenus en France de 1933 à 1945*. Vol. I, pp. 89–90).

[10] See Beloff, *The Foreign Policy of Soviet Russia 1929–1941*, I, p. 160; Kerillis, *Français! Voici la guerre*, p. 117; Charles A. Micaud, *The French Right and Nazi Germany, 1933–1939*, p. 68; Tabouis, *Ils l'ont appelée Cassandre*, pp. 244–5. Some idea of what the French Foreign Office, even at the time of the Popular Front Government, thought of the Franco-Soviet Pact may be gathered from the following extract taken from a memorandum by the Acting State Secretary of the German Foreign Office following a conversation on September 1, 1936, with the French Ambassador, François-Poncet. Referring to the proposed meeting of the five Locarno Powers (Great Britain, France, Belgium, Italy, and Germany) to negotiate a new Western Pact to take the place of the Locarno Agreement, the memorandum states: "M. François-Poncet was particularly interested in hearing whether we were willing to go to the conference and negotiate on the first points on the agenda without bringing up the fifth point, or whether we wanted to force the French Government now, in advance, expressly to renounce the fifth point, that is, the ties in the East. In other words, did the German Government take the stand that it was possible to start out by negotiating on a Western Pact, leaving the Eastern questions open? Or did it demand from the very first that France renounce her Eastern ties, before Germany would enter into a discussion concerning a Western Pact? If Germany followed the first course, he believed he could say that the Franco-Russian ties

might eventually be disregarded, and it thus became a vital task for French Communists to ensure that France would honour her commitments.

"We can congratulate ourselves on the Franco-Soviet treaty," declared Vaillant Couturier, the French Communist leader, "but as we have no confidence that the French bourgeoisie and the fascist cadres of the French army will observe its clauses, *we shall act accordingly*. We know that whatever may be the interests that lead certain French political circles towards a rapprochement with the U.S.S.R., the champions of French imperialism hate the Soviet Union."[11]

It is of course true that there were powerful forces both in France and Britain who were opposed to any hard and fast commitments in Eastern Europe that might entangle the West in a war with Germany and who seemed ready to countenance the latter's expansionist aims at the expense of the Soviet Union. "In those prewar years," writes Sumner Welles, who became U.S. Under-Secretary of State in 1937, "great financial and commercial interests of the Western democracies, including many in the United States, were firm in the belief that war between the Soviet Union and Hitlerite Germany could only be favourable to their own interests. They maintained that Russia would necessarily be defeated, and with this defeat Communism would be destroyed; also that Germany would be so weakened as a result of the conflict that for many years thereafter she would be incapable of any real threat to the rest of the world."[12]

---

would gradually cool, particularly since they had never been popular with a large sector of the French people; we would then attain our objective slowly but surely. If, on the other hand, we should apply pressure to the French Government now and demand that it give up the Russian alliance, the French Government could only refuse to do so. In a long discourse M. François-Poncet tried to convince me of the rightness of the one alternative and the wrongness of the other, emphasizing solemnly during the course of his statements that there were no special military ties between France and the Soviet Union."— *Documents on German Foreign Policy 1918–1945. III. Germany and the Spanish Civil War 1936–1939*, p. 67.

[11] *L'Humanité*, May 17, 1935. Italics in text. See also *ibid.*, May 16, 1935, article by M. Magnien.

[12] *The Time for Decision*, p. 321. On May 6, 1935, William Dodd, U.S. Ambassador to Berlin, noted in his diary the following lines regarding a letter he had received from Lord Lothian: "He [Lothian] indicated clearly that he favours a coalition of the democracies to block any German move in their direction and to turn Germany's course eastwards."—Ambassador Dodd, *Ambassador Dodd's Diary*, p. 241. In an article entitled, "Why not a Franco-British Alliance?" (*Daily Mail*, November 28, 1933), Viscount Rothermere wrote: "The new bond between France and Britain would have another effect

That the rulers of Western Europe were confronted with a fateful choice is indubitable:

On the one hand, they could oppose and destroy the Nazi régime while it was still weak, leaving the Soviet Union free to develop its resources and become in time, with allied Communist parties, the greatest menace in the world;[13] on the other hand, they could, though not without opprobrium and extreme peril to themselves, allow the Nazi régime to overrun the non-totalitarian states in Central and South-Eastern Europe lying west of Russia's border in the hope that it would in time come into collision with the rising power of the Soviet Union.[14] How far their attitude towards Germany was determined by this hope is illustrated by Lord Lloýd, a leading British diplomat. In his pamph-

---

of inestimable importance. It would turn Germany's territorial ambitions in the direction where they can do least harm and most good—towards the east of Europe." See also Micaud, *The French Right and Nazi Germany, 1933–1939,* pp. 71–4.

[13] "I feel that if the Nazi régime in Germany is destroyed then the country will go Communist and we shall find a lining-up of France, Germany and Russia and the menace of Communism as the most powerful policy in the world."—The Marquess of Londonderry in a letter to Winston Churchill, May 9, 1936, quoted by Londonderry in *Wings of Destiny,* p. 171. The Marquess of Londonderry was Secretary of State for Air from 1931 to 1935. ". . . these parties [of the French Right]," wrote Thierry Maulnier in *Combat* (November, 1938), "felt that in the event of war not only would the disaster be tremendous, not only would the defeat and devastation of France be within the bounds of possibility, but, even more, that Germany's defeat would mean the collapse of those authoritarian systems which form the principal bulwark against Communist revolution and that it would perhaps lead to the immediate Bolsheviza-tion of Europe. In other words, a French defeat would indeed have been a defeat of France, while a French victory would have been less a victory for France than for the principles quite rightly regarded as leading directly to the ruin of France and of civilization itself. It is a pity that the men and parties in France who shared in that belief did not in general admit it, for there was nothing inavowable about it. Indeed, in my opinion, it was one of the principal and well-founded reasons, if not the best-founded, for not going to war in September, 1938." See also extract from article by Léon Bailby, quoted p. 96, below.

[14] It is only right to record here the view of one of the staunchest right-wing opponents of any policy involving the sacrifice to Nazi Germany of the small states in Central and South-Eastern Europe. "We all wish to live on friendly terms with Germany," wrote Winston Churchill to the Marquess of London-derry. "We know the best Germans are ashamed of the Nazi excesses and recoil from the paganism on which they are based. We certainly do not want to pursue a policy inimical to the legitimate interests of Germany, but you must surely be aware that, when the German Government speaks of friendship with England, what they mean is, that we shall give them back their former colonies,

let, *The British Case*, which was written shortly after the outbreak of war in 1939 between Britain and Germany, and which was given the stamp of official endorsement by the commendatory preface of Lord Halifax, then Secretary of State for Foreign Affairs, Lord Lloyd wrote:

"However abominable [Hitler's] methods, however deceitful his diplomacy, however intolerant he might show himself of the rights of other European peoples, he still claimed to stand ultimately for something which was a common European interest, and which therefore could conceivably provide some day a basis for understanding with other nations equally determined not to sacrifice their traditional institutions and habits on the blood-stained altars of the World Revolution."[15]

In order to prevent the Western democracies from compounding their differences with the Third Reich at the possible expense of Russia, in order to guarantee that the Franco-Soviet Pact of Mutual Assistance would not fall by the wayside, and, moreover, in order to conclude similar alliances with other countries, notably Great Britain, it was essential for the Soviet Union that governments hostile to German aims in Eastern Europe should be brought into office. It was with this end in view that the Popular Front line was formally adopted at the Seventh World Congress of the Comintern in August, 1935.[16] The Congress decided that one of the immediate tasks of Communists in all countries was to bring the peasantry and the small urban bourgeoisie into a "wide anti-fascist people's front." Contending that the

---

and also agree to their having a free hand, as far as we are concerned, in Central and Southern Europe.

"This means that they would devour Austria and Czechoslovakia as a preliminary to making a gigantic Middle-European bloc. It would certainly not be in our interest to connive at such policies of aggression. It would be wrong and cynical in the last degree to buy immunity for ourselves at the expense of smaller states in Central Europe.

"It would be contrary to the whole tide of British and United States opinion for us to facilitate the spread of Nazi tyranny over countries which now have a considerable measure of democratic freedom. In my view we should build up so strong a Federation of Regional Agreements under the League of Nations, that Germany will be content to live within her own bounds in a law-abiding manner, instead of seeking to invade her smaller neighbours, slay them and have their farms and homes for themselves."—Quoted Londonderry, *Wings of Destiny*, p. 187.

[15] p. 55.

[16] It should be noted that some of the sections of the Comintern had, in accordance with the new trend in Soviet foreign policy, been seeking co-operation with other parties before that date. This attempt had been most successful in France.—See Beloff, *The Foreign Policy of Soviet Russia 1929–1941*, I, pp.188–9.

"dominant circles of the British bourgeoisie support German arma-ments[17] in order to weaken the hegemony of France on the European Continent . . . and to direct Germany's aggressiveness against the Soviet Union,"[18] the Congress declared that the struggle for peace opened up the greatest opportunity for creating the broadest united front, and that "all those interested in the preservation of peace should be drawn into this united front." This was to be achieved by mobilizing the people against "the plundering price policy of monopoly capital and the bourgeois governments" and against "increasing taxation and the high cost of living."[19] Although the Congress reaffirmed the aims of the Communist International, namely, the revolutionary overthrow of the rule of the bourgeoisie and the establishment of the dictatorship of the proletariat in the form of soviets,[20] the policy of unity with the middle classes could not but lead sooner or later to an attempt on the part of the Comintern's various sections to live down their revolu-tionary past and to disarm the suspicion with which they were once regarded.

[17] On February 6, 1935, Sir John Simon, then Secretary of State for Foreign Affairs, had stated in the House of Commons: "Germany's claim to equality of rights in the matter of armaments cannot be resisted, and ought not to be resisted."—*The Times*, London, February 7, 1934. And on June 18, 1935, the Anglo-German Naval Agreement had been signed, giving the German Navy thirty-five per cent of British naval tonnage. Referring to the agreement in the House of Commons on July 11, 1935, Winston Churchill declared: "We have condoned, and even praised the German treaty-breaking in fleet-building."—Quoted in Churchill, *Arms and the Covenant*, p. 249. See also Churchill, *The Gathering Storm*, pp. 137–41. "In Russia," writes Max Beloff (*The Foreign Policy of Soviet Russia 1929–1941*, I, pp. 133–4), "the pact was interpreted as a sign of Britain's weakness and of her desire to divert Germany from air preparations to naval building, where she felt stronger. It might also serve to divert Germany's attention eastward and to allow Britain to disengage herself from Europe, so as to salvage her menaced position in the Far East. A new field of activity would be open for British advocates of an entente with Germany. The Germans would not, the Russians argued, observe the agreement, and only welcomed it as a breach in the treaties. It was clear that the German command of the Baltic [the gateway to Russia] would be unassailable. Nor does there seem any reason to doubt that it was the Baltic situation which Herr Hitler had chiefly in mind." In the summer of 1935, Germany reintroduced conscription in violation of the Versailles Treaty. This too was condoned by Britain. See Churchill, *The Gathering Storm*, p. 189.

[18] *International Press Correspondence*, September 19, 1935.

[19] *Ibid.*

[20] *Ibid.*

8

Concealing the Revolution

FOR a time the Popular Front policy met with appreciable success. In the early months of 1936, both in France and Spain, the Communists participated in general elections on a broad basis and helped to bring liberal governments into office, uniting not only with the Socialists, but also with the moderate parties.

That Germany should have viewed with alarm the success of a policy designed to establish an anti-German front by reinforcing and extending Russia's political and military ties with Western Europe is natural, but not until the outbreak of the revolt in Spain in July, 1936, did an opportunity arise, by direct intervention on the side of the rebellion, to counter this threat to her own plans.[1] In going to the aid

[1] Contrary to the opinion widely held, no promises of German military aid were given to the organizers of the revolt prior to the outbreak of hostilities. According to the documents relating to Spain in the archives of the German Foreign Ministry, published in Washington by the Department of State, 1950, Hitler did not promise assistance until several days after the outbreak of the rebellion, when General Franco sent a German businessman resident in Spanish Morocco and the local Nazi leader to Germany to request planes and other support.—*Documents on German Foreign Policy 1918–1945*. III. *Germany and the Spanish Civil War 1936–1939*, pp. 1–2. This request, to be sure, was promptly acceded to, for according to Nazi sources German airplanes were active on the side of General Franco in the first weeks of the war either in transporting Moors and Foreign Legionaries from Spanish Morocco to the mainland or in bombing operations.—See Werner Beumelburg, *Kampf um Spanien*, pp. 22–9; Wulf Bley, *Das Buch der Spanienflieger*, pp. 23–7, 31–2; Max Graf Hoyos, *Pedros y Pablos*, pp. 15–22; Otto Schempp, *Das autoritäre Spanien*, pp. 69–71; Rud. Stache, *Armee mit geheimem Auftrag*, pp. 10–26; Hannes Trautloft, *Als Jagdflieger in Spanien*, p. 29; official account of German intervention published in the German Press (as reported in the *Daily Telegraph*, May 31, 1939); special number of *Die Wehrmacht* entitled *Wir Kämpften in Spanien*, issued in May, 1939, by the German High Command. According to the official account published in the German Press referred to above, the first armoured car detachment was sent out in October, 1936. It consisted of staff, two companies, and a transport

of General Franco, she had no doubt a twofold objective. On the one hand, while fearful of the international complications that might arise from being drawn too deeply into the Spanish conflict[2] at a time when she was not yet ready for a large-scale war, she hoped to secure strategic advantages in preparation for the coming struggle in Western Europe;[3] on the other hand she hoped that the defeat of the Popular Front and the resurgence of the Right in Spain would weaken the French Popular Front and strengthen those forces in France who were opposed to blocking German expansion eastwards and who regarded the Franco-Soviet Pact of Mutual Assistance as likely to entangle their country in a struggle which, in the event of a German defeat, would result in the enthronement of Communism in Europe. "What Moscow wants," ran an article that was typical of an appreciable segment of French opinion, "is a war between French and German soldiers. At some time or another, on some pretext or another, Russia hopes that she will be able to force us to throw our troops against the [German] frontier and deal a double blow by weakening the dreaded German power and by delivering our country up to a foreign war, which would ring in the hour of the Bolshevik Revolution."[4]

company, and, in addition to taking part in the fighting, formed a school of instruction for Spaniards in the use of armoured cars, guns, and flame-throwers. In November, according to the same account, a complete air force corps arrived in Spain, composed of combat, pursuit, and reconnaissance planes, as well as intelligence and anti-aircraft detachments. In an article published in the special number of *Die Wehrmacht*, mentioned above, General Sperrle stated that six thousand five hundred German "volunteers" reached Spain at the beginning of November, 1936.

[2] See memorandum by the Acting State Secretary of the German Foreign Office, Hans Heinrich Dieckhoff, as reprinted in *Documents on German Foreign Policy 1918–1945*. III. *Germany and the Spanish Civil War 1936–1939*, pp. 155–6; also *ibid.*, pp. 168, 222, 230, 265, 391–2, and Ernst von Weizsäcker, *Memoirs of Ernst von Weizsäcker*, pp. 113–14.

[3] In this connection the extract of a report (quoted in n. 8, pp. 98–9, below) by the German Ambassador in Rome to the Wilhelmstrasse, dated December 18, 1936, on the interests of Germany and Italy in the Spanish conflict is instructive. In a communication to the Wilhelmstrasse, dated May 1, 1937, the German Ambassador to General Franco wrote: "There is no doubt that [after] a war won because of our intervention a Spain socially ordered and economically reconstructed with our help will in the future be not only a very important source of raw materials for us, but also a faithful friend for a long time to come."— *Documents on German Foreign Policy 1918–1945*. III. *Germany and the Spanish Civil War 1936–1939*, p. 279.

[4] Léon Bailby in *Le Jour*, September 24, 1936. See also Pierre Bernus in *Journal des Débats*, August 15, 1936; Pierre Gaxotte in *Candide*, August 27, 1936; Pierre Dominique in *La République*, October 8, 9, 1936.

Russia was not blind to the dangers of German intervention in Spain, but anxious not to give body and colour to attacks that pictured her as the open patron of world revolution, lest she antagonize the moderate parties in the Western democracies on whom she based her hopes of an anti-German front, she adhered in August, 1936, to the international non-intervention agreement, which had been proposed by France in order to prevent an extension of the conflict,[5] and undertook together with the other countries participating in the accord not to send arms to Spain.[6] "Had the Soviet Union not agreed to the French proposal for neutrality," commented the London *Daily Worker*, "it would have very seriously embarrassed that Government, and considerably assisted Fascists in France and England, as well as the governments of Germany and Italy, in their campaign against the Spanish people. . . .

[5] An account of the non-intervention system can be found in Norman J. Padelford's *International Law and Diplomacy in the Spanish Civil Strife.*

[6] This concern for Western opinion ill accords with the charge put forward by rebel sources, in order to justify the military revolt, that the Communists had been conspiring to set up a Soviet régime in Spain in the summer of 1936 (see Manuel Aznar, *Historia militar de la guerre de España*, pp. 25–30; also *Exposure of the Secret Plan to Establish a Soviet in Spain*), for it is obvious that had they even attempted to establish such a régime they would have ruined the Comintern's hopes of a rapprochement with the Western powers. For this reason alone—to say nothing of the fact that they certainly did not have the necessary strength—the charge may be safely discounted. In spite of the seemingly revolutionary character of the language they sometimes employed so as not to lose touch with the radical temper of the masses after the victory of the Popular Front in the February, 1936, elections, and in spite of their warnings to the liberal government that the agricultural workers would divide up the estates of the big landed proprietors by force of arms if it did not carry out the agrarian reform more expeditiously (see speech by José Díaz, secretary of the Communist Party, April 5, 1936, as given in *Tres años de lucha*, p. 134), the Communists were careful to maintain their alliance with the moderates. "The Popular Front must continue," wrote José Díaz. "We have still a long way to travel in company with the left-wing Republicans." (Article in *La Correspondencia Internacional*, April 17, 1936, as given in Díaz, *Tres años de lucha*, pp. 116–21). Again, in spite of their threat just before the military insurrection that unless the government fulfilled the Popular Front programme they would strive for the creation of a government of a "revolutionary popular character" (speech by José Díaz, July 5, 1936, *ibid.*, pp. 183–6), this language was designed more to propitiate the prevailing revolutionary sentiment and to goad the government into positive action against the Right than to encourage an immediate social overturn. Indeed, during the Madrid building strike which seriously embarrassed the government before the military uprising, the Communists did what they could to induce the Anarchosyndicalists to terminate it.—See *Mundo Obrero*, July 6, 8–11, 13, 15–17, 1936; also José Bullejos (former secretary of the Communist Party), *Europa entre dos guerras*, pp. 189–90.

"If the Soviet Government took any step which added further fuel to the present inflammable situation in Europe, it would be welcome by the Fascists of all countries and would split the democratic forces, thus directly preparing the way for so-called 'preventive warfare' against Bolshevism as represented by the U.S.S.R."[7]

Nevertheless, in face of continued assistance by Germany and Italy to General Franco in the first months of the war in violation of the non-intervention agreement,[8] Russia was soon forced to reverse her

[7] September 9, 1936.

[8] On the matter of Italian intervention in the early stages of the war, Fascist sources later affirmed that Italian aeroplanes and naval units were in operation at the beginning of August.—Generale Francesco Belforte, *La guerra civile in Spagna*, III, p. 28; Guido Mattioli, *L'aviazione legionaria in Spagna*, pp. 22–8; *Le Forze Armate* (official organ of the Italian War Office), June 8, 1939. According to the latter publication, Italian warships assisted General Franco's forces in the defence of Majorca and the occupation of the neighbouring island of Ibiza in September, 1936. With regard to Italian ground forces, the first contingent of black shirts, numbering three thousand, did not leave Italy until December 18, 1936.—See telegrams from the German Ambassador in Rome to the Wilhelmstrasse, as given in *Documents on German Foreign Policy 1918–1945*. III. *Germany and the Spanish Civil War 1936–1939*, pp. 169, 173. The first shipment of Italian artillery, anti-aircraft guns, and armoured cars, however, reached Spain towards the end of September, according to Manuel Aznar, *Historia militar de la guerra de España*, p. 316. As for the motives of Italian intervention in Spain, it is worth recording here the following extract from a report, dated December 18, 1936, by the German Ambassador in Rome to the Wilhelmstrasse on the interests of Germany and Italy in the Spanish Civil War: "The interests of Germany and Italy in the Spanish troubles coincide to the extent that both countries are seeking to prevent a victory of Bolshevism in Spain or Catalonia. However, while Germany is not pursuing any immediate diplomatic interests in Spain beyond this, the efforts of Rome undoubtedly extend towards having Spain fall in line with its Mediterranean policy, or at least towards preventing political co-operation between Spain on the one hand and France and/or England on the other. The means used for this purpose are: immediate support of Franco; a foothold on the Balearic Islands, which will presumably not be evacuated voluntarily unless a central Spanish government friendly to Italy is set up; political commitment of Franco to Italy; and a close tie between Fascism and the new system of government to be established in Spain. . . .

"In connection with the general policy indicated above, Germany has in my opinion every reason for being gratified if Italy continues to interest herself deeply in the Spanish affair. The role played by the Spanish conflict as regards Italy's relations with France and England could be similar to that of the Abyssinian conflict, bringing out clearly the actual, opposing interests of the powers and thus preventing Italy from being drawn into the net of the Western powers and used for their machinations. The struggle for dominant political influence in Spain lays bare the natural opposition between Italy and France; at the same time the position of Italy as a power in the Western Mediterranean

policy, and the first Soviet artillery, tanks, and aeroplanes, together with pilots and tank operators, reached Spain in October.[9] But in supplying arms, Russia was careful not to become involved in a major conflict with Italy and Germany. According to Walter Krivitsky, the GPU agent in charge of the foreign end of Soviet arms shipments to Spain: "[Stalin] doubly cautioned his commissars that Soviet aid to Spain must be unofficial and handled covertly, in order to eliminate any possibility of involving his government in war. His last phrase passed down by those at that Politburo meeting as a command to all high officers of the service was: *Podalshe ot artillereiskovo ognia!* 'Stay

---

comes into competition with that of Britain. All the more clearly will Italy recognize the advisability of confronting the Western powers shoulder to shoulder with Germany—particularly when considering the desirability of a future general understanding between Western and Central Europe on the basis of complete equality. In my opinion the guiding principle for us arising out of this situation is that we should let Italy take the lead in her Spanish policy, but that we ought simultaneously to accompany this policy with so much active good will as to avoid a development which might be prejudicial to Germany's direct or indirect interests, whether it be in the form of a defeat for Nationalist Spain or in the nature of a direct Anglo-Italian understanding in case of further stagnation in the fighting. We surely have no reason for jealousy if Fascism takes the fore in the thorny task of creating a political and social content behind the hitherto purely military and negatively anti-Red label. . . . We must deem it desirable if there is created south of France a factor which, freed from Bolshevism and removed from the hegemony of the Western powers but on the other hand allied with Italy, makes the French and British stop to think—a factor opposing the transit of French troops from Africa and one which in the economic field takes our needs fully into consideration."—*Documents on German Foreign Policy 1918–1945*. III. *Germany and the Spanish Civil War 1936–1939*, pp. 170–3.

[9] In spite of all that has been said to the contrary, they did not arrive in Spain before then. The military men of high rank (Generals José Miaja, Sebastián Pozas, Ignacio Hidalgo de Cisneros) with whom the author was able to converse freely after the war confirmed this. Hidalgo de Cisneros, the Chief of the Air Force, informed the author that the first Russian bombers, tanks, and artillery reached Spain in October and the first combat aeroplanes on November 2. True, the German Consul General at Barcelona reported to the Wilhelmstrasse on September 16 that he had learned from a reliable source that thirty-seven aeroplanes were landed by the Russians in a small Spanish harbour a week before (*Documents on German Foreign Policy 1918–1945*. III. *Germany and the Spanish Civil War 1936–1939*, p. 89), but the author has found no evidence in support of this. It is of course not unlikely, as Walter Krivitsky, the GPU agent in Western Europe in charge of the foreign end of Soviet arms shipments to Spain affirms, that the Soviet decision to send arms was actually taken at the end of August.—*In Stalin's Secret Service*, p. 80. At all events the German Chargé d'Affaires in the Soviet Union sent the following significant report to

out of range of the artillery fire!' "[10] And, in a speech made after the war, when he had ceased to belong to the Spanish Communist Party, Jesús Hernández, a former member of the Politburo, declared: "... to the direct requests of our party [for war material], Moscow replied with vague excuses about the gigantic technical difficulties that surrounded the shipment of arms and with cunning arguments to the effect that the international situation was so tense and delicate that a more overt aid to Republican Spain could create very grave complications for the U.S.S.R. *vis-à-vis* the fascist Powers and frighten the Chamberlains, Daladiers, and Roosevelts, thereby increasing both the isolation of the Spanish Republic and the danger to the U.S.S.R. This was the road that was to lead the Soviet Union into collaboration with the monstrous policy of non-intervention."[11]

Because of her fear of involvement in a war with Italy and Germany, Russia limited her aid to bolstering the resistance of the anti-Franco forces until such time as Britain and France, faced by the threat to their interests in the Mediterranean of an Italo-German overlordship of

---

the German Foreign Ministry on September 28, 1936: "An expert foreign observer has noted that in the Black Sea harbour of Novorossiisk access to the harbour area has been more severely restricted since the summer months. The old entrance permits have been annulled and replaced by new ones. The same observer felt he had grounds for assuming that there was more than food in the heavy crates composing the cargo of the *Neva*, which left Odessa for Spain. So far, however, it has been impossible to obtain reliable proof of violation of the arms embargo by the Soviet Government. Since the wide expanse of the Soviet Union, the position of her harbours, and the well-known Soviet system of surveillance and of restricted areas greatly facilitate any camouflage manoeuvres, it is quite naturally extremely difficult to obtain such information."—*Documents on German Foreign Policy 1918–1945. III. Germany and the Spanish Civil War 1936–1939*, p. 100. As for other Soviet military aid to Spain, Segismundo Casado, Operations Chief on the General Staff of the War Ministry in the left zone, affirms that in the second half of September "there made their appearance at the Ministry of War certain Generals and Chiefs of the Soviet Army who were supposed to be 'Military technicians' and were known as 'friendly advisers,'" and that from that day onwards light arms began to arrive.—*The Last Days of Madrid*, p. 51. Although the Russians sent no Soviet infantrymen to Spain, the first units of the International Brigades—which were organized on the initiative of the Comintern (see Manuilsky's report to the Eighteenth Congress of the Communist Party of the Soviet Union on March 10, 1939, as given in *The Land of Socialism Today and Tomorrow*, pp. 57–100), and whose leaders, according to a commander of the Garibaldi Brigade (Carlo Penchienati, *Brigate Internazionali in Spagna*, p. 30), were, with rare exceptions, all Communists—went into action early in November.

[10] *In Stalin's Secret Service*, p. 81. See also *ibid.*, p. 85.

[11] As given in *Acción Socialista*, February 1, 1952.

Spain, might be induced to abandon the policy of non-intervention. Moreover, Russia was careful not to throw her influence on the side of the left wing of the revolution or to identify herself with it. To have done otherwise would have revived throughout the world, among the very classes whose support the Comintern was seeking, fears and antipathies it was striving most anxiously to avoid. It would have given a deathblow to the French Popular Front—in which the cleavage of opinion was already running deep[12]—and rendered sterile of result every effort to establish a basis of agreement with the moderate parties in other countries, particularly in Britain,[13] where the Communists' campaign for a Popular Front was already meeting with opposition from the Labour Party.[14] Indeed, it was for these reasons that, from the very inception of the war, the Comintern had sought to minimize the profound revolution that had taken place in Spain by defining the struggle against General Franco as one for the defence of the democratic republic.

"The working-class parties in Spain, and especially the Communist Party," wrote André Marty, a member of the Executive Committee of the Comintern, in an article widely published in the world Communist press, "have on several occasions clearly indicated what they are striving for. Our brother party has repeatedly proved that the present struggle in Spain is not between capitalism and socialism but between fascism and democracy. In a country like Spain, where feudal institutions and roots are still very deep, the working class and the entire people have the immediate and urgent task, *the only possible task*[15]—and all recent appeals of the Communist Party repeat it and prove it—not to bring about the socialist revolution, but to defend, consolidate, and develop the bourgeois democratic revolution.

"The only slogan of our party which was spread right across *Mundo Obrero*, its daily paper, on July 18, was 'Long Live the Democratic Republic!'

"All this is well known. Only dishonest people can maintain the contrary. . . .

[12] See, for example, speeches at the Radical Party congress, reported in *L'Ere Nouvelle*, October 25, 1936.

[13] "The People's Front in France," wrote a British Communist, "has driven back the fascist reaction and stands united with the Soviet Union for peace. If we could do the same in Britain, if the criminal opposition to unity could be overcome, if we could combine a corresponding Anglo–Soviet Pact with the Franco-Soviet Pact, then we could build a front which could hold in check the fascist war offensive."—R. Palme Dutt in *The Labour Monthly*, August, 1936.

[14] See, for example, the *Daily Herald*, October 10, 1936.

[15] Italics in text.

"The few confiscations which have been made—for example, the offices and newspapers of the rebels—constitute sanctions against proven enemies and saboteurs of the régime, and were made not as socialist measures, but as measures for the defence of the republic."[16]

And a French Communist Party manifesto declared:

". . . We speak for the Communist comrades, for the Socialists, and for all fighters for freedom in Spain, *when we declare that it is not a question of establishing socialism in Spain.*[17]

"*It is simply and solely a question of the defence of the democratic republic by the constitutional government, which, in face of the rebellion, has called upon the people to defend the Republican régime.*"[18]

Before many weeks had passed, the Communists took advantage of German and Italian intervention to tone down the class character of the war still further. "In the beginning," declared a Spanish Communist Party manifesto, "it was possible to describe the struggle simply as one between democracy and fascism, between progress and reaction,

---

[16] *L'Humanité*, August 4, 1936; *Communist International*, October, 1936; *International Press Correspondence*, August 8, 1936; *Daily Worker*, London, August 5, 1936. "The Central Committee of the Spanish Communist Party," ran a statement issued by the Communist Party of France (*L'Humanité*, August 3, 1936), "has asked us to make known to public opinion, as a reply to interested and fantastic reports in a certain press, that the Spanish people in their struggle against the rebels, are not striving for the establishment of the dictatorship of the proletariat, but have only one aim: THE DEFENCE OF THE REPUBLICAN ORDER AND RESPECT FOR PROPERTY."

[17] "The people of Spain," wrote Harry Pollitt, secretary of the British Communist Party (*International Press Correspondence*, August 8, 1936), "are not fighting to establish Soviets, or the proletarian dictatorship. Only downright lying scoundrels, or misguided self-styled 'Lefts' declare that they are—and both combine to help the aims of the fascist rebels."

[18] *L'Humanité*, August 3, 1936 (italics in text). See also statement to the foreign press representatives in Madrid by Jesús Hernández, as given in *Mundo Obrero*, August 8, 1936. "Really, people are sometimes surprising," wrote one observer. "Representative members of the PSUC [the Communist-controlled United Socialist Party of Catalonia] express the opinion that there is no revolution at all in Spain, and these men (with whom I had a fairly long discussion) are not, as one would suppose, old Catalan socialists, but foreign communists. Spain, they explain, is faced with a unique situation: the Government is fighting against its own army. And that is all. I hinted at the fact that the workers were armed, that the administration had fallen into the hands of revolutionary committees, that people were being executed without trial in thousands, that both factories and estates were being expropriated and managed by their former hands. What was revolution if it was not that? I was told that I was mistaken; all that had no political significance; these were only emergency measures without political bearing."—Borkenau, *The Spanish Cockpit*, p. 110.

between the past and the future. But now it has broken through these bounds and become transformed into a holy war, into a national war, into a defensive war of the people who feel that they have been betrayed and that their deepest sentiments have been wounded."[19]

[19] *Mundo Obrero*, August 18, 1936; *International Press Correspondence*, August 29, 1936.

9

The Communists Undermine
the Socialist Movement

THAT the Communist Party's policy of camouflaging the revolution could only have been initiated with the acquiescence or active support of other organizations can be open to no doubt; nor can there be any doubt that in order to feel sure of the successful continuation of its policy it had to become the ruling party in the left camp. This could be accomplished only at the expense of the Socialist movement, and more especially of its predominant left wing, the most powerful force in Madrid on the morrow of the revolution.

In the months before the Civil War the official relations between the left-wing Socialists and the Communist Party had been on a most friendly footing, so much so that their leader, Francisco Largo Caballero, the general secretary of the trade union federation, the UGT, and virtual leader of the Socialist youth movement, had given his encouragement to the fusion of the Socialist and Communist trade union federations[1] as well as to the merging of the two youth organizations.[2] Moreover, in March, 1936, the Madrid section of the Socialist Party, presided over by Largo Caballero, had decided to propose at the next National Congress the fusion of the Socialist and Communist Parties.[3] Largo Caballero himself had personally advocated this amalgamation in several public statements,[4] and had replied favourably to a Communist proposal that a contact committee be set up with a programme designed "to facilitate the development of the democratic revolution

---

[1] See speech by Wenceslao Carrillo in *La Correspondencia de Valencia*, September 4, 1937.

[2] See p. 115, below.

[3] *Claridad*, March 19, 1936; *La Libertad*, April 4, 1936.

[4] See, for example, interview reported in *Claridad*, December 7, 1935, speech, *ibid.*, April 11, 1936.

and to carry it to its final consequences."[5] This policy of the left-Socialist leader, in strident contrast to that of Indalecio Prieto, the leader of the numerically smaller centre faction of the Socialist Party, who at that time was hostile through and through to the Communists, had been warmly praised by José Díaz, the Communist leader, as "one that approaches most the revolutionary path, the path of the Communist Party and the Communist International."[6]

A moderate Socialist for more than forty years, except for an occasional spurt of revolutionary activity, a target of the Anarchists and of the Communists in the first years of the Republic, Largo Caballero had been fired towards the end of 1933, after two years of disillusionment as Minister of Labour during the Republican–Socialist coalition, by revolutionary ideas and had become metamorphosed overnight into the exponent of the left wing of Spanish Socialism.[7] Around him had gathered the mass of Socialist workers who, dissatisfied with the results of collaboration with the liberal Republicans, wished to swing the Socialist movement into a revolutionary channel and who had been drawn to him by his simplicity, personal integrity, and incorruptibility.[8] In March, 1936, four months before the outbreak of the Civil War, the Madrid Socialist organization over which he presided had drafted a new programme for the Socialist Party to be

[5] See article by José Díaz, general secretary of the Communist Party, in *Correspondencia Internacional*, April 17, 1936, as reprinted in Díaz, *Tres años de lucha*, pp. 116–21.

[6] *Ibid.*

[7] "The refusal of the Republican parties to treat agrarian reform seriously lay . . . at the root of the Socialists' disillusion with the Republic. It was a feeling that welled up from below, affecting the young more than the old, the recently joined rather than the confirmed party men. . . . This feeling found a leader in Largo Caballero. As President of the UGT he was especially alive to the danger of losing ground to the Anarchosyndicalists. And he had also a personal grievance. First of all he had quarrelled with Azaña [Prime Minister at the time]. Then as Minister of Labour he had been especially disgusted at the way in which much of the legislation drawn up by him had been sabotaged. . . . Caballero had found that even the officials in his own ministry refused to obey the directions given them. There was a conspiracy to make nonsense of everything. Thus it came about that already in February, 1934, he was saying that 'the only hope of the masses is now in social revolution. It alone can save Spain from Fascism.' "—Brenan, *The Spanish Labyrinth*, pp. 273–4.

[8] These characteristics are acknowledged even by opponents inside and outside his own party. See, for example, Gorkin, *Caníbales políticos*, p. 62; Madariaga, *España*, p. 547; Federica Montseny and Indalecio Prieto in *Francisco Largo Caballero*, pp. 71, 138; Andrés Saborit in *Adelante*, Marseilles, May 3, 1946; Zugazagoitia, *Historia de la guerra en España*, p. 208.

submitted to its next National Congress, calling for the immediate conquest of political power by the working class and for the dictatorship of the proletariat under the Socialist Party.[9] In the succeeding months, Caballero toured the provincial capitals, proclaiming before rapt audiences that the Popular Front programme could not solve the problems of Spain and that a working-class dictatorship was necessary.[10]

The Communists, who were then endeavouring to strengthen the Popular Front both by reinforcing their contacts with the liberal Republicans and by prodding the government into vigorous action against the Right,[11] were, in spite of the smooth course of official relations between themselves and Caballero, secretly embarrassed by his revolutionary ardour. In fact, José Díaz, while praising his collaboration with the Communist Party, declared in an oblique reference to the Socialist leader's revolutionary conduct that the Communists would oppose "every manifestation of exaggerated impatience and every attempt to break up the Popular Front prematurely."[12] However, they could not afford to press their differences with Caballero, for his popularity had reached its peak, and they valued his utility as a link between themselves and the masses that followed him.[13] Moreover, the idea of working-class unity had laid hold of his imagination, and this promised to facilitate the fusion of the Socialist and Communist Parties as it had already facilitated the merging of their respective trade union organizations and youth movements. "The important point for the unity movement," wrote José Díaz, "and for the whole advance of the revolution in Spain is that the line represented by Largo Caballero gains the victory in the Socialist Party."[14] And, writing shortly after the fusion of the Young Communist League and the Young Socialist Federation in April, 1936, Santiago Carrillo, the leader of the united

[9] *Claridad*, March 19, 1936.

[10] See, for example, speech in Oviedo, *La Libertad*, June 16, 1936.

[11] See n. 6, p. 97, above.

[12] Article in *Correspondencia Internacional*, April 17, 1936, as reprinted in Díaz, *Tres años de lucha*, pp. 116–21. See also his speech on July 5, 1936, *ibid.*, pp. 183–91. It is worth recording that José Duque, who became a member of the Central Committee of the Communist Party in 1937, confirmed to the author that in the months before the Civil War leading Communists were secretly hostile to Caballero's policy. According to Frank Manuel (*The Politics of Modern Spain*, p. 164), José Díaz, during a private discussion that took place shortly before the military uprising, "assented to 'infantile leftist' as the proper term for Caballero's tendencies."

[13] See José Bullejos (a former secretary of the Communist Party), *Europa entre dos guerras*, pp. 191–2.

[14] *International Press Correspondence*, May 9, 1936.

organization, stated with reference to conversations he and other representatives of the two youth movements had previously held in Moscow: "As Manuilski, the old Bolshevik, told us . . . , the important thing now for the movement of unity and for the whole course of the Spanish revolution is that the tendency represented by Largo Caballero should triumph in the Socialist Party. If this victory does not occur, unity and the very future of the revolution—I continue to quote Manuilski—would be compromised."[15]

But in view of the underlying differences between the Communists and the left-wing Socialists over Largo Caballero's revolutionary zeal, it is not surprising that the outbreak of the revolution should have thrown their disparate attitudes into sharp focus. "When the Communist Party raised the necessity of defending the democratic republic," declared José Díaz in a report to the Central Committee some months later, "the Socialists, a large proportion of our Socialist comrades, took the stand that the democratic republic had no longer any *raison d'être* and advocated the setting up of a Socialist Republic. This would have divorced the working class from the democratic forces, from the petty bourgeois and popular layers in the country. It was natural that our policy of uniting all the democratic forces with the proletariat should have met with certain difficulties owing to the failure of some Socialist comrades to understand that . . . this was not the moment to speak of a Socialist Republic."[16] Although there is no record that any leading Socialist made a public declaration, either oral or written, at the outbreak of the revolution urging the establishment of a Socialist Republic, a proposal of this nature may conceivably have been made in backstage discussions with the Communists. Certainly it would have been entirely consistent with Largo Caballero's policy and with the aims of his most ardent followers up to the very inception of the conflict, and it is significant that the Communist leader's assertion was never challenged. Nor indeed did an assertion by André Marty, French Communist leader and organizer of the International Brigades in Spain, to the effect that the Socialists abandoned their proposal to establish a Socialist Republic as a result of Communist influence,[17]

[15] *Claridad*, April 9, 1936.

[16] Díaz, *Tres años de lucha*, pp. 288–339.

[17] "When from the first day of the rebellion," he affirmed, "the Communist Party declared that the prime need was the defence of the democratic republic, many top-ranking Socialist leaders held, on the contrary, that a Socialist Republic should be immediately established. This would have immediately smashed the Popular Front and led to the victory of fascism. Today, thanks to our influence, many leaders of the Socialist Party have changed their attitude

elicit any denial.[18] At all events, by mid-August Caballero had so tempered his pre-Civil War language, at least as far as the outside world was concerned, as to declare in a letter to Ben Tillett, the British trade union leader, that the Spanish Socialists were fighting only for the triumph of democracy and had no thought of establishing Socialism.[19] What arguments the Communists may have adduced in order to sway Caballero were not disclosed by André Marty, but if his assertion be true, as would seem most likely, they no doubt held that the setting up of a Socialist Republic would have antagonized the Western Powers and destroyed the advantages to be gained from keeping in office the legally constituted government of José Giral, which, in accordance with the rules of international law applicable to cases of rebellion against a legitimate government, was entitled to buy arms in the world market.

But however much Largo Caballero may have allowed himself to be influenced by these impelling considerations in behind-the-scenes discussions with the Communists, it is clear from the following editorial in his newspaper *Claridad* that he was not ready to turn his back completely upon the revolution. "Some persons," this editorial declared, in a veiled reference to the Communists, "are saying: 'Let us crush fascism first, let us finish the war victoriously, and then there will be time to speak of revolution and to make it if necessary.' Those who express themselves in this way have obviously not reflected maturely upon the formidable dialectical process which is carrying us all along. The war and the revolution are one and the same thing. Not only do they not exclude or hinder each other but they complement and support each other. The war needs the revolution for its triumph in the same way that the revolution needed the war to bring it into being.

---

and adopted the platform of the Communist Party."—André Marty, *En Espagne ... où se joue le destin de l'Europe*, p. 34. "Even those who used to speak of proletarian revolution without taking into account the present situation," declared Antonio Mije, a member of the Politburo (speech reported in *Mundo Obrero*, September 9, 1936), "understand today the correctness of the Communist Party line in defending the democratic republic."

[18] In fact, Largo Caballero's followers—anxious no doubt to protect their leader from the stigma of bowing to Communist policy—have sedulously avoided any explanation for his sudden change of position. Many years after the war, it should be stated, an intimate associate of the Socialist leader, when questioned by the author with regard to José Díaz' and André Marty's assertions, dismissed them as "pure nonsense" and as a "Communist lie," while other prominent left-wing Socialists ignored the author's written requests for information on the matter.

[19] See report from London in *La Humanitat*, August 13, 1936.

"The revolution is the economic annihilation of fascism, and is consequently the first step towards its military annihilation. . . . The people are not fighting for the Spain of July 16, which was still dominated socially by hereditary castes, but for a Spain from which those castes have been finally rooted out. The most powerful auxiliary of the war is the complete economic extinction of fascism. That is the revolution in the rear, which will make more assured and more inspired the victory on the battlefields."[20]

Nor was Largo Caballero ready to go along with the Communist Party when in August, 1936, it opposed his suggestion that the Socialists and Communists should enter the government. ". . . The Communist Party," wrote César Falcón, editor during the first months of the war of *Mundo Obrero*, the Communist organ, "maintained a position contrary to that of Caballero. Why change the government when for various reasons the national and international situation was not opportune for the participation of Socialists and Communists?"[21] This divergence of opinion became manifest when, shortly after the capture of Badajoz on August 14 by General Franco's forces and his rapid advance up the Tagus valley towards Madrid, José Giral, tired of presiding over a government that lacked the confidence of the major working-class organizations, informed President Azaña that he wished to resign, and, at the latter's suggestion, asked Caballero to head a new administration.[22] But although the Communists at first opposed the left Socialist leader when he offered to form a new Cabinet on condition that they shared the responsibilities of office,[23] they finally agreed to do so in face of his inflexible attitude and orders from Moscow.[24] The new Cabinet, in which Largo Caballero took over the War Ministry in addition to the Premiership, and in which minor posts were reserved for the liberal Republican parties, had six Socialist and two Communist ministers.[25]

But the two portfolios held by the Communist Party furnished no real index of its strength in the country, either at the time the Cabinet was constituted, when the number of its adherents had swollen far

[20] August 22, 1936.

[21] *Madrid*, p. 159.

[22] *Claridad*, September 4, 1936.

[23] Jesús Hernández, *Yo fuí un ministro de Stalin*, p. 47. See also Alvarez del Vayo, *Freedom's Battle*, p. 212.

[24] Jesús Hernández, *Yo fuí un ministro de Stalin*, p. 47. Hernández was a member of the Politburo.

[25] The members of the new Cabinet and the portfolios they held (as given in

beyond the pre-war total of forty thousand,[26] or a few months later, when it became, with an officially estimated membership of nearly a quarter of a million, the strongest political party in the anti-Franco camp.[27] If a large number of its new adherents, such as peasant owners, tenant farmers, tradesmen, small manufacturers, civil servants, army and police officers, doctors, teachers, writers, artists, and other intellectuals, had been members of the liberal Republican parties or even right-wing sympathizers before the Civil War and had been attracted to the party by the hope either of rescuing something from the ruins of the old régime or of sharing in the Communists' growing power;[28] if, moreover, a large number had been members of the Socialist Party or the UGT before the war, an even greater number had never cast

the *Gaceta de Madrid*, September 5, 1936) as well as the parties to which they belonged were as follows:

Francisco Largo Caballero (Socialist)	Prime Minister and War
Julio Alvarez del Vayo (Socialist)	Foreign Affairs
Angel Galarza (Socialist)	Interior
Anastasio de Gracia (Socialist)	Industry and Commerce
Juan Negrín (Socialist)	Finance
Indalecio Prieto (Socialist)	Navy and Air
Jesús Hernández (Communist)	Education and Fine Arts
Vicente Uribe (Communist)	Agriculture
José Giral (Left Republican)	Minister without portfolio
Mariano Ruiz Funes (Left Republican)	Justice
Bernardo Giner de los Rios (Republican Union)	Communications
José Tomás y Piera (Left Republican Party of Catalonia)	Labour and Health

Later in the month Julio Just (Left Republican) was made Minister of Public Works (*Gaceta de Madrid*, September 16, 1936), and Manuel de Irujo (Basque Nationalist Party) was appointed minister without portfolio (*ibid.*, September 26, 1936). The CNT was asked to participate, but declined for reasons that will be seen in a later chapter.

[26] See p. 81, above.

[27] The precise figure, as given by José Díaz, general secretary of the Communist Party, in a report to the Central Committee in March, 1937, was 249,140, of which 87,660 (35·2 per cent) were industrial workers, 62,250 (25 per cent) agricultural labourers, 76,700 (30·7 per cent) peasants, that is, peasant owners and tenant farmers, 15,485 (6·2 per cent) members of the urban middle classes, and 7,045 (2·9 per cent) intellectuals and members of the professional classes.—Díaz, *Tres años de lucha*, pp. 288–339.

[28] The following passages from a variety of sources are worth quoting: "The Republican middle class, surprised by the moderate tone of Communist propaganda and impressed by the unity and realism which prevailed in this party, flocked in great number to join its ranks," writes A. Ramos Oliveira. "... Army officers and officials who had never turned the pages of a Marxist leaflet

their faith into any political mould and, like the converts from the Socialist movement, had been drawn to the Communist Party by its proselytizing zeal, its immensely skilful propaganda, its vigour, its organizing capacity, and the prestige it derived from Soviet arms sold to the government.

Hardly inferior to all these factors as a source of Communist strength was the relative weakness or even impotence of other organizations. The liberal Republicans, lacking influence among the masses, had retired into the background, ceding to the Communists the delicate work of opposing the left wing of the revolution and defending the interests of the middle classes. Not only did they give favourable publicity to the Communist Party,[29] whose declared policy coincided with their own,[30] but not a few, to quote Indalecio Prieto, the Socialist

---

became Communists, some through calculation, others through moral weakness, others inspired by the enthusiasm which animated this organization."—*Politics, Economics and Men of Modern Spain, 1808–1946*, p. 599. "Actually, bourgeois generals and politicians, and many peasants who approve the Communist Party's policy of protecting small property-holders, have joined its ranks. I think these people influence and are influenced. But essentially their new political affiliation reflects a despair of the old social system as well as a hope to salvage some of its remnants."—Louis Fischer, *The Nation*, August 7, 1937. "Whenever Poldi took us along to his many conversations with young officials of the various Ministries," writes a Socialist, "I tried to assess them. It struck me that most of them were ambitious young men of the upper middle classes who now declared themselves Communists, not, as we had done in Madrid, because to us it meant the party of revolutionary workers, but because it meant joining the strongest group and having a share in its disciplined power. They had leaped over the step of humanist socialism; they were efficient and ruthless."—Barea, *The Forging of a Rebel*, pp. 706–7. As for the intellectuals, another Socialist affirms: "Traditional Spanish pride was transformed into humiliation in the hands of the intellectuals. Nearly all of them bowed to the will of the Communist Party."—F. Ferrándiz Alborz, *La bestia contra España*, p. 95. Illustrative of the efforts made by the Communist Party to capture the sympathy of the Spanish intellectuals and scientists were the elaborate measures taken by the Communist-controlled Fifth Regiment to evacuate them from Madrid in the early days of the siege, giving them every comfort and protection.—See, for example, *Política*, November 24, December 1, 1936.

[29] A consultation of the files of *Política*, the organ of the Left Republican Party, will substantiate this. "The change in the attitude of the bourgeois Republicans is . . . very interesting," ran an article in *Pravda* (November 6, 1936). "Previously they tried not to notice the Communist Party and spoke of it with animosity and disdain. Now some organs of the Republican press devote whole laudatory articles to it."

[30] In a speech reported in *La Voz Valenciana*, of March 10, 1937, José Giral observed that the coincidence of views between his party and the Communists was almost identical.

leader, actually served the ambitions of the Soviet Union.[31] Furthermore, the Anarchosyndicalists, in spite of their numerical strength,
were, owing largely to their lack of centralized direction, an unequal
match for the Communists with their monolithic organization, their
discipline, and their cohesion.

As for the Socialists, who at the outbreak of the revolution were the
strongest force in the capital and in Old and New Castile, they were
not only undermined by open and secret defections to the Communist
Party, for which their own passivity was in some degree responsible,[32]
but were entangled in factional strife, the Executive Committee of the
party, in the hands of the centrists led by Indalecio Prieto, being in a
state of irreconcilable belligerence with local units sympathetic to
Largo Caballero.[33] ". . . The life of the Socialist movement," writes
Gabriel Morón, a prominent member of the party, "was reduced to a
faint breath, manifesting itself in internal dissensions.[34] . . . In the rear,

[31] Speech on April 21, 1940, as given in *Inauguración del círculo 'Pablo Iglesias'
de México*, p. 13. See also article by Juan López in *CNT*, June 19, 1937.

[32] A leading left-wing Socialist, at one time very much influenced by the
Communist Party, confesses that the "dynamic quality of the Communists was
very congenial to me as compared with the extreme sluggishness of many
Socialists."—Carlos de Baraibar in *Vía Libre*, August 5, 1939. See also extract
from his article in *Timón*, Buenos Aires, June, 1940, as quoted on p. 286, below,
and extract from article by the left Socialist leader, Rodolfo Llopis, as quoted
on p. 274, below. Another left-wing Socialist writes: "I had lost all confidence in [the Socialist Party's] power of assuming responsibility and authority
in a difficult situation, and my companion Torres, an old member of the
Socialist Youth Organization, had recently joined the Communists."—Barea,
The Forging of a Rebel, p. 579. See also editorial in *El Socialista*, March 9, 1937,
referring to a letter from a group of Socialists, in which they stated that they
were joining the Communist Party because their own party showed no sign of
life at the fronts. For an account by a left-wing Socialist of how the Socialist
Party in the provincial capital of Alicante, where it was the strongest political
organization, had failed to compete successfully with the Communists and
Anarchists for the control of leading positions, see F. Ferrándiz Alborz, *La
bestia contra España*, pp. 64-5.

[33] "Each provincial federation and division acted on its own initiative,"
attests Wenceslao Carrillo, one of the leading Caballero Socialists in the Madrid
section of the party, which was controlled by the left wing. "Only the Madrid
division maintained contact with a number of federations and sections, which
asked it for directives."—Report to the Labour and Socialist International,
dated May 23, 1939, published in special issue of *Independent News* [June, 1939?].

[34] Of these the Communists took full advantage. Referring some years after
the war to the dissensions among the leaders of the Socialist Party (Prieto,
Caballero and Besteiro), Jesús Hernández, one of the two Communist ministers
in the Government, wrote: "We managed to derive the utmost benefit for
ourselves from their suicidal antagonisms. One day we supported one man

as at the front, the boldest, the most zealous and unscrupulous imposed their views, made their influence felt, and asserted their personality." And in a later passage he attests: "There were no individuals with these moral and temperamental traits left in the Socialist Party. On the other hand the Communist Party was filled with them to the point of congestion."[35]

In view of all these factors, the drive that the Communists initiated to engulf the Socialist movement began under the most promising auspices. That the successes they rapidly achieved, particularly at the expense of its predominant left wing, should have irked Largo Caballero was, of course, inevitable; for when, before the war, he had advocated fusion with the Communists, he may have believed, as he later contended, that he could absorb them,[36] but never had he anticipated the absorption of his own following. Acute therefore was his resentment when, within a few days of the inception of the war, the Catalan Federation of the Spanish Socialist Party led by Rafael Vidiella, hitherto a stout supporter, merged with the Catalan section of the Communist Party and two other organizations to form the PSUC, the United Socialist Party of Catalonia, which accepted the discipline of the Third International[37] and which brought the local

---

against the other; the following day we did the reverse, and on all occasions we incited them against one another so that they would destroy themselves, a game we played in full view and not without success.—*Yo fuí un ministro de Stalin*, p. 135.

[35] *Política de ayer y política de mañana*, pp. 79, 88.

[36] See his letter to José Bullejos of November 20, 1939, as given in Francisco Largo Caballero, *¿Qué se puede hacer?*, pp. 20–4.

[37] For reference to this by Caballero, see his speech as given in Largo Caballero, *La UGT y la guerra*, p. 32. Although the question of the PSUC lies outside the purview of this volume, the following may be said: The two other organizations that merged to form the new party were the Catalan Proletarian Party and the Socialist Union of Catalonia, whose secretary, Juan Comorera, became the leader of the united organization. From the beginning, the latter adhered to the Communist International, and almost immediately the Communists became the ruling nucleus. In addition to controlling its organizational work, its press, and trade union activities, they were in charge of internal vigilance, all party records being in their hands. A Comintern delegate, known as "Pedro" (whose name was Ernö Gerö and who, after World War II, became a member of the Soviet-controlled Hungarian Government), was placed at Comorera's elbow, and Spanish Communist leaders were sent regularly to Barcelona with directives. For some of the above details I am indebted to Miguel Serra Pamies, a member of the Central Committee of the PSUC. Within a few months, both Comorera, the secretary of the PSUC, and Vidiella, the leader, before the fusion, of the Catalan Federation of the Socialist Party,

organization of the UGT under its dominion.[38] But it was in other parts of the left zone, particularly in Madrid, the stronghold of the left-wing Socialists, where the danger to Caballero's influence revealed itself in its full stature. Lacking directives from their own party, which was racked and torn by internal discord, a large number of left Socialist workers, swayed by the dynamism and proselytizing methods of the Communists,[39] were ebbing away and attorning to the rival movement. To make matters worse, some of Caballero's most trusted aides, both in the Socialist Party and the UGT, had transferred their attachment to the Communists, either in secrecy or without disguise, such as Julio Alvarez del Vayo, Foreign Minister and vice-president of the Madrid section of the Socialist Party,[40] Edmundo Domínguez, secretary of the National Federation of Building Workers and president of the Madrid headquarters of the UGT, Amaro del Rosal, a member of the UGT Executive, Felipe Pretel, the treasurer of the UGT,[41] as well as Margarita Nelken[42] and Francisco Montiel,[43] two well-known Cortes deputies and intellectuals.

A still more important development that told on Largo Caballero's

---

were appointed to the Central Committee of the Spanish Communist Party.— See Pedro Checa, *A un gran partido, una gran organización*, p. 23.

[38] This matter also lies beyond the scope of the present volume. But see Largo Caballero, *La UGT y la guerra*, p. 32, and *Adelante*, Caballero's organ in Valencia, April 8, 1937.

[39] For complaints in the left-wing Socialist press regarding some of these methods, such as flattery, offers of material gain, and coercion, see article in the *Boletín de la Unión General de Trabajadores*, as given in *Claridad*, March 11, 1937; also article by S. Esteve Gregori in *Adelante*, March 27, 1937.

[40] See pp. 120–1, below.

[41] See report by Wenceslao Carrillo to the Labour and Socialist International, May 23, 1939, in which the Communist sympathies of Domínguez, Rosal, and Pretal are mentioned, as published in special issue of *Independent News* [June, 1939?].

[42] See article by left Socialist leader, Rodolfo Llopis in *Tribuna*, March, 1949, and Zugazagoitia, *Historia de la guerra en España*, p. 170.

[43] Addressing the plenary session of the Central Committee of the Communist Party in March, 1937, Montiel stated: ". . . it is wonderful, for those of us who were outside the Communist Party until a few weeks ago, to contemplate how, in the very midst of the revolutionary struggle, one organization which was for many years a powerful political force, and which had almost a monopoly of the political leadership of the Spanish proletariat, was disintegrating, ruined by its mistakes, and how another organization, composed in the early days of little more than a handful of men, but guided to perfection by Marxism and Leninism, could become after July 18 the real force in the struggle against fascism and the real directing force of the Spanish masses."—Francisco Montiel, *Por qué he ingresado en el partido comunista*, p. 4.

political influence was the loss of his authority over the Unified Socialist Youth Federation, known in short as the JSU,[44] which was formed shortly before the outbreak of the Civil War, as a result of the amalgamation of the Union of Young Communists and the Socialist Youth Federation, whose representatives had met in Moscow with the Executive Committee of the Young Communist International to draw up plans for the fusion of the two organizations.[45] The preparatory operations for this merger, writes Luis Araquistain, a close collaborator of Caballero, were conducted in the home of Alvarez del Vayo. "I lived in Madrid, one floor above him, and witnessed the daily visits paid to him by young Socialist leaders for the purpose of interviewing the Comintern agent then prominent in Spain, a certain Codovila, who used the false name of Medina, and spoke Spanish with a strong South American accent. It was there that a voyage to the Muscovite Mecca was organized for them; it was there that it was agreed to deliver the Socialist youth, the new working-class generation of Spain, to Communism."[46]

In spite of everything that has since been said to the contrary, Caballero had encouraged the fusion of the two youth movements, although it is true that in a joint statement issued in March, 1936, before the merger had taken place, it was agreed that until a National Congress of Unification had determined democratically the principles, programme, and definitive structure of the united organization and elected a directive body, the fusion would be effected on the basis of the entry of the Young Communists into the Socialist Youth Federation.[47] However, stimulated by Largo Caballero's policy of uniting the working-class movement, the fusion of the two organizations took place in a precipitate fashion without any congress of unification being held.[48] Caballero, to be sure, had not opposed this, because the Union

[44] *Juventudes Socialistas Unificadas.*

[45] See José Díaz in *International Press Correspondence*, May 9, 1936; Segis Alvarez, *Nuestra organización y nuestros cuadros*, p. 7. Santiago Carrillo, general secretary of the JSU, claimed that its membership which, according to his figures, had been forty thousand at the time of the fusion, had risen to one hundred and fifty thousand just before the outbreak of the Civil War (Carrillo, *En marcha hacia la victoria*, p. 13), and to three hundred thousand in April, 1937 (see his speech, reported *Frente Rojo*, April 2, 1937).

[46] *El comunismo y la guerra de España*, p. 9.

[47] Passages from this statement are quoted by Carlos Hernández Zancajo, *Tercera etapa de octubre*, pp. 9–11.

[48] See L. Romero Solano, *Vísperas de la guerra de España*, p. 77. Romero Solano represented Estremadura on the National Committee of the Socialist Youth Federation.

of Young Communists was incomparably smaller than his own Socialist Youth Federation—only three thousand members against fifty thousand, according to one estimate[49]—and because he had believed that through his supporters he would be able to control the united movement. But in the sequel he was rudely undeceived; for within a few months of the inception of the Civil War Santiago Carrillo, general secretary of the JSU, and hitherto a sedulous admirer,[50] quietly joined the Communist Party together with other former leaders of the Socialist Youth Federation[51]—some of them, including Carrillo himself, later becoming members of its Central Committee[52]—and transformed the JSU into one of the main props for Communist policy. Commenting on this defection, Carlos de Baraibar, the left Socialist leader, who, according to his own confession, was very much influenced by the Communists early in the war, recalls: ". . . A group of leaders of the Unified Socialist Youth visited me in order to inform me that they had decided to join the Communist Party *en masse*. . . I considered it monstrous that such a thing could have happened . . . with no one's knowledge other than that of Alvarez del Vayo who, as I learnt later, was informed of every step taken. And all of them were advised by the person whom we used to call 'the eye of Moscow,' the secret representative of the Comintern [Codovila]."[53]

Before long the Communists consolidated their hold over the JSU still further.

[49] That of Antonio Escribano, organizational secretary of the JSU in Alicante province, in a letter to the author. However, Santiago Carrillo, the general secretary of the JSU, gives 40,000 as the figure for the combined membership at the time of the fusion (see n. 45, p. 115, above). It is worth noting that the Communist writer, E. Varga, in his book, *Ispaniia i revoliutsiia* (Moscow), gives the number of Young Communists as 50,000, obviously an exaggerated figure. Quoted, Catell, *Communism and the Spanish Civil War*, p. 220.

[50] See, for example, his article in *Claridad*, May 13, 1936; speech in Saragossa, reported *ibid.*, June 1, 1936.

[51] For example, Alfredo Cabello, José Cazorla, José Laín, Federico Melchor, Serrano Poncela. The Spanish Communist refugee periodical *España Popular* of June 15, 1940, gives the date of José Cazorla's entry into the Communist Party as November 7, 1936. For Santiago Carrillo's defence of their action, see Carrillo, *La juventud factor de la victoria*, p. 14.

[52] According to Pedro Checa, himself a member of the Central Committee, in a speech in March, 1937. *A un gran partido, una gran organización*, p. 23.

[53] *Timón*, Buenos Aires, June, 1940. During the first year of the Civil War Codovila (an Argentinian) was the real head of the Spanish Communist Party. See Castro (former member of the Central Committee), *Hombres made in Moscú*, p. 374. His successor was Togliatti, the Italian Communist, known in Spain as Ercoli.

Instead of holding the projected National Congress of Unification, Santiago Carrillo convened, in January, 1937, a National Conference, to which he appointed as delegates not only the representatives of the local sections of the JSU, but a large number of young Communists from the fronts and factories, a strategem that enabled him to control the Conference from start to finish and to secure the election then and there of a National Committee packed with Communist Party nominees.[54] In this coup he had undoubtedly been aided not only by his liberal praise of Largo Caballero[55] and by the fact that few of the young Socialist delegates were aware at the time that Carrillo had joined the Communist Party, believing that he and other leaders of the JSU were acting in full accord with Caballero and his supporters in the Socialist Party, but also by the avoidance of any debate. "Nothing at all was debated at the Conference," recalls Antonio Escribano, the delegate for Alicante province. "Those who did speak confined them-

[54] "Could we," he asked, defending his action from criticism a few months later, "could we, in wartime, and considering the changes that have taken place in our country and in our own organization, hold a congress attended exclusively by the representatives of the local sections? Could we, with our youth at the fronts, hold the same type of congress that we should have held before July 18, when our youth was not yet defending its liberty with arms? No, we could not have held such a congress. We had to adapt ourselves to the situation. And the situation made it compulsory that our congress, our National Conference, should be attended not only by the representatives of the local sections, but also by those young men who were striving with great sacrifice to increase war production in the factories and by those who were giving their blood for our liberty on land, on sea, and in the air; in other words, by that part of our youth, the best part—not in the local sections, but at the front—that has a legitimate right to direct and control the life of its federation."—As given in *Nuestra lucha por la unidad*, p. 34. See also Carrillo, *Somos la organización de la juventud*, pp. 6–9. The following extract from a letter sent to the author some years after the war by Antonio Escribano, a delegate to the Conference, is of interest: "I remember when the National Committee of the JSU was elected. . . . Several veterans of the youth movement met with Carrillo and his associates and elected representatives for each province. Later they read the 'election' of the National Committee which everyone approved by acclamation because instructions had been given to agree to everything proposed by the leadership."

[55] "It is necessary to say here and now," he had declared in his speech at the Conference, ". . . that as ever, and even more than ever, Largo Caballero enjoys the support of the Spanish youth in the factories and at the fronts. I must also add that Comrade Largo Caballero is for us the same as he was before: the man who helped our unification. He is the man from whom we are expecting much useful advice so that, in the interests of the common cause we are defending, the unity of the Spanish youth may be a reality."—As given in Carrillo, *En marcha hacia la victoria*, p. 9.

selves to making a report or address, but no discussion followed. A certain Carrasco spoke on behalf of the anti-tankists on how to destroy tanks; a sailor spoke on his own subject, an aviator likewise, and so on and so forth. The fact is that nothing regarding the unification of the two organizations was debated. On the contrary, everything that had happened was taken for granted. Those of us who were loyal to Caballero did not raise any objections at the Conference for two reasons, both fairly ingenuous when I look back on them today, although justifiable at the time. These reasons were: 1. Ninety per cent of the young Socialists who attended the Conference did not know that Carrillo, Laín, Melchor, Cabello, Aurora Arnaiz, etc., had gone over outright to the Communist Party. We believed that they were still young Socialists and that, strange as it seemed to us, they were acting in agreement with Caballero and the Socialist Party. Had we known that this group of recreants had betrayed us, I can assure you that an entirely different situation would have arisen. But we were taken off our guard. That is the truth of the matter, which, for my part, I am not ashamed to confess. 2. The atmosphere and the manner in which the Conference was conducted took us by surprise, and when we wished to react the assembly had already come to an end. We members of the Socialist Youth Federation had been accustomed to discuss the agendas of our congresses and assemblies democratically and exhaustively, and had firmly believed that the Conference would be conducted in the same way. . . . Nothing of the kind occurred. When we realized what had happened, it was too late. The Conference had ended."[56]

Indeed, it was not until a few weeks after the Conference had taken place, when the struggle between Largo Caballero and the Communists had entered upon an acute stage, that the first fissure in the JSU appeared with the publication of open letters to Santiago Carrillo from two of Caballero's supporters, declining the seats on the National Committee to which they had been elected at the Conference, on the ground that their local sections had not been consulted.[57]

If, in conjunction with all these developments, the skill of the

[56] Letter to the author after the war.

[57] The letters were from José Gregori Martínez, general secretary of the Provincial Committee of the Valencia JSU, and Rafael Fernández, general secretary of the JSU of the Asturias, and were published in *La Correspondencia de Valencia*, March 31, April 1, 1937, respectively. See also statement by José Gregori Martínez in *Adelante*, as given in *La Correspondencia de Valencia*, April 9, 1937.

Communists in using artifice and subterfuge, in playing one hostile faction against another, in packing pivotal positions with secret party members or with fellow travellers, in bestowing patronage and exerting pressure upon anyone who joined their ranks or served their interests, is taken into consideration, their emergence before long as the real power in the anti-Franco camp should be readily appreciated.

10

The Communists Pilot
the Cabinet

JUST as the two ministries the Communist Party held in the
government furnished no real index of its strength in the country
so too did they afford no true indication of the influence it wielded
in its councils.[1] This was so because the real weight of the Communists
in the government lay not so much in the two portfolios they held as
in the secret influence they enjoyed over Caballero's Foreign Minister
and man of confidence, Julio Alvarez del Vayo, and over the Minister
of Finance, Dr. Juan Negrín.

Though Vice-President of the Madrid section of the Socialist Party
and officially a left-wing Socialist, Alvarez del Vayo soon came to be
regarded by the leading figures in his party as a Communist at heart.[2]
A supporter of the Soviet Union and of Comintern policy before the
Civil War,[3] he had played an important part, as has been shown, in
bringing about the fusion of the Socialist and Communist youth
movements,[4] and during the war itself he endorsed the Communists'

[1] For the composition of the government, see n. 25, p. 109, above.

[2] See, for example, Largo Caballero, *Mis recuerdos*, p. 212; Araquistain, *El
comunismo en la guerra de España*, p. 8, and his letter to Diego Martínez Barrio,
as given in *Vía Libre*, May 15, 1939; also Carlos de Baraibar in *Timón*, Buenos
Aires, June, 1940; Wenceslao Carrillo, *ibid.*, November, 1939; Indalecio Prieto
in *Correo de Asturias*, July 10, 1943. Because of his political conduct, the Madrid
section of the Socialist Party decided, a few days before the end of the war, to
suspend Alvarez del Vayo and to propose to the National Executive his expulsion from the Socialist Party.—See *Claridad*, March 15, 1939; also report of
Wenceslao Carrillo to the Labour and Socialist International, May 23, 1939,
as given in special issue of *Independent News* [June, 1939?].

[3] See his articles in *Claridad*, October 5, November 9, 1935; also *The Times*,
London, March 2, 1936 (dispatch from Madrid); speech reported in *Verdad*,
August 13, 1937, showing his position prior to the war.

[4] See p. 115, above.

campaign for the fusion of the Socialist and Communist Parties.[5] As the Premier's trusted adviser, he not only possessed his ear on matters of foreign policy, but was appointed by him to head the vital Commissariat of War, which directed the political orientation of the armed forces. And in this body, according to Pedro Checa, a member of the Politburo, he served the Communist Party "scrupulously."[6] He was also in charge of appointments to the Foreign Press Bureau, which censored the dispatches of correspondents with an eye to opinion abroad. "During the three months that I was director of propaganda for the United States and England under Alvarez del Vayo, . . . I was instructed not to send out one word about this revolution in the economic system of loyalist Spain," wrote Liston Oak. "Nor are any foreign correspondents in Valencia [the provisional seat of government] permitted to write freely of the revolution that has taken place."[7]

But valuable as were Alvarez del Vayo's services to the Communists in helping them to implement their strategy of infiltration and domination in the early stages of the Civil War, the main instrument in bringing their plans to fruition in its final stages was Dr. Juan Negrín. An adherent, at the outbreak of the conflict, of Indalecio Prieto's anti-Communist centre faction of the Socialist Party,[8] a professor of physiology at the Madrid School of Medicine, Minister of Finance in Largo Caballero's government, Prime Minister from May, 1937, to April, 1938, and Premier and Defence Minister from April, 1938, until the end of the war in March, 1939, he was more responsible than any one Spaniard for the later success of Communist policy.[9]

[5] See his articles in *Frente Rojo*, June 19, 28, 1937, and speech, *Verdad*, August 13, 1937; also Dolores Ibarruri's reference to him in her speech at the plenary session of the Central Committee of the Communist Party, June 17, 1937, *Frente Rojo*, June 21, 1937. In spite of this record, he denied some years later that he had ever advocated a merger of the two parties.—*The Last Optimist*, p. 228.

[6] Quoted Enrique Castro, *Hombres made in Moscú*, p. 659. See also pp. 230, 289–91, below. But in spite of Vayo's many services, the party had no respect for him. See Castro, *ibid.*, pp. 553, 555–7.

[7] Article in *Socialist Review*, September, 1937. It is worth noting that Alvarez del Vayo appointed the foreign Communist, André Simone, as director of the propaganda press agency in Paris, the *Agencia Española*.—See letter by Simone in *Tiempo*, August 27, 1943.

[8] Because of his services to the Communist cause, some Spaniards have concluded that at the beginning of the war he was a member of the left wing of the Socialist Party. This is untrue. See, for example, Zugazagoitia (a moderate Socialist), *Historia de la guerra en España*, p. 138, who shows that he was a follower of Prieto's.

[9] Although a detailed account of Negrín's subservience to the Communists

Although Prieto's own man and recommended by him to head the Ministry of Finance in Caballero's government,[10] Negrín was, long before the war had run its course, to free himself, at first secretly and then openly, from the bonds that tied him to the moderate Socialist leader.

As Minister of Finance in Largo Caballero's administration, Negrín maintained constant and easy relations with Arthur Stashevsky, officially the Soviet trade representative, to whom Stalin, in the words of General Krivitsky, the head of Soviet Intelligence in Western Europe, had assigned the task of "manipulating the political and financial reins of Loyalist Spain."[11] According to Louis Fischer, who was personally acquainted with most of the leading Russians in Spain, the Soviet trade envoy "not only arranged Spanish purchases of Russian arms but was Negrín's friendly adviser on many economic problems."[12]

---

and of his vast contribution, as Premier and Defence Minister, to the success of their policy in the last twelve months of the war lies beyond the scope of the present volume, the interested reader is referred to the testimony of the following top-ranking Socialists: Luis Araquistain (letter to Martínez Barrio, as given in *Vía Libre*, May 15, 1939; *El comunismo y la guerra de España*, pp. 14, 17); Carlos de Baraibar (*Timón*, Buenos Aires, June, 1940); Wenceslao Carrillo (speech in May, 1946, as given in *2° congreso del partido socialista obrero español en el exilio*, pp. 95–107; *El último episodio de la guerra civil española*, p. 10); Gabriel Morón (*Política de ayer y política de mañana*, pp. 108–9); Indalecio Prieto (*Cómo y por qué salí del ministerio de defensa nacional*, prologues to the Mexican and French editions, pp. 12, 25; *Epistolario Prieto y Negrín*, pp. 17, 99–100; article in *Correo de Asturias*, July 10, 1943; article in *El Socialista*, Paris, November 9, 1950; interview given to the United Press, reported in *El Universal*, July 30, 1939); Julián Zugazagoitia (*Historia de la guerra en España*, pp. 408, 464, 535). But see also the testimony of Colonel Segismundo Casado, *The Last Days of Madrid*, pp. 101, 281, and Pérez Salas, *Guerra en España*, pp. 141, 162, as well as editorials in *Política*, March 16, 20, 1939. Like Alvarez del Vayo, Negrín was also suspended towards the end of the war from the Madrid section of the Socialist Party because of his political conduct.—See *Claridad*, March 15, 1939; also report of Wenceslao Carrillo to the Labour and Socialist International, May 23, 1939, as given in special issue of *Independent News* [June, 1939?].

For confirmation by a former leading Communist that Negrín was controlled by the party, see Castro, *Hombres made in Moscú*, p. 660. Too many people, in a position to know otherwise, have appeared blind to Negrín's subservience to the Communists. See, for example, Claude Bowers (U.S. Ambassador to Spain during the Civil War), *My Mission to Spain*, p. 358, who says that Negrín was "as remote from Communism as it is possible to be."

[10] See Angel Galarza in *El Socialista Español*, December 2, 1946.

[11] *In Stalin's Secret Service*, pp. 96–7.

[12] *The Nation*, January 13, 1940. Alvarez del Vayo in *The Last Optimist*, p. 291, remarks that "the Russian with whom Negrín had the most contact was Stashevsky; they formed a real friendship." However, he adds (p. 292):

Indeed, it would appear that it was at Stashevsky's suggestion that in October, 1936, Negrín shipped more than half the Spanish gold reserves to the Soviet Union.[13] This important transfer, with a value

"Another point Negrín considered essential to the maintenance of good relations with the Russians was a clear understanding that he would not tolerate, from anyone, even the suggestion of intervention in the affairs of the republican government or in the internal policy of Spain."

[13] "[Stashevsky]," writes Krivitsky (*In Stalin's Secret Service*, pp. 99–100), "discovered in Juan Negrín, Finance Minister in the Madrid cabinet, a willing collaborator in his financial schemes. Madrid found it almost impossible to buy arms openly anywhere in the world market. The Spanish republic had deposited a considerable quantity of the Spanish gold reserve in Paris banks hoping to import war materials from France. But an insuperable difficulty developed: the French banks refused to release the gold because Franco threatened to file claims against them in the event of his victory. Such claims would little disturb the distant Kremlin, once the gold was in its possession. Stashevsky offered to take the Spanish gold to Soviet Russia, and to supply Madrid with arms and munitions in exchange. Through Negrín he made the deal with Caballero's government." There has been some controversy, however, as to whether all the ministers knew of the plan to transfer the gold to Russia. The Navy and Air Minister, Indalecio Prieto, for his part, affirms that they did not. After stating that on October 25, 1936, seven thousand eight hundred cases of gold, in coin and bars, were shipped from the naval base of Cartagena to Russia, he continues: "Previously, Señor Negrín, as Minister of Finance, obtained the consent of the government and the signature of the President of the Republic for a decree empowering him to take whatever measures he deemed necessary to safeguard the gold of the Bank of Spain. As a member of that government I accept my share of responsibility for the decree, although neither I nor the other ministers knew of the aim pursued. I do not know whether Largo Caballero, who was then head of the government, was aware of it. The loading was surrounded with great secrecy. I found out about it by pure accident just when the gold was being loaded under the direction of Negrín and Méndez Aspe [Under-Secretary of Finance], having arrived at Cartagena to attend to matters connected with my department."—*Como y por qué salí del ministerio de defensa nacional* (preface to the Mexican edition), p. 15. Alvarez del Vayo, on the other hand, states that a Commercial Agreement was concluded between the two governments providing for the use of the facilities of the Soviet state bank by the Spanish Government and that after its ratification "Largo Caballero and Negrín jointly decided that a considerable part of the gold reserves—something more than half—should be remitted to Moscow." They were agreed, he said, that the greatest secrecy should be observed. "As it was necessary to assure and protect the transportation by sea, Indalecio Prieto, as Minister of Marine and Aviation, was made a co-partner in the secret, . . . and directly and personally took charge, arranging that a squadron should accompany the convoy nearly to Tunis."—*The Last Optimist*, pp. 283–5. Angel Galarza, Minister of the Interior and a left-wing Socialist at the time of the events, but writing after the war as a supporter of Negrín, likewise affirms that Largo Caballero and Prieto were aware of the shipment from Cartagena at the

of 578 million dollars[14]—prompted by the imminent danger to Madrid as well as by the difficulty of purchasing arms in other countries owing to the non-intervention agreement—was forthwith to make the Cabinet dependent in large measure on the good will of Moscow by depriving it of any bargaining power with Soviet agents in Spain.

Still another factor weighing heavily in favour of Communist influence in the affairs of government was the arrival in September and October, 1936, of military advisers and political agents, who exercised, in fact if not in form, the authority of ministers in various departments.[15] This they were able to do not because there were Soviet forces

---

time it was made.—*El Socialista Español*, December 2, 1946. For his part, Largo Caballero writes: "As the rebels were at the gates of Madrid [Negrín] asked the Government for authority to transfer the gold from the Bank of Spain to a safe place without stating where. This was a natural thing to do in order to prevent the treasure, through misadventure, from falling into the hands of the rebels; for without gold with which to purchase arms the defeat of the Republic would have been inevitable. . . . The first step taken by Negrín was to transfer the gold to the naval base of Cartagena. Later, fearing a landing, he decided to send it abroad. Where? England and France were the very soul of 'non-intervention.' . . . Could we have had any faith in them? No. Then, where else could we have sent it? There was no other place but Russia, the country that was helping us with arms and food. . . . With this gold we paid Russia for the war material she was sending us. . . . Also we used what gold we needed for other purchases, these transactions being made through a bank in Paris located on the Avenue de l'Opéra. The letters of withdrawal had to be signed by Negrín and myself. I signed two or three of them. Later, without giving me any explanation, Negrín alone signed them."—*Mis recuerdos* (Cartas a un amigo), pp. 203–4. It is not undeserving of interest that according to the ex-Communist "El Campesino," who was entrusted with the transfer from Madrid to Cartagena, the withdrawal of the gold from the vaults of the Bank of Spain was undertaken only by Communists "several of them dressed in the uniform of Assault Guards."—*La vie et la mort en U.R.S.S., 1939–1949*, p. 177.

[14] Luis Araquistain (*El comunismo y la guerra de España*, p. 20) writes: "According to a communication dated February 10, 1937, from Marcelino Pascua, Spanish Ambassador in Moscow, the amount deposited in Russia was 510,079,529·3 grams of gold." At $35 per ounce, this was the equivalent of approximately $578,000,000, a figure confirmed indirectly by the combined data furnished by Alvarez del Vayo and Louis Fischer. While the former states that something more than half the gold reserves was sent to Moscow (*The Last Optimist*, p. 284), the latter discloses, on the basis of figures given to him by Negrín, that in September, 1936, the Spanish Government's total assets in gold and silver amounted to almost one billion paper dollars (*Men and Politics*, p. 364).

[15] "As time went on," writes Colonel Segismundo Casado, Operations Chief on the General Staff of the War Ministry in the early months of the war, "Russian influence was increased at the War Ministry. They [the Russian military advisers] looked over the plans of the General Staff and through the

in Spain strong enough to coerce the government by mere numbers. "I am sure," affirms Indalecio Prieto, Navy and Air Minister in the Cabinet, and Minister of Defence after the fall of Largo Caballero, "that at no time did the Russians in our territory aggregate more than five hundred, including aviators, industrial technicians, military advisers, naval men, interpreters, and secret agents.[16] Most of them were aviators who, like the Germans and Italians, were relieved after short periods.[17] . . . Russia could not use coercion because of the military forces she sent to Spain. Her ability to do so stemmed from the fact that she was, owing to the attitude of the other Powers, our sole purveyor of war material."[18]

In addition to all this, the position of the Communists in the government was greatly strengthened by the fact that they could rely for support, in major issues of domestic and foreign policy, on the Republican and moderate Socialist representatives,[19] and that Largo

Minister they rejected many technical proposals and imposed others."—*The Last Days of Madrid*, p. 52. And in a later passage (p. 54), he says: "These 'friendly advisers' exercised authority just as much in the Air Force, and in the Tank Corps." Of Russian influence in high places, Luis Araquistain, close collaborator of Largo Caballero for many years, writes: "The Air Force, directed by the Russians, operated when and where they pleased, without any co-ordination with the land and sea forces. The Navy and Air Minister, Indalecio Prieto, meek and cynical, made fun of his office to anyone who visited him, declaring that he was neither a minister nor anything else, because he received absolutely no obedience from the air force. The real Air Minister was the Russian General Duglas."—*El comunismo y la guerra de España*, pp. 24–5. And later on, he adds (p. 26): "Behind [the Russian officers] were innumerable political agents who were disguised as commercial agents and were in real control of Spanish politics. . . . They directed the Russian officers, the Communist Party, and Rosenberg himself [the Soviet Ambassador], who in reality was only an ambassador of straw. The real ambassadors were those mysterious men who entered Spain under false names and were working under direct orders from the Kremlin and the Russian police."

[16] Louis Fischer, an authority on this subject, claims that at no time were there more than seven hundred Soviet Russians in Spain (*Men and Politics*, p. 498). Krivitsky, on the other hand, places the figure at under two thousand (*In Stalin's Secret Service*, p. 95).

[17] Ignacio Hidalgo de Cisneros, the Spanish Chief of the Air Force, when interviewed by the author after the war, stated that Soviet pilots were relieved every few months and that altogether one thousand flew in Spain during the war.

[18] *Cómo y por qué salí del ministerio de defensa nacional* (prologue to the French edition), pp. 24–5. See also extract from Largo Caballero's unpublished memoirs, quoted on p. 233, below.

[19] José Giral, Premier of the government formed on July 19 and minister without portfolio in Caballero's administration, representing the Left Repub-

Caballero, in spite of Russian pressure and the ravages on his following, maintained tolerable relations with the Communist Party during the first months of his incumbency; for, however provoked he may secretly have been, a large measure of agreement still existed between them. In fact, from the day his government was formed, he adopted the Communist viewpoint that it should impress the outside world with its moderation. Not that he or the other non-Communist members of his Cabinet were concerned with the broader aims of Russian policy. They simply hoped that by proclaiming respect for legal forms, Britain and France, fearful of an Italo-German vassalage of Spain, would finally raise the arms embargo. It was necessary, Caballero declared, during a private conversation shortly after taking office, "to sacrifice revolutionary language to win the friendship of the democratic Powers."[20] In this respect he was not remiss. "The Spanish Government is not fighting for socialism but for democracy and constitutional rule," he stated to a delegation of British Members of Parliament.[21] And in a communiqué to the foreign press, he said: "The Government of the Spanish Republic is not aiming at setting up a Soviet régime in Spain in spite of what has been alleged in some quarters abroad. The Government's essential aim is to maintain the parliamentary régime of the Republic as it was set up by the Constitution which the Spanish people freely assumed."[22]

Illustrative of his Cabinet's regard for foreign opinion was the declaration it issued after its first session. Avoiding all reference to the

---

lican Party, declared in a speech in March, 1937, that the coincidence of views between his party and the Communists was almost identical.—Reported in *La Voz Valencia*, March 10, 1937. ". . . We have to take into account the attitude of the states that surround us . . . ," said *El Socialista* (October 4, 1936), which expressed the opinions of Prieto, the moderate Socialist leader and Navy and Air Minister. "We still hope that the estimate of Spanish events made by certain democracies will be changed, and it would be a pity, a tragedy, to compromise these possibilities by accelerating the revolution."

[20] Quoted by Julián Gorkin in *Workers' Age*, May 31, 1939.

[21] Extracts from his statement, which was made on December 4, 1936, were given to the author by the delegation itself when he was representing the United Press in Valencia, and were approved for transmission to the United Press office in London by the Foreign Press Censorship. They were not published in any of the newspapers the author consulted.—See bibliography: "Burnett Bolloten. Dispatch from Valencia to the United Press."

[22] *Manchester Guardian*, November 25, 1936. See also his statement to the Duchess of Atholl and other women Members of Parliament as given in *Claridad*, April 22, 1937.

profound revolutionary changes that had taken place or to any social programme, it stated:

"1. In view of its composition, [the Government] considers itself the direct representative of all those political forces that are fighting at the fronts for the maintenance of the democratic Republic, against which the rebels have taken up arms. . . .

"2. The programme of the Government consists essentially of the firm intention to accelerate victory over the rebellion, co-ordinating the forces of the people by the necessary unity of action. . . . To this end all other political interests are subordinated, ideological differences being set aside. . . .

"4. . . . The Government affirms the feelings of friendship of Spain towards all nations and its most devoted adherence to the Covenant of the League of Nations, hoping that, in just return, our country will receive from others the same consideration it will give to them. . . .

"6. The Government greets with the utmost enthusiasm the land, sea and air forces, as well as the People's Militia who are defending the Republican Constitution. Its highest aim is to be worthy of such heroic fighters, whose legitimate desires for social betterment will find in it a determined champion."[23]

As it was essential for the sake of foreign opinion that legal forms be observed, the Cortes, or Parliament, met on October 1, as stipulated in the Constitution. Commenting on this, the director of the Communist organ, *Mundo Obrero*, wrote:

"The deputies of the nation, the legal representatives of the people, the deputies elected by the free will of the people on February 16, have assembled this morning. The government has appeared before the Congress in accordance with the Republican Constitution.

"In the midst of civil war, while the struggle to impose republican legality and the will of the people is proceeding at the fronts, the government is ratified by the Chamber. Constituted as the genuine representative of the people, it has functioned as such until today. The head of the state gave it his confidence, and today it reinforces its legal origin . . . with the confidence of Parliament.

". . . On the one side is the Republic, with its legal organs. . . . On the other are the military traitors, the fascist blackguards, the adventurers of all classes in Spain and abroad. . . .

"The civilized world has now been able to judge; it is on our side in its entirety. To help the legal authorities of Spain is a duty imposed

[23] *Política*, September 5, 1936.

by international law; to help the rebels is a crime against civilization and against humanity."[24]

And after the next session of the Cortes in December, the organ of the Left Republican Party declared:

"Legality has only one medium of expression. This is what yesterday's session of the Parliament of the Republic demonstrated. . . . It was also the most eloquent demonstration of the continuity of the democratic republican régime and of the unshakeable determination of the country not to allow the legality of its public life to disappear in the whirlwind of passions and appetites unleashed by this bloody civil war.

"At this time, . . . when the world is contemplating the unique struggle of the people of Madrid and of the Spanish people as a whole, the Republic maintains a rich and vigorous constitutional life. All its basic institutions, allowing for the exigencies of the times and the particular circumstances of a country at war, function normally. Not one has been supplanted. . . .[25]

"The session of the Cortes of the Republic that took place yesterday once again destroys the specious arguments of those who, particularly outside Spain, take delight in stridently censuring a people fighting to defend rights that are so legitimate that in countries with an older democratic tradition they are not even mentioned because they are taken for granted. Spain is today waging a struggle for republican and democratic consolidation such as other countries experienced many years ago.

"Would it be too much to ask those governments that are tolerating the international crime being committed in Spain by German and Italian intervention to appreciate what this signifies? Face to face with the enemy at home, the Spanish people, victorious in the February elections, would have triumphed over the barbarous rebellion within a few days. But face to face with the military apparatus of Germany and Italy, it has no course but to appeal frankly and sincerely to world opinion.

"The same government, or rather a legal continuation of that government, the same Parliament, the same President of the Republic, the same institutions with which every country in the world had

[24] October 1, 1936.

[25] It should be mentioned that the Left Republican Party was not the only liberal party that attempted to conceal the changes in the economic, social, and political life of the left camp. See, for example, radio address to world opinion by Diego Martínez Barrio, Vice-President of the Republic and leader of the Republican Union Party, as reported in *Política*, August 2, 1936.

maintained friendly and cordial relations until July 17 exercise today, more than four months after the outbreak of the rebellion that is striving to put an end to the legal constitution of Spain, the same powers and the same functions. Does this mean nothing at all? Or, in face of the inexcusable aggression of which these institutions have been the object, has the world lost all feeling?"[26]

In order to ensure that the Western democracies would continue to recognize the government as the legally constituted authority, it was essential that Manuel Azaña, the President of the Republic, should remain in office to sanction its decrees and perform the diverse functions laid down in the Constitution. Whether he could be persuaded to do so indefinitely was open to grave doubt, not only because his hostility to the revolution was a matter of common knowledge, but because in October, 1936—three weeks before the government's own transfer to Valencia as a result of the enemy's threatening advance towards the capital—he had decided to take up residence in Barcelona, from where, it was feared, he might cross the border into France and there resign the presidency.[27] "Reports reaching us regarding the attitude of Señor Azaña . . . were by no means reassuring," testifies Alvarez del Vayo. "We feared that his habitual pessimism, exacerbated by isolation, might lead him to make some irrevocable decision."[28]

The state of mind of President Manuel Azaña was also well known to

[26] *Política*, December 2, 1936. It is worth noting that after the war the Communists, Republicans, and Socialists in exile, still hoping to influence world opinion in favour of the Spanish Republican cause, did what they could to conceal the depth of the 1936 revolution. Some, in fact, even maintained that the Republican Constitution had remained inviolate during the Civil War. See, for example, article in *The Left News*, January, 1943, by Pablo de Azcárate, former Spanish Ambassador in London and a Negrín supporter, in which he affirmed that "from July 16, 1936, to March 5, 1939 [the date of the overthrow of the Negrín government by a coalition of left-wing parties], the constitution was in force, *in fact* and *in law*, throughout the territory under the legitimate authority of the Republic, and *in law only* in that ruled by the rebels."

[27] If he did not do so, it was partly because of the pressure that was brought to bear upon him by Republicans as well as by Indalecio Prieto with whom he was always in close contact. Relating after the war how Azaña informed him in April, 1938, of his intention to resign, because of his inability to settle a governmental crisis in accordance with his own wishes, Prieto records his reply as follows: "You cannot resign . . . [because] your resignation would bring down everything, and because you personify the Republic, which to a certain degree the countries not allied to Franco respect. If you were to resign, that respect, thanks to which we are still able to exist, would disappear."—*Palabras al viento*, p. 282.

[28] *Freedom's Battle*, p. 214.

Moscow, and, in December, 1936, Stalin, Molotov, and Voroshilov, showing how much they appreciated his diplomatic utility, gave Largo Caballero the following advice: "It is above all necessary," they wrote to him in a letter, "that the government should be assured of the support of Azaña and his group, doing everything possible to help them to overcome their hesitation. This is necessary in order to prevent the enemies of Spain from considering her as a Communist Republic."[29]

[29] Quoted by Luis Araquistain, *El comunismo y la guerra de España*, p. 30. A facsimile of the page of the letter in which the above-quoted passage appears was published in *The New York Times*, June 4, 1939. "The participation of the bourgeois parties in the Loyalist government is . . . a symbol," wrote Louis Fischer (*Spain Fights On*, p. 37). "To capitalists in fascist Spain, and to the outside world, it is intended as an indication that the Republic has no plan now of setting up a Soviet State or a Communist régime after victory in the civil war." See also extract of article by Marcel Rosenberg (Soviet Ambassador to Spain until April, 1937) in the *Journal de Moscou*, as quoted by *Le Temps*, May 1, 1937. The fact that the Catholic Basque Nationalist Party, a middle-class organization, had opposed the military rebellion and had agreed to participate in the Largo Caballero government—this on condition that the Basque Country be granted autonomy (see Jesús de Galíndez, *Los vascos en el Madrid sitiado*, p. 19)—was exploited to the full by the Communists and by fellow travellers in their domestic and foreign propaganda. The following extract from a letter reproduced in the pro-Franco newspaper *Heraldo de Aragón* on June 10, 1937, and allegedly written by Alvarez del Vayo to another member of the government, whose identity was not given, is worth quoting in view of its credibility: "How many times I have remembered what you said four months ago in my presence! It was necessary, you said—and you will recall that I immediately assented—to give the outside world the impression of a bourgeois tendency [in the government]. Nothing has favoured us so much abroad as unity with the Basque Nationalist Party." Communist praise of José Antonio Aguirre, who became premier of the autonomous Basque Government, was at times so extravagant as to embarrass him. "I must confess," he stated in a report to the central government, "that as far as I am concerned the eulogies and headlines of the newspapers, principally the Communist newspapers, were sometimes so exaggerated, the adjectives so friendly and laudatory, that instead of feeling flattered I blushed with shame. This old tactic has no place in the customs of the Basque people, who are forthright and not double-faced."—This passage is on p. 68 of the report. (See bibliography.)

II

Wooing Britain and France

THAT Soviet leaders saw great advantages in the continued recognition of the Spanish Government as the legally constituted authority is indubitable. They knew that as long as it was recognized as such by Britain and France, it would not only be in a position to bring the question of Italo-German intervention before the League of Nations, but could demand that, in accordance with the rules of international law applicable to cases of insurrection against a legitimate government, it be permitted to purchase arms freely in the markets of the world.[1] They knew, moreover, that if Britain and France were to abandon their policy of neutrality, the Civil War in Spain might ultimately develop into a large-scale conflict, a conflict from which they could remain virtually aloof until the warring parties had fought to the point of mutual exhaustion and from which the Soviet Union would emerge master of the European continent.[2]

But before many months had passed, it became clear that except for occasional lapses of French neutrality, both Britain and France, in spite of the risks involved to themselves of a Spain under bondage to Italy and Germany,[3] were not to be diverted from the policy of non-

[1] "Juridically there was no possible defence for Non-Intervention," writes Alvarez del Vayo (*Freedom's Battle*, p. 44). "To refuse a legitimate Government, with whom the United Kingdom and France were maintaining normal diplomatic relations, their indisputable right to acquire the material necessary to subdue the revolt of a few rebel generals was the very extreme of arbitrary conduct."

[2] In 1925 Stalin had declared in a speech at a plenary session of the Central Committee of the Communist Party: ". . . if war begins, we shall hardly have to sit with folded arms. We shall have to come out, but we ought to be the last to come out. And we should come out in order to throw the decisive weight on the scales, the weight that should tilt the scales."—J. Stalin, *Sochineniia*, VII, pp. 13–14, as quoted by Deutscher, *Stalin*, p. 411.

[3] It is worth recording that by mediation, Britain, though sceptical of the possibility of putting it into practice, hoped that she might be able to avoid

intervention they had pursued since the inception of the conflict. Although Léon Blum, the Socialist premier of the Popular Front government of France, is alleged to have adopted a neutral stand mainly under strong British pressure,[4] it should be emphasized that he had also been subject to pressure from some of the Radical ministers in his Cabinet, from the President of the Republic,[5] from the combined forces of the French Right, as well as from the powerful Radical Party itself,[6] which represented a large segment of the middle classes.

Equally indicative of the opposition of influential quarters in both Britain and France to any military commitment that might involve them in a war with Germany was their hostility to the Franco-Soviet Pact of Mutual Assistance. If this hostility was undisguised by an important section of French opinion,[7] to say nothing of the antipathy in official quarters,[8] it was no less patent in authoritative British newspapers. "British opinion," said *The Times*, the unofficial mouthpiece

---

the entrenchment of Italy and Germany in Spain and an extension of the conflict to Western Europe.—See the proposal for mediation made to Germany in December, 1936, by Anthony Eden, British Foreign Secretary, as outlined in a communication from Joachim von Ribbentrop, Germany Ambassador in Great Britain, to the Wilhelmstrasse (*Documents on German Foreign Policy 1918–1945*. III. *Germany and the Spanish Civil War 1936–1939*, pp. 158–9).

[4] Pertinax (André Géraud) in prologue to Dzelepy, *The Spanish Plot*, p. vii. See also Maurice Pujo in *L'Action Française*, July 25, 1936; Vincent Auriol, quoted by Indalecio Prieto in *España Republicana*, July 17, 1948; Fenner Brockway, *Workers' Front*, pp. 159–60; Pierre Lazareff, *Deadline*, p. 134; Alexander Werth, *Which Way France?*, p. 379.

[5] According to Louis Lévy, an intimate of Léon Blum, *Vérités sur la France*, p. 114.

[6] See his testimony before the Parliamentary Commission of Inquiry set up in 1947 to investigate the events that took place in France between 1933 and 1945, as given in *Les événements survenus en France de 1933 à 1945*, Vol. I, pp. 216–17. At the Radical Party Congress held in October, 1936, a resolution was approved commending the government for having "averted a grave international peril" by proposing the Non-Intervention Agreement.—See *L'Ere Nouvelle*, October 24, 1936.

[7] See p. 96, above.

[8] See p. 90, above. ". . . The foreign policy of the Popular Front was weakened by the fact that the Franco-Soviet Pact, which should have been its solid basis, was really accepted only by the Communist deputies, by a small part of the Socialist Party, and by barely half the radicals. Were not the arguments of Léon Blum himself, in his articles in the *Populaire*, perhaps the most difficult to dismiss by those who wished to see the pact ratified? His policy was one of weakness. His personal views on collective security—'Fundamentally, can we logically be expected to run the risk of a war now in order to avoid another later on?'—were floating around more than ever."—Tabouis, *Ils l'ont appelée Cassandre*, p. 297.

of the Government, "is not prepared to accept . . . the leadership of France over the whole field of foreign politics, or to admit responsibility for all the liabilities which she had been accumulating . . . in the shape of alliances on the farther side of Germany. . . . The Franco-Soviet Pact is not regarded here as a helpful diplomatic achievement."[9]

"France," wrote "Scrutator" in the *Sunday Times*, "has made alliances in Eastern Europe for power—its motive is still power, even if there is no idea of aggression but only self-defence. Rightly or wrongly—wrongly, as some of us think—she convinced herself that the benefits to herself of an alliance with Russia and the Little Entente outweighed the risk of entanglements in disputes not really her own. In this regard, France's policy is not ours."[10]

"These pacts [the Franco-Soviet and Czech–Soviet treaties]," affirmed J. L. Garvin, editor of the *Observer*, an influential conveyor of Conservative opinion, "mean war and can mean nothing else. If we support them they mean war between Britain and Germany and can mean nothing else. If Britain is to give countenance or patronage to those fatal instruments; if we are to have any lot or part in them whatever; if we are to stand behind France and Czechoslovakia as the potential allies of Russia and Communism against Germany—then the situation becomes inherently deadly to peace, and it is no use talking of anything else. We cannot have it both ways. If we are to interfere with Germany in the East she must ultimately strike us in the West. Nothing else is possible."[11]

If such expressions of opinion were more outspoken than official declarations, they nevertheless corresponded closely to the attitude of the British Government, an attitude of which the Kremlin was fully conscious. Indeed, the fear that both Britain and France might arrive at some agreement with Germany at the expense of Eastern Europe was deeply grounded in Moscow. In a conversation with Joseph E. Davies, U.S. Ambassador to Russia, in February, 1937, Litvinov, Soviet Commissar for Foreign Affairs, did not conceal this disquietude: ". . . he could not understand," Davies informed the Secretary of State, "why Great Britain could not see that once Hitler dominated Europe he would swallow the British Isles also. He seemed to be very much stirred about this and apprehensive lest there should be some composition of differences between France, England, and Germany."[12]

[9] July 6, 1936.
[10] December 20, 1936.
[11] November 1, 1936.
[12] Letter dated February 6, 1937, quoted in *Mission to Moscow*, pp. 57–60. See also letter dated February 19, 1937, *ibid.*, pp. 77–9.

It was undoubtedly the fear that the impetus of German militarism might ultimately be directed against the East rather than against the West, augmented by the disappointment over the continued neutrality of Britain and France with regard to the Spanish conflict despite increasing Italo-German intervention,[13] over the failure of the French Government to supplement the Franco-Soviet Pact by any positive military agreement,[14] and over the rejection of a Popular Front by the British Labour Party[15] that prompted the Kremlin to redouble its efforts in Spain with a view to enticing Britain and France from their neutrality.

At the end of January, 1937, a leader of the PSUC, the Communist-controlled United Socialist Party of Catalonia, told the Central Committee of his party in words that reflected discussions that had taken place with "Pedro," a top-ranking Comintern agent in Spain,[16] who had just returned from Moscow,[17] that "the essential thing at this time is to seek the collaboration of the European democracies, particularly that of England."[18]

". . . in the democratic bloc of powers," he declared two days later at a public meeting, "the decisive factor is not France; it is England. It is essential for all party comrades to realize this so as to moderate [their] slogans at the present time. . . .

"England is not a country like France. England is a country governed by the Conservative Party. England is a country of slow evolution, which is constantly preoccupied with Imperial interests. England is a

[13] In a frank account published after the Civil War of Italian assistance to General Franco, *Forze Armate*, the official organ of the Italian War Office, revealed (June 8, 1939) that between mid-December, 1936, and mid-April, 1937, the Navy had transported 100,000 men to Spain in addition to 4,370 motor vehicles, 40,000 tons of war material, and 750 heavy guns. Furthermore, the paper revealed that units of the Italian Fleet had been employed in the early stages of the war not only in escorting Italian transports from Italian to Spanish ports but in naval operations against the Republican fleet and coast as well as against ships bringing cargoes to Republican ports, many of which had been sunk. For an equally frank account of German intervention in the early part of the war, see the special number of *Die Wehrmacht* entitled *Wir Kämpften in Spanien*, issued in May, 1939, by the German High Command.

[14] See p. 90, above.

[15] See reference in the *Daily Herald*, January 13, 1937, to the Labour Party's statement, appealing to the Labour Movement to "establish unity within its own ranks and not by association with organizations in conflict with the aims of the Party."

[16] See n. 37, p. 113, above.

[17] According to a leader of the PSUC, who prefers to remain anonymous.

[18] *El Día Gráfico*, January 31, 1937.

country of plutocrats, a country with a profoundly conservative middle class that reacts with great difficulty. . . .

". . . Some persons say that England could never on any account agree to the triumph of Germany over Spain because that would signify a danger to her own vital interests. But we should realize that the big capitalists in England are capable of coming to an understanding at any time with Italian and German capitalists if they should reach the conclusion that they have no other choice with regard to Spain.

"[Therefore] we must win, cost what it may, the benevolent neutrality of that country, if not its direct aid."[19]

That this was to be achieved not merely by accentuating the moderate tendencies initiated by the Communists at the outbreak of the revolution but by more tangible means was evident from a sensational Note sent by the Spanish Government, in February, 1937, to Britain and France—undoubtedly inspired by Comintern agents acting through a Spanish diplomat or Cabinet minister secretly in their service[20]—offering to transfer Spanish Morocco to these two Powers in return for the adoption of measures designed to prevent further Italo-German intervention.[21] As this territory was in the hands of General Franco, and inasmuch as there had recently been insistent reports that Germany was fortifying the coast opposite Gibraltar,[22] it must have been obvious to Moscow that no such assignment could have been made in favour of Britain and France and accepted by them without the risk of precipitating an international conflict, although it is doubtful whether the majority of the members of the Spanish Government, concerned solely with the Spanish scene and with securing Anglo-French support, were aware of the wider objectives

[19] *Treball*, February 2, 1937.

[20] According to information in the author's possession, the proposals contained in the Note were suggested to the government by a prominent Spanish diplomat sympathetic to the Communists. This, however, does not preclude the possibility that they were also recommended by a pro-Communist member of the Cabinet.

[21] It is significant that during his discussions with the PSUC leaders at the end of January, after his return from Moscow (approximately two weeks before the Note was delivered to Britain and France), "Pedro," the Comintern agent, spoke of the advisability of offering Spanish Morocco and the Canary Islands (also in the hands of General Franco) to Britain and France in order to win the support of these two Powers. Russia, during her revolution, he added, had also been compelled to make sacrifices. For this information, the author is also grateful to the PSUC leader mentioned in n. 17, p. 134, above.

[22] See, for example, *Daily Telegraph* and *Le Temps*, January 11, 1937.

of Soviet policy in Spain or even of the Russian provenance of the Moroccan proposals.

Signed by Alvarez del Vayo, the philo-Communist Foreign Minister, the Note stated in part:

I

1. The Spanish Government wishes Spain's future foreign policy, so far as Western Europe is concerned, to assume the form of active collaboration with France and the United Kingdom.

2. To this end, Spain would be ready to take into consideration, both in the matter of economic reconstruction and in her military, naval and air relations, the interests of these two Powers, in so far as this is compatible with her own interests.

3. In the same manner, Spain would be ready to examine, in conjunction with these Powers, the advisability or otherwise of modifying the present status of North Africa (Spanish Morocco) on condition that such modification is not made in favour of any Power other than Great Britain and France. . . .

II

. . . If these proposals, which are made in a spirit of full international collaboration, are appreciated at their true worth by the British and French Governments, these governments would henceforth be responsible for the adoption of any measures within their power designed to prevent further Italo-German intervention in Spanish affairs, in view of the fact that the interests of peace, which are synonymous with the national interests of the Western democracies, demand the effective prosecution of this aim.

If the sacrifices which the Spanish Government is willing to make prove insufficient to prevent the further supplying of men and material to the rebels by Italy and Germany, and if, in consequence, the Republican Government is compelled to fight the rebel generals, aided by two foreign Powers, until victory is attained, then the proposals made in the first part [of this Note] will be considered null and void, in view of the fact that their essential aim, which is to spare the Spanish people further suffering, would be frustrated. . . .[23]

". . . The Spanish Memorandum . . . gave the most conclusive proof of the Republic's desire for an understanding with Great Britain and France," writes Alvarez del Vayo. "Though it could not, in view of the existing circumstances, take the form of a pact of mutual assistance or

[23] *El Adelanto*, March 17, 1936. A copy of this Note fell into the hands of General Franco's administration (see *The Times*, London, April 12, 1937), and the text was published for the first time by the Franco press. Later, excerpts or summaries were published in the British and French press and elicited no denial from the Spanish Government.

an alliance, it was to all intents and purposes the same."[24] And in a later passage, he says:

"Neither of the two Governments received the Republican initiative favourably,[25] and the international 'leakage' by which the text of the Spanish Memorandum was made known to the public[26] gave evidence of an active hand behind the scenes which was doing everything possible to frustrate attempts to help the cause of the Spanish Government. . . .

"Although the February Memorandum was an official statement of the Republic's foreign policy during the war, it must not be thought that it represented the extent of our efforts to persuade Great Britain and France to adopt an attitude more in keeping with their own interests. By every relevant argument, by communicating reports on Italo-German activity to both Governments, by the submission of concrete proposals for combating the Italian menace in Majorca—by every means in our power we endeavoured to bring about a change of attitude in London and Paris.[27]

"We were not crying for the moon. We made no request for armed assistance. We only asked that in strict accordance with the policy of Non-Intervention—which Great Britain and France have imposed on us and should for that very reason have enforced—'Spain should be left to the Spaniards'; and that if those two democracies did not feel able to prevent Germany and Italy from continuing to intervene in Spain, they should make honourable recognition of the failure of their policy and re-establish in full the right to freedom of trade. In a word, we asked that international law should be respected.

"The way in which the British and French Governments ignored

[24] *Freedom's Battle*, p. 235.
[25] For the British and French replies, see *The. Times*, London, April 22, 1937.
[26] See n. 23, above.
[27] "When, after Munich, it became clear that the British Government had decided to follow very closely the policy of friendship with Rome which had already been initiated with the Anglo-Italian Agreement of the previous April," he writes (*Freedom's Battle*, p. 255), "the Spanish Government—in spite of its tremendous opposition to Italian intervention in Spain—did not hesitate to inform the British Government categorically that if the latter would put an end to this intervention, the victory and consolidation of the Republic in Spain would afford no obstacle whatever to a policy of collaboration with Italy in the Mediterranean. They even went so far as to declare that they would themselves be willing to collaborate with Italy on the basis of mutual respect for the integrity and political independence of either state. This declaration, which I communicated personally to M. Fouques Duparc, the French Chargé d'Affaires in Barcelona, was also ignored by the British Government."

our warnings, suggestions, and requests was truly heartbreaking."[28]

Notwithstanding these disappointments, Russia continued to bolster the resistance of the anti-Franco forces in the stubborn belief that Britain and France could not permit an Italo-German vassalage of Spain and would sooner or later be forced to intervene in defence of their own interests, undermining or destroying Germany's military power before she had time to prepare for war in Eastern Europe. "[Moscow]," affirmed Stepanov, Soviet adviser to the Spanish Politburo, "will try by every means to avoid being isolated, to force . . . the Western democracies to fight Hitler."[29]

"We want [the democratic states] to help us," declared José Díaz, the general secretary of the Spanish Communist Party, reflecting Moscow's policy, "and believe that in this way they will be defending their own interests. We try to make them understand this and to enlist their help. . . . We know full well that the fascist aggressors find bourgeois groups in every country to support them, such as the Conservatives in England and the Rightists in France, but fascist aggression is going forward at such a pace that national interests, in a country like France, for instance, must convince all men who desire the liberty and independence of their country of the necessity of standing up to this aggression. And today there is no more effective way of doing this than by giving concrete help to the Spanish people."[30]

"Moscow tried to do for France and England what they should have done for themselves," Juan Negrín, Prime Minister during the last two years of the war, declared after the end of the conflict. "The promise of Soviet aid to the Spanish Republic was that ultimately Paris and London would awake to the risks involved to themselves in an Italo-German victory in Spain and join the U.S.S.R. in supporting us."[31]

At this stage it is important to anticipate the course of events so far as to say that even after the loss of Catalonia in February, 1939, a few weeks before the close of the war, when the anti-Franco forces had been deprived of the French border and the area of their resistance had been reduced to the central and south-eastern parts of Spain, Moscow— prior to taking the drastic step of negotiating a non-aggression pact

[28] *Freedom's Battle*, pp. 238–9.

[29] As quoted by Jesús Hernández, *Yo fuí un ministro de Stalin*, p. 159.

[30] *Frente Rojo*, March 30, 1938, as reprinted in Díaz, *Tres años de lucha*, pp. 461–3.

[31] Address in May, 1939, before the Council of Foreign Relations in New York, as quoted by Alvarez del Vayo, *Freedom's Battle*, p. 76.

with Germany in a last endeavour to turn German military might against the West[32]—still clung to the belief, much diminished, to be sure, that Britain and France would reverse their policy of neutrality, and instructed the Spanish Communists and the Communist-dominated Negrín government to continue the struggle in the hope that the latent antagonisms between the Western Powers might finally burst into flame.[33]

[32] Although it is most likely that Stalin, quite early in the Spanish Civil War, had in mind the idea of striking a bargain with Hitler in the event that his hopes of a conflagration in Western Europe should be disappointed, it was only after the overthrow of the Communist-dominated Negrín government in March, 1939, a few weeks before the end of the war, that the first hint was thrown out by him of his desire for a rapprochement with Germany. "Marshal Stalin, in March, 1939, delivered a speech in which he made certain hints of his desire to have better relations with Germany," testified the former Reich Foreign Minister, Joachim von Ribbentrop, during his trial at Nuremberg. "I had submitted this speech to Adolf Hitler and asked him whether we should not try to find out whether this suggestion had something real behind it. Hitler was at first reluctant, but later on he became more receptive to this idea. Negotiations for a commercial treaty were under way, and during these negotiations, with the Führer's permission, I took soundings in Moscow as to the possibility of a definite bridge between National Socialism and Bolshevism and whether the interests of the two countries could not at least be made to harmonize."—*Trial of the Major War Criminals before the International Military Tribunal*, X, p. 267. The extremely cautious manner in which both sides broached the question of a political settlement from the time of Stalin's speech, as revealed by documents found in the archives of the German Foreign Ministry (*Nazi–Soviet Relations*, 1939–1941), establishes beyond a vestige of doubt, in spite of everything that has been alleged regarding Stalin's secret negotiations with Hitler during the Spanish Civil War, that no such negotiations had been going on before that time. In actual fact, up to the end of July, 1939, less than four weeks before the signing of the German–Soviet Non-Aggression Pact, matters, according to these documents, had not gone beyond vague soundings. This of course was because each side feared that the other would use any concrete proposal for a political agreement as a means of strengthening its own bargaining position *vis-à-vis* the Western Powers.

[33] Referring to an earlier period, namely to the occupation of the Basque provinces and the Asturias by General Franco and by his Italian and German allies in the summer and autumn of 1937, Wenceslao Carrillo, leading left-wing Socialist, writes: "Nevertheless, the hope of victory that the Communist Party and the Negrín government held out to us, based on the possibility of world war, had not disappeared. Neither France nor England, they argued, can consent to an out-and-out triumph of fascism in Spain, because that would put them in a critical position in the Mediterranean. As I am ready to tell the whole truth, I refuse to conceal the fact that, in the beginning, I too shared this belief. If France and England had created the Non-Intervention Committee in their desire not to become involved in a war surely they could not go to the extreme

"It is a profound error to believe that we can hope for nothing or for very little from abroad and that the democratic countries, which have allowed Catalonia to be invaded by the Germans and Italians, will not help us now that we have lost such an important position," declared the Politburo of the Spanish Communist Party on February 23, 1939. "The international situation has never been more unstable than it is today. Furthermore, the successes of the fascist invaders in Catalonia have increased their boldness, encouraging them to reveal still more clearly their plans of conquest, plunder, and war, and this in turn opens the eyes of those who until now have not wanted to face reality, and increases the possibilities of direct and indirect aid for the Spanish people. On the side of the Spanish Republic is the Soviet Union, that powerful country, the firm defender of liberty, justice, and peace throughout the world. The working class, as well as the sincerely democratic forces of France, England, the United States, and other democratic countries, have until now given Spain very substantial material aid and will continue to do so. What they have not been able to do, partly because of lack of unity and determination in the struggle, and partly because they have not yet completely understood the importance to them of a just solution of the Spanish problem, is to change radically in our favour the policy of their governments. But what has not been achieved up to now can still be accomplished if we increase our resistance.

"For all these reasons, we say that resistance is not only necessary but possible, and we affirm that, as on previous occasions when many persons believed that everything was lost . . . , our resistance can change the situation. It will permit new factors to develop, both in Spain and abroad, which will redound to our advantage and will open the prospect of victory."[34]

And when the Civil War had ended, Alvarez del Vayo wrote: "Not a day passed until almost the end, when we did not have fresh reasons to hope that the Western democracies would come to their senses and restore us our rights to buy from them. And always our hopes proved illusory."[35]

But if these expectations were disappointed, it was not because those

---

of providing their possible enemies with the means of opposing them with greater possibilities of success. But I did not think of profiting from war; nor was I in the service of interests other than those of my country."—*El último episodio de la guerra civil española*, pp. 5–6.

[34] *Mundo Obrero*, February 26, 1939.

[35] *Freedom's Battle*, p. 66.

who determined policy in Britain and France were blind to the possible dangers of a Franco victory, or because they contemplated lightly the extension of German power; it was because the purview of their foreign policy went beyond the situation in Spain, and embraced the whole of Europe. If they refused to challenge Germany in Spain; if, moreover, they sacrificed Austrian and Czechoslovakian independence to Nazi totalitarianism, as well as their own economic interests in these two countries; if, finally, the British Government under the premiership of Neville Chamberlain strove right up to the outbreak of World War II to come to an understanding with Germany, an understanding that would have laid the whole of Eastern Europe west of Russia's borders open to German penetration,[36] this was not only because of lack of military preparedness, but because the government

[36] Evidence of this lies in the papers of Herbert von Dirksen, German Ambassador to London until the outbreak of World War II, which were found on his estate at Gröditzberg by the Soviet Army. "When Herr Wohlthat [emissary of Goering] was in London for the whaling negotiations in July [1939]," testifies Dirksen in a memorandum on the development of Anglo-German political relations, written after the outbreak of war, "Wilson [Sir Horace Wilson, Chamberlain's chief collaborator and adviser] invited him for a talk, and, consulting prepared notes, outlined a programme for a comprehensive adjustment of Anglo-German relations. . . .

"In the political sphere, a non-aggression pact was contemplated, in which aggression would be renounced in principle. The underlying purpose of this treaty was to make it possible for the British gradually to disembarrass themselves of their commitments towards Poland, on the ground that they had by this treaty secured Germany's renunciation of methods of aggression.

"In addition, a pact of non-intervention was to be signed, which was to be in a way a wrapper for a delimitation of the spheres of interest of the Great Powers.

"The basic idea of these proposals, Sir Horace Wilson explained, was that they would broach and settle questions of such great importance that the deadlocked Near East questions, such as Danzig and Poland, would be pushed into the background, and then could be settled by Germany directly with Poland.

"The importance of Wilson's proposals was demonstrated by the fact that Wilson invited Wohlthat to have them confirmed by Chamberlain personally, whose room was not far from Wilson's. Wohlthat, however, declined this in order not to prejudice the unofficial character of his mission. . . .

"In the following days the British side continued to press the suggestion that reconciliation moves be inaugurated and put the matter on official lines. After a conversation I was to have with Mr. Butler [Under-Secretary of State for Foreign Affairs] before we both went on leave fell through owing to the fact that Butler left prematurely, he let me know through Herr Kordt that Sir Horace Wilson wanted to talk with me. In order to avoid all publicity, I visited Wilson at his home on August 3 and we had a conversation which lasted nearly two hours. In the main, it followed the same lines as the Wohlthat conversations. I thought it valuable to have him confirm the proposals he had made to

knew that the frustration of German aims at this stage, even if it did not lead to war, would weaken the Nazi régime and enhance Russia's influence on the Continent. Above all, those who moulded policy in Britain and France wished to avoid war in the West until Germany had weakened herself in the East. To have resisted Germany before she had blunted her teeth on Russian soil would have left the Soviet Union arbiter of the Continent, infinitely more powerful than if she had to bear the main burden of the fighting.[37]

Wohlthat. This Wilson did, so that the authenticity of the project is beyond question.

"I considered it particularly important to elucidate what connection there was between Wilson's proposals and the British encirclement policy. Again Wilson affirmed, and in a clearer form than he had done to Wohlthat, that the conclusion of an Anglo-German entente would practically render Britain's guarantee policy nugatory. Agreement with Germany would enable Britain to extricate herself from her predicament in regard to Poland on the ground that the non-aggression pact protected Poland from German attack; England would thus be relieved of her commitments. Then Poland, so to speak, would be left to face Germany alone.

"Sir Horace Wilson, on my insistence, also touched on the question of how the negotiations were to be conducted in face of the inflamed state of British public opinion, and how they were to be protected from the fate which befell the conversations with Wohlthat. He admitted quite frankly that by taking this step Chamberlain was incurring a great risk and laying himself open to the danger of a fall. But with skill and strict secrecy, the reefs could be avoided. The British Government must however be sure that its initiative met with equal readiness on the German side. There was no sense in beginning negotiations if a new crisis was in the offing. It would therefore very much like to know how the Führer had received Wohlthat's report, whether he foresaw a quiet period of negotiation in the next few months, and, lastly, whether he himself was ready to manifest a willingness for negotiations, whether by means of a public statement or confidentially. However that might be, it would be a great disappointment to the British Government if no response to the British initiative were forthcoming from our side. The only alternative would then be catastrophe. . . .

"The tragic and paramount thing about the rise of the new Anglo-German war was that Germany demanded an equal place with Britain as a world power and that Britain was in principle prepared to concede. But, whereas Germany demanded immediate, complete and unequivocal satisfaction of her demand, Britain—although she was ready to renounce her Eastern commitments, and therewith her encirclement policy, as well as to allow Germany a predominant position in East and South-east Europe and to discuss genuine world political partnership with Germany—wanted this to be done only by way of negotiation and a *gradual* revision of British policy. This change could be effected in a period of months, but not of days or weeks."—*Documents and Materials Relating to the Eve of the Second World War.* II. Dirksen Papers 1938–1939, pp. 183–9.

[37] "In no case, whatever," affirmed J. L. Garvin, editor of the influential

The attitude, then, of the controlling forces in Britain and France towards the Spanish Civil War was determined not merely by their hostility to the revolutionary changes—of which they were fully apprised in spite of the efforts to conceal them—but by the whole field of foreign politics. Hence, no attempt at dissimulation and persuasion on the part of successive Spanish Governments, prompted mainly by the Communist Party, no attempt even at curbing the revolution, could have altered their policy with regard to the Spanish conflict.

From what has been said in the preceding pages it would be wrong to assume that all the Spanish Communists, while following unhesitatingly the directives of the Kremlin,[38] necessarily understood its purely

---

Observer (November 29, 1936), "can it be to the interest of Britain and the British Empire that Germany should be overthrown to exalt still further and beyond restraint the Soviet Power of the future, and to make Communism supreme, whether in Europe or Asia." But it goes without saying that in the long run Britain and France could no more have desired Germany to obtain a complete mastery over the greater part of Europe than they could Russia. They wished for the domination of neither, and of this German leaders were supremely conscious. Hence, if, after the occupation of Czechoslovakia and Poland, Germany invaded France before attacking the Soviet Union, this was because the subjection of Western Europe and the control of the Atlantic coastline were, in the German mind, indispensable prerequisites for war on the Soviet Union; for although Britain and France might appear to connive at German ambitions at the expense of Russian, Germany could not feel certain that once she was involved in an exhausting struggle on Soviet soil, these Powers would not attempt, with the help of allies, to restore the balance in their favour. It was undoubtedly the conviction that Germany would not attack Russia before assailing the West that lay at the root of some of the opposition in Britain and France to the policy of giving Germany a free hand in Eastern Europe. See, for example, Henri de Kerillis (right-wing French deputy), *Français! Voici la guerre*, pp. 147–8.

[38] "During the war and the long, bloody years of Franco repression and Falangist revenge," declared Jesús Hernández (Communist Minister of Education in the Largo Caballero government) in a speech delivered after the war, when he had ceased to belong to the Communist Party, "our men entered the jails, or fell riddled with bullets . . . the flags of Stalin and the U.S.S.R. unfurling from their lips. It is not at all surprising, therefore, that the Spanish Communist Party should have subordinated its entire policy to the 'guidance' of Moscow. Nor is it surprising that those of us who 'directed' the Spanish Communist Party should have been and should have acted more like Soviet subjects than sons of the Spanish people. It may seem absurd, incredible, but our education under Soviet tutelage had deformed us to such an extent that we were completely denationalized; our national soul was torn out of us and replaced by a rabidly chauvinistic internationalism, which began and ended with the towers of the Kremlin."—As given in *Acción Socialista*, January 15, 1952.

selfish moves in rendering aid to the anti-Franco zone. "I sincerely believed," writes Valentín González, more commonly known as "El Campesino," an important Communist figure during the war, "that the Kremlin sent us its arms, its military and political advisers, and the International Brigades under its control, as a proof of its revolutionary solidarity. . . . Only later did I realize that the Kremlin does not serve the interests of the peoples of the world, but makes them serve its own interests; that, with a treachery and hypocrisy without parallel, it makes use of the international working class as a mere pawn in its political intrigues, and that, on the pretext of fomenting world revolution, it consolidates its own totalitarian counter-revolution and prepares for world domination."[39]

[39] *Solidaridad Obrero*, Paris, March 11, 1951. After the close of the Civil War "El Campesino" took refuge in Russia, whence he escaped ten years later completely disillusioned. See his book *La vie et la mort en U.R.S.S.* (*1939–1949*).

PART III

CURBING THE REVOLUTION

12

Anarchism and Government

THE efforts of the Communists from the outset of the Civil War to gain the support of Britain and France and to ensure the continued recognition first of the Giral and later of the Caballero government as the legally constituted authority could not but have an important effect on the course of the revolution. If these two countries were to be influenced even in the smallest measure, it was obvious that the government would have to re-construct the shattered machinery of state not upon revolutionary lines but in the image of the deceased Republic. Moreover, if the Caballero administration were to be a government in essence rather than in name, it would have to assume control of all the elements of state power appropriated by the revolutionary committees in the first days of the Civil War.[1] On this point all members of the Cabinet were of one mind, and there can be little doubt that they would have been so irrespective of the need to impress foreign opinion.

But the work of reconstructing the state power could not be achieved or, at least, would be extremely difficult of achievement without the participation in the government of the extreme left wing of the revolution, the powerful Anarchosyndicalist or Libertarian movement, as it was more frequently called, represented by the CNT (the National Confederation of Labour) and by the FAI (the Iberian Anarchist Federation), its ideological guide, whose mission it was to protect the CNT from deviationist tendencies[2] and to lead the trade union federa-

---

[1] See pp. 37–8, 42, above.

[2] See, for example, *Tierra y Libertad*, October 29, 1938; Horacio Prieto, *Marxismo y socialismo libertario*, pp. 62–4. The FAI accomplished its directive mission by virtue of the fact that its members, with few exceptions, belonged to the CNT and held many positions of trust. Furthermore, it was an established principle that any person belonging to a political party should not occupy any official position in the trade union organization. (See CNT *Memoria del congreso extraordinario celebrado en Madrid los días 11 al 16 de junio de 1931*, p .38.) Finally,

tion to the Anarchist goal of Libertarian Communism.[3] Although
views were divided in the Cabinet as to the advisability, from the
standpoint of foreign opinion, of allowing the Libertarians to participate in the government,[4] the advantages of having them share
responsibility for its measures were indubitable.[5] But would the
Anarchosyndicalists themselves wish to become Cabinet members and
join in the reconstruction of the state? This was questionable.

Rootedly opposed to the state, which they regarded as "the supreme
expression of authority of man over man, the most powerful instrument for the enslavement of the people,"[6] the Libertarians were equally
opposed to every government whether of the Right or Left. In the
words of Bakunin, the great Russian Anarchist, whose writings had a
far-reaching influence on the Spanish working-class movement, the
"people's government" proposed by Marx would simply be the rule
of a privileged minority over the huge majority of the working
masses. "But this minority, the Marxists argue, would consist of
workers. Yes, I dare say, of *former* workers, but as soon as they become
rulers and representatives of the people they would cease to be proletarians and would look down upon all workers from their political
summit. They would no longer represent the people; they would
represent only themselves. . . . He who doubts this must be absolutely

---

it should be pointed out that the FAI kept a close and constant supervision over
the unions of the CNT, often threatening to use force when argument failed
in order to prevent deviationist tendencies. This domination by the FAI, to
be sure, was not openly acknowledged by the Anarchosyndicalists, and indeed
was emphatically denied (see, for example, *Solidaridad Obrera*, April 18, May 8,
1937) but it was nevertheless very real and was frankly admitted to the author
by Victor Zaragoza, secretary of the National Committee of the CNT National
Transport Federation.

[3] See p. 60, above.

[4] See, for example, letter of Luis Araquistain, published in *The Left News*,
December, 1942, on the opposition of Juan Negrín to Anarchosyndicalist
participation in the government.

[5] See quotation from *Claridad*, Caballero's organ, n. 32, p. 159, below.

[6] Abad de Santillan, *La bancarrota del capitalismo*, p. 55. "The entire dialectic
of the officials of the Russian Government cannot erase one palpable, one
evident fact regarding the Russian experiment that we have always affirmed,"
said *Tierra y Libertad*, the FAI organ (July 3, 1936). "The study of the last
nineteen years of the Russian scene has given a most eloquent demonstration
of the correctness of our view. In proportion as the Soviet state became stronger
the revolution perished in the iron grip of decrees, bureaucrats, repressive
machinery, and taxation. The revolution is a thing of the people, a popular
creation; the counter-revolution is a thing of the state. It has always been so,
and will always be so, whether in Russia, Spain, or China."

ignorant of human nature."[7] And the Italian Anarchist, Malatesta, whose influence on the Spanish Libertarian movement was appreciable, stated: "The primary concern of every government is to ensure its continuance in power irrespective of the men who form it. If they are bad, they want to remain in power in order to enrich themselves and to satisfy their lust for authority; and if they are honest and sincere they believe that it is their duty to remain in power for the benefit of the people. . . .

"The Anarchists . . . could never, even if they were strong enough, form a government without contradicting themselves and repudiating their entire doctrine; and, should they do so, it would be no different from any other government; perhaps it would be even worse."[8]

The establishment of the Spanish Republic in 1931, following the fall of the Monarchy and the Berenguer Dictatorship, did not cause the Libertarians to modify their basic tenets: "All governments are detestable and it is our mission to destroy them."[9] "All governments without exception are equally bad, equally contemptible."[10] "All governments are destroyers of liberty."[11] "Under the Monarchy and the Dictatorship," wrote an Anarchist at the time of the Republican–Socialist coalition in 1933, "the workers suffered hunger and a thousand privations and they continue to do so today under the Republic. Yesterday it was impossible to satisfy their most urgent needs and today conditions are the same. We Anarchists say this without fear that any worker will contradict us, and we say more. We say that at all times, under whatever type of government, the workers have been tyrannized and have had to wage bitter struggles so that their right to live and enjoy themselves after exhausting hours of labour would be respected."[12] Just as the Libertarians made no distinction between governments of the Left and governments of the Right so did they make no distinction between individual politicians: "For us, all politicians are equal—in electoral demagogy, in filching the rights from the people, in their desire for fame, in their opportunism, in their ability to criticize when in the opposition, and in their cynicism when justifying themselves once in power."[13]

[7] *Gosudarstvennost i anarkhiia (State and Anarchy)*, p. 234.
[8] Article in *L'Adunata dei Refrattari*, March 12, 1932.
[9] *Tierra y Libertad*, September 15, 1933.
[10] *Ibid.*, October 27, 1933.
[11] Germinal Esgleas in *La Revista Blanca*, January 18, 1935.
[12] José Bonet in *Tierra y Libertad*, September 22, 1933.
[13] Isaac Puente in *CNT*, Madrid, June 19, 1933, as reproduced in Puente, *Propaganda*, pp. 129–30.

In contrast to other working-class organizations the CNT and FAI shunned parliamentary activity.[14] They held no seats in central or local governments, refrained from nominating candidates for parliament, and, in the crucial November, 1933, elections which brought the parties of the Right to power, they had enjoined their members to abstain from voting. "Our revolution is not made in Parliament, but in the street," *Tierra y Libertad*, the FAI organ, had declared[15] a month before the elections. "We are not interested in changing governments," Isaac Puente, an influential Anarchosyndicalist had written at the time. "What we want is to suppress them. . . . Whatever side wins, whether Right or Left, will be our enemy, our jailor, our executioner, and will have at its disposal the truncheons of the Assault Guards, the bullying of the secret police, the rifles of the Civil Guard, and the outlook of prison wardens. The working class will have just what it has today: sombre jails, spies, hunger, cardinals, and executioners."[16] And a few days before the elections, *Tierra y Libertad* declared: "Workers! Do not vote! The vote is a negation of your personality. Turn your backs on those who ask you to vote for them. They are your enemies. They hope to rise to power by taking advantage of your trustfulness. Urge your parents, your children, your brothers and sisters, your relatives, and your friends not to vote for any of the candidates. As far as we are concerned they are all the same; all politicians are our enemies whether they be Republicans, Monarchists, Communists, or Socialists. Honorio Maura is just as shameless as Rodrigo Soriano and Barriobero. Largo Caballero and Prieto are just as cynical and despicable as Balbontin and his associates. . . . We need neither a state nor a government. The bourgeoisie needs them in order to defend its interests. Our interests lie solely in our working conditions and to defend them we require no parliament. No one should vote. . . . Do not be concerned whether the rightists or the leftists emerge triumphant from this farce. They are all die-hards. The only left-wing organization that is genuinely revolutionary is the CNT, and, because this is so, it is not interested in Parliament, which is a filthy house of prostitution toying with the interests of the country and the people. Destroy the ballots! Destroy the ballot boxes! Crack the heads of the ballot supervisers as well as those of the candidates!"[17]

[14] See, for example, Germinal Esgleas in *La Revista Blanca*, January 18, 1935.
[15] October 27, 1933.
[16] *CNT*, Madrid, October 24, 1933, as reproduced in Puente, *Propaganda* p. 126.
[17] November 10, 1933.

In the February, 1936, elections, however, the CNT and FAI changed their posture; for, while opposing the Popular Front programme—which they regarded as a "profoundly conservative document"[18] out of harmony with "the revolutionary fever that Spain was sweating through her pores"[19]—they decided not to urge their members to abstain from voting, not only because the left coalition promised a broad amnesty for thousands of political prisoners in the event of victory,[20] but because a repetition of the abstentionist policy of 1933 would have meant as great a defeat for the Libertarian movement as for the parties that adhered to the Popular Front coalition.[21] But this change of posture, which ensured the victory of the Popular Front coalition, did not imply any fundamental change of doctrine, and, having regard to the Anarchosyndicalists' impressive background of hostility to all governments and to all politicians, it was not easy to conceive that they would join the Cabinet of Largo Caballero, the more so as they had been, for many years before the outbreak of the Civil War, at sword's point with the Socialist leader and his rival trade union organization, the UGT.

[18] *Solidaridad Obrera*, January 17, 1936.

[19] *Ibid.*, April 2, 1936.

[20] See speech by Juan López, *Fragua Social*, February 16, 1937, also Federica Montseny, *María Silva. La Libertaria*, p. 28.

[21] Diego Abad de Santillán, the CNT–FAI leader, makes this point clear in *La revolución y la guerra en España*, p. 30.

13

The Anarchosyndicalists
Enter the Government

AS leader of the Socialist UGT, Largo Caballero's relations with the Anarchosyndicalists in the years before the Civil War had been marked by almost constant enmity. During the dictatorship of Primo de Rivera, who had proscribed the CNT, Caballero had served as Councillor of State in the dictator's Cabinet, partly with the object of protecting and strengthening his own organization and partly in the hope of gaining ground from the Anarchosyndicalists.[1]

[1] See Brenan, *The Spanish Labyrinth*, pp. 223–4. Before being outlawed the CNT had been increasing in strength very rapidly. "With the aid of its *sindicato único* and the prestige of its great strikes," writes Brenan (*ibid.*, p. 224), "it had not only swept away all the recent gains of its rival in the Andalusian campo, but it had invaded the Socialist preserve of the centre and north. Here it had seized half the builders' union in Madrid, which was one of the first strongholds of the UGT, had drawn off many of the railwaymen and planted itself firmly in the Asturias, in the port of Gijón and in the great iron foundries of Sama and La Felguera.

"To Caballero, who had the whole organization of the UGT in his hands, this was a serious matter: the fear of losing ground to the CNT was almost an obsession with him. As a Marxist he felt the supreme importance of the unification of the proletariat. He sensed therefore in the Dictatorship a good opportunity for making some progress in this direction. Possibly the UGT would be able to absorb the CNT altogether.

"This hope was not fulfilled. By using the *comités paritarios* (arbitration boards in industrial disputes) of the Dictatorship as a starting point, the UGT greatly increased their strength in the country districts, especially in Extremadura, Granada, Aragon and New Castile, but they failed completely in Catalonia and made no progress among the industrial proletariat." It should not be overlooked that at one time the CNT had likewise hoped to monopolize the entire trade union movement. At an Anarchosyndicalist congress held in 1919, a resolution was passed to the effect that a manifesto should be addressed to all the workers of Spain granting them a period of three months in which to enter the CNT, failing which they would be denounced as scabs.—Quoted by

In these circumstances, it is no wonder that he became the object of the CNT's unsparing criticism. Nor did relations between them improve with the advent of the Republic in 1931, when Caballero became Minister of Labour; for he used his powers to augment the influence of the UGT at the expense of the rival organization,[2] and clashed with the CNT owing to his defence of state interference in labour disputes.

In distinction from the UGT, the CNT rejected arbitration courts for settling conflicts between labour and management, not only because they increased the power of the state in industrial matters, but because their purpose, in the opinion of a prominent CNT–FAI member, was "to castrate the Spanish proletariat in the interests of 'class conciliation.' "[3] Not conciliation, then, but continual and implacable war between labour and management was what the CNT wanted, and direct action was its method: violent strikes, sabotage, and boycott.[4] This was not simply a means of improving the standard of living of the workers; above all it was a method of agitation, of stimulating and keeping alive a spirit of revolt in preparation for the day of insurrection. "Direct action," declared the International Workingmen's Association, with which the CNT was affiliated, "finds its highest expression in the

H. Ruediger, *Ensayo crítico sobre la revolución española*, p. 25. During the Civil War Ruediger was representative in Spain of the International Workingmen's Association, with which the CNT was affiliated.

[2] "The Minister of Labour, Largo Caballero," writes Gerald Brenan (*The Spanish Labyrinth*, pp. 258–9), "had introduced a series of laws regulating the rights of the working classes in their dealings with capital. The most important of these, the law of December 24, 1931, laid down the conditions which all contracts between workers and employers must fulfil in order to be valid. A special tribunal was set up to decide alleged infractions. Another law, the *Ley de Jurados Mixtos*, established tribunals at which labour disputes were to be compulsorily settled. . . . Another law required eight days' notice to be given of every strike. Apart from the fact that these laws ran contrary to the Anarchosyndicalist principles of negotiating directly with the employers and interfered with the practice of lightning strikes, it was clear that they represented an immense increase in the power of the State in industrial matters. A whole army of Government officials, mostly Socialists, made their appearance to enforce the new laws and saw to it that, whenever possible, they should be used to extend the influence of the UGT at the expense of the CNT. This had of course been the intention of those who drew them up. In fact the UGT was rapidly becoming an organ of the State itself and was using its new powers to reduce its rival." See also Peirats, *La CNT en la revolución española*, pp. 35–6; S. Cánovas Cervantes, *Durruti y Ascaso. La CNT y la revolución de julio*, p. 15.

[3] Jacinto Toryho, a prominent CNT–FAI member, in *Vía Libre*, May 19, 1940.

[4] See, for example, Rudolf Rocker, *Anarcho-Syndicalism*, p. 116.

general strike, which should be a prelude to the social revolution."[5] Famed for their frequent uprisings in the years before the military rebellion, the Anarchosyndicalists were the classic force of Spanish insurrection. It mattered little whether these uprisings, invariably confined to a few localities, failed for lack of support elsewhere; what was important was that they should rouse the revolutionary temper of the working class. Today they might fail, but tomorrow they would be victorious. "If yesterday ten villages revolted," wrote Isaac Puente, a leading Anarchosyndicalist, "one thousand villages must rise tomorrow, even if we have to fill the holds of a hundred [prison] ships like the *Buenos Aires*. Defeat is not always failure. The future does not always belong to those who triumph. We never play our last card."[6]

The sharp divergence between the CNT and UGT was not in any way lessened by Largo Caballero's leftward swerve towards the end of 1933,[7] for the Anarchosyndicalists continued to regard him with unrelenting animosity. Nor did his advocacy of the dictatorship of the proletariat under the Socialist Party[8] and of the unification of the CNT and UGT[9] a few months before the outbreak of the Civil War temper this animosity; for they held that Caballero was a "dictator in embryo" who favoured "the absolute hegemony of the Socialist Party on the morrow of the triumphant insurrection of the working class,"[10] and that under the cover of unification his "crooked aim" was to absorb the CNT in those localities where the UGT was stronger.[11] No practical discussions to bring about the fusion ever took place, and the somewhat more cautious attitude adopted by the leadership of the UGT towards the developing strike movement, just before the military insurrection,[12] tended to increase still further the hostility of the CNT, which was sweeping the rank and file of the UGT along with it in several places.[13] Then came the Civil War and the revolution,

[5] "Declaración de Principios de la Asociación Internacional de Trabajadores," as reproduced in *Internacional*, May, 1938.

[6] In *Solidaridad Obrera*, April 15, 1932, as given in Puente, *Propaganda*, p. 132.

[7] See pp. 104–5, above.   [8] Referred to on p. 106, above.

[9] Speech published in *Claridad*, April 11, 1936.

[10] *Solidaridad Obrera*, April 24, 1936.

[11] *Ibid.*, June 7, 1936.

[12] See, for example, *Claridad*, July 7, 9, 1936.

[13] ". . . The mass of workers were desperate," wrote an acute observer (Manuel, *The Politics of Modern Spain*, p. 167), "and were prepared to follow the most ardent leaders." ". . . In Madrid," said the Madrid paper, *El Sol* (June 3, 1936), "we are witnessing the astonishing spectacle of the CNT . . . declaring general strikes, continually organizing partial strikes, and inspiring intransigent and rigid attitudes that cause the government to despair."

creating fresh points of friction between the two trade union federations.[14]

Yet, in spite of this discord, in spite of the traditional anti-government stand of the Anarchosyndicalists and of their hostility towards him personally, Largo Caballero hoped to secure their participation in his Cabinet. But much as he needed them to share the responsibilities of office, in order to forestall any criticism of his government's decrees, he offered them only a single seat without portfolio,[15] a meagre reward for what would have entailed a flagrant breach of principle for the Libertarian movement. Moreover, according to the Madrid Anarchosyndicalist organ, *CNT*, the offer was "neither generous nor enticing" and was "absolutely disproportionate to the strength and influence of the CNT in the country."[16] To be sure, the CNT, if smaller than the UGT in Madrid province and the Basque Country, as well as in most of the provinces controlled by General Franco, yielded nothing to it in the majority of provinces within the left zone, such as Albacete, Guadalajara, Jaen, and Toledo (to mention but a few where the two federations had approximately the same number of adherents), and, in addition to being more powerful in the regions of Aragon, Catalonia, and Valencia, had, in all probability, more members than its Socialist rival in the total area controlled by the left-wing forces.[17]

After Largo Caballero had actually formed his government without the participation of the Anarchosyndicalists, *CNT* declared: "Perhaps many wonder how it is that the CNT, one of the principal forces preparing for the victory of the people at the front and in the rear . . . does not form part of this government. Undoubtedly, if the CNT

[14] For some idea of these, see the following materials: speeches by Pascual Tomás, vice-secretary of the UGT, as reported in *La Correspondencia de Valencia*, December 21, 1936, February 17, 1937; *CNT*, February 26, March 3, 1937; *Claridad*, April 13, 1937; document signed by the National Committee of the CNT and the Executive Committee of the UGT, dated November 26, 1936, as given in Peirats, *La CNT en la revolución española*, pp. 252–3; excerpts from speeches of delegates at a meeting of the CNT unions of the central region, as given in *CNT*, October 8, 1936.

[15] See *Claridad*, October 27, 1936.

[16] October 28, 1936.

[17] The author realizes that some persons may not accept the whole of this statement, but it has not been made without very careful research. As for the total number of persons in the anti-Franco camp belonging to each federation, this may have been between 1,500,000 and 1,750,000, but no figures can be given with any degree of exactitude. Estimates above and below these figures by sources siding with one organization or the other have been made, but as there is no way of checking their accuracy nothing would be gained by burdening the text with them.

were inspired by political ideas, the number of its seats in this government would have to be at least as large as that of the UGT and the
Socialists.[18] However, the CNT once again affirms its unshakeable
adhesion to its anti-authoritarian postulates and believes that the
Libertarian transformation of society can only take place as a result of
the abolition of the state and the control of the economy by the working
class."[19] But although the Anarchosyndicalists could not join the
government without striking at the very roots of official doctrine, they
were loth to leave the affairs of state entirely in the hands of rival
organizations.[20] They therefore decided, at a plenary meeting of
representatives of the regional committees of the CNT, that the
government should be replaced by a National Council of Defence
composed of five members of their own organization, five of the
UGT, and four members of the Republican parties.[21] This Council,
of course, would have been a government in everything save in name,
although the title of National Council of Defence would have been
less offensive to the Libertarian movement.[22]

[18] In other words it would have required the same number of seats as both
the Caballero faction of the Socialist Party, which the paper identifies with the
UGT because of its control of the trade union executive, and the Prieto faction,
which controlled the party executive.

[19] September 5, 1936.

[20] "The organization should not have declined [to enter the government] in
view of the important role we were playing in the war," writes Horacio Prieto,
secretary at that time of the National Committee of the CNT, "but fear of
violating the ideological principles of the movement, respect for its ideas, for
its tenets, and fear of shouldering this responsibility acted as a brake on initiative,
with the result that indecision prevailed."—*El anarquismo español en la lucha
política*, p. 7.

[21] See resolution published in *CNT*, September 17, 1936.

[22] In an unpublished work, written after the war, a Spanish Anarchosyndicalist comments that when the Caballero government was formed the
Anarchist leaders still had doctrinal scruples that made it difficult for them to
join it. "They certainly wanted to enter the government, but they demanded
that it should change its name to National Council of Defence. The purpose of
this purely nominal change was to reconcile their fervent desire to enter the
government with their anti-state doctrine. What childishness! A movement that
had cured itself of all prejudices and had always scoffed at mere appearances
tried to conceal its abjuration of fundamental principles by changing a name.
. . . This behaviour is as childish as that of an unfortunate woman, who,
having entered a house of ill fame and wishing to preserve a veneer of morality,
asks to be called a hetaera instead of a whore."—Lazarillo de Tormes (Benigno
Bejarano), "Les morts ne vous pardonnent pas," p. 69. It is worth noting that
foreign Anarchists, who later criticized the Spanish Libertarians for entering
the government, had previously approved of the idea of a National Council of

In the hope of avoiding any resistance to the proposed Council on the part of Communists, Socialists, and Republicans, because of possible repercussions in moderate circles abroad, the CNT suggested that Manuel Azaña continue as President of the Republic.[23] "Our position abroad," declared *Solidaridad Obrera*, "cannot deteriorate as a result of the new structure we propose; for it must be borne in mind that the decorative figures which characterize a petty-bourgeois régime would be retained so as not to frighten foreign capitalists."[24] For several weeks the CNT waged a ceaseless campaign in favour of the National Council of Defence,[25] but its efforts were unavailing. Caballero himself was adamant in his opposition, his attitude, which was identical with that of the Communists and Republicans,[26] finding expression in the following passage taken from an editorial in his mouthpiece, *Claridad*: "A radical transformation of the organs of the state would occasion a loss of continuity, which would be fatal to us. Furthermore, we are waging a battle in Geneva [at the League of Nations], which, in the event of victory, could have far-reaching consequences for us, because the scales would be tipped in our favour in view of the fact that we should obtain the material elements indispensable for winning the war. What would be the repercussions of the leap outside the bounds of the Constitution peremptorily demanded by the comrades of the CNT? We fear that it would put things just where our enemies want them."[27]

Defence. "It is a curious thing," wrote Helmut Ruediger, representative in Spain of the International Workingmen's Association, with which the CNT was affiliated, "that nearly all the dissenting comrades [abroad] accepted the programme providing for the direction of the anti-fascist movement by a National Council of Defence. . . . Let us be frank. *This was also a programme for the exercise of power*, the only difference being that the *name* was a little more pleasant to our Anarchist comrades in other countries."—*Internacional*, July–August, 1938. Ruediger was also director of the German language papers, *CNT-FAI-AIT Informationsdienst* and *Soziale Revolution*, both published in Barcelona.

[23] Resolution approved at the plenary meeting of representatives of the regional committees of the CNT, published in *CNT*, September 17, 1936.

[24] September 25, 1936.

[25] For some of the most interesting editorials in the Anarchosyndicalist press, see *CNT*, September 19, October 6, 1936; *Solidaridad Obrera*, September 30, October 2, 4, 1936.

[26] For the attitude of the Republicans and Communists, see, for example, *El Mercantil Valenciano*, October 8, 1936 (speech by Angel Moliner, Cortes deputy representing the Left Republican Party); *Treball*, October 1, 1936; *Verdad*, September 22, 1936.

[27] September 30, 1936. That this was the personal attitude of Largo Caballero was confirmed to the author by Mariano Cardona Rosell, who became a

Faced by Caballero's unbending attitude and by opposition from other quarters, the CNT leaders decided to relinquish their campaign for a National Council of Defence and to open negotiations for seats in the Cabinet. "We are taking into consideration the scruples that the members of the government may have concerning the international situation," the Madrid Anarchosyndicalist organ explained, ". . . and for this reason the CNT is ready to make the maximum concession compatible with its anti-authoritarian spirit: that of entering the government. This does not imply renouncing its intention of fully realizing its ideals in the future; it simply means that . . . in order to win the war and to save our people and the world, it is ready to collaborate with anyone in a directive organ, whether this organ be called a council or a government."[28] In their negotiations with Caballero the CNT representatives asked for five ministries, including War and Finance, but he rejected their demand.[29] Finally, they accepted four: Justice, Industry, Commerce, and Health, none of which, however, was vital;[30] moreover, the portfolios of Industry and Commerce had previously been held by a single minister.[31] Neverthe-

---

member of the National Committee of the CNT at the end of September, 1936, and who was one of the members of that body who conducted the negotiations with the Premier. The following extract from an editorial in *Claridad* (October 31, 1936) is also worth recording: "Quite as important as attending to the purely military needs of the Civil War—perhaps even more so—is to give to the institutions of the régime a form that will awaken the least suspicion in foreign countries."

[28] *CNT*, October 23, 1936. It is worth noting that Horacio Prieto, secretary at that time of the National Committee of the CNT, was one of the main advocates of collaboration in the government. "I was convinced," he writes (*El anarquismo español en la lucha política*, p. 6), "of the necessity of collaboration, and I smothered my own ideological and conscientious scruples." See also *ibid.*, p. 7.

[29] See *CNT*, October 30, 1936, and Caballero's statement to the correspondent of the *Daily Express*, published in *Claridad*, October 29, 1936.

[30] Lazarillo de Tormes (Benigno Bejarano), *España, cuña de la libertad*, p. 83, affirms that the CNT ministers knew, when they took possession of their departments, that they could not influence the war or revolution. See also quotation from article by Federica Montseny, one of the four CNT ministers, in n. 39, pp. 161–2, below.

[31] The composition of the reorganized government was as follows:
    Francisco Largo Caballero (Socialist)—Prime Minister and War
    Julio Alvarez del Vayo (Socialist)—Foreign Affairs
    Angel Galarza (Socialist)—Interior
    Anastasio de Gracia (Socialist)—Labour
    Juan Negrín (Socialist)—Finance
    Indalecio Prieto (Socialist)—Navy and Air

less, this representation was an improvement as compared with Caballero's original offer on forming his government, and there is evidence that he agreed to it not only because of the CNT's constant pressure and his desire to invest his government with greater authority,[32] but also because of General Franco's threatening advance upon the capital[33]—an advance which within a few days was to force the government to move to Valencia—and the fear, whether grounded or not, that if the Cabinet should move to another city without first incorporating representatives of the Libertarian movement, the CNT and FAI might set up in Madrid an independent administration.[34]

The decision of the CNT and FAI to enter the Cabinet caused a profound stir in the Libertarian movement. Not only did it represent a complete negation of the basic tenets of Anarchism, shaking the whole structure of Libertarian theory to the core, but, in violation of democratic principle, it had been taken without consulting the rank and file.[35]

Jesús Hernández (Communist)—Education and Fine Arts
Vicente Uribe (Communist)—Agriculture
Juan García Oliver (CNT)—Justice
Juan López (CNT)—Commerce
Federica Montseny (CNT)—Health and Public Assistance
Juan Peiró (CNT)—Industry
Carlos Esplá (Left Republican)—Propaganda
José Giral (Left Republican)—Minister without portfolio
Julio Just (Left Republican)—Public Works
Bernardo Giner de los Rios (Republican Union)—Communications
Jaime Aiguadé (Left Republican Party of Catalonia)—Minister without portfolio
Manuel de Irujo (Basque Nationalist)—Minister without portfolio

The new appointments and the shifts they entailed are given in the *Gaceta de Madrid*, November 5, 1936.

[32] "The entry of the representatives of the CNT into the present Council of Ministers would certainly endow the directive organ of the nation with fresh energy and authority," said *Claridad*, Caballero's mouthpiece (October 25, 1936), "in view of the fact that a considerable segment of the working class, now absent from its deliberations, would feel itself bound by its measures and its authority."

[33] "The grave problems created by the encirclement of Madrid and the urgent necessity of avoiding internal disorders had decided [Caballero] to bring the CNT into the government, thereby forming a bloc of all the anti-Fascist forces of the country."—Alvarez del Vayo, *Freedom's Battle*, p. 215.

[34] See, for example, *ibid.*, p. 216.

[35] See resolution approved by the regional congress of the Catalan CNT in April, 1937, as given in article by P. Bernard (Bernardo Pou) in *Universo*, May 1, 1948, in which this fact is mentioned; also report of Mariano Vázquez,

From the day the Cabinet was reorganized, the leading Anarcho-syndicalist newspaper, *Solidaridad Obrera*, in an attempt to overcome the scruples of the purists, sought to justify the decision by minimizing the divergence between theory and practice.

"The entry of the CNT into the central government is one of the most important events in the political history of our country. Both as a matter of principle and by conviction, the CNT has been anti-statist and an enemy of every form of government.

"But circumstances . . . have transformed the nature of the Spanish Government and the Spanish state.

"At the present time, the government, as the instrument that controls the organs of the state, has· ceased to be a force of oppression against the working class, just as the state no longer represents a body that divides society into classes. And both will oppress the people even less now that members of the CNT have intervened."[36]

In subsequent months, as the friction between the "collaborationist" and "abstentionist" tendencies in the Libertarian movement increased, some supporters of government collaboration argued that the entry of the CNT into the Cabinet had marked no recantation of Anarchist ideals and tactics,[37] while others frankly acknowledged the violation of doctrine and contended that it should yield to reality. ". . . The philosophico-social conceptions of Anarchism are excellent, wonderful, in theory," wrote Manuel Mascarell, a member of the National Committee of the CNT, "but they are impractical when confronted with the tragic reality of a war like ours. The conduct of Anarchists and Anarchosyndicalists should be inspired by and should be in harmony with our Anarchist ideology, but when circumstances, when particular events demand a modification of tactics, Anarchists should not confine themselves to the limited framework of what, theoretically, in normal

---

secretary of the National Committee of the CNT, to the Extraordinary Congress of the AIT, as reproduced in *L'Espagne Nouvelle*, March 15, 1939, and J. Capdevila in *Solidaridad Obrera*, Paris, April 7, 1951.

[36] November 4, 1936.

[37] See manifesto issued by the Regional Federation of Anarchist Groups of Catalonia, as given in *Tierra y Libertad*, December 19, 1936. In a manifesto issued by the Federation of Anarchist Groups of the Central Region it was affirmed that in spite of the CNT's entry into the government "there is not the slightest contradiction with our doctrines."—As given in *Cultura Proletaria*, March 20, 1937. See also speech by Juan López (CNT Minister of Commerce), *Solidaridad Obrera*, February 11, 1937; *Tierra y Libertad*, May 22, 1937, October 30, 1937, and the manifesto of the Peninsular Committee of the FAI, addressed to the international Libertarian movement, as reproduced in *Cultura Proletaria*, October 23, 1937.

times, was held to be their line of action, because to cling obstinately to principles, to follow a rigid line without departing one iota from what is laid down in Anarchist textbooks and declarations is the most comfortable attitude one can adopt in order to justify doing nothing or risking nothing."[38]

But in spite of this reasoning, the CNT–FAI leaders had not entered the government without an inner struggle with conscience and principle. Not all of them admitted this conflict, but the confession of Federica Montseny, one of the four CNT ministers in the government and a member of the Peninsular Committee of the FAI, gave unerring expression to the doubts and misgivings that had assailed, not only the majority of CNT–FAI leaders, but the entire Libertarian movement. "As the daughter of veteran Anarchists," she declared at a meeting of the CNT after she had ceased to belong to the Cabinet, "as the descendant, I might say, of a whole dynasty of anti-authoritarians, with an achievement, with a record, with a life of struggle in continual defence of the ideas I inherited from my parents, I regarded my entry into the government, my acceptance of the post to which the CNT assigned me, as having more significance than the mere appointment of a minister. Other parties, other organizations, other sectors cannot appreciate the struggle inside the movement and in the very consciences of its members, both then and now, as a result of the CNT's participation in the government. They cannot appreciate it, but the people can, and if they cannot then they should be informed. They should be told that for us—who had fought incessantly against the state, who had always affirmed that through the state nothing at all could be achieved, that the words 'government' and 'authority' signified the negation of every possibility of freedom for men and for nations—our intervention in the government as an organization and as individuals signified either an act of historical audacity of fundamental importance, or a rectification of a whole work, of a whole past, in the field of theory and tactics.

"We do not know what it signified. We only know that we were caught in a dilemma. . . .

"When I was appointed by the CNT to represent it in the government, I was in the Regional Committee of Catalonia; I had lived through the whole epic from July 19 to November without a stain. . . .

". . . What inhibitions, what doubts, what anguish, I had personally to overcome in order to accept that post![39] For others it could have

---

[38] *Internacional*, October 1938.
[39] In a letter to the author after the war, Severino Campos, who was secre-

meant their goal, the satisfaction of their inordinate ambitions. But for me it implied a break with my life's work, with a whole past linked to the ideals of my parents. It meant a tremendous effort, an effort made at the cost of many tears. But I accepted the post. I accepted it, conquering myself. I accepted it, ready to clear myself of responsibility before my own eyes for what I considered to be a rupture with everything I had been, on condition that I always remained loyal, upright, honest, always faithful to the ideals of my parents and of my whole life. And that is how I entered the government."[40]

Such a complete departure by the CNT and FAI from their anti-governmental creed could only have been determined by very powerful motives. Of these motives, the following given by leading members of the CNT were undoubtedly among the most important:

"We were compelled by circumstances," Montseny herself declared shortly after entering the Cabinet, "to join the Government of the Republic in order to avoid the fate of Anarchist movements in other countries which, through lack of foresight, resolution, and mental agility, were dislodged from the revolution and saw other parties take control of it."[41]

---

tary of the Regional Committee of Anarchist Groups of Catalonia and was present at the meeting of CNT–FAI leaders at which the entry of the CNT into the government was decided upon, stated that Federica Montseny at first vigorously opposed her appointment as one of the four ministers, but finally yielded to pressure. The other appointees, he said, were not present at the meeting. In a letter to the author after the war, Montseny stated that the four persons designated to represent the CNT in the government were selected by Horacio Prieto, secretary of the National Committee. Juan Peiró and Juan López, she pointed out, represented the right wing and Juan García Oliver and herself the left. "[Horacio Prieto]," she added, "hoped that I would check the opposition of the puritans." In an article written several years after the war, she affirmed that she personally never had any illusions as to the possibility of achieving anything in the government. "I knew, we all knew . . . ," she continued, "that in spite of the fact that the government was not at that time a real government, that power was in the street, in the hands of the combatants and producers, [governmental] power would once again be co-ordinated and consolidated, and, what is worse, with our complicity and our help, and that it would ruin many of us morally."—*Inquietudes*, special number, July, 1947.

[40] As given in *Fragua Social*, June 8, 1937.

[41] Speech in Barcelona, *Solidaridad Obrera*, January 5, 1937. See also her speech reported in *Fragua Social*, June 8, 1937. "At that time," wrote Federica Montseny in a letter to the author after the war, "we only saw the reality of the situation created for us: the Communists in the government and ourselves outside, the manifold possibilities, and all our conquests endangered." In a speech shortly after becoming Minister of Commerce, Juan López, one of the four CNT representatives in the government, asked: "Were we going to

Diego
Abad de Santillán

Bruno
Alonso

Julio
Alvarez del Vayo

Francisco
Antón

Luis
Araquistain

General José
Asensio

Manuel
Azaña

Carlos
de Baraibar

Crescenciano
Bilbao

"El Campesino"

Mariano
Cardona Rosell

Santiago
Carrillo

Wenceslao
Carrillo

Segismundo
Casado

Santiago
Casares Quiroga

Medina
Codovila

Juan
Comorera

Carlos
Contreras

Antonio
Cordón

José
Díaz

Marcelino
Domingo

Edmundo
Domínguez

José
Duque

Buenaventura
Durruti

Antonio
Escribano

Manuel
Estrada

General Francisco
Franco

Angel
Galarza

Alejandro
García Val

Gabriel
García Maroto

J. García Pradas

Juan
García Oliver

José
Giral

Ramón
González Peña

General Goriev

Jesús
Hernández

Juan
Hernández Sarabia

Ignacio Hidalgo
de Cisneros

General Kleber

Ramón
Lamoneda

Francisco
Largo Caballero

Enrique
Lister

Juan
López

José Ignacio
Mantecón

Diego
Martínez Barrio

José
Martín Blázquez

Federico
Melchor

Cipriano
Mera

General José
Miaja

Antonio
Mije

General Emilio
Mola

Federica
Montseny

Juan
Negrín

Margarita
Nelken

"La Pasionaria"
(Dolores Ibarruri)

"Pedro"
(Ernö Gerö)
(*World Wide Photos*)

Juan
Peiró

Jesús
Pérez Salas

General Sebastián
Pozas

Felipe
Pretel

Indalecio
Prieto

Vicente
Rojo

Amaro del
Rosal

Marcel
Rosenberg

Felipe
Sánchez Román

José
Silva

Pascual
Tomás

Vicente
Uribe

Mariano
Vázquez

Rafael
Vidiella

Ricardo
Zabalza

Julián
Zugazagoitia

". . . The CNT," wrote Manuel Villar, a director early in the war of *Fragua Social*, the CNT newspaper in Valencia, "was compelled to participate in the government for the specific purpose of . . . preventing an attack on the conquests of the workers and peasants . . . , of preventing the war from being conducted in a sectarian manner and the army from being transformed into an instrument of a single party, of eliminating the danger of dictatorship, and of preventing totalitarian tendencies in every aspect of our economic and social life."[42] And, finally, one of the CNT's fundamental objectives in entering the government was, in the words of Juan López, the Anarchosyndicalist Minister of Commerce, to regulate the political life of Spain by giving legal validity to the revolutionary committees that had sprung up in the first months of the Civil War.[43]

---

entrust the interests of the workers . . . exclusively to the political parties? On no account."—Reported, *Boletín de Información*, CNT–FAI, December 23, 1936.

[42] *Internacional*, June, 1938. See also resolution approved by the regional congress of the Catalan CNT in April, 1937, as given in article by P. Bernard (Bernardo Pou) in *Universo*, May 1, 1948.

[43] Speech reported in *Fragua Social*, May 29, 1937. Another reason for entering the government given by García Oliver, the CNT Minister of Justice, was that in order to secure military aid from the "international bourgeoisie" it was necessary "to give the impression that not the revolutionary committees were in control but rather the legal government."—Speech in Paris after he had left the Cabinet, reported in *Le Libertaire*, June 24, 1937.

14

Against the Revolutionary Committees

WHILE the Anarchosyndicalist leaders fostered the hope that the Libertarian movement's participation in the Cabinet would enable it the more successfully to defend its revolutionary conquests, the Communist leaders, on the other hand, their eyes turned towards the Western democracies, hoped that this participation, by enhancing the government's authority among the rank and file of the CNT and FAI, would facilitate the reconstruction of the shattered machinery of state, and would, moreover, enable them, under cover of a democratic superstructure, to gather into their hands all the elements of state power appropriated by the revolutionary committees at the outbreak of the Civil War. Furthermore, they hoped that the CNT's entry into the government would hasten the supplanting of these committees—which, in addition to assuming powers of state, had superseded the normal functions of the municipalities and of other local governing bodies—by regular organs of administration, organs which had either been thrust into the shade or had ceased to function from the first day of the revolution.[1]

This policy represented a radical change for the Communists, who, at the time of the left-wing rising in the Asturias in 1934, had called for the substitution of the Republican state by revolutionary organs of power.[2] It was also in contrast to the policy pursued by the Russian Bolsheviks in 1917; for whereas the latter had directed their efforts during the first months of the Revolution to supplanting the old governing bodies by the soviets, in the Spanish Revolution the Communists strove to replace the revolutionary committees by regular

[1] See p. 38, above.
[2] See, for example, *Los soviets en España* (La lucha por el poder, por la república obrera y campesina en España).

organs of administration. ". . . An epidemic of exclusivist committees of the most varied shades and performing the most unexpected functions has broken out," complained the Communist organ, *Mundo Obrero*, early in the war. "We declare that each and every one of us should be interested in the defence of the democratic republic, and for this reason all bodies should reflect accurately the composition of the [Caballero] government as well as the aims that inspire it, aims which we have all undertaken to support and defend. This is a prerequisite for winning the war, imposed by numerous factors, both of a national and international character, and to which we must adapt our step."[3]

In contrast to the Communist view—shared by Socialists and Republicans—that the committees, which in most cases were dominated by the more radical members of the CNT and UGT, and whose authority was practically unlimited in their respective localities, should give way to regular organs of administration, in which all the parties forming the government would be represented, and whose powers would be circumscribed by the laws of the state, the Anarchosyndicalists contended that these revolutionary bodies should, on the contrary, become the foundation stones of the new society. "The committees . . . ," declared *CNT*, the principal Libertarian newspaper in Madrid, "are organs created by the people to oppose the fascist insurrection. . . . Without these committees, which replaced the municipal and provincial administrations as well as . . . many other organs of bourgeois democracy, it would have been impossible to resist fascism. They are revolutionary committees which the people created in order to make the revolution. . . .

"By this we do not mean to say that Spain should be split up by the work of hundreds of scattered committees. We want the reconstruction of Spanish society . . . to be based on the organs that have sprung up from the people, and we should like them to work in agreement with one another. Our prime motive in defending them is to prevent the resurgence of those bourgeois organs and norms that were shipwrecked so pitifully on July 19."[4]

Inside the Cabinet, however, the CNT–FAI ministers yielded step by step to their opponents, who applied constant pressure to end the power of the committees on the ground of placating foreign opinion and enhancing the government's prospects of securing arms from the

---

[3] September 9, 1936. See also *Verdad*, December 30, 1936.

[4] December 20, 1936. The text given here is a retranslation from the Anarchosyndicalist German language periodical *Die Soziale Revolution*, Barcelona, February, 1937, No. 5–6. The Spanish text was unavailable.

Western Powers. Writes Federica Montseny, one of the four Anarcho-syndicalists in the Cabinet: ". . . The arguments of the Communists, Socialists, and Republicans were always the same: It was essential to give an appearance of legality to the Spanish Republic, to calm the fears of the British, French, and Americans. As a consequence the state recovered the positions it had lost, while we revolutionaries, who formed part of the State, helped it to do so. That was why we were brought into the government. Although we did not enter it with that intention, we were in it, and therefore had no alternative but to remain imprisoned in the vicious circle. But I can state positively that, although we lost in the end, we defended our ground inch by inch and never voted for anything that curbed the conquests of the revolution without first being authorized by the National Committee of the CNT, on which there was a permanent representative of the FAI."[5]

As a result, the government, with the acquiescence of the CNT members, approved decrees which, far from giving legal validity to the committees, as the CNT had hoped on entering the Cabinet,[6] provided for their dissolution and replacement by regular provincial and municipal councils, in which all the parties adhering to the Popular Front as well as the trade union organizations were to be represented,[7] thus threatening the predominant position of the

[5] Letter to the author. In February, 1937, Juan Peiró, CNT Minister of Industry, while acknowledging his fear that Britain and France would not reverse their stand on the matter of supplying arms to the government, stated that victory depended on these two Powers "on condition that we prosecute the war and not the revolution." This, he added, did not imply renouncing the revolution. "The road to follow is this: We must wage the war, and, while waging it, limit ourselves to preparing for the revolution by means of a conscientious and discreet control of the factories, for this is equivalent to taking up revolutionary positions and equipping ourselves in a practical way for the final assault on capitalist society after the end of the war."—Article published in *Política*, February 23, 1937. A prominent member of the left wing of the Libertarian movement wrote: "It was feared that we would lack the 'help' of the 'democratic' nations, if they were to see us driving ahead with the revolution, and with this argument the politicians succeeded in causing the promoters of the movement for liberty in Spain to hesitate."—Solano Palacio in *Tiempos Nuevos*, September 28, 1938.   [6] See p. 163, above.

[7] See *Gaceta de la República*, December 25, 1936, January 7, 1937. In addition, a decree was published providing for the suppression of all controls on highways and at the entrance to villages set up by local committees and by parties or trade union organizations, and for the taking over of their functions by the police forces under the Ministry of the Interior.—*Ibid.*, December 26, 1936. None of these decrees, it should be noted, applied to the semi-autonomous region of Catalonia, where events took a somewhat different course.

Anarchosyndicalists in numberless towns and villages, and throwing the more extreme spirits into a position of antagonism to the leadership of the CNT and FAI.

That Largo Caballero, despite his revolutionary stand before the war and the fact that the UGT, which he controlled, held a dominant position on the committees in many towns and villages, should have found common ground with the Communists and other members of the government on the matter of their dissolution is understandable, if only because of his concern for foreign opinion. When, shortly after taking office, he had declared that it was necessary to sacrifice revolutionary language in order to win the friendship of the democratic powers,[8] he must have realized that his efforts to secure Anglo-French aid could not be confined solely to verbal adhesions to the Republican Constitution and that it would be necessary to dissolve the revolutionary organs that had assumed state functions. But apart from the question of foreign opinion, the supporters of the government had other cogent motives for opposing the committees, chief of which was the fact that they impinged on its authority and obstructed its work in almost every sphere.[9] "At the present time," commented *Claridad*, the mouthpiece of Largo Caballero, "these organs can only serve as impediments to a function that belongs solely and exclusively to the Popular Front government, in which all parties and labour organizations in the country participate with full responsibility."[10] And the Communist *Mundo Obrero* declared: "There may be some doubt as to whether or not the numerous bodies created at the beginning of the Civil War in the towns and villages of Loyalist Spain were necessary. But there can be no doubt that at the present time they . . . greatly hinder the work of the government."[11] Criticism of the committees on this score came not only from the Communists and Socialists; even Juan Peiró, the Anarchosyndicalist Minister of Industry, avowed that they interfered

[8] See p. 126, above.

[9] For attacks by the Communists on the committees for levying taxes and requisitioning harvests, see *Verdad*, December 30, 1936, January 12, 1937 (speech by Juan José Escrich); *Frente Rojo*, March 31, 1937; also pp. 84–5, above.

[10] February 19, 1937. See also speech by Largo Caballero at the session of the Cortes held on February 1, 1937, as reported in *El Día Gráfico*, February 2, 1937. For other criticisms of the committees by moderate as well as by left-wing Socialists, see *Claridad*, February 16, 1937 (article by Leoncio Pérez); *La Correspondencia de Valencia*, November 30, 1936 (speech by Molina Conejero), February 1, 1937 (speech by Jerónimo Bugeda), February 2, 1937 (speech by Angel Galarza), February 16, 1937 (speech by Rodolfo Llopis); *El Socialista*, March 2, 10, 11, 1937 (editorial articles); *Verdad*, January 9, 1937 (speech by Juan Tundidor). [11] December 25, 1936.

with governmental functions. "The government issues an order," he declared at a public meeting of the CNT a few weeks before the promulgation of the decrees, "but the local committees interpose their directives. While it tries to put order into things, they disorganize everything. (Murmurs from the audience.) Either the government is superfluous or the committees. (Cries of 'Yes!') What do these inter-jections mean? That the committees are superfluous? (More cries of 'Yes!' 'No!' 'Yes!') . . . The committees are not superfluous, but they must become auxiliary bodies of the government."[12]

Because of the cleavage in the Libertarian movement on the question of dissolving the committees, it was a far cry from the promulgation of the decrees to their actual implementation, and in a large number of localities, where the Anarchosyndicalists were in undisputed ascen-dancy, and even in some where the less radical UGT was dominant, the committees subsisted in the teeth of government opposition.[13] "Those who defend the existence of a network of committees of all kinds," the Communists remonstrated, "forget one important thing: that at the present time nothing can be more prejudicial to us than the division of power. We know that the comrades who uphold the committees do not want Spain to be atomized by the scattered efforts of hundreds of these committees. On the other hand, they consider that the democratic organs [of the Republic] are useless at the present time. This is an error. As we have to defend the democratic structure of the state, because it conforms to the present period of the revolution and because it is a vital requisite for winning the war, it is inexplicable that anyone should think of converting that structure and the organs that give it life into a mere decoration."[14]

But persuasion alone could not ensure the enforcement of the decrees. Only by reconstructing the police corps of the Republic could the government impose its will and centralize in its hands all elements of state power assumed by the revolutionary committees. And of this the Cabinet of Largo Caballero had long been conscious, as will now be seen.

[12] Speech reported by *Solidaridad Obrera*, November 29, 1936.

[13] It should be noted, however, that according to the Anarchosyndicalists, the delay in setting up the new municipal councils in some places was due to the efforts of the Popular Front parties to secure a representation out of propor-tion to their strength. "In spite of the time that has elapsed since the promulga-tion of the decree providing for the formation of the new municipal councils," wrote *Castilla Libre* (March 30, 1937), with regard to the province of Ciudad Libre (previously Ciudad Real), "they have been set up in only three or four localities. The Popular Front, which represents no one, wants to appropriate the majority of posts. We want proportional representation."

[14] *Verdad*, January 26, 1937.

15

The Police

IT has already been shown early in this volume that the police power of the Republic crumbled under the impact of the military rebellion and the social revolution. The Civil Guard, the secret police, and the Assault Guards disintegrated as a result of wholesale desertions to the rebel cause and the taking over of police functions by militia units improvised by the left-wing organizations. These forces, declared Angel Galarza, Minister of the Interior in the Caballero government, "either well or badly, efficiently or inefficiently, some in absolute good faith, others driven by base ambitions and evil instincts, performed a function in the rear . . . ," and "were the only forces that at one time could be used against the fascists in the towns and villages."[1]

With only the bare remnants of the Republican police corps at its disposal,[2] the liberal government formed by José Giral on July 19, 1936, was impotent in face of the revolutionary terror exercised by the working-class organizations through their police squads and patrols, which carried out searches, arrests and summary executions.[3] Nor

[1] Speech reported in *La Correspondencia de Valencia*, August 5, 1937. "Fascism in the rear areas," wrote *Política* (September 18, 1936), the organ of the Left Republican Party, "has been put down principally as a result of the intelligent and skilful work of the militia."

[2] See pp. 36–7, above.

[3] In Madrid, according to Arturo Barea, a Socialist, each of the branches and groups of the trade unions and political parties set up "its own police, its own prison, its own executioners, and a special place for its executions."—*The Forging of a Rebel*, p. 536. For testimony by opponents of the military rebellion on the excesses committed by the Left during this early period of revolutionary terror, see speech by Wenceslao Carrillo, *La Correspondencia de Valencia*, August 4, 1937; Juan José Domenichina in *Hoy*, November 30, 1940; Galíndez, *Los vascos en el Madrid sitiado*, pp. 15–19, 42–3, 67–9; Miguel Peydro in *Correo de Asturias*, January 25, 1941; Indalecio Prieto, *ibid.*, August 15, 1942; Sánchez Roca, interview published in *Solidaridad Obrera*, September 17, 1937; Zugaza-goitia, *Historia de la guerra en España*, pp. 111–12.

could the Giral Cabinet or any government that succeeded it hope to curb this terror and establish its authority in the eyes of the Western world without reconstructing and expanding the police forces under its control. On this point the Communists, Socialists, and Republicans were of one mind, although it is true that they had their respective views as to who should ultimately control the regular police corps.

The first significant step in the reconstruction of the regular police forces was taken by the Giral Cabinet on August 31, 1936, with the promulgation of a decree providing for the purging and reorganizing of the Civil Guard, which henceforth was to be known as the National Republican Guard.[4] Under the Largo Caballero government thousands of new members were recruited for this corps,[5] the same being true of the Assault Guards, whose numbers increased by twenty-eight thousand at the beginning of December, according to Angel Galarza, the left-wing Socialist Minister of the Interior.[6] No less important was the growth of the *carabineros*, or carabineers, a corps composed of customs and excise officials and guards dependent on the Ministry of Finance, which, like the Assault and Civil Guards, had fallen to pieces under the blow of the military insurrection and the revolution. Although the Giral government planned to reorganize and use the corps as a force of public order against the extreme wing of the revolution, its reconstruction and expansion were not seriously undertaken for this purpose until Juan Negrín assumed control of the Ministry of Finance, when the Caballero Cabinet was formed in September, 1936. Within a few months, the *carabineros*, who before the war had numbered approximately 15,600 in the entire country,[7] were reported in April, 1937, to total forty thousand men in the left camp alone, that is, in about half the area of Spain.[8] Some of them, to be sure, were serving at the front, but it was well known that the major part was kept in the rear.[9] That this corps was reorganized partly with an eye to the left wing of the revolution was emphasized by the threatening tone of a speech by Jerónimo Bugeda, Negrín's undersecretary, addressed to a body of

[4] *Gaceta de Madrid*, August 31, 1936.
[5] See n. 6, p. 36, above, for figures on its growth.
[6] Speech reported in *La Correspondencia de Valencia*, August 5, 1937.
[7] According to Diego Abad de Santillán, *Por qué perdimos la guerra*, p. 236.
[8] James Minifie in *The New York Herald Tribune* (dispatch from Valencia), April 28, 1937. See also Henry Buckley, *Life and Death of the Spanish Republic*, p. 311. Negrín himself estimated in mid-November, 1936, that the force would soon number thirty thousand.—*Gaceta de la República*, November 18, 1936.
[9] Buckley, *Life and Death of the Spanish Republic*, p. 311.

carabineers: "You are," he declared, ". . . the guardians of the state that Spain wishes to create for herself, and those visionaries who believe that a chaotic situation of social indiscipline and licentiousness is permissible are utterly mistaken, because the army of the people, as well as you *carabineros*, who are a glorious part of that army, will know how to prevent it."[10]

Concurrently with the reconstruction of the police corps, the government of Largo Caballero took steps to bring the independent squads and patrols of the working-class organizations under its control. Shortly after taking office it published a decree providing for their incorporation into a "Vigilance Militia," which, under the authority of the Ministry of the Interior, was to collaborate with the official police forces in the maintenance of internal order.[11] All militiamen performing police functions who did not belong to the new corps were to be regarded as "disaffected elements," while the members themselves were given priority if they wished to enrol in the regular police forces.[12] Actually, the decree soon proved to be but a preparatory step towards the incorporation of the squads and patrols of the working-class organizations into the armed forces of the state.[13] But whereas members of the Communist, Socialist, and Republican parties were quick to avail themselves of the opportunity to enter the official police corps, the Anarchosyndicalists held back, and in many places clung tenaciously to their own police squads and patrols in defiance of the government. Far from acquiescing in the absorption of their own militia by the state, some of the more resolute elements demanded, on the contrary, that the government police corps should be dissolved and their members incorporated into the militia of the working-class

[10] Reported, *Verdad*, December 27, 1936. The Anarchists did not conceal their fears lest the carabineers should eventually be used against them.—See, for example, speech by Fidel Miró, reported in *Ruta*, February 18, 1937. James Minifie in a dispatch from Valencia published in *The New York Herald Tribune*, April 28, 1937, reported: "A reliable police force is being built up, quietly but surely. The Valencia government discovered an ideal instrument for this purpose in the *carabineros*. . . . The anarchists have already noticed and complained about the increased strength of this force 'at a time when we all know there's little enough traffic coming over the frontiers, land or sea.' They realize that it will be used against them."

[11] *Gaceta de Madrid*, September 17, 1936.

[12] *Ibid.*

[13] See speech by Angel Galarza, reported in *La Correspondencia de Valencia*, August 5, 1937. The decree did not apply to Catalonia. The reconstruction of the regular police corps in that region lies beyond the scope of the present volume.

organizations.[14] But it was a vain demand; for the government, strengthened by the reorganized police corps and by the tacit if not open consent of the CNT–FAI ministers, was beginning to disarm and arrest recalcitrants and take over the administration of public order in one locality after another where the Anarchosyndicalists had been in control since the first days of the Civil War.[15]

Parallel with the reconstruction of the government police corps, important changes were taking place in the field of justice. The revolutionary tribunals set up by the working-class organizations in the early days of the war[16] were gradually being displaced by a legalized form of tribunal composed of three members of the judiciary and fourteen members of the Popular Front parties and trade union federations, two representing each organization.[17] Although decrees providing for the creation of the new courts were promulgated by the Giral government at the end of August, 1936, it was not until several weeks after the CNT had entered the Caballero government in November that they began to function in all the provinces of the left camp.[18]

While the reorganization of the regular police corps was gradually taking place, the Communists were making full use of their skill in proselytism, defamation, and infiltration to secure for themselves a

[14] Resolution approved at the Congress of the Valencia CNT in November, 1936, *Fragua Social*, November 18, 1936. See also *Frente Libertario*, April 10, 1937.

[15] For protests against the disarming and arrest of Anarchosyndicalists and the occupation of villages by the police, see speech by Tomás Cano Ruiz at the closing session of the Congress of the Valencia CNT, reported in *Fragua Social*, November 17, 1936; manifesto issued by the CNT of the central region, published in *El Día Gráfico*, December 23, 1936; *Fragua Social*, April 23, 1937; *Nosotros*, March 13, April 5, 7, 8, 10, 1937. See also *Memoria del pleno regional de grupos anarquistas de Levante celebrado en Alicante, durante los días 11, 12, 13, 14, y 15 del mes de abril de 1937*, pp. 128–31, 133; *Actas del congreso regional de sindicatos de Levante celebrado en Alicante, en el Teatro Verano, los días 15, 16, 17, 18 y 19 de julio de 1937*, pp. 199–205. It is worth noting that some of the measures taken by the police in different localities were in accordance with instructions issued by the Ministry of the Interior to local authorities under his jurisdiction to collect arms in the possession of all persons not belonging to official bodies under the control of the Ministries of Finance, Interior, Justice, and War. See, for example, instructions published in *La Correspondencia de Valencia*, February 15, 1937; also *Gaceta de la República*, March 13, 1937.

[16] See pp. 38–9, above.

[17] *Gaceta de Madrid*, August 24, 26, 1936; see also *ibid.*, October 7, 1936.

[18] See speech by García Oliver, CNT–FAI Minister of Justice in the Caballero government, reported in *Fragua Social*, June 1, 1937.

position of predominance.[19] Moreover, aided by their supporters, both overt and covert, in high places, by the timidity, if not the complaisance, of many leading Socialists and Republicans, they secured pivotal positions in the reconstructed police apparatus. For instance, Lieutenant-Colonel Burillo, an open Communist, became police chief of Madrid; Justiniano García and Juan Galán, also members of the party, were made chief and sub-chief respectively of the *Servicios Especiales*, the Intelligence department of the Ministry of the Interior,[20] while two others were appointed to vital posts in the police administration, one being made Commissar General in the *Dirección General de Seguridad*, in charge of the appointment, transfer, and discipline of the police, and the other becoming head of the training centre of the secret police, the *Escuela de Policía*, which formed the cadres of the new secret police corps.[21]

From the time of its creation this corps, more important, in the last analysis, than any of the uniformed forces of public order, became a mere arm of the Soviet secret police, which, because of the paramount position that Spain now occupied in Soviet diplomacy, had established itself in the left camp quite early in the war. According to General Walter Krivitsky, chief of Soviet Intelligence in Western Europe, an emergency conference had been held in Moscow on September 14, 1936, at which Sloutski, chief of the Foreign Division of the GPU, was present. "From Sloutski . . . ," he adds, "I learned that at this conference a veteran officer of his department was detailed to establish the Ogpu [GPU] in Loyalist Spain. He was Nikolsky, alias Schwed, alias Lyova, alias Orlov."[22] Within a few weeks, the GPU, operating in

[19] See, for example, *Frente Libertario*, March 10, 1937; also General José Asensio on Margarita Nelken, as quoted by Gorkin, *Caníbales Políticos*, p. 218; interview given to *CNT* by Wenceslao Carrillo, Director General of Security from December, 1936, to May, 1937, as reported in *La Correspondencia de Valencia*, August 11, 1937; Pérez Salas, *Guerra en España*, p. 160.

[20] For this information I am grateful to José Muñoz López, a member of the secret police and later a high-ranking official of the SIM (Military Investigation Service). At the end of April, 1937, Juan Galán was made inspector of the armed forces under the control of the Ministry of the Interior, see *Gaceta de la República*, April 30, 1937.

[21] For this information I am likewise indebted to José Muñoz López (see previous note).

[22] *In Stalin's Secret Service*, p. 8. It was under the alias of Orlov that Nikolsky operated in Spain, and his presence there in mid-September, as head of the GPU, is confirmed by Louis Fischer who met him personally.—*Men and Politics*, pp. 361, 383. See also the book by the former Communist, El Campesino, *La vie et la mort en U.R.S.S. (1939–1949)*, p. 206.

intimate association with Spanish Communists, with crypto-Communists, and with the Spanish secret police, and focusing its attention mainly on left-wing opponents of Soviet policy, became the decisive force in determining the course of events in the anti-Franco camp. Writes Krivitsky: "The Ogpu had its own special prisons. Its units carried out assassinations and kidnappings. It filled hidden dungeons and made flying raids. It functioned, of course, independently of the Loyalist government. The Ministry of Justice had no authority over the Ogpu, which was an empire within an empire. It was a power before which even some of the highest officers in the Caballero government trembled. The Soviet Union seemed to have a grip on Loyalist Spain, as if it were already a Soviet possession."[23]

[23] *In Stalin's Secret Service*, p. 102. See also *ibid.*, pp. 106–7. The tale of arrests without judicial warrant, of detentions in clandestine jails, of tortures, kidnappings, and assassinations by the GPU and the Communist-controlled Spanish secret police is amply confirmed by left-wing sources: see, for example, *CNT*, April 17, 1937 (statement by Melchor Rodríguez); *La Correspondencia de Valencia*, February 24, 1937 (open letter of the provincial secretariat of the Valencia UGT); *Cultura Proletaria*, September 25, December 18, 1937; *L'Espagne Nouvelle*, September 17, 1937 (article by Ethel MacDonald); *Fragua Social*, April 16, 17, 1937; *Frente Libertario*, April 9, 1937; *Independent News*, November 7, December 4, 1937; *Modern Monthly*, September, 1937 (article by Anita Brenner); *La Révolution Prolétarienne*, July, 1947 (article by Jordi Arquer); *El Socialista*, April 20, 1937; *Solidaridad Obrera*, April 25, 1937; *Workers' Age*, February 22, 1937 (article by George Kopp), January 15, 1938 (extract from report by John McGovern); Abad de Santillán, *Por qué perdimos la guerra*, pp. 183, 185–90; Borkenau, *The Spanish Cockpit*, pp. 239–40; Brockway, *Workers' Front*, pp. 123–4; Gorkin, *Canibales Políticos*, pp. 133, 176–9, 184, 227–40; Krivitsky, *In Stalin's Secret Service*, pp. 72–3; Katia Landau, *Le stalinisme en Espagne*, pp. 14–17, 24, 27, 33–4, 45–8; John McGovern, *Terror in Spain*, pp. 5, 9; Morón, *Política de ayer y política de mañana*, p. 99; *L'assassinat de Andres Nin*, pp. 18–19.

16

Nationalization Versus Socialization

IF, in order to impose the will of the government, it was necessary to reconstruct the regular police corps and dissolve the revolutionary committees that had assumed functions formerly belonging to the state, it was also necessary, in the opinion of the Communists, as well as of the Socialists and Republicans, to break the power of the revolutionary committees in the factories by bringing the collectivized enterprises, particularly in the basic industries, under the control of the government.[1] Nationalization, the Communists knew, would enable the central authority not only to organize the manufacturing capacity of the anti-Franco camp in accordance with the needs of the war and to control the output and allocation of war material, often assigned by the labour unions to their own locals or militia units,[2] but also to weaken the left wing of the revolution at one of the principal sources of its power. They did not, of course, openly acknowledge the political motive of their desire for nationalization and defended it only on military and economic grounds.[3] In the campaign they waged they were aided by the fact that collectivization suffered from palpable defects. In the first place, the collectivized enterprises were unconcerned with the problems of provisioning and distributing skilled labour, raw

[1] Although the Communists at first called for government ownership only of the basic industries, there can be no doubt that, in the long run, they aimed at taking the rest of the economy out of the hands of the labour unions.

[2] See statement issued by the Executive Committee of the UGT Metallurgical Federation, *La Correspondencia de Valencia*, March 2, 1937.

[3] See, for example, *Verdad*, December 8, 1936 (speech by José Díaz), December 17, 1936 (Communist Party manifesto), December 23, 1936 (editorial); speech by José Díaz on February 8, 1937, as given in *Tres años de lucha*, pp. 274–82; *Frente Rojo*, February 27, 1937 (editorial), March 19, 1937 (manifesto of the Central Committee of the Communist Party).

materials, and machinery in accordance with a single and rational plan of production for military needs. "We have been satisfied with throwing out the proprietors from the factories and putting ourselves in them as committees of control," declared Diego Abad de Santillán, CNT–FAI leader in Catalonia. "There has been no attempt at connection, there has been no co-ordination of economy in due form. We have worked without plans and without real knowledge of what we were doing."[4] Furthermore, non-essential civilian goods and even luxury items were being produced simply because they yielded a high profit, with the resultant wastage of raw materials and human effort.[5] And, finally, in some enterprises there was a complete lack of proper accounting and control, the workers distributing to themselves as wages everything they received from sales without allowing for replacement of stocks and depreciation of capital.[6]

Although the Communists made good use of these deficiencies in order to press their campaign in favour of nationalization, the CNT and FAI, contrary to what has been generally believed, also had their own plans for the co-ordination of industrial production. In order to remedy the defects of collectivization, as well as to iron out discrepancies in the living standards of the workers in flourishing and impoverished enterprises, the Anarchosyndicalists, although rootedly opposed to nationalization,[7] advocated the centralization—or socializa-

[4] Abad de Santillán, *After the Revolution*, p. 122. See also *Boletín de Información*, CNT–FAI, June 21, 1937; speech by Juan López in *Fragua Social*, October 6, 1936; *Solidaridad Obrera*, September 25, 1936 (interview with *España Industrial*); manifesto of the Communist Party, as given in *Verdad*, December 17, 1936; report of Helmut Ruediger, representative in Spain of the AIT (International Workingmen's Association), with which the CNT was affiliated, *Informe para el congreso extraordinario de la AIT, el día 6 de diciembre de 1936*.

[5] See joint statement issued by the national committees of the CNT and UGT textile federations, as given in *Claridad*, March 3, 1937; *Tierra y Libertad*, January 2, 1937; speech by Jesús Hernández in May, 1937, as given in Hernández, *El partido comunista antes, durante y después de la crisis del gobierno Largo Caballero*, p. 41; speech by Antonio Mije, as given in Mije, *Por una potente industria de guerra*, p. 4.

[6] "When the war broke out," Juan Negrín, Minister of Finance, told Louis Fischer (*Men and Politics*, p. 421), "working-men's committees, often Anarchist, took over the factories. . . . They paid themselves in wages everything they took in from sales. Now they have no money. They are coming to me for running expenses and for raw materials. We will take advantage of their plight to gain control of the factories."

[7] See statement by the secretary of the National Committee of the CNT at the Extraordinary Congress of the Catalan CNT in *Memoria del congreso*

tion, as they called it—under trade union control, of entire branches of production.[8] This was the Anarchosyndicalist conception of socialization, without state intervention, which was to eliminate the wastes of competition and duplication, render possible industry-wide planning for both civilian and military needs, and halt the growth of selfish tendencies among the workers of the more prosperous collectives by using their profits to raise the standard of living of the workers in the less favoured enterprises.[9] Already in the early months of the war, the leaders of some of the local CNT unions had undertaken limited forms of socialization, confined to a branch of industry in a single locality, such as the cabinet-makers' trade in Madrid, Barcelona, and Carcagente, the dressmaking, tailoring, metal, and leather goods trades in Valencia, the shoemaking industry in Sitges, the metal and textile industries of Alcoy, the lumber trade of Cuenca, the brickmaking industry of Granollers, the tanning trade of Barcelona and Vich, to mention but a few examples.[10] These partial socializations were not regarded as ends in themselves but rather as transitional stages in the integration of atomized branches of production into a Socialist (i.e. a Libertarian) economy under trade union control.

This work of socialization, however, could not go forward as rapidly as the Libertarian planners desired, not only because they encountered the opposition of many factories in a privileged position, controlled by

---

extraordinario de la confederación regional del trabajo de cataluña celebrado en Barcelona los días 25 de febrero al 3 de marzo de 1937, p. 197. "If nationalization were carried out in Spain, as the Socialists and Communists desire," said *Nosotros*, the Anarchist newspaper (March 9, 1937), "we should be on the way to a dictatorship, because by nationalizing everything the government would become the master, the chief, the absolute boss of everyone and everything." See also Juan Negre, *Qué es el colectivismo anarquista?*, p. 5.

[8] See, for example, *Tierra y Libertad*, December 26, 1936 ("Posición de la FAI" and article by Gaston Leval); January 30, 1937 ("Se impone la socialización" and "Hacia nuevas realizaciones"); February 6, 1937; also *Boletín de Información*, CNT–FAI, December 23, 1936; M. Cardona Rosell, *Aspectos económicos de nuestra revolución*, pp. 3, 6; *Collectivisations. L'oeuvre constructive de la révolution espagnole*, pp. 13–16.

[9] For data from Anarchosyndicalist sources on the development of these tendencies, see *Boletín de Información*, CNT–FAI, June 21, 1937 (speech by C. Bassols); *Cultura y Acción*, July 24, 1937 (article by Maximo Llorca); *Regeneración*, March 15, 1938 (article by H. N. Ruiz); *Solidaridad Obrera*, April 24, 1937 (speech by Playan); *Tierra y Libertad*, May 1, 1937 (article by Juan P. Fábregas).

[10] See pp. 50–2, above, for these and other examples; also *Documentos Históricos de España*, March, 1938; *Tierra y Libertad*, October 9, 16, November 13, 1937.

workers of the UGT as well as by those of the CNT, who did not wish to sacrifice any of their profits to help the less successful collectives,[11] but also because the leadership of the Socialist UGT, which, like the Communist Party, advocated government ownership and control of the basic industries,[12] was opposed to the confiscation of the property of the small bourgeoisie,[13] on which complete Socialist planning, in accordance with the ideas of the CNT leaders, depended.[14] These divergent attitudes of the CNT and UGT rendered the establishment of a centrally co-ordinated industry impossible, either through social- ization or nationalization, and perpetuated the prevailing state of economic chaos.

Of this chaos the Communists took full advantage in order to further their campaign in favour of government ownership and control of industry and against collectivization and socialization. Referring to what he called the "premature experiments in collectivization and socialization," José Díaz, the secretary of the Communist Party, declared: "If, in the beginning, these experiments were justified by the fact that the big industrialists and landlords had abandoned their factories and estates and that it was necessary to continue production, later on they were not. . . . At first it was understandable that the

[11] See, for example, *Las Noticias*, April 14, 1937 (speech by Riera); *Solidaridad Obrera*, April 24, 1937 (speech by Playan); also *Tiempos Nuevos*, September– October, 1937.

[12] See speeches by Pascual Tomás, vice-secretary of the UGT, in *La Correspon- dencia de Valencia*, December 21, 1936, January 11, February 17, April 9, 1937, and other references by him to nationalization in *Adelante*, February 13, 1937, and *Claridad*, April 6, 1937. "The divergence of outlook between the CNT and UGT on economic matters was constant owing to the fact that while the CNT advocated a more and more effective socialization it met with lack of co-opera- tion on the part of the national, regional, and local leaders of the UGT, who paid little or no attention to this vital problem. As a result, the rank and file of the UGT followed the directives of the CNT in many localities."—Mariano Cardona Rosell (a member of the National Committee of the CNT) in reply to a questionnaire sent to him by the author.

[13] See n. 1, p. 48, above.

[14] Another obstacle to the integration of industry into a Socialist economy under trade union control lay in the fact that a large number of firms were in a state of insolvency or semi-insolvency and were compelled, owing to the fact that the banks were controlled mainly by the UGT, to have recourse to state intervention in order to secure financial aid from the government, such inter- vention being recommended even by the CNT Minister of Industry, Juan Peiró—see his statements published in *La Correspondencia de Valencia*, January 6, 1937, and in *El Día Gráfico*, February 9, 1937; also his decree providing for state intervention in industrial enterprises, as given in *Gaceta de la República*, February 24, 1937, and his order of March 2, 1937, *ibid.*, March 7, 1937.

workers should take possession of the abandoned factories in order to continue production at all costs. . . . I repeat that this was understandable, and we are not going to censure it. . . . [But] today when there is a government of the Popular Front, in which all the forces engaged in the fight against fascism are represented, such things are not only inadvisable, but they have the opposite effect from that intended. Today, we must co-ordinate production rapidly, and intensify it under a single direction so as to provision the front and the rear with everything they need. . . . To rush into these premature experiments in 'collectivization' and 'socialization' when the war is still undecided and at a time when the internal enemy, aided by foreign fascism, is violently attacking our positions and endangering the future of our country, is absurd and is tantamount to aiding the enemy."[15]

[15] Report to the Central Committee of the Communist Party, reprinted in Díaz, *Tres años de lucha*, pp. 288-339.

17

"A Democratic and Parliamentary Republic of a New Type"

IT should be stressed that at the root of the Communist Party's opposition to the CNT's plans for the socialization of industry lay the fact not merely that socialization was a threat to its own programme of nationalization, but that, in order to be effective, it had of necessity to impinge on the property of the middle classes, on whose support the Kremlin was relying for the success of its foreign policy. To counter this danger, the Spanish Communists argued that the attempts to further the revolution at the expense of the middle classes were due to a lack of political understanding on the part of the workers. "In the first days of the rebellion," declared a Communist leader, referring to Valencia, "many workers fell into a mania of confiscating and socializing, because they believed that we were in the midst of a social revolution. Nearly all industries were socialized. . . . This fever of 'socialization' not only laid hold of factories and workshops abandoned by bosses who supported the rebellion but even encroached on the small property of liberal and Republican employers. . . .

"Why have the workers fallen into these errors? Mainly owing to a lack of understanding of the present political situation, which leads them to believe that we are in the midst of a social revolution."[1]

And Federico Melchor, a member of the Executive Committee of the JSU, the Communist-oriented Unified Socialist Youth Federation, affirmed:

"We are not making a social revolution today; we are developing a democratic revolution, and in a democratic revolution, the economy . . . cannot be launched into socialist channels. If we are developing

[1] Speech reported in *Frente Rojo*, March 30, 1937.

a democratic revolution and say we are fighting for a democratic republic, how can we attempt in the economic field to introduce methods of a totalitarian socialist type? . . .

"Comrade Alvarez del Vayo said the other day, 'In order to triumph, a correct political line is necessary.' To that we should add: a correct political line based on a clear economic line, on a correct economic line, is necessary. These economic aberrations, these economic trends, these experiments that are carried out in our country, are not due to any accident; they stem from a whole ideology, from the ideological deformation of a broad section of the working-class movement, which is trying to carry forward the economic development of our country without adapting itself to the stages that this economic development requires."[2]

To argue along these lines in the prevailing state of revolutionary exultation was for the Communists a heavy task; for they had to contend not only with the Libertarian movement, but also with the more radical members of the UGT, of the Socialist Party, and of the JSU. From this task they did not shrink. ". . . At a time of the greatest revolutionary effervescence," recalled Antonio Mije, a member of the Politburo, "we Communists did not blush on the platforms of Madrid and the rest of Spain, when we came out in defence of the democratic republic. Whereas some people were afraid even to mention the democratic republic, we Communists had no objection to explaining to impatient elements, who did not understand the situation, that politically it was advisable to defend it against fascism."[3]

"We are fighting for the democratic republic, and we are not ashamed to say so," declared Santiago Carrillo, the secretary of the JSU, in a speech at the National Conference in January, 1937, in which he outlined, for the first time since the fusion of the Socialist and Communist youth movements,[4] the policy of the united organization. "Confronted by fascism and the foreign invaders, we are not fighting at the present time for the socialist revolution. There are some who say that at this stage we should fight for the socialist revolution, and there are others who even say that we are practising a deception, that we are manoeuvring to conceal our real policy when we declare that we are defending the democratic republic. Nevertheless, comrades, we are fighting for a democratic republic, and, furthermore, for a democratic and parliamentary republic. This is not a stratagem to deceive Spanish

[2] Speech in January, 1937, as published in Melchor, *Organicemos la producción*, pp. 6–8.

[3] Speech reported in *Mundo Obrero*, May 18, 1938.

[4] See p. 115, above.

democratic opinion, nor to deceive democratic opinion of the world. We are fighting sincerely for the democratic republic, because we know that if we should commit the mistake of fighting at this time for the socialist revolution in our country—and even for some considerable time after victory—we should give the victory to fascism; we should see in our fatherland not only the fascist invaders but side by side with them the bourgeois democratic governments of the world, which have already stated explicitly that in the present European situation they would not tolerate a dictatorship of the proletariat in our country."[5]

Although there is no record that any democratic government ever made such a threat, there can be no doubt that the fear of incurring the open hostility of the democratic Powers carried considerable weight among the rank and file of the JSU. Nevertheless, dissatisfaction with the policy adumbrated at the Conference was not long in manifesting itself; for, within a few weeks it was denounced by Rafael Fernández, general secretary of the JSU of the Asturias, as "anything but Marxist."[6] This was more than a personal opinion. It was the opinion of a substantial number of Socialists in the JSU who felt themselves betrayed by what they regarded as a rightward swing, and their mood is accurately reflected in the following protest sent from the battle front:

"I have read several times in different newspapers the speeches made by Carrillo . . . to the effect THAT THE UNIFIED SOCIALIST YOUTH IS FIGHTING FOR A DEMOCRATIC AND PARLIAMENTARY REPUBLIC. I believe that Carrillo is completely mistaken. As a young Socialist and revolutionary I am fighting for the collectivization of the land, of the factories, of the entire wealth of Spain, for the benefit of everyone, for the benefit of humanity.

"Do Carrillo and the others who aim at leading us along that prejudicial and counter-revolutionary road believe that the militants of the JSU are sheep? No, we are not sheep; we are revolutionaries!

"What would our comrades who have perished on the battlefields do if they could raise their heads and see that the JSU has been an accomplice in betraying the revolution for which they gave their lives? They would do only one thing. They would spit in the face of the culprits."[7]

[5] Carrillo, *En marcha hacia la victoria,* p. 10.

[6] Open letter to Carrillo published in *La Correspondencia de Valencia,* April 1, 1937.

[7] Letter published in *Juventud Libre,* May 1, 1937. See also article by Federico Fernández López in *Adelante,* May 28, 1937.

If it was difficult for the Communists to convince the radical members of the JSU of the correctness of their policy, it was still more difficult to convince the Libertarian movement. Yet, in order to ensure the success of that policy, it was essential to secure the compliance, if not the wholehearted approval, of this powerful movement. With this end in view, Soviet diplomatic representatives, according to Federica Montseny, the Anarchosyndicalist Minister of Health, held frequent conversations with CNT–FAI leaders. ". . . the advice they gave us," she writes, "was always the same: it was necessary to establish in Spain a 'controlled democracy' (euphemistic term for a dictatorship); it was not advisable to create the impression abroad that a profound revolution was being carried out; we should avoid awakening the suspicion of the democratic Powers."[8] But whatever political concessions at the expense of the revolution the CNT–FAI ministers felt compelled to make to Soviet policy in the hope of influencing the democracies, they did not adhere undeviatingly to the Communist slogan of the democratic republic,[9] and, if, on entering the government, they had agreed to adopt it, this was, according to one of them, "in order to produce an impression beyond the frontiers, but never to strangle the legitimate revolutionary conquests of the working class."[10]

Even less than the CNT–FAI ministers did the Libertarian movement as a whole accept the Communist slogan of the democratic republic. This was clearly reflected in its press:

"The thousands of proletarian combatants at the battle fronts," declared the *Boletín de Información*, "are not fighting for the 'democratic republic.' They are proletarian revolutionaries, who have taken up arms in order to make the revolution. To postpone the triumph of the latter until after we win the war would weaken considerably the fighting spirit of the working class . . .

[8] Letter to the author. The behaviour of the Russians, she adds, was very courteous. "I never heard them utter a threatening word. . . . When I went to Geneva in January and February of 1937 to attend the Congress of Hygiene, Rosenberg [the Soviet Ambassador] urged me to go to Russia, saying, 'Comrade Stalin would be very happy to meet you. Go there, Federica! You will be received like a little queen.' [The Russians] never made any concrete offer that would have forced me to break relations with them. They were too subtle for that. But on various occasions, Rosenberg suggested that I send my daughter to Valencia to live with his wife and children in a villa they occupied on the outskirts. When I heard these suggestions the blood froze in my veins."

[9] See, for example, speech by Juan López, February 7, 1937, reprinted in López, *Concepto del federalismo en la guerra y en la revolución*, pp. 3–4.

[10] Juan López in *CNT*, June 19, 1937.

". . . If we wish to raise the enthusiasm of our fighters and inject the anti-fascist masses with revolutionary zeal, we must drive the revolution forward with determination, liquidate the last vestiges of bourgeois democracy, socialize industry and agriculture, and create the directing organs of the new society in accordance with the revolutionary aims of the proletariat.

"It should be clearly understood that we are not fighting for the democratic republic. We are fighting for the triumph of the proletarian revolution. The revolution and the war are inseparable. Everything that is said to the contrary is *reformist counter-revolution.*"[11]

And *CNT* exclaimed:

" 'Democratic revolution.' 'Parliamentary republic.' 'This is not the moment for carrying out the social revolution.' Here are a few slogans worthy of the political programmes of the Republican parties but degrading to the working-class organizations. . . . [If] the Socialist and Communist parties as well as their youth movement had honoured their Socialist principles 'the entire apparatus of the old bourgeois state' (Marx) and the structure of capitalist economy would have been destroyed. In the *Communist Manifesto* Marx and Engels never referred to a transitional period of a 'democratic and parliamentary republic.' . . . For this reason, the Marxism of the Spanish Marxist parties is a Marxism that has nothing in common with revolutionary Marxism but much with social-democratic reformism, against which Lenin directed his revolutionary theories outlined in *State and Revolution.*"[12]

To counter the embarrassing denunciations of their policy in the CNT and FAI press, the Communists—who, at the beginning of the Civil War, as has already been seen, had likened the revolution taking place in Spain to the bourgeois democratic revolution which had been achieved over a century before in France,[13] were compelled, for the purposes of home consumption, to modify their language. "What do the comrades of *CNT* accuse us of?" asked *Mundo Obrero* in reply to the Anarchosyndicalist organ. "According to them, we have diverged from the path of revolutionary Marxism. Why? Because we defend the democratic republic . . . [We] should like to define the character of the republic in our country at the present time. . . . First, the working class, the peasants, and the small bourgeoisie have ALL THE

---

[11] January 19, 1937.

[12] February 2, 1937. See also *Juventud Libre*, February 6, 1937; *Solidaridad Obrera*, February 9, 1937; *Tierra y Libertad*, January 23, 1937.

[13] See speech by Pasionaria, p. 87, above.

ARMS; second, the peasants have the land: the agricultural labourers are working the former large estates collectively or individually and the tenant farmers now possess their own land; third, working-class control has been established in all factories, and the big political bosses who joined the military rising have been expropriated and therefore deprived of their social and political power; fifth, the greatest influence, the principal directing influence in the development of the democratic revolution is in the hands of the entire working class; sixth, the former army of oppression has been destroyed and we have a new army of the people. Hence, our republic is of a special type; it is a democratic and parliamentary republic with a social content that has never existed before. And this republic . . . cannot be considered in the same light [as those republics] where democracy is a fiction, a democracy based on the absolute hegemony of the exploiters. This point having been established, we must inform the comrades of *CNT* that by defending democracy and the republic we do not abjure or contradict the doctrines of revolutionary Marxism. It was Lenin who taught us that to be revolutionary one should not jump into space. It was Lenin who taught us that to be revolutionary one should always bear in mind the concrete situation of a given country so as to apply to it the most suitable revolutionary tactics."[14]

And at the plenary session of the Central Committee of the Communist Party in March, 1937, José Díaz, the secretary, declared: "We are fighting for the democratic republic, for a democratic and parliamentary republic of a new type and with a profound social content. The struggle taking place in Spain is not aimed at the establishment of a democratic republic like that of France or of any other capitalist country. No. The democratic republic for which we are fighting is different. We are fighting to destroy the material foundations on which reaction and fascism rest; for without their destruction no true political democracy can exist. . . .

"And now I ask: To what extent have [they] been destroyed? In every province we control big landowners no longer exist. The Church, as a dominant power, has likewise ceased to exist. Militarism has also disappeared never to return. Nor are there any big bankers and industrialists. That is the reality of the situation. And the guarantee that these conquests will never be lost lies in the fact that the arms are in the hands of the people, of the genuine anti-fascist people, of the workers, the peasants, the intellectuals, and the small bourgeoisie, who were always the slaves of those castes. That is the best guarantee that

[14] February 3, 1937. See also *Mundo Obrero*, February 5, 1937.

the past will never return. And precisely for that reason, because we have a guarantee that our conquests will not be lost, we should not lose our heads . . . by trying to introduce experiments in 'Libertarian Communism' and 'socialization.' . . . The present stage of political development in Spain is that of the democratic revolution, the victory of which depends on the participation of all the anti-fascist forces, and these experiments can only serve to drive them away and estrange them."[15]

But the efforts of the Communists to convince their critics were unavailing; for the adherents of the Libertarian movement, particularly of its extreme wing, the Libertarian Youth, were in their immense majority immovably hostile to Communist slogans and, in distinction from the CNT–FAI leadership, were becoming more and more sceptical as to whether any advantage could be gained by making concessions to foreign opinion. Some hint of the temper of the movement may be gleaned from the following quotations. In an attack on the Communist-led JSU, which, in January, 1937, had officially espoused the cause of the democratic republic, *Juventud Libre*, the leading organ of the Libertarian Youth, declared:

"The strongest argument that the Unified Socialist Youth can put forward in order to defend the democratic and parliamentary republic is that we should desist from speaking of revolution so as not to make our position with regard to the European democracies more difficult. Childish argument! The European democracies know only too well who we are and where we are inevitably going; they know, just as the fascist countries know, that in Spain practically all the soldiers who are fighting against fascism are revolutionaries and will not permit this magnificent occasion for making the revolution . . . to be snatched from them. Whether we speak either of the democratic and parliamentary republic or of the revolution, the European democracies will help us only if it suits them. . . .

". . . To deceive our soldiers, who are dying heroically on the battlefields, to deceive our peasants and workers, who are labouring in the rear areas, with a democratic and parliamentary republic, is to betray the Spanish Revolution. . . .

"The economic wealth of the country as well as the arms are in our hands. Everything belongs to us. . . . We are defending everything we have against the international fascist criminals. The traitors who try to

[15] Díaz, *Tres años de lucha*, pp. 295–7. See also his speech at the plenary session of the Central Committee of the PSUC, reported in *Treball*, February 9, 1937.

steal what belongs to us should be denounced as fascists and shot without mercy."[16]

"Anyone who comes to us at this time, when we have the possibility of transforming Spain socially, with the story that this transformation would not be approved of by the international bourgeoisie, is a scoundrel," declared J. García Pradas, director of *CNT*. "From the very moment that he aspires to make a revolution with the licence of the international bourgeoisie, he has no authority to tell us what to do.

"If we have to refrain from making the revolution in order to prevent the international bourgeoisie from clashing with us, if we have to conceal our every aim, if we have to renounce our every aim, then why are our comrades fighting? Why are we all fighting? Why have we thrown ourselves into this struggle, into this war without mercy against Spanish and foreign fascism?"[17]

And *Fragua Social*, the CNT organ, stated:

". . . At the very moment when our country is being lashed by a tempest, by a real social revolution that has changed everything, the Communist Party comes out with the demand for a parliamentary republic, a republic that has already been left far behind by the march of events. Paradoxically, this results in a situation where the Communists form the extreme right wing of Loyalist Spain, the last hope of the small bourgeoisie, which sees its world going under. However strange it may appear, the Communists are the nerve centre of a policy and of a campaign of propaganda aimed at pushing us back to the first years of the bourgeois republic, a policy that ignores the existence of a triumphant and regenerating July 19."[18]

It was, of course, incorrect to ascribe to the Communists the intention of rolling back the revolution to before July 19. All their propaganda for abroad notwithstanding, they could not return to the days of the 1931 Republic without restoring the property of the big landowners and industrialists, in other words, without giving them a share in the affairs of state. This would have been incompatible with the Kremlin's purpose in Spain, which was to control her domestic and foreign policy in conformity with its own diplomatic needs. By curbing the revolution, the Communist Party aimed not at restoring the property of the

---

[16] April 10, 1937.

[17] Speech at a meeting of the Libertarian Youth, reported in *CNT*, May 4, 1937.

[18] May 22, 1937. For other attacks in the Libertarian press accusing the Communists of trying to return to the Republic of 1931, see *Juventud Libre*, May 9, 1937; *Ruta*, April 1, 17, 1937.

big landowners and industrialists but at finding a backing for itself among the middle layers of the population and at using them, as long as it suited its purpose, to offset the power of the revolutionary segment of the anti-Franco camp. If this was its policy in the field of industry and trade, it was no less so in the field of agriculture, as will be seen in the succeeding chapter.

18

Balancing the Class Forces

AIDED by the Ministry of Agriculture which they controlled, the Communists were able to influence substantially the course of events in the countryside. By far the most resounding of the decrees issued by Vicente Uribe, the Communist minister, was that of October 7, 1936, by which all rural properties belonging to persons who had intervened either directly or indirectly in the military insurrection were confiscated without indemnity and in favour of the state.[1] "This decree," commented *Mundo Obrero*, the Communist Party organ, "breaks the foundation of the semi-feudal power of the big landlords who, in order to maintain their brutal caste privileges and to perpetuate salaries of two pesetas a day and labour from dawn to dusk, have unleashed the bloody war that is devastating Spain."[2] Under the terms of the decree the estates that had been cultivated directly by the owners or by their stewards, or had been leased to large tenant farmers, were given in perpetual usufruct to organizations of peasants and agricultural workers to be cultivated individually or collectively in accordance with the wishes of the majority of beneficiaries. In cases where the estates had been leased to small cultivators, the latter were promised the permanent use of their holdings, which, however, were not to exceed thirty hectares in dry sections, five in irrigated districts, and three in fruitgrowing areas.[3] "[The decree of October 7]," affirmed the Communist organ, *Frente Rojo*, "is the most profoundly revolutionary measure that has been taken since the military uprising. . . . It has abolished more than forty per cent of private property in the countryside."[4]

Although the language of the decree gave the impression that it was

[1] *Gaceta de Madrid*, October 8, 1936.
[2] October 10, 1936.
[3] One hectare is equivalent to approximately two and a half acres.
[4] March 20, 1937.

the government that had taken the initiative in confiscating the properties of supporters of the military insurrection, in point of fact the measure merely set the seal of legality on expropriations already carried out by agricultural labourers and tenant farmers. The Communists, however, frequently represented the measure as having been instrumental in giving the land to the peasants. ". . . In Communist newspapers," wrote Ricardo Zabalza, left-wing Socialist and general secretary of the powerful Federation of Land Workers affiliated with the UGT, "we have read such things as this: 'Thanks to the decree of October 7, a measure of a Communist minister, the peasants have the land today.' Such statements no doubt make very effective propaganda among the ignorant, but they cannot convince anyone who is half-acquainted with the facts. . . . Before any Communist minister was in the government, the peasant organizations, on instructions from our federation, had already confiscated *de facto* all the land belonging to the rebels."[5] And, in an article written after the Civil War, Rafael Morayta Nuñez, secretary-general of the Institute of Agrarian Reform during the first months of the conflict, writes: "I can state positively, and this everyone knows, that it was not the government that handed the land to the peasants. The latter did not wait for a governmental decision, but appropriated the estates and cultivable lands themselves. . . . Hence the much-vaunted decree of October 7, which a certain political party practically claims to be exclusively its own creation, did not give those estates to the peasants or to anyone else; for the peasants were already working them several months before, and the only thing the decree accomplished—a decree which was of course approved by the government—was to give legal status to those expropriations."[6]

Because the decree applied only to the estates of persons charged with participating directly or indirectly in the military revolt and thereby exempted from legal confiscation the properties belonging to Republican and other landowners who had not identified themselves with General Franco's cause, the Anarchosyndicalists considered that it was inadequate to the situation. "The Minister of Agriculture," commented *CNT*, "has just promulgated a decree confiscating in favour of the state all rural properties whose owners intervened directly or indirectly in the fascist insurrection of July 19. As usual, of course, the state arrives late. The peasants did not wait for such a vital problem to be settled by decree: they acted in advance of the government, and from the very beginning . . . they seized the property of the land-

[5] Article published in *CNT*, May 26, 1937.
[6] *Tribuna*, October, 1948.

owners, making the revolution from below. With a real understanding of the land problem, they were more expeditious than the state. They expropriated without making any distinction between owners who had intervened and owners who had not intervened in the rebel conspiracy. . . . The expropriation of those who have intervened directly or have helped the fascists leaves the supreme problem of the Spanish Revolution unsolved.

"Our authorities should understand once and for all that the 19th of July destroyed the régime of unjust privileges and that a new life is springing up all over Spain. As long as they do not understand this, as long as they cling to institutions and methods that became obsolete on July 19 they will always lag behind the conquests of the people."[7]

Criticism of the limitations of the decree came also from the Federation of Land Workers, controlled by the left-wing Socialists. At a National Conference held in June, 1937, the federation demanded that the decree should be so amended as to include within its scope not only persons implicated in the military uprising, but also those who had been regarded as enemies of the working class for having "violated labour contracts, discharged workers unjustly because of their ideas, denounced them [to the police] without good reason, [and] encouraged strike breaking."[8] But it was impossible for the Communist Party even to countenance such an amendment. Seeking support among the propertied classes in the anti-Franco camp, it could not afford to repel the small and medium proprietors who had been hostile to the working-class movement before the Civil War, and, indeed, through the Ministry of Agriculture and the Institute of Agrarian Reform, which it controlled, it seconded, on the basis of the limitations of the decree of October 7, many of their demands for the restitution of their land. "I can tell you about the Castilian countryside . . . ," declared a leader of the Libertarian Youth movement, "because I am in daily contact with all the agricultural districts of Castile, districts to which the delegates of the Ministry of Agriculture go . . . with the object of returning to the bourgeoisie, to the fascists, to the landowners, the property they once possessed. The Minister of Agriculture claims that these are small proprietors. Small proprietors, with a splendid number of acres! Are the political bosses of the villages and those who used to conspire against the workers small proprietors? Are those who have twenty or twenty-five workers and three or four pairs of bullocks small proprietors? I must ask where the policy of the Minister of Agriculture

[7] October 12, 1936.
[8] *Por la revolución agraria*, p. 44.

is leading and just what is the limit to the term 'small proprietor.' "[9]

The protection that the Communist Party gave even to farmers who had belonged to right-wing parties before the Civil War—particularly in the province of Valencia, where it organized them into the Peasant Federation[10]—irrevocably antagonized a large segment of the rural population. "The Communist Party," complained a Socialist, referring to the Peasant Federation, "devotes itself to picking up in the villages the worst remnants of the former *Partido Autonomista*, who were not only reactionary, but also immoral, and organizes these small proprietors into a new peasant union by promising them the possession of their land.[11]

There can be no doubt that the Communist Party's championship of the small, to say nothing of the medium proprietor, irrespective of his political antecedents, was one of the many important reasons for the bitter strife that soon developed between itself and the left-wing of the Socialist Party, which controlled the Federation of Land Workers.[12] Whereas the Communists demanded that collectivization be entirely voluntary,[13] thereby implying that the property of the right-wing as well as of the Republican farmer should be respected,[14] the left-wing

[9] Speech published in *Juventud Libre*, July 24, 1937. See also article in *Castilla Libre*, March 30, 1937, quoting a member of the provincial committee of the CNT of Ciudad Libre (formerly Ciudad Real) as saying that a delegate of the Minister of Agriculture in that province had demanded the return of their land to persons who were not fascists; and letter sent to the Minister of Agriculture by Ricardo Zabalza, general secretary of the Federation of Land Workers (published in *Adelante*, May 29, 1937), complaining that a delegate of the Institute of Agrarian Reform had ordered the restoration of a large estate to its original owner in the village of Garvayuela, Badajoz.

[10] See p. 86, above.

[11] *Claridad*, December 14, 1936.

[12] For indications of the hostility created among left-wing Socialists, see replies of various provincial secretaries of the Federation of Land Workers to questions posed by the Socialist newspaper, *Adelante*, regarding Communist policy in the countryside, as given in *Adelante*, June 17, 20, 1937, and *CNT*, June 14, 21, 1937. See also *Colectivismo*, May 1, 1938 (article by A. Fernández Ballesteros).

[13] See, for example, speech by Vicente Uribe, the Minister of Agriculture, reported in *Verdad*, December 8, 1936.

[14] It is worth noting that in their efforts to win the support of the middle layers of the rural population, both right-wing and Republican, the Communists were forced to restrain the collectivist tendencies even in their own youth movement. "Not only have we seen certain organizations advocate collectivization," said Santiago Carrillo, general secretary of the Unified Socialist Youth Federation, "but in the beginning we also saw our own youth defending it through failure to understand the character of the present struggle.

Socialists, while against the compulsory collectivization of the land of the small Republican farmer,[15] were opposed to sacrificing the growth of the collective farm movement to the small owner who had been in open conflict with the rural wageworker before the Civil War. "The loyal small proprietor," declared the left Socialist paper, *Claridad*, the mouthpiece of the UGT, "should not be forced to enter the collective farms, but generous technical, economic, and moral aid should be given to every spontaneous initiative in favour of collectivization. When we say 'loyal small proprietor' we deliberately exclude both the small owners who were brazen enemies of the working class and the venomous and petty political bosses, who are now snivelling and trying to keep in the background and who constitute a real Fifth Column in the rural areas. As for these, we must draw their teeth and claws. It would be a veritable catastrophe if, on the basis of these elements, an attempt were made to create an organization of kulaks, while ignoring the courageous peasants fighting at the front who suffered imprisonment, torture, and misery in the past."[16]

The policy of the Communists, as expressed by the Minister of Agriculture's decree of October 7 and by its practical application, was criticized for other reasons than those given in the foregoing pages. Ricardo Zabalza, general secretary of the Federation of Land Workers which enrolled small tenant farmers as well as farm hands, affirmed, when interviewed about conditions in the province of Albacete: "There are many landowners whose properties have not been confiscated, either because they are adherents of the Left or because they have passed themselves off as such. Their tenants are compelled by law to continue the payment of rent, and this is an injustice, because the

---

However, the comrades of Badajoz and other peasant provinces know very well that when the federation told them they were pursuing the wrong policy and that when they started to follow the correct one the situation in the countryside began to change. . . .

"It is hardly necessary for us to point out how the only country in the world that has made the revolution, the Soviet Union, began to collectivize the land after nine years of proletarian power. How, then, in a democratic republic, are we going to do what the Soviet Union did after nine years of workers' power? We declare that, as long as the situation in our country does not permit any other course, our line for a long time to come will be the defence of the small peasant, the defence of the legitimate interests of the small proprietor of the countryside."—Speech at the National Conference of the Unified Socialist Youth Federation in January, 1937 (Carrillo, *En marcha hacia la victoria*, p. 41).

[15] See p. 58, above.

[16] December 16, 1936.

tenants of rebel landowners are freed from such payment."[17] Zabalza also criticized the decree on the ground that it prevented a distribution of land in favour of the village poor. This criticism was based on the fact that the tenant farmers and sharecroppers who benefited from the decree were legally entitled to retain all the land they had cultivated before the revolution, provided that it did not exceed the specified limits, and were therefore unwilling to cede any portion of their holdings to the rural wageworkers. "As a result," Zabalza argued, "the [wageworkers] remain without land in many places or have to content themselves with the worst soil or with that which is farthest from the villages, because the rest of the land, or nearly all of it, is in the hands of small owners and tenant farmers. This makes friction inevitable for it is impossible to accept the galling injustice of a situation whereby the sycophants of the former political bosses still enjoy a privileged position at the expense of those persons who were unable to rent even the smallest parcel of land, because they were revolutionaries."[18]

But more important still as a source of friction in the countryside was the fact that the Communists used the decree in order to stimulate the personal interest of those tenant farmers and sharecroppers who, before its publication, had been caught up by the collective farm movement or had agreed to a redistribution of land in favour of the agricultural labourers.

". . . Then came the decree of October 7," declared the Federation of Land Workers, "offering tenant farmers the possibility of retaining in perpetual usufruct all the land they formerly cultivated, provided that it did not exceed thirty hectares in dry sections, five in irrigated districts, and three in fruitgrowing areas. This represented . . . a guarantee that no lessee, provided that he was not an open supporter of the rebellion, could be dispossessed of his land. . . . [And] the practical effect of this decree has been to create, among the tenant farmers and sharecroppers who had accepted the new order of things, a desire to recover their former parcels."[19]

Encouraged by the support they received from the Communists, many right-wing tenant farmers and sharecroppers who had accepted

[17] *Adelante*, July 3, 1937.

[18] *Ibid*. See also *Por la revolución agraria*, pp. 42–3, and statement by Ramón Arcos Arnau, provincial secretary of the Madrid section of the Federation of Land Workers, as given in *CNT*, June 14, 1937.

[19] *Por la revolución agraria*, pp. 42–3. See also *Adelante*, June 17, 1937 (reply by Jesús Pérez Pérez to questions posed by the newspaper regarding Communist policy in the countryside); *Colectivismo*, September 15, 1937; January–February, 1938; May 1, 1938 (article by A. Fernández Ballesteros).

collectivization in the first months of the revolution demanded the return of their former parcels. At the peak of their offensive against the collective farms, Ricardo Zabalza declared: "Our most fervent aim today is to guarantee the conquests of the revolution, especially the collective farms which were organized by the different branches [of our federation] and against which a world of enemies is rising up, namely, the reactionaries of yesterday and those who held land on lease, because they were lackeys of the political bosses, whereas our members were either denied land or evicted from their wretched holdings. Today, these reactionaries, protected by the famous decree of October 7, and enjoying unheard-of official aid, are endeavouring to take by assault the collectivized estates with the object of dividing them up, distributing their livestock, their olives, their vineyards, and their harvests, and of putting an end to the agrarian revolution. . . . And in order to do this they are taking advantage of the absence of our best comrades, who are at the front and who would weep with rage if they should find on their return that their efforts and sacrifices had only served to enthrone their eternal enemies, who, to increase the mockery, are now protected by membership cards of a working-class organization."[20]

In their campaign against the collective farms, the Communists also endeavoured to mobilize the agricultural labourers. Early in April, 1937, Mariano Vázquez, the secretary of the National Committee of the CNT, accused them of going to areas where the CNT and UGT had established collective farms by mutual agreement and of "stirring up egotistic impulses . . . by promising personal advantages to the labourers and inciting them to divide up the land."[21] Nor did the Communists limit themselves to this procedure; for Vázquez also charged that they had assassinated dozens of Anarchosyndicalists in the province of Toledo,[22] and, a few months later, the general secretary of the CNT Peasants' Federation of Castile, declared: "We have fought terrible battles with the Communists, especially with brigades and divisions under their control, which have assassinated our best peasant

[20] Interview given to *Adelante*, reprinted in *Solidaridad Obrera*, May 28, 1937. See also his letter to the Minister of Agriculture, published in *Adelante*, May 29, 1937, and articles by José España in *Cultura y Acción*, June 5, 1937, and in *Nosotros*, June 3, 1937.
[21] *Castilla Libre*, April 10, 1937. See also Zabalza's letter to the Minister of Agriculture, published in *Adelante*, May 29, 1937.
[22] *Loc. cit.* See also *Castilla Libre*, March 31, 1937 (article by Isabelo Romero); *CNT*, March 26, May 29, 1937; *Frente Libertario*, March 20, April 6, 1937; *Spanish Revolution*, July 2, 1937.

militants, and savagely destroyed our collective farms and our harvests, obtained at the cost of infinite sacrifice."[23]

It was inevitable that the attacks on the collectives should have had an unfavourable effect upon rural economy and upon morale, for while it is true that in some areas collectivization was anathema to the majority of peasants, it is no less true that in others collective farms were organized spontaneously by the bulk of the peasant population.[24] In Toledo province, for example, where even before the war rural collectives existed,[25] eighty-three per cent of the peasants, according to a source friendly to the Communists, decided in favour of the collective cultivation of the soil.[26]

As the campaign against the collective farms reached its height just before the summer harvest—a period of the year when even the more successful farms were beset with economic difficulties—a pall of dismay and apprehension descended upon the agricultural labourers. Work in the fields was abandoned in many places or only carried on apathetically, and there was danger that a substantial portion of the harvest, vital for the war effort, would be left to rot.

It was then that the Communists suddenly changed their policy.

The first intimation of this about-face came early in June, 1937, when the Minister of Agriculture issued a decree promising various forms of aid to the collectives[27] so that they could carry out "as

[23] Interview given to *Juventud Libre*, July 10, 1937. See also *Acracia*, March 19, 1937 (article by M. Salas); *CNT*, May 29, 1937; Peirats, *La CNT en la revolución española*, pp. 320, 323.

[24] A commissar in the Communist-controlled International Brigades, an authority on the Spanish Revolution, wrote to the author after he had severed his ties with the Communist Party: ". . . the C.P. drive against collectivization was absolutely wrong, for while there were plenty of abuses, forced collectivization, etc., there were plenty of good collectives, i.e. voluntary ones."

[25] Anibal Ponce, *Examen de la España actual*, p. 75, says there were nearly fifty; Capo, *España Desnuda*, p. 88, puts the number at thirty-five. See also *Claridad*, April 7, 9, 1936.

[26] Cordoba Iturburu, *España bajo el comando del pueblo*, p. 154.

[27] This did not mean that no assistance had been given in the past. According to the Communist organ, *Frente Rojo* (June 11, 1937), the Institute of Agrarian Reform, which was controlled by the Minister of Agriculture, and which, under the decree of October 7, had been charged with the task of apportioning aid to the beneficiaries, had since that date provided collective farms with fifty million pesetas in credits, farm implements, seed, and fertilizers. This is not unlikely. But this assistance must have gone solely to those collectives that accepted the intervention of the Institute; for the CNT, which rejected state intervention because it threatened the autonomy of its collectives, charged that the latter were denied all help from the Minister of Agriculture. See, for

satisfactorily and as speedily as possible the agricultural labours appropriate to the season."[28] It was necessary, said the preamble, to avoid "economic failures that might chill the faith of the land workers in the collective form of cultivation they chose freely when they confiscated the land of the rebel exploiters." Said Article I of the decree: "For the purposes of assistance by the Institute of Agrarian Reform, all collective farms set up since July 19, 1936, are considered legally constituted *during the current agricultural year,*[29] and no claim will be handled by the subsidiary departments of the Institute of Agrarian Reform for the return of land occupied by the said collectives . . . even in cases where it is alleged that errors have been made of a legal character or in defining the political status of the former owner or beneficiary of the collectivized land." "This means," commented *Frente Rojo,* the Communist organ, "that the only thing that counts in guaranteeing the legality of the collectives is the very act, the revolutionary act of having formed them, and that they are thus saved from any legal or political stratagem that might be devised against them."[30] Although the measure offered no guarantee of legality beyond the current agricultural year,[31]

---

example, interview given to *Juventud Libre,* July 10, 1937, by the general secretary of the CNT Peasants' Federation of Castile; report on the Madrid Congress of the Libertarian Youth, *ibid.,* July 31, 1937; *Castilla Libre,* March 30, 1937 (article on Ciudad Libre); *Fragua Social,* October 21, 1937. It is noteworthy that according to Mariano Cardona Rosell, a member of the National Committee of the CNT, and its representative on the Executive Commission of the National Service of Agricultural Credit, although the Institute of Agrarian Reform was not empowered to extend credits and assistance to collectives outside its jurisdiction, such collectives could apply for aid from the National Service without any danger of control other than that arising from the credit transactions involved.—Letters to the author. But this service, which operated under the auspices of the Ministry of Agriculture, and on whose Executive Commission there were representatives of the CNT and UGT as well as officials of that department (see composition as given in the decree of January 30, 1937, *Gaceta de la República,* February 2, 1937), did not begin to function properly until late in the summer of 1937. Moreover, although, according to Cardona Rosell, it extended very substantial credits to those collective farms that applied for assistance, some CNT collectives did not take advantage of it for a long time owing to their suspicion of official bodies and the fear that they might curb their independence.

[28] *Gaceta de la República,* June 9, 1937.

[29] Author's italics.

[30] June 11, 1937.

[31] It is noteworthy that the above-quoted article in *Frente Rojo* did not mention the fact that the status of legality had been conceded only temporarily. "[The decree]," it said, "grants to the agricultural collectives formed since

it produced a sense of relief in the countryside during the vital period of the harvest, and in that respect it achieved its purpose.

But no sooner had the crops been gathered than apprehension again set in. On August 10, the central government, then in the hands of Communists and moderate Socialists, had decreed the dissolution of the Anarchosyndicalist-dominated Defence Council of Aragon,[32] and the

---

July 19, 1936, an indestructible legal position. Since its publication, the legal existence of the agricultural collectives is perfectly assured. What began as a spontaneous impulse among a large section of the agricultural workers has now been converted, by virtue of the decree, into a legal form of agricultural labour." Nevertheless, many months later, in a programme of common action drawn up by the CNT and UGT (reprinted in *Alianza CNT-UGT*, pp. 131-41), it was found necessary to demand that the collective farms be legalized. This did not change matters, for towards the end of the war *CNT* of Madrid (October 3, 1938) was still insisting on this point. Indeed, Vicente Uribe, who remained in charge of the Ministry of Agriculture until the end of the war, never granted a permanent status of legality to the collectives.

[32] This body was set up by the CNT early in the war to control the revolution in that part of Aragon occupied by the anti-Franco forces, predominantly Anarchosyndicalist. In a report to Largo Caballero (*Solidaridad Obrera*, November 2, 1936), Joaquín Ascaso, its Anarchist president, stated that the absence of all governing organs in the three provinces of Aragon and the occupation of part of this region by militia, "not all subjected to the necessary and desirable discipline," had given rise to a chaotic situation that threatened economic ruin in the rear and disaster at the front. For these reasons, he added, it had been essential to create a body that would assume all the functions exercised by the former organs of administration, "a body adequate both in its structure and functioning to the present situation." (See also "De julio a julio," *Fragua Social*, July 19, 1937, as reprinted in *De julio a julio*, pp. 9-18). Although the CNT later gave representation to other organizations, it retained in its hands the key positions: presidency, public order, propaganda, agriculture, economy, transport, and supplies. (See *El Día Gráfico*, December 9, 1936.) While the Communists joined the Council, they did so with the intention of opposing it. This is natural, because they could not be in agreement with an arch-revolutionary body that fomented Libertarian Communism in the countryside and eluded the control of the government. But only after the power of the CNT and FAI had been broken in the neighbouring region of Catalonia in May, 1937, and Largo Caballero had been replaced by Juan Negrín, the moderate Socialist leader and ally of the Communists, was it possible for the government to take decisive measures against the Council. After the Communists had prepared the way for its dissolution by a short though fierce campaign at the beginning of August (see *Frente Rojo*, August 4, 1937; *Verdad*, August 5, 1937; *Fragua Social's* comments, August 5, 1937; Duque, "La situación en Aragón al comienzo de la guerra," pp. 36-43), and the 11th Division commanded by the Communist Enrique Lister had been ordered to move into the region, a decree was issued dissolving the Council (*Gaceta de la República*, August 11, 1937). Commenting on the decree, *Adelante*, mouthpiece

newly appointed Governor General, José Ignacio Mantecón, a member of the Left Republican Party, but a secret Communist sympathizer,[33] basing his authority on the Communist-controlled 11th Division under Enrique Lister, which had just been sent to Aragon, ordered the break-up of the collective farms. According to a report of the Aragon CNT, the land, farm implements, horses, and cattle confiscated from right-wing supporters were returned to their former owners or to their families; new buildings erected by the collectives, such as stables and hen-coops, were destroyed, and in some villages the farms were deprived even of the seed necessary for sowing, while six hundred members of the CNT were arrested.[34] Of this repression the tenant farmers and small owners who had entered the collective farms in the early weeks of the revolution took full advantage. They divided up the land as well as the crops and farm implements, and, with the aid of the Assault Guards and Communist military forces, even raided those collectives that had been established in accordance with the wishes of their members.

The situation became so serious that the Communists, although evading personal responsibility, later acknowledged that a dangerous

---

at that time of the moderate Socialists in the government, said (August 12, 1937): "Perhaps the change that took place yesterday in Aragonese territory may not have extraordinary repercussions abroad. No matter. It deserves to have them, because by this action the government offers the firmest testimony of its authority."

[33] After the Civil War, when in exile, Mantecón joined the Communist Party. See the Spanish Communist refugee periodical, *España Popular*, January 23, 1948.

[34] *Fragua Social*, October 23, 1937. In a conversation with the author a few years after the war, José Duque, one of the two Communist members of the Defence Council of Aragon, stated, when he was no longer a Communist, that in his opinion Lister's measures were more severe than they need have been. This view was also held by Manuel Almudí, the other Communist on the Defence Council, who, when interviewed by the author after the war, stated (speaking as a Communist): "Lister's measures in Aragon were very harsh. He could have acted with greater discretion. Great ill feeling was aroused as a result of his conduct." Accounts of the dissolution of the Defence Council and the repression that followed can be found in *Acción Libertaria. Boletín Inform-ativo sobre España*, September 22, 1937; *Cultura Proletaria*, January 17, 1948 (article by Miguel Jiménez); *Documentos Históricos de España*, May, 1939 (summary of a report of the Aragon CNT to the central government); *L'Espagne Nouvelle*, October 1, 29, 1937; *Frente Libertario*, August 27, 1937; *Juventud Libre*, September 4, 1937; *Spanish Labour Bulletin*, February 3, 1938; *Spanish Revolution*, October 22, 1937, February 28, 1938; Prats, *Vanguardia y retaguardia de Aragón*, pp. 157-8.

policy had been adopted. "It was in Aragon," wrote José Silva, general secretary of the Institute of Agrarian Reform and a Communist Party member, "where the most varied and strange experiments in collectivization and socialization were made, where undoubtedly the most violence was used in order to compel the peasants to enter the collective farms, and where a manifestly false policy tore open serious breaches in rural economy. When the Government of the Republic dissolved the Council of Aragon, the Governor General tried to allay the profound uneasiness in the hearts of the peasant masses by dissolving the collectives. This measure was a very grave mistake, and produced tremendous disorganization in the countryside. Under cover of the order issued by the Governor General, those persons who were discontented with the collectives—and who had good reason for being so, if the methods employed in forming them are taken into account—took them by assault, carrying away and dividing up the harvest and farm implements without respecting the collectives that had been formed without violence or pressure, that were prosperous, and that were a model of organization, like the one in Candasmo.

"It is true that the Governor's aim was to repair injustices and to convince the workers of the countryside that the Republic was protecting them, but the result was just the opposite from that intended. The measure only increased the confusion, and violence was exercised, but this time by the other side. As a result, labour in the fields was suspended almost entirely, and a quarter of the land had not been prepared at the time for sowing."[35]

In order to redress this situation the Communist Party had once again to change its policy, and some of the dismantled collectives were restored. "The recognition of the rights of the collectives," Silva added, "and the decision to return what had been unjustly taken away from them, together with the efforts of the Governor General of Aragon in this direction, brought things back to normal. Tranquillity returned, and enthusiasm was revived among the peasants, who gave the necessary labour for sowing the abandoned land."[36] But although the situation in Aragon improved in some degree, the hatreds and resentments generated by the break-up of the collectives and by the repression that followed were never wholly dispelled. Nor was the resultant disillusionment that sapped the spirit of the Anarchosyndicalist forces on the Aragon front ever entirely removed, a disillusionment that no doubt contributed to the collapse of that front a few months later.

[35] *La revolución popular en el campo*, p. 17.
[36] *Ibid.*, pp. 17–18.

If, after the destruction of the collective farms in Aragon, the Communist Party was compelled to modify its policy, and support collectives also in other regions against former owners who sought the return of confiscated land,[37] this was due not only to the damage inflicted on rural economy and on morale at the front and in the rear by its previous policy, but to another important factor: much as the Communist Party needed the backing of the small and medium tenant farmer and proprietor in the anti-Franco camp, it could not allow them to become too strong, lest, under the leadership of the liberal Republicans, they should, in conjunction with the urban middle classes, endeavour to take the affairs of state into their own hands. In order to guide domestic and foreign policy in accordance with Russia's diplomatic needs, the Communists themselves had to be supreme. And this they could be only by a careful interplay of the pieces on the board; for their influence rested not only on the inherent strength of their own party, powerful that it was, but on a careful balancing of class forces, which, because of their mutual antagonisms, could not combine against the arbiter that stood between. Hence, if in the beginning it was essential for the Communists to destroy the power of the extreme Left by an alliance with the middle strata of the population, it was no less important at a later stage to prevent these layers from acquiring too much strength and threatening the supremacy of their party.

But no attempt on the part of the Communists to balance one class against another could succeed for long unless they could gain control of the armed forces, both at the front as well as in the rear, unless they could incorporate the independent revolutionary militia into a regular army under the command of a staff of officers and political commissars amenable to their wishes.

[37] See, for example, *Frente Rojo*, January 27, 1938.

PART IV

FROM THE REVOLUTIONARY
MILITIA TO A REGULAR ARMY

19

The Revolutionary Militia

THE reader will remember that the government of liberal Republicans formed by José Giral at the outset of the military rebellion inherited a régime without an army. As a result, the weight of the struggle at the fronts fell upon the trade unions and proletarian parties, which organized militia forces under commanders appointed or elected from among the most resolute and respected of their men. These militia units, or "columns," as they were called, to which army officers were attached under the watchful eye of party or trade union representatives,[1] were controlled exclusively by the organizations that had created them, the office of the War Minister being an empty title and possessing no authority as far as they were concerned.[2]

In order to create a counterpoise to the revolutionary militia, no less than to organize additional armed units for service at the front, the liberal middle-class government of José Giral decided, during the last days of July, to call up two years of conscripts,[3] a measure that met with trifling response, not only because many of the men were already in the militia, but also because the government did not possess any coercive machinery for enforcing the draft. Furthermore, it published a decree providing for the creation of "volunteer battalions,"[4] and two weeks later, in a still more significant move, it issued a series of decrees

---

[1] "When, out of absolute necessity, [the working-class organizations] had to make use of us," complains a Republican army officer, "they employed only the minimum of loyal officers strictly indispensable to their needs; these were kept under constant vigilance and were, in addition, menaced because of their alleged fascist sympathies."—Pérez Salas, *Guerra en España*, p. 259. See also Romero Solano, *Vísperas de la guerra de España*, p. 308.

[2] See Martín Blázquez (an officer in the War Ministry), *I Helped to Build an Army*, p. 189; Pérez Salas, *Guerra en España*, p. 115.

[3] *Gaceta de Madrid*, July 28, 1936.

[4] *Ibid.*, August 3, 1936.

aimed at the formation of a "volunteer army," which was to be raised
from among men in the first-line reserve, with cadres composed of
retired officers and of non-commissioned officers not then on active
service, whose loyalty had been attested by a Popular Front organization.[5] But the effect of these measures too was negligible, because the
average volunteer preferred to enlist in one of the militia units organized by his party or labour union; moreover, the idea of an army under
the control of the government—a government whose Premier, José
Giral, and War Minister, Hernández Sarabia, were both stalwart supporters of the conservative-minded President of the Republic, Manuel
Azaña—was viewed with alarm not only by the Anarchosyndicalists of
the CNT[6] but also by the left-wing Socialists of the UGT, whose
secretary, Largo Caballero, had several violent interviews with José
Giral on this account.[7] In an editorial published two days after the
promulgation of the decree, *Claridad*, the mouthpiece of Largo
Caballero, declared that the measures could not be justified either on
the ground that the militia forces were not large enough numerically
to carry on the war or on the ground that they lacked efficiency; that
the number of men incorporated in them or who desired to join them
could be considered "virtually unlimited," and that as far as their
military efficiency was concerned "it could not be greater and we doubt
whether it could be surpassed by any other armed organization."
Furthermore, it affirmed that the reserve soldiers who had not yet
volunteered for service in any other force were "not animated, however great their loyalty to the Republic, by the same political and
combative ardour that had induced the militiamen to enlist," and that
the preferential right granted them under the terms of the decree to
enrol in the regular army units that would be organized after the war
would not stimulate the fighting zeal of the militia. Having disposed
of the military arguments in favour of the volunteer army, the editorial
continued:

"The new army, if there must be one, should have as its foundation
the men who are fighting today and not merely those who have not
yet fought in this war. It must be an army that is in keeping with the
revolution . . . to which the future state will have to adjust itself. To
think of replacing the present combatants by another type of army

---

[5] *Ibid.*, August 18, 1936.

[6] See p. 246, below.

[7] Information given to the author by Giral himself, who also stated that
Caballero had a "violent temper" and "put up a terrible opposition to the
formation of the volunteer army."

which, to a certain extent, would control their revolutionary action, is to think in a counter-revolutionary way. That is what Lenin said (*State and Revolution*): 'Every revolution, after destroying the state apparatus, shows us how the governing class attempts to re-establish special bodies of armed men at "its" service, and how the oppressed class tries to create a new organization of this type capable of serving not the exploiters but the exploited.' "[8]

Unlike the left-wing Socialists, the Communists entertained no misgivings about the projected army, and, indeed, aided the Giral Cabinet in implementing its decrees.[9] Yet, if, as has already been shown, their championship of this government sprang from the need to keep it in office as a democratic veil to influence the Western world,[10] if, in particular, their support of the military decrees was inspired by a desire to create a centralized force of greater combat efficiency than the militia, it also had a more subtle motive; for the Communists not only regarded the decrees as a step towards a permanently organized army of the state, over which they hoped, in the course of time, by systematic and adroit penetration, to establish their supremacy, but they knew that as long as the trade unions and parties possessed their own armed units, that as long as these units had not been merged into a regular army whose pivotal positions they themselves controlled, their own party could never be master of the anti-Franco camp.

In their endeavours to quiet the fears of the Caballero Socialists with regard to the creation of the volunteer army, the Communists were careful to conceal the political motive of their support under the sole and powerful argument of military efficiency, and to refrain, as yet, from calling for the fusion of the militia into a government-controlled army, a demand that was soon to become an important item in their declared programme.

". . . We believe," wrote their central organ, *Mundo Obrero*, "that all the parties and organizations belonging to the Popular Front will agree with us on the necessity of creating in the shortest possible time an army with all the technical efficiency required by a modern war. There can be no doubt that the cornerstone of our army is our heroic popular militia. But it is not enough to romance about its self-sacrifice and heroism. We must give thought to the measures that should be put into effect immediately with a view to increasing the efficiency of the people in arms. . . .

[8] August 20, 1936.
[9] According to Giral, when interviewed by author.
[10] See p. 108, above.

"Some comrades have wished to see in the creation of the new volunteer army something like a detraction from the role of the militia, possibly because the decree lacks sufficient clarification. Undoubtedly the militia should enjoy all the advantages conceded to the volunteer army, and we do not entertain the least doubt that the government will say so immediately, because no one under present circumstances could think of creating anything that runs counter to our glorious popular militia. Actually, the aim of the decree is to complement and reinforce the popular army, to give it greater efficiency, and to end the war as soon as possible."[11]

But the issue of a further decree granting militiamen the same preferential right as conceded to members of the volunteer army[12] did nothing to remove the uneasiness that the government's project had created in the minds of the left-wing Socialists; and the appointment of Diego Martínez Barrio—who had formed the ill-starred Cabinet of conciliation on the morning of July 19,[13] and whose party, the Republican Union, stood on the right flank of the Popular Front coalition—to head the commission charged with the organization of this army,[14] only tended to deepen their suspicion of the government's intentions. It was this suspicion, superimposed upon the imminent threat to Madrid consequent upon the rapid advance of General Franco's forces—an advance that had carried them more than 230 miles in twenty days after their capture of Badajoz on August 14—that impelled José Giral, weary of presiding over a government to which the power of state belonged on paper only and which would certainly be held responsible if Madrid should fall, to resign his post.

It was in these circumstances, as has already been shown, that a new government was formed on September 4, with Largo Caballero as Premier and War Minister.

The first major problems that confronted Largo Caballero in his new capacity were undoubtedly the defects of the militia system; for, in spite of *Claridad's* claim that the efficiency of the militia could not be greater, these defects were indubitably among the principal reasons for General Franco's swift advance up the Tagus valley towards the Spanish capital. True, they did not spring from any lack of combativity, for in street fighting or in small battles against a localized enemy, the

[11] August 21, 1936.
[12] *Gaceta de Madrid*, August 27, 1936.
[13] See p. 29, above.
[14] See *Política*, August 19, 1936.

militiamen showed great courage; they sprang rather from lack of training and discipline,[15] from the absence of any effective unity, either of conception or of action, among the militia units, and from the rivalry existing between the various organizations. On the Aragon front, for example, according to Jesús Pérez Salas, a professional officer and a loyal Republican who commanded the *Macià-Companys* column in the early months of the war, it was impossible to carry out a combined operation involving different units. "Whenever the staff decided upon an operation of this kind, . . . it was obliged to call the [militia] commanders to headquarters and explain to all of them the fundamental objective of the operation and the role that each column was to play. Thereupon, a debate was initiated, during which the militia commanders expressed their agreement or disagreement, often forcing a change in the original plan by their vetoes. After a great struggle, an agreement was reached but always with respect to an operation on a reduced scale and of much smaller scope. Even so, it was never carried out, because when the time came for undertaking the operation there

[15] "It is hardly necessary to say," wrote a left-wing observer, "that these troops made every mistake that can be made. Night attacks were launched with *vivas* for the revolution; artillery was often placed on the same line as the infantry. Sometimes there were really grotesque incidents. One day a militiaman told me that after lunch a whole detachment went into a neighbouring field to eat grapes; when it returned its position was occupied by the enemy."— Kaminski, *Ceux de Barcelone*, p. 244. Referring to the offensives launched by Catalan militia forces against the besieged town of Huesca, Manuel Aznar, a supporter of General Franco, writes in his *Historia militar de la guerra de España*, pp. 601–2: ". . . in the early days, the attacks of the Catalan columns, nearly all of which were made up of Anarchist militia, were so completely uncoordinated and so divorced from the norms of military technique that their movements resembled the arbitrary efforts of disintegrated hordes rather than genuine military operations. As a result, Nationalist headquarters gained two to three months in which to assemble reinforcements, to learn from their own weaknesses, to concentrate war material, and to prepare for the transition from an elastic to a rigid defence. Furthermore, it could be seen from the concentration of artillery fire, the disposition of machine guns, the preparation of assaults, the bad organization of the troops, the irresolution of the subaltern commanders, and from the weakness of the offensives that the besieging army lacked the most essential pyschological and technical elements for war." See also *ibid.*, p. 106. For materials on the matter of discipline, see, for example, Pérez Salas, *Guerra en España*, p. 145; verbatim report of a meeting of political and military leaders on the Aragon front in September, 1936; speech by Enrique Lister, quoted in *Mundo Obrero*, October 12, 1936. For a frank account of the behaviour of the Socialist militia on the Toledo front, see Romero Solano (former Socialist deputy for Cáceres), *Vísperas de la guerra de España*, pp. 308–10.

was always somebody who acted tardily, upsetting that co-ordination which is the key to success.

"This was due to the fact that orders, even within each sector, were never carried out precisely, and that, as forces of very distinct ideology existed on the front, each one of them looked upon the failure of the others with a certain degree of satisfaction. The CNT, which formed the bulk of the forces, wished for the defeat of its political enemies of the POUM and the PSUC with all its heart. These, in their turn, held the men of the CNT in abomination."[16]

". . . Sectarianism, differences in outlook, and proselytizing zeal," wrote a prominent member of the CNT and FAI, "resulted not only in the militia units being indifferent to one another's existence and forgetting that they had a common foe, but also, on many occasions, in really dangerous situations arising between them."[17]

"Party pride seemed stronger than the feeling of common defence," writes Arturo Barea, who was in frequent contact with militiamen returning from the Madrid front. "A victory of an Anarchist battalion was paraded in the face of the Communists; a victory of a Communist unit was secretly lamented by the others. The defeat of a battalion was turned into ridicule for the political group to which it belonged. This strengthened the fighting spirit of the individual units, but also created a hotbed of mutual resentment damaging the military operations as a whole, and circumventing a unified command."[18]

But the most striking overall account of the situation obtaining at the fronts in the early months of the Civil War is given by the Republican officer, Major Aberri, who was sent from Barcelona to assist in the reorganization of the Aragon front:

"On approaching Sariñena [headquarters of the militia forces], I came across a truck halted on the other side of the highway, and, at the request of a group of soldiers, I stopped my car. Their truck has broken down, but they did not know what was wrong with it. . . .

" 'Where are you going?' I asked them with surprise.

" 'To Barcelona, to spend the Sunday there.'

" 'But aren't you supposed to be at the front?'

" 'Sure, but as there's nothing doing we are going to Barcelona.'

" 'Have you been given leave?'

" 'No. Can't you see we are militiamen?'

"They did not understand my question, because it was the most

---

[16] *Guerra en España*, pp. 131–2.
[17] Miguel González Inestal in *Internacional*, July–August, 1938.
[18] *The Forging of a Rebel*, pp. 536–7.

natural thing in the world for them to leave the front when it was quiet. They knew nothing of discipline, and it was clear that nobody had bothered to instruct them on the subject. After a forty-hour week at the front they got bored and left it. . . .

"... Once [in Sariñena] I reported to the commander of the [Aragon] front [a professional officer] and informed him of my assignment. I told him what plans I had in mind, what I thought it necessary to do. He looked at me pityingly, and then replied:

" 'We shall see. We shall see. Things are not what they used to be, and you have to be pretty smart to get along with these fellows. At any rate I am having a conference with the heads of the [militia] columns very soon, and you will have an opportunity to judge for yourself. Meanwhile, stay and have lunch with me. . . .' We spoke at length during the meal and he told me about his tragedy; he had no authority and could not make himself obeyed by anybody. The leaders of the columns were demigods who accepted neither orders, advice, nor suggestions.

" 'You will see for yourself! The war cannot be waged in this way. I have no supplies; war material is distributed by the parties and trade unions; arms are not sent where they are most needed, but where [these organizations] decide. . . .'

"The leaders of some of the columns arrived. . . . The majority of them had never served in the army. Some were accompanied by professional officers, who were called technicians, but who unfortunately were without authority. Their role was an auxiliary one and their advice was to no purpose. Also to no purpose were the mortifications we officers had to suffer in spite of the fact that we had been loyal to our oath and had risked our all. Nobody had any confidence in us: any Tom, Dick, or Harry thought he had a right to spy on us and ignore our suggestions. . . .

"... The commander of the Aragon front recommended that a decisive operation be launched against Huesca. Everything pointed to the fact that the historic Aragonese town was almost without protection, and that with an intelligent and well co-ordinated attack it could have fallen into the hands of the Republic. . . . Those present listened to his plan, which was discussed in detail, but unfortunately they finally decided to consult their respective trade union organizations before accepting anything. In the end the discussion took a very regrettable turn, because the Commander's request that some of the columns should hand over to other units the additional material they needed was rejected out of hand. In other words, the commander of the front had absolutely no authority to decide on the disposition of men and arms.

"I point these things out, even though briefly, since they accurately reflect the predicament of a people who, because of a lamentable indiscipline and a tremendous lack of equipment, had to perform prodigies of heroism in order to resist a regular army. . . . What could they not have achieved with good leaders, with sufficient war material, and with military discipline? I saw this later when I visited the different sectors of the front. There were no fortifications at that time. A position was taken by sheer courage, but since nobody bothered to fortify it, it was lost during the next enemy counter-attack. The employment of war material was equally absurd. I was once in a position where there were several 10·5 guns, but there were no munitions. These were in the possession of a nearby column, which refused to part with them although it had no artillery itself. . . .

"The system of trenches was also in keeping with the situation. At some points parapets had been thrown up with an eye to a neighbouring column, which belonged to a different political organization. There was a certain amount of satisfaction when a rival got a beating from the enemy. . . .

"During my mission on the Huesca front, I had to pass a night very near the enemy lines. I was tired and I lay down to sleep, but shortly after wrapping myself up in my blanket, I heard someone singing at the top of his lungs. I got up and found a sentinel singing a jota for all he was worth.

" 'Listen,' I said. 'Don't you know that a sentinel should keep quiet?'

" 'Who the hell cares! That's what things were like in the past.'

" 'No, man, no! They should be the same now. Don't you realize that they could spot you and plug a bullet into you from the other side?'

" 'Nuts! We have agreed not to plug one another. Besides, if I don't sing, I'll fall asleep.'

"In face of such reasoning I retired to my improvised 'dormitory'— a blanket, the earth, and the grass—ready to sleep when this yokel of a guard had finished his repertoire. But no sooner had he stopped singing than I heard him speaking with a loud voice, as though carrying on a discussion with someone at a distance. I got up from my nook again and saw with amazement—afterwards nothing amazed me—that our sentinel was talking to the sentinel on the fascist side of the lines, who was asking him what he had eaten for dinner. Our man, laying it on thick, gave him a pantagruellian menu. Lucullan had eaten at his own table.

" 'You've eaten that!' retorted the other. 'You've only eaten potatoes and you've had to be thankful for them!'

" 'You mean that's all you've had, and things are going to get even worse for you. We have everything we want here. Come over and you'll soon see.'

"Turning down this offer, the other fellow replied with an invitation to a certain member of his enemy's family, whom he qualified in not very academic language [your whore of a mother],[19] to come over to his own lines, adding, 'And shut up, you starving rat!'

" 'Starving rat!' exclaimed our sentinel. 'Just to show you that we have more food than we need, here's a sausage for you.'

"And without further ado, he flung a hand grenade over the parapet. The result was inevitable. Within a few seconds the firing became general along the entire front. Hand grenades, rifles, and machine guns performed their fantastic symphony for a good quarter of an hour.

"Then silence fell, but only after several thousand cartridges had been wasted stupidly."[20]

In addition to all the aforementioned defects, the militia system had other notable shortcomings: there was no central General Staff in the proper sense of the word,[21] nor any central body that could review the situation on all the battle fronts, formulate a common plan of action, and decide on the allocation of available supplies of men, munitions,

[19] This typically Spanish insult is what Major Aberri implies.

[20] *Hoy*, August 12, 1939.

[21] Martín Blázquez, an officer in the War Ministry under Hernández Sarabia and Largo Caballero, writes (*I Helped to Build an Army*, p. 143): "There was, of course, no General Staff, but its functions were partly fulfilled by the Intelligence Department, which received all cables and wireless messages. . . . Most of the other departments of the General Staff were not created until after . . . Largo Caballero became Minister of War." It is worthy of remark that the War Ministry under Hernández Sarabia had to rely upon the working-class organizations for much of its information. "In the offices of the UGT in Madrid," writes Alvarez del Vayo, *Freedom's Battle*, p. 28, "a permanent Information Bureau was set up, and this for some time was the War Ministry's finest news agency. From every province, from every village where a representative of this organization was installed, the slightest movement of rebel troops was telephoned immediately to the central office." See also Romero Solano, *Vísperas de la guerra de España*, p. 308, and speech by Rodolfo Llopis reported in *La Correspondencia de Valencia*, August 13, 1937.

arms, and motor vehicles[22] in such a way as to produce the best results on the most promising front. Each party and trade union had its own military headquarters, its own supply services, its own transport section, which, in most cases, attended to the requirements of its own militia without any knowledge of, and without regard to, the needs of other units on the same or neighbouring sector, least of all on distant fronts, and, frequently, supplies of one unit were stolen by another.[23]

Whereas the strength of General Franco's forces during the first few months of the war lay largely in the Moors and Foreign Legionaries with their stern discipline, training, and professional cadres,[24] and in the modern aircraft that had been arriving from Italy and Germany since the first weeks of the war,[25] the militia units, with few exceptions, had no staff of officers they would trust to lead them into the field; were, for the most part, ignorant of the organization of war, of co-operation between sections and companies, of the use of cover and camouflage, of the digging of trenches; were subject to the orders

[22] In the first months of the war, it should be observed, the War Ministry did not exercise any authority in the field of transport and had to reply upon a National Committee of Road Transport, dominated by representatives of the CNT and UGT transport unions (see decree published in the *Gaceta de Madrid*, August 3, 1936, and subsequent amendments, *ibid.*, September 20, October 4, 1936). Not only did the committee pay little attention to the demands of the War Ministry (see, for example, Martín Blázquez, *I Helped to Build an Army*, pp. 131–4, whose testimony was amply confirmed to the author by Alejandro García Val, Director of Road Transport later in the war), but its orders were very often disregarded by militia units, committees, trade union branches, and local party headquarters, which retained what vehicles they could for their own use without regard to general requirements.—See Carreño España on the Madrid transport problem, as recorded in the minutes of the Madrid Defence Council (*Actas de la Junta de Defensa de Madrid*, p. 456).

[23] See, for example, Manuel Azaña, *La velada en Benicarló*, p. 107. Alejandro García Val, a commander at one time of the Communist Party's Fifth Regiment, told the author after the war that the regiment often stole vehicles from the CNT in order to compensate for its own deficiency.

[24] This is confirmed by German diplomats in General Franco's territory.—See Hans Hermann Voelckers' and Lieutenant General Wilhelm Faupel's communications to the German Foreign Ministry, as given in *Documents on German Foreign Policy 1918–1945.* III. *Germany and the Spanish Civil War 1936–1939*, pp. 137–9, 159–62. It should be mentioned here that the Carlist (Monarchist) and Falangist (fascist) militia units, which, in the early months of the war, were not subordinate to the regular army, suffered from some of the defects of the left-wing militia. According to Ramón Serrano Suñer, Foreign Minister and member of the Falange, they were "not always sufficiently disciplined."—*Entre Hendaya y Gibraltar*, p. 43.

[25] See n. 1, pp. 95–6, n. 8, pp. 98–9, above.

of no central military authority; had little or no discipline, and had no modern aircraft to protect them until the adversary reached the very gates of Madrid at the beginning of November.[26] In such circumstances, they were not only incapable of any sustained offensive action in the first months of the war, and at many points wasted month after month in fruitless sieges,[27] but they often crumbled under the onset of the enemy.

[26] Although Russian bombers reached Spain in October, the first combat aeroplanes did not arrive until November 2. See n. 9, pp. 99–100, above.

[27] "It is a phenomenon of this war that when towns held by the fascists are attacked they hold out for a long time and that [when we are attacked] we do not resist at all. They surround a small town, and after a couple of days it is taken; but when we surround one we spend our entire life there."—García Oliver, CNT–FAI leader, at a meeting of political and military leaders on the Aragon front in September, 1936.—See verbatim report. For two revealing accounts by eye-witnesses in the anti-Franco camp of the chaos during the siege of the Alcazar of Toledo, see Louis Fischer, *Men and Politics*, pp. 359–62, 365–9; article by Clara Candiani in *La Dépêche de Toulouse*, October 3, 1936.

20

Discipline and the Anarchosyndicalist Militia

O F the manifold defects of the militia system that General Franco's victories forced to the front during the first weeks of the war, none was more hotly debated, none called for more urgent correction than the lack of discipline. If this problem beset all the militia units, whatever their ideology, it was only in those formed by the Libertarian movement that its solution encountered a philosophical impediment, for the liberty of the individual is the very core of Anarchism and nothing is so antipodal to its nature as submission to authority. "Discipline is obedience to authority; Anarchism recognizes no authority," said *La Revista Blanca*, a leading Anarchist journal, in an issue published before the Civil War.[1]

The CNT–FAI militia reflected the ideals of equality, individual liberty, and freedom from obligatory discipline integral to the Anarchist doctrine. There was no officers' hierarchy, no saluting, no regimentation. "A CNT member will never be a disciplined militiaman togged up in a braided uniform, strutting with martial gait through the streets of Madrid, and rhythmically swinging his arms and legs," said an article in *CNT*.[2] And a resolution approved at a regional congress of the Valencia CNT stated: "When a comrade enters the CNT barracks, he must understand that the word barracks does not signify subjection to odious military regulations consisting of salutes, parades, and other trivialities of the kind, completely theatrical and negating every revolutionary ideal."[3] If there was no discipline in the CNT–FAI militia units in the early days of the Civil War, there were also no military titles, badges, or distinctions in the way of food, clothing, and quarters, and the few professional military men whose

[1] June 22, 1934. [2] August 22, 1936.
[3] *Fragua Social*, November 18, 1936.

216

services were accepted acted only in an advisory capacity.[4] The basic unit was the group, composed generally of ten men;[5] each group elected a delegate, whose functions were somewhat akin to those of a non-commissioned officer of the lowest rank, but without the equivalent authority. Ten groups formed a century which also elected its own delegate, and any number of centuries made up a *columna,* or "column,"[6] at whose head stood a committee of war.[7] This committee was likewise elective and was divided into various sections in accordance with the needs of the column.[8] The gradation into group and century delegates and a committee of war did not imply the existence of any permanent staff with special privileges since all delegates could be removed as soon as they failed to reflect the wishes of the men who had elected them.[9] "The first impression one gets," ran a CNT–FAI account, "is the total absence of hierarchy. . . . There is no one giving orders by authority."[10] Nevertheless, duties had to be assigned, and in such a way as to avoid friction. In the Anarchist Iron Column, for example, lots were drawn by the militiamen to decide on who should stand guard at night and who in the early morning.[11]

But so serious were the drawbacks of this anti-authoritarian system, particularly in the field of battle, that there was soon a widespread call for discipline. "On repeated occasions we have stated that we do not believe in the discipline of the convent or of the barracks," declared *Solidaridad Obrera,* the leading organ of the CNT, "but that in actions in which a large number of persons participate a precise coincidence of views and a perfect co-ordination of effort are indispensable.

"In the course of the last few days we have witnessed certain things that have broken our hearts and made us somewhat pessimistic. Our

---

[4] For further details see the Anarchist *Nosotros,* February 16, March 12, 13, 15–17, 1937, the CNT papers, *Fragua Social,* September 8, November 14, 18, 1936, and *Solidaridad Obrera,* September 24, 1936, also Lazarillo del Tormes (Benigno Bejarano), *España, tumba del fascismo,* p. 82.

[5] On the Madrid front the group consisted of twenty men.—Guzmán, *Madrid, rojo y negro,* p. 78.

[6] On the Madrid front there were also battalions composed of a certain number of centuries.—*Ibid.*

[7] See, for example, resolution passed at the Regional Congress of the Valencia CNT establishing a uniform structure for the CNT–FAI columns formed in that region, *Fragua Social,* November 18, 1936.

[8] *Ibid.*

[9] *Ibid.* See also statement by Buenaventura Durruti in *CNT,* October 6, 1936.

[10] *Boletín de Información,* CNT–FAI, as given in *Spanish Revolution,* January 8, 1936.

[11] *Fragua Social,* September 8, 1936.

comrades act independently and in a great number of cases ignore the slogans issued by the [directing] Committees [of the CNT].

"The revolution will escape from our hands; we shall be massacred from lack of co-ordination if we do not make up our minds to give the word discipline its real meaning.

"To accept discipline means that the decisions made by comrades assigned to any particular task, whether administrative or military, should be executed without any obstruction in the name of liberty, a liberty which in many cases degenerates into wantonness."[12]

Gaston Leval, the well-known Anarchist writer, maintained that it was incongruous to try to wage war on the basis of Anarchist ideas, because "war and Anarchism are two conditions of humanity that are mutually repugnant; one is destruction and extermination, the other is creation and harmony; one implies the triumph of violence, the other the triumph of love." There were in the rear, he said, a large number of comrades who at first had rejected discipline altogether and then had accepted self-discipline, but "if self-discipline results in an effectual collective discipline in a particular column, this does not justify dangerous generalizations, because this is not the case in the majority of militia forces, and, to avoid disasters, a discipline imposed from without is essential."[13]

[12] August 7, 1936.

[13] *Fragua Social*, November 21, 1936. For other appeals for discipline, see *ibid.*, November 17, 1936 (speech by Juan Peiró), November 24, 1936 (article by Claro J. Sendón); *Solidaridad Obrera*, October 1, 1936 (article by Jaime Balius), October 3, 1936 (editorial note), October 27, 1936 (article by Luka-Zaga); December 5, 1936 (speech by García Oliver); *CNT*, October 3, 1936 (editorial), October 5, 1936 (report by the CNT of the Central Region), October 8, 1936 (speech by Federica Montseny). The following revealing anecdote about Buenaventura Durruti, the most revered of Anarchist leaders who was regarded as a purist in matters of doctrine, was contained in an article published by an Anarchosyndicalist refugee periodical: A group of young militiamen belonging to the column he commanded had left the front in panic with the object of returning to Barcelona. Apprised of their intention, Durruti hastened to intercept them: "Springing out of his car, and brandishing his revolver, he cowed them and made them face the wall. Meanwhile, a militiaman from the locality arrived on the scene and asked him for a pair of shoes, to which he replied vigorously, 'Look at the shoes these fellows are wearing; if they are all right you can have the pair you like. There's no need for the shoes to rot in the soil.' It was very far from Durruti's mind to shoot those young-sters, because he was accustomed to say: 'Here no one is under compulsion. Those who are afraid to remain at the front can return to the rear.' But he was so convincing that all of them asked to return to the front, where they fought with unexampled heroism."—*España Libre*, Toulouse, September 11, 1949.

Nevertheless, it was not an easy task to secure acceptance of ideas that slashed at the roots of Anarchist doctrine, and not a little ingenuity was at times necessary. In an article that appeared in the organ of the Peninsular Committee of the FAI, a leading Anarchist argued: "If the war is being prolonged, this is due not only to the material help the rebels receive from the fascist countries, but also the lack of cohesion, discipline, and obedience of our militia. Some comrades will object, 'We Anarchists cannot accept the command of anyone.' To these we should reply that Anarchists also cannot accept any declaration of war, yet we have all accepted the declaration of war against fascism, because it is a question of life and death, and involves the triumph of the proletarian revolution.

"If we accept war, we must also accept discipline and authority, because without them it is impossible to win any war." Then, criticizing a statement made by a delegate at a recent FAI congress to the effect that Anarchists had always been enemies of discipline and that they should so continue, he said: "The Tarragona delegate starts from a fundamental error. We Anarchists have encouraged indiscipline against the institutions and power of the bourgeoisie, not against our own movement, nor against our own cause and our own interests. To lack discipline where the general interests of our anti-fascist movement are concerned is to condemn ourselves wittingly to failure and defeat."[14]

Whereas on static fronts the idea of obligatory discipline was slow in taking root among the CNT–FAI militia, on the fluid central front, where the advantages of General Franco's superior military organization were presented in dramatic terms, the breakdown of traditional Anarchist principles had gone so far by the beginning of October that the CNT Defence Committee of Madrid, which was in charge of the Madrid CNT–FAI militia, was able to introduce regulations that included the following articles:

> Every militiaman shall fulfil the regulations issued by battalion committees and century and group delegates.
>
> He shall not act on his own account in matters of war and will accept without discussion any post and any place to which he is assigned, both at the front and in the rear.
>
> Any militiaman not obeying the regulations issued by battalion committees and century and group delegates will be punished by his group, if the offence is slight, and by the battalion committee, if the offence is serious.
>
> Every militiaman must understand that, although he joined the militia voluntarily, he now forms part of it as a soldier of the Revolution and that his duty is to take orders and to execute them.[15]

[14] A. G. Gilabert in *Tierra y Libertad*, December 12, 1936.
[15] Published in *CNT*, October 3, 1936.

Although many Libertarians yielded to the idea of discipline as "one of the great sacrifices that the victory of redemptive ideals imposes,"[16] there were others who saw in the acceptance of the concept of authority by the Libertarian movement a blow so deadly to Anarchist principles, a threat so real to the future course of the revolution, that they could not conceal their anxiety. "We know," stated a propaganda committee of the Anarchist youth movement, "that present circumstances have compelled us, for the time being, to forget some of our dearest principles . . . but do not let us forget that the basic tenet of Anarchism is anti-authoritarianism, and that if we sail along with the authoritarian current by which some comrades have already been carried away nothing will remain of Anarchist ideas. Let us remember that other revolutions were arrested in their ascending movement and were brought to disaster when they were warped by the authoritarian disease that every revolution breeds. . . .

"No, comrades, for the sake of the ideals that animate us all, for the sake of the revolution, the Anarchist youth begs of you not to follow this path. The authoritarian germ will lead to hatred, and we must not forget that hatred in our midst is the worst enemy of the revolution."[17]

[16] *Frente Libertario*, October 20, 1936.
[17] *Ruta*, November 28, 1936.

21

The Fifth Regiment

FOR the Marxist organizations, particularly for the Communist Party, whose members were indoctrinated with the principles of leadership and control, the problem of military discipline caused no heart-searching. This is not to suggest that indiscipline did not exist in the ranks of the Communist militia;[1] it is rather that no conscientious scruples had to be overcome, no ethical principles had to be laid aside, as in the case of the Anarchosyndicalists, before the problem could be solved. The Civil War had been in progress but a few days when *Mundo Obrero*, the Communist organ, affirmed that every militiaman should get used to the idea that he belonged to a militarized corps. "Discipline, Hierarchy and Organization," it demanded. "Every man must obey his group, each group the body directly above it, and so on and so forth. In this way our victory will be assured."[2] The Communists saw in military discipline and organization the central problem of the war. They lost no time in vesting the commanders of their militia with adequate powers to enforce discipline, and undertook, through their Fifth Regiment, the training of military cadres and the formation of units with technical staffs and specialized departments.

The Fifth Regiment was their outstanding military achievement. "We had to create an army and staff at once, for most of the armed forces were with the rebels," the Italian Communist Vittorio Vidali, known in Spain as Carlos Contreras,[3] who was political commissar

---

[1] That it did exist is proved by the following extract from an article in a Communist military paper: "There are still cases, though not as frequent as before, of comrades who have no sense of responsibility, who abandon their posts in order to roam around the town, and we know that the result of such excursions is the purchase of liquor."—*Pasaremos*, December 31, 1936.

[2] July 22, 1936.

[3] Leader, after World War II, of the Trieste Communist Party.

of the regiment, told a foreign reporter. "We had at first just groups of comrades, old and young, men and women, many of whom did not even know how to use a rifle. We had no leaders, no central command, for the central command of the old army led the revolt against the Republic. We had only enthusiastic, determined people, seizing any weapons they could find, following any leaders that arose, rushing to any front which they heard it was necessary to seize from the enemy.

"In those days we took anyone who knew anything and made him an officer. Sometimes it was enough just to look into a face and see that the eyes were intelligent and determined, and say to the man: 'You are a captain. Organize and lead these men.'

"After two days we occupied the Salesian Convent—six hundred of us, of whom two hundred were Communists. We decided to organize and the War Department said: 'You will be the Fifth Battalion; already we have four other applications.'

" 'No,' we said, 'we shall be the Fifth Regiment, for we shall get at least a thousand men.'

"Well, those first four battalions remained on paper, but the fifth had six thousand men in less than ten days. During this time the [Giral] Government wrote us: 'Comrades of the Fifth Battalion,' and we answered back: 'We of the Fifth Regiment.' After we got six thousand men they admitted that we were a regiment. . . .

"We decided to create a special company which should give an example of discipline. We called it the 'Steel Company.' . . . For this company we established special slogans designed to create an iron unity. 'Never leave a comrade wounded or dead, in the hands of the enemy,' was one of these. 'If my comrade advances or retreats without orders, I have the right to shoot him' was another.

"How Madrid laughed at that. The Spaniard is such an individualist that nobody will accept such discipline, they said. Then our first Steel Company—mostly Communists and metalworkers—paraded through the city: it made a sensation.[4] After that we created twenty-eight such companies of picked men, besides the ordinary muster of our regular Fifth Regiment militia."[5]

So successful was the Fifth Regiment in its recruiting of Communists, Socialists, non-party workers and peasants, that at the peak of its development in December, 1936, it claimed that it had, no doubt

[4] See, for example, *Política*, organ of the Left Republican Party, July 30, 1936.
[5] Anna Louise Strong (associated editor at that time of the *Moscow Daily News*), *Spain in Arms*, pp. 41–3.

with some exaggeration, sixty thousand men serving on different fronts,[6] and had become metamorphosed into what its first commander-in-chief called "a great centre of political and military education."[7] Out of this centre, which supervised every aspect of the volunteers' lives, political and spiritual, as well as economic and domestic, there flowed a large number of units possessing uniformity of method and organization. "They were parts of a building set," wrote one authority, "which could be rebuilt into an army when the time came. Their officers had precise rank and their orders received the backing of a disciplinary code which the volunteers accepted on enlistment. At the same time the political enthusiasm of the combatants was watched over and fostered by the political commissars."[8]

One of the great assets of the Fifth Regiment was the collaboration not only of professional military men who had been Communist Party members before the war—such as Lieutenant-Colonel Luís Barceló, a commander of the regiment, and head of the *Inspección General de Milicias*, to which the militia units were required to apply for whatever arms and funds they needed from the War Ministry[9]—but also of other professional officers, who, though liberal Republicans in sentiment, were attracted to the Communists because of their moderate propaganda[10] and because of their superior discipline and organization, which alone seemed capable of building an army that could carry the

---

[6] Carlos Contreras, speech reported, *Mundo Obrero*, December 21, 1936; see also José Díaz, *Tres años de lucha*, p. 254, who also gives the same figure. Although the number of Fifth Regiment troops on all fronts was given as seventy thousand by one leading Communist (Pasionaria, speech reported, *Treball*, February 3, 1937) and as high as one hundred and thirty thousand by another (Enrique Lister, who succeeded Enrique Castro as commander-in-chief of the Fifth Regiment in September, 1936, quoted Simone Téry, *Front de la liberté*, p. 182), the figure of sixty thousand is more sober.

[7] Enrique Castro, quoted by Hernández, *Negro y rojo. Los anarquisatas en España*, p. 332.

[8] Ralph Bates in *The New Republic*, October 20, 1937.

[9] See notices issued by the *Inspección General de Milicias* published in *Claridad*, August 19, 25, 1936. At the outbreak of the conflict, Barceló was aide-de-camp to Casares Quiroga, the Left Republican Premier and War Minister (see Martín Blázquez, *I Helped to Build an Army*, p. 121). Although he figured publicly as a member of the Left Republican Party (see his speech reported in *La Libertad*, August 11, 1936), his real allegiance was to the Communist Party, of which he had actually been a member, according to a Spanish Communist refugee newspaper (*España Popular*, March 11, 1940) since 1935. This paper erroneously refers to him as Eduardo instead of Luís Barceló, but there is no mistaking his identity.

[10] See, for example, Pérez Salas, *Guerra en España*, p. 146.

war through to victory.[11] An advantage no less important than the collaboration of these professional officers, to say nothing of the foreign Communists with military experience, who were associated with the regiment for varying periods before helping to organize the International Brigades,[12] was the preferential treatment the regiment received, as compared with other units, in the distribution of the arms that reached Spain from the Soviet Union.[13] Indeed, it was because of this preferential treatment, because of the opportunity given to a large number of men of the regiment to train in Russia as tank operators,[14] no less than because of the pull of the Communists' efficiency, that the regiment was able to recruit heavily from non-Communist sources.

If the influx of many Socialists and Republicans would appear to support the Communist contention that the Fifth Regiment was not a Communist force but a force that belonged to the Popular Front as a whole,[15] it was, nevertheless, under the rigid and all-embracing control

[11] "The Communist Party must be granted the credit of having set the example in accepting discipline," writes a non-Communist professional officer (Martín Blázquez, *I Helped to Build an Army*, p. 205). "By doing so it enormously increased not only its prestige, but its numbers. Innumerable men who wished to enlist and fight for their country joined the Communist Party.

"It often happened that, when I came across a man who was just leaving for the front, I asked him:

" 'But why did you join the Communist Party? You were never a Communist, were you? You were always a Republican.'

" 'I joined the Communists because they are disciplined and do their job better than anybody else,' was the answer."

[12] According to information given to the author by Carlos Contreras.

[13] Referring to the light arms which began to arrive in September, Segismundo Casado, who was Operations Chief on the War Ministry General Staff, when Largo Caballero became Minister of War, writes: "I noticed that these were not being given out in equal quantities, but that there was a marked preference for the units which made up the so-called Fifth Regiment."—*Last Days of Madrid*, p. 51. The commander-in-chief of the Fifth Regiment declared, at the time of its dissolution (speech reported in *Pasaremos*, January 31, 1937), that it had thousands of machine guns and hundreds of pieces of artillery —a wealth of material certainly unequalled by any other force in the anti-Franco zone at that stage of the war. A commissar of one of the International Brigades, a Communist at that time, confirmed to the author after the war that the units of the Fifth Regiment received "the cream of the weapons." For complaints by the CNT that its units were being discriminated against in the distribution of arms, see, for example, *Frente Libertario*, October 24, 27, 1936.

[14] According to information given to the author by Carlos Contreras.

[15] "The story has been spread by interested persons that the Fifth Regiment was the military organization of the Communist Party, a military force of the party," wrote its commander-in-chief. "No, the fact that a large number of the

of the Communist Party,[16] and was to all intents and purposes the principal element of its armed power in Central and Southern Spain.

---

officers were Communists does not mean that the Fifth Regiment was an auxiliary of the Communist Party, and anyone affirming this would be departing from historical truth. The Fifth Regiment was this: the military organization of the Popular Front. Its political composition was as follows: Communists 50 per cent; Socialists 25 per cent; Republicans 15 per cent; without party affiliation 10 per cent."—Quoted by Hernández, *Negro y rojo. Los anarquistas en España*, p. 331. See also Díaz, *Tres años de lucha*, p. 254; Pasionaria, speech in Valencia, reported in *Frente Rojo*, February 20, 1937.

[16] "From the beginning," ran an article in the Communist *International Press Correspondence*, February 6, 1937, "the Fifth Regiment was recruited and politically influenced by the Communist Party." See also "El Campesino" (an ex-Communist), *La vie et la mort en U.R.S.S.*, p. 12.

22

Honeycombing the Army

IMPORTANT though the Fifth Regiment was to the Communist Party as an element of armed power, there were potent reasons of a political as well as of a military nature why it soon proposed that the independent party and trade union militia should be incorporated into a government-controlled force. Not only did it hold that the war could not be carried through to victory without a single command that could decide on the disposition and manner of employment of all the fighting forces—in default of which there could be neither an organized army nor any planned strategy—but it knew that as long as the parties and trade unions possessed their own militia under the control of their own leaders, that as long as these forces had not been fused into a regular army consolidated by the power of discipline and authority, an army of whose levers of command it aimed to secure control, it could never be the ruling force in the anti-Franco zone, determining, behind the curtain of democratic institutions, its domestic and foreign policies.

During the life of the Giral Cabinet, it will be recalled, the Communists had refrained from calling for the merging of the militia into a government-controlled army because of the Caballero Socialists' distrust of that Cabinet's intentions,[1] but once Largo Caballero himself was at the helm they could do so without equivocation.[2] Indeed, it was in no small degree due to the insistence of the Communist minister and the Soviet military advisers who, in urging their demands, made full use of the succession of defeats on the central front—highlighted on September 27 by the capture of Toledo, fifty-one miles from the capital—that measures were promulgated providing for the militarization of the militia and the creation of a military force, or People's Army, as it was called, on a conscripted basis and under the supreme

[1] See p. 207, above.
[2] See, for example, *Mundo Obrero*, September 17, 1936.

command of the War Minister.[3] But it was a long way, as events will show, from the publication to a thoroughgoing execution of these measures, and in succeeding months, the Communists, in barracks and trenches, in public addresses, and in the Cabinet itself, pressed for their enforcement.[4]

In order to set an example to others, the Communist Party progressively broke up its own Fifth Regiment,[5] whose battalions, together with other forces, were welded into the "mixed brigades"[6] of the embryonic regular army, Enrique Lister, head of the Fifth Regiment at that time, being made commander (with a Soviet officer at his side)[7] of the first of these units.[8] Because they took the lead in disbanding their own militia, the Communists secured for themselves the control of five of the first six brigades of the new army.[9]

While they were thus gathering into their hands the control of the first units of the new army, the Communists were not neglecting its commanding summits. Indeed, during the early weeks of Caballero's

[3] See *Gaceta de Madrid*, September 29, 30; October 16, 30, 1936. "Largo Caballero," writes Louis Fischer (*Men and Politics*, p. 354), whose personal contact with most of the leading Russians in Spain gives his testimony particular authority, ". . . long resisted the idea of a regular army, and it was only with difficulty that his Soviet military advisers persuaded him to abandon the popular but inefficient form of party armies."

[4] See editorials and speeches published in *Mundo Obrero, Verdad,* and *Milicia Popular* of the period.

[5] See *Milicia Popular*, December 17, 19, 28, 1936; also *The Volunteer for Liberty*, June 1, 1937, which gives an account of the disbanding of the Fifth Regiment.

[6] So called because they were to be composed of all arms (see Martín Blázquez, *I Helped to Build an Army*, p. 293; Colonel Segismundo Casado in *The National Review*, July, 1939, who, according to his book, *The Last Days of Madrid*, p. 52, helped to organize the brigades). The word "mixed" was also appropriate, because in addition to the old militia volunteers, the brigades consisted of recruits, professional army officers, members of the police corps, and *carabineros* (excise and customs officials).

[7] Louis Fischer, *Men and Politics*, p. 383, gives the name of this officer as "Fritz."

[8] See *Milicia Popular*, October 17, 1936.

[9] According to information given to the author by Carlos Contreras, political commissar of the Fifth Regiment, their respective commanders and the majority of their members had served in the regiment. Enrique Castro, commander-in-chief of the regiment during the first weeks of the war, informed the author that, in addition to Enrique Lister of the 1st Brigade, José María Galán, commander of the 3rd, and Gallo, commander of the 6th (not to be confused with Luigi Gallo, or Longo, of the International Brigades) were Communist Party members.

tenure of the War Ministry, they had already secured a promising foothold. This they were able to do partly because their relations with the War Minister, notwithstanding his many grievances, were still of a tolerable nature, as a result of which two of their adherents, Antonio Cordón and Alejandro García Val, were appointed to the operations section of the General Staff,[10] but mainly because in key positions in the War Ministry there were men of supposedly unquestioned loyalty to Caballero, such as Lieutenant-Colonel Manuel Arredondo, his aide-de-camp, Captain Eleuterio Díaz Tendero, the head of the vital Information and Control Department,[11] and Major Manuel Estrada, the Chief of the General Staff,[12] who had already been drawn or were being drawn into the Communist orbit.[13]

By the same open and disguised occupation of directing posts the Communists became firmly embedded in the vital General Commissariat of War, which was set up for the purpose of exercising a politico-social control over the armed forces through the medium of political commissars or delegate commissars, as they were officially called.[14] The custom of installing commissars in the militia units had already been adopted by the different parties and trade union organizations at the outbreak of the Civil War with the object of keeping a constant vigil over the morale of the militiamen and the reliability of the professional officers,[15] but now, in accordance with the general tendency

[10] A few weeks later Cordón was made head of the technical secretariat of the Under-secretaryship of War which controlled the personnel, matériel, army pay, audit, co-ordination, court-martial, engineering, and supply departments as well as the war experiments committee.—See Martín Blázquez (one of the two technical secretaries who assisted Cordón), *I Helped to Build an Army*, p. 279; also *Diario Oficial del Ministerio de la Guerra*, November 2, 1936.

[11] This department examined the antecedents of every man before he could enter the army.—See Martín Blázquez, *I Helped to Build an Army*, p. 121; Casado, *The Last Days of Madrid*, pp. 49–50.

[12] He was appointed to this post when Caballero became War Minister (*Diario Oficial del Ministerio de la Guerra*, September 5, 1936). His adjutant was Alejandro García Val, the Communist Party member mentioned above, who, in accordance with the procedure governing such appointments, was nominated by Caballero on the proposal of the Chief of the General Staff.

[13] For this information the author is indebted to Communists as well as non-Communists. For further details regarding these officers, see pp. 236, 277–8, below.

[14] See circular order signed by Largo Caballero, *Gaceta de Madrid*, October 16, 1936. The Communists later claimed that they had, on repeated occasions, urged the War Minister to establish the Commissariat.—See, for example, Francisco Antón in *Nuestra Bandera*, January–February, 1938.

[15] "Many of the militia battalions . . . were led by commanders who,

towards centralization, a government body was created in October, 1936, to regularize this practice. While the commissar was still expected to guard against disloyalty on the part of professional officers,[16] he was also expected to establish concord between the officers and men of the new regular army, and uphold the former's prestige and authority.[17] But, in addition to these duties, in addition to the tasks of enforcing discipline[18] and watching over the morale of the soldiers,[19] the commissar had other responsibilities. "The commissar is the soul of the combat unit, its educator, its agitator, its propagandist," said Carlos Contreras, political commissar of the Fifth Regiment. "He is always, or should be always, the best, the most intelligent, the most capable. He should occupy himself with everything and know about everything. He should interest himself in the stomach, in the heart, and in the brain of the soldier of the people. He should accompany him from the moment he enlists and receives his training until he leaves for the front and returns from it; he should interest himself in how he eats, how he sleeps, how he educates himself and how he fights. He must see that his political, economic, cultural and artistic needs are satisfied."[20] To be sure, not all commissars conducted themselves in a way expected of them. "There are political commissars," affirmed Contreras, "who do not maintain close contact with the mass of the soldiers, who are not with them in the trenches, and who only want to be near the commanding officer."[21]

---

conniving with the enemy, deserted at the first opportunity. This resulted in a natural distrust on the part of the men for their officers, and made it necessary for them to have their own delegate in the military command in order to guarantee the loyal conduct of the officers. These delegates were the first political commissars."—Lieutenant-Colonel Rovira, chief of the 42nd Brigade, in *Mundo Obrero*, April 26, 1937. See also *Informaciones*, August 8, 1936; *Claridad*, October 15, 1936.

[16] See, for example, José Díaz' speech, October 22, 1936, as reprinted in *Tres años de lucha*, pp. 215-221.

[17] See circular orders signed by Largo Caballero, *Diario Oficial del Ministerio de la Guerra*, October 16, 1937; also regulations issued by the General Commissariat of War, published in *Claridad*, November 5, 1936.

[18] "The political commissar must make his men understand the necessity of a conscious and iron discipline," ran one of the regulations issued by the General Commissariat of War. "By constant work he must ensure this discipline as well as obedience to the officers."—Published in *Claridad*, November 5, 1936.

[19] "The political commissar," said the organ of the CNT Defence Committee of Madrid, "must at every moment analyse the psychological condition of his troops, so as to harangue them in moments of moral depression."—*Frente Libertario*, February 20, 1937.

[20] *Verdad*, January 27, 1937.   [21] *Ibid.*

Having regard to the influence the commissar could exert upon the ranks, to say nothing of the opportunity his position gave him to sway the minds and hearts of the officers,[22] it is not strange that predominance in the Commissariat of War was for the Communist Party a vital factor in its bid for control of the regular army. Of this predominance it was well assured, to some extent because Antonio Mije, a member of the Politburo, occupied the Sub-Commissariat of Organization—the most important of the four sub-commissariats created[23]—but principally because Felipe Pretel, the Secretary General, and Julio Alvarez del Vayo, the Commissar General, both of whom Largo Caballero had nominated because they possessed his unstinted confidence, secretly promoted the interests of the Communist Party.[24] Before long, the latter increased its influence still further owing to the appointment of José Laín, a JSU leader and recent Communist convert, as Director of the School of Commissars,[25] and to the illness of Angel Pestaña, the leader of the Syndicalist Party,[26] who had occupied one of the four sub-commissariats, and who was replaced by Gabriel García Maroto, a friend of Alvarez del Vayo's and a left-wing Socialist with pronounced Communist leanings, although critical of some of the party's methods. As Caballero was not apprised until some months later of the defection of Alvarez del Vayo and Felipe Pretel and of the consequent extent of Communist penetration of the Commissariat of War,[27] the Communist Party and its allies were able to exploit their

[22] "He should also carry on political agitation among the officers and infuse them with the same spirit that animates the soldiers."—Antonio Mije, member of the Politburo of the Communist Party, in *Frente Rojo*, April 17, 1937.

[23] The other three sub-commissariats were held by Crescenciano Bilbao, a moderate or Prieto Socialist, Angel Pestaña, the leader of the Syndicalist Party, and Angel G. Gil Roldán, a CNT member.—See *Diario Oficial del Ministerio de la Guerra*, October 16, 1936.

[24] See Carlos de Baraibar (left Socialist leader) in *Timón*, Buenos Aires, June, 1940; Enrique Castro, *Hombres made in Moscú*. For other references to Alvarez del Vayo's pro-Communist activities as Commissar General see Wenceslao Carrillo, *ibid.*, November, 1939; Araquistain, *El comunismo y la guerra de España*, p. 8; Largo Caballero, *Mis recuerdos*, p. 212, *La UGT y la guerra*, pp. 10–11; Indalecio Prieto in *Correo de Asturias*, July 10, 1943; Casado, *The Last Days of Madrid*, p. 57; also, for Communist praise of his work in the Commissariat, see *Frente Rojo*, April 16, May 19, 1937, and *Pasaremos*, May 8, 1937.

[25] See *Nuestra lucha por la unidad*, p. 35. For his entering the Communist Party, see p. 116, n. 51, above, also Checa, *A un gran partido, una gran organización*, p. 23.

[26] This was only a small party, formed by dissident members of the CNT, and had no influence on the course of events.

[27] See pp. 288–90, below.

privileged position without hindrance by appointing an overwhelm-ingly large number of Communist commissars at the expense of and to the extreme displeasure of other organizations,[28] whose complaints, it may be added, could not reach Largo Caballero through the Com-missariat itself, and did so, eventually, through independent channels.[29]

Because the precise functions and powers of the political commissar were not strictly delimited by law, he possessed a broad measure of independence, which the Communist commissar—who was instructed to be "the organizer of the party in his unit, boldly and systematically recruiting the best elements from among the best fighters and recom-mending them for positions of responsibility"[30]—used to the full in helping to extend his party's dominion over the armed forces. ". . . Dozens, hundreds of party and JSU 'organizers' invaded the fronts and military units," declared Jesús Hernández, Communist Minister in the Largo Caballero government, in a speech delivered some years later, after he had ceased to belong to the party, "and our officers were given categoric instructions to promote the maximum number of Com-munists to higher ranks, thus reducing the proportion of promotions open to members of other organizations. But it is my duty to state that, while this reckless policy was being carried out, the Communists did not cease fighting the enemy and their resolution and discipline at the fronts showed them to be better than the best, a fact that facili-tated the proselytizing work we had undertaken.

". . . The zeal of some Communist officers and commissars was so unbridled and so undiplomatic that it went to the unspeakable extreme

[28] This matter is dealt with more fully in a later chapter. Meanwhile, suffice it to say that Gabriel García Maroto, who occupied one of the four sub-commissariats, told the author after the war that, at the beginning of 1937, on the central front, Socialist battalions frequently complained to him that Com-munist commissars had been appointed to them, and stated that they found this intolerable. He also told the author that, about the same time, Alberto F. Ballesteros, a Caballero Socialist, holding the position of Inspector-Commissar on the southern front, had protested that Antonio Mije, in appointing thirty commissars for that front, had selected only Communists.

[29] See Carlos de Baraibar in *Timón*, Buenos Aires, June, 1940.

[30] Clavego, *Algunas normas para el trabajo de los comisarios políticos* (Com-munist Party handbook on the commissar's functions), p. 24. Even before the creation of the General Commissariat of War, the Communists had not neglected party activity at the front. "Teams of agitators must be created to inform militiamen of the attitude of the party with regard to all problems. . . . The Communists should take upon themselves the task of recruiting for the party the best fighters at the front."—From speech by Antonio Mije, member of the Politburo, reported in *Mundo Obrero*, September 9, 1936.

of removing officers and of sending men to the front line for refusing to become members of the Communist Party or of the JSU.[31]

"By this procedure the strength of the party was 'reinforced' at the fronts by thousands of new adherents, but at the same time . . . the party destroyed unity, spread discord, and inflamed rivalry among military units of a different political complexion.[32]

"That was the practical result of the policy which we were ordered to carry out and which we were stupid enough to follow."[33]

In addition to the work of the Communist political commissars and officers and to the help of crypto-Communists and philo-Communist Socialists in promoting the influence of the party in the armed forces, there was yet another factor of greater consequence that militated in its favour: this was the arrival, first of Soviet officers, then of Soviet arms.

"Shortly after [Largo Caballero's] government had been formed in September, 1936," writes Luis Araquistain, friend and political associate of the premier for many years, "the Russian Ambassador presented to it a serving Soviet General [General Goriev], stating that he was military attaché of the Embassy and offering his professional services. Later on fresh 'auxiliaries' sprang up spontaneously without

[31] Indalecio Prieto, the moderate Socialist leader, affirms that the Communists actually assassinated at the front Socialists who refused to join their party.—*Correo de Asturias*, July 10, 1943. See also Prieto, *Inauguración del círculo "Pablo Iglesias" de México*, p. 22.

[32] "In accordance with their usual tactics and with the slogans they received," writes a professional officer, "the Communist commissars, who formed the majority, endeavoured to increase their party membership by ceaseless propaganda among those soldiers of their units who did not share their ideas. They employed every means at their disposal, from the promise of future promotions to the threat of execution for offences that had not been committed. This could not be viewed favourably by the other parties, observing as they did a continual reduction in the number of their members, who were compelled to change their party cards in order to avoid victimization. As a result of all this a contest ensued between commissars representing different political views, with consequent prejudice to the armed forces."—Pérez Salas, *Guerra en España*, p. 144. See also Casado, *The Last Days of Madrid*, p. 57. The atmosphere created by the conduct of the Communist political commissars was certainly the very opposite to that which Largo Caballero had hoped would be encouraged when the Commissariat of War was formed. "When at the battle fronts or in the barracks and other places where the troops are billeted," ran a circular order signed by him (*Gaceta de Madrid*, October 7, 1936), "disagreements or conflicts arise between soldiers or militiamen belonging to different trade union organizations delegate commissars shall act with perfect equanimity, and in such a way that brotherly acts shall efface all divergences of opinion between the combatants as well as all selfish aims of individuals or groups."

[33] *Acción Socialista*, March 15, 1952.

being requested, and they introduced themselves *motu proprio* into the military staff and army corps, where they gave orders at will."[34] While it might be incorrect to infer that the Russian officers invariably acted on their own accord without the prior consent of the War Ministry or the General Staff, there is irrefragable evidence that in many cases they disregarded the views of these two bodies and conducted themselves high-handedly. Colonel Segismundo Casado, the Chief of Operations on the War Ministry General Staff, affirms that "their influence reached such a point as to control every project of the General Staff and often entirely to reverse technical plans, replacing them with their own. These generally contained some political end; in questions of organization, appointing commanders; in news, in making propaganda in a party sense; in operations, putting on one side incontrovertible tactical and strategical considerations in order to impose their policy."[35] And the War Minister himself testifies: "The Spanish Government, and in particular the minister responsible for the conduct of operations, as well as the commanding officers, especially at headquarters, were not able to act with absolute independence because they were obliged to submit, against their will, to irresponsible foreign interference, without being able to free themselves from it under pain of endangering the assistance that we were receiving from Russia through the sale of war material. Sometimes, on the pretext that their orders were not being carried out as punctually as they desired, the Russian Embassy and the Russian generals took the liberty of expressing to me their displeasure, stating that if we did not consider their co-operation necessary and fitting, we should tell them so plainly so that they could inform their government and take their departure."[36]

There can be no doubt that the minatory and imperious behaviour of the Russian officers[37] accelerated the deterioration of Caballero's relations with the Communists that had already set in as a result of

[34] *El comunismo y la guerra de España*, p. 24.

[35] *The National Review*, July, 1939. See also Casado, *The Last Days of Madrid*, pp. 52–3.

[36] Quoted by Luis Araquistain, *El comunismo y la guerra de España*, p. 25. This passage is taken from Caballero's unpublished memoirs.

[37] The behaviour of Russian civilians was no less imperious if one may generalize from the conduct of Michael Koltzov, leading Soviet newspaper correspondent, influential in the Kremlin, who, towards the end of 1936, established himself in the Madrid Commissariat of War, where, according to Arturo Barea, then in charge of the censorship of foreign press reports—a function which Koltzov placed under the control of the Commissariat—he "intervened in most of the discussions on the authority of his vitality and arrogant will,"—*The Forging of a Rebel*, pp. 585. See also *ibid.*, p. 604.

their absorption of the Socialist movement in Catalonia, of the JSU, and of many of his followers in the UGT and the Socialist Party.[38] While, for a time, these relations showed no manifest impairment, a significant crack in the smooth surface soon appeared. This was his appointment, on October 22, of General José Asensio to the Under-secretaryship of War.

As a commander of the militia forces in the Sierra de Guadarrama, defending the north-western approaches to Madrid, Asensio, at that time a colonel, had so inspired the confidence of the Socialist leader during the latter's frequent visits to the Sierra, that, on becoming Premier and Minister of War in September, Caballero had made him a general and placed him in charge of the threatened central front. The Communists, who had already been striving to win his adherence to their party acclaimed his promotion and new assignment, praised the military accomplishments of "this hero of the democratic republic"[39] under whose direction their steel companies in the Sierra had "won victory after victory,"[40] and made him an honorary commander of their Fifth Regiment.[41] When, however, in the succeeding weeks Asensio showed no inclination to follow the trajectory of other professional military men who had yielded to their courtship, and even evinced for them a profound antipathy, they demanded his removal from the command of the central front,[42] a demand in which they were

[38] See pp. 113–18, above.

[39] *Milicia Popular*, September 6, 1936.

[40] Enrique Castro (Commander-in-Chief of the Fifth Regiment) in *Mundo Obrero*, September 10, 1936; see also *ibid.*, September 8, 1936.

[41] *Ibid.*; see also letter to Asensio from Alejandro García Val on behalf of the Fifth Regiment, notifying him of its decision to make him an honorary commander, published in Asensio, *El General Asensio. Su lealtad a la república*, p. 105. García Val informed the author after the war that the reason for his party's attentions to Asensio was that it had hoped to wean him from Caballero's influence.

[42] See Falcón, *Madrid*, p. 177. "I may as well point out here," writes Colonel Segismundo Casado (*The Last Days of Madrid*, pp. 75–6), "what tactics the Communist Party usually followed in their relationships with the commanders of the People's Army. They treated as subordinate those commanders who were affiliated to their party, demanding simply that their orders should be carried out in whatever way best served their party ends, often in contradiction to their duty as soldiers. These officers generally obeyed blindly, paying more attention to the orders of the party than to those of the Military High Command. Other commanders on many occasions opposed their plans and rejected suggestions which sounded more like orders, or refused to take part in activities which would not have left them with a clear conscience. They [the Communists] pretended to show the greatest consideration to these, but only for a short time,

aided by the series of military disasters that towards the end of October had brought General Franco's forces close to the gates of Madrid. Yet, in spite of these defeats, the more balanced appraisals of Asensio concur in the view that he possessed great military capacity and exceptional mental gifts,[43] and that the debacle was inevitable in view of the defects of the militia system and the lack of tanks, artillery, and aircraft.[44] These, it is true, did not arrive from Russia until the end of October, while the International Brigades which, under Communist leadership, were to play a cardinal role in the defence of Madrid, entered the field only in the first days of November.[45]

Although for a time Caballero refused to remove Asensio, he finally yielded. But while propitiating the Communists with one hand, he

---

and in a wholly superficial way. They asked them to dine, they told them of the great admiration they had for them, for their intelligence or bravery. In a word, they attempted to stir their private ambitions, but when they were convinced that it was not possible to captivate them by such means, they started an insidious campaign of libel against them, so that the High Command was obliged to relieve them. More than one commander lost his life or his freedom through simply doing his duty."

"The commander who accepted Communist Party membership without hesitation," wrote the organ of the moderate Socialists towards the end of the war, "soon acquired, in the Communist press, military qualities superior to those of Napoleon and Alexander, while those who dared to reject a membership that they had not requested were obliquely or openly criticized."—*El Socialista*, March 12, 1939. See also, Alonso, *La flota republicana y la guerra civil de España*, pp. 89–90.

[43] See, for example, Martín Blázquez, *I Helped to Build an Amy*, pp. 264, 280, 291. Even Alvarez del Vayo, who read and approved the rough draft of a letter written by Louis Fischer to Largo Caballero on October 11, in which Fischer questioned the loyalty of Asensio (see Fischer, *Men and Politics*, pp. 372–4) and who later voted in the Cabinet for his removal from the Under-secretaryship of War (see p. 276, below), contends that he was "unquestionably one of the most capable and intelligent officers in the Republican army" and that he could "have become the greatest military genius."—Alvarez del Vayo, *Freedom's Battle*, p. 126. It is noteworthy that the day before he approved Fischer's letter to Caballero, Alvarez del Vayo had written the following lines in a note to Asensio: "I am aware of the very important operation due to begin at dawn. To know that you will be there personally directing it adds very much to my hopes. Owing to recent bitter experiences, we can only trust in your skill. For that reason I have decided to send you these intimate lines, which, under all circumstances, should remain between us."—As given in Asensio's book, *El General Asensio. Su lealtad a la república*, p. 107.

[44] See, for example, Zugazagoitia, *Historia de la guerra en España*, pp. 141–3, 1852–3; Martín Blázquez, *I Helped to Build an Army*, p. 263.

[45] See n. 9, pp. 99–100, above.

diminished their victory with the other by elevating him to the Under-secretaryship of War. His determination to pursue an independent course found practical expression in two further moves: the reinstatement of Segismundo Casado, whom he had dismissed at the pressing instance of the Communists from his post as Chief of Operations on the General Staff,[46] and the replacement of Major Manuel Estrada, Chief of the General Staff—who a month before had become a member of the Communist Party[47]—by General Martínez Cabrera, a friend of Asensio's. These shifts, which in the whirl of events passed almost unnoticed by the general public, gave the Communists cause for disquietude and convinced them of the rough weather ahead with Caballero.

But while strengthening Largo Caballero's authority inside the War Ministry itself, the shifts did nothing to curtail the power of the Communists on the vital central front. And this for the following reasons: on November 7, with the enemy in the outskirts of Madrid, the government had abandoned the capital for Valencia, and left it in the hands of a *Junta de Defensa*, or Defence Council, under General José Miaja, the military commander of Madrid. Although the General—who, it is worth stating, had secretly belonged to the right-wing military organization, the *Unión Militar Española*, before the war[48] and

[46] In his book (*The Last Days of Madrid*, p. 51), Casado states that he had been dismissed because of a campaign waged against him by the Communist Party after he had informed the high command that the marked preference with which Russian arms were being distributed to the Fifth Regiment would inevitably cause suspicion and jealousy among the men, and, what was more, would soon bring about the accession of the Communist Party to power. "This party," he adds, "observing what my opinion was, with the underhandedness which characterized it, started a campaign of discredit against me and convinced the Minister of War that I was not the most suitable person to fill the office of Operations Chief because I had the faults of violence and pessimism." For his reinstatement by Largo Caballero, see *ibid.*, p. 63.

[47] According to information given to the author by Enrique Castro, a member of the Central Committee. Letter to the author.

[48] A documentary work published by General Franco's Government, *Datos complementarios para la historia de España. Guerra de liberación 1936–1939*, has the following to say (pp. 291–2) with regard to José Miaja and Vicente Rojo, the former's chief of staff during the defence of Madrid: "In order to appreciate the lack of sincerity in the conduct of these two officers, who were caught at the time of the [insurrectionary] movement in territory dominated by the Red Government, it is sufficient to bear in mind that both were enrolled in the *Unión Militar Española* (UME), which had been formed . . . with the patriotic aim of throwing up, at the opportune moment, a dyke capable of protecting Spain from the Communist tide. But once this moment had arrived and the

had, at its outset, refused to serve as War Minister in the Giral Government on the ground that the victory of the military insurrection was inevitable[49]—had at first resented Largo Caballero's action in giving him a post which in those days of peril to the capital, seemed to promise only a fatal end,[50] he soon became, by a singular twist of fortune, the most glorified figure in the defence of Madrid.[51] Elevated

Nationalist Rising in Madrid had failed, General Miaja and Major Rojo—who had seen the fate that had befallen so many general and lesser officers of the Army, a large number having been assassinated precisely because they had belonged to the UME—instead of siding with their comrades, hastened to offer their services to the Popular Front. But as their consciences were not clear, and inasmuch as they believed that, by doing away with the filing cards recording their membership of this organization, all trace of their previous conduct would disappear, General Miaja . . . went, on July 18, 1937, to the [police department in charge of political records] and demanded that both his card and that of Vicente Rojo, a colonel at the time, be shown to him. Once in his possession, he put them away in his pocket." A photostatic copy of a document signed by officials of the department, testifying to this occurrence, is published in Appendix X of the same book. The authenticity of this document has been confirmed to the author by a supporter of the anti-Franco camp. Miaja's and Rojo's membership in the UME is attested by Caballero, who saw the official list of members—*Mis recuerdos*, pp. 213–14.

[49] The author is obliged to Giral himself for this information. Miaja, when interviewed by the author after the war, stated that he refused to join the government because it had neither an army nor a police force with which to combat the rebellion. It is worth noting that he had a few hours previously formed part of Martínez Barrio's ill-fated government of conciliation.—See n. 50, p. 31–2, above.

[50] General Sebastián Pozas, who succeeded Asensio in command of the central front, told the author after the war that he was present when Miaja learned of his assignment and that the latter nearly wept with rage at what he regarded as a deliberate attempt to sacrifice him to General Franco.

[51] "Thanks to his great prestige as a result of his achievement," wrote Martínez Cartón, member of the Central Committee of the Communist Party (*International Press Correspondence*, May 17, 1938), "General Miaja became the best loved General in Spain." That Miaja was intoxicated by the Communists' heady propaganda and by his popularity is attested by the following quotations: "When I am in my car," he told Julián Zugazagoitia, director of *El Socialista* (*Historia de la guerra en España*, p. 197), "women call out to me, 'Miaja!' 'Miaja!' And they scream to each other, 'There goes Miaja! There goes Miaja!' . . . I greet them and they greet me. They are happy and so am I." And Colonel Segismundo Casado writes (*The Last Days of Madrid*, pp. 63–4): "I managed to apply a cold douche to lower the fever which he had caught from the people, the Press, and above all, the clique which surrounded him, and which had brought him to a state of actual danger. More than once he told me that the popular enthusiasm had reached such a pitch that women even kissed him in the streets." See also Castro, *Hombres made in Moscú*, pp. 452–3.

to the rank of national hero by the propaganda of the Communist Party, and prodded by Francisco Antón, Inspector-Commissar of the Central Front and secretary of the Madrid party organization, his principal activator and mentor,[52] Miaja shortly entered the Communist fold.[53] Even more important for the Communists than their control of General Miaja, the President of the Junta, was their control of the vital councils of public order, supplies, and war,[54] and the fact that the operations Miaja nominally commanded were planned and

---

It is worth recording that after the war, following Miaja's participation in the National Council of Defence, which revolted against the Communists and the Negrín Government in March, 1939, Antonio Mije, a member of the Politburo of the Communist Party, wrote: "In order to distort the true situation regarding the defence of Madrid, there have been and there still are persons interested in attributing it to the traitor Miaja. Those who have made and continue to make such propaganda know nothing of what happened, nor of the military 'fruits' which Miaja is capable of giving. He never knew more than what he was told as to what was going on in Madrid. He never felt the terrible and difficult situation in its full intensity. The tragedy of those days in Madrid could not penetrate the skull of a dull-witted general, lacking any knowledge of the people."—*España Popular*, November 9, 1940.

[52] See Martínez Cartón, member of the Central Committee of the Communist Party, in *International Press Correspondence*, May 17, 1938; also Edmundo Domínguez (*Los vencedores de Negrín*, p. 203), who likewise confirms the guiding role of Antón. Domínguez, a left-wing Socialist and secretary of the UGT National Federation of Building Workers in July, 1936, followed Communist policy during the war, finally becoming Inspector-Commissar of the Central Front.

[53] The Comintern organ, *International Press Correspondence*, February 6, 1937 (article by Hugh Slater, datelined Madrid, January 28, 1937), stated that he was then a member of the party. See also speech by Jesús Hernández, Communist Minister of Education (May 28, 1937), referring to Largo Caballero's hostility to Miaja because he was "impregnated with Communist policy."—Hernández, *El partido comunista antes, durante y después de la crisis del gobierno Largo Caballero*, p. 24. "General Miaja," writes Louis Fischer (*Men and Politics*, p. 593), "was under Communist influence and carried a Communist Party card though he probably knew as much about Communism as Francisco Franco. Communist propaganda had inflated him into a myth."

[54] The composition of the Defence Council and the affiliation of its members, as given in *Mundo Obrero*, November 10, 1936, were as follows:

General José Miaja, President.
Fernando Frade (Socialist), Secretary.
Antonio Mije (Communist), War.
Santiago Carrillo (JSU), Public Order. [Member of the Communist Party.
Amor Nuño (CNT), War Industries.
Pablo Yagüe (UGT), Supplies. [Member of the Communist Party.]
José Carreño (Left Republican), Communications and Transport.

directed by the Soviet General, Goriev, the real organizer of Madrid's defence,[55] and by his Russian aides who controlled the air force, the tank corps, the artillery, as well as the anti-aircraft defences,[56] and who acted to all intents and purposes independently of the War and Air Ministries in Valencia.[57] Furthermore, the power of the Soviet officers,

Enrique Jiménez (Republican Union), Finance.
Francisco Caminero (Syndicalist), Civilian Evacuation.
Mariano García (Libertarian Youth), Information and Liaison.

Although Fernando Frade figures in the list as a Socialist, he was actually a Communist. This was confirmed to the author by several Socialists. See also Barea, *The Forging of a Rebel*, p. 579.

[55] See Fischer, *Men and Politics*, pp. 395, 398. What he says of Goriev's role is corroborated by information given to the author by Carlos Contreras, chief political commissar of the Fifth Regiment. For the best descriptive account of General Goriev, see Barea, *The Forging of a Rebel*, pp. 628–30.

[56] For this information I am grateful to Carlos Contreras, chief political commissar of the Fifth Regiment, as well as to Ludwig Renn, officer in the Eleventh (International) Brigade, and Manuel Schwartzmann, officer in the DECA (anti-aircraft defence).

[57] This was confirmed to the author by Ignacio Hidalgo de Cisneros, the Spanish Chief of the Air Force, whose adviser was the Russian General Shmoushkievich (known in Spain as Duglas), and who became a member of the Communist Party in January, 1937. According to Luis Araquistain, close political associate of Largo Caballero, the air force "operated when and where [the Russians] pleased, without any co-ordination with the land and sea forces. The Navy and Air Minister, Indalecio Prieto, meek and cynical, made fun of his office to anyone who visited him, declaring he was neither a minister nor anything else, because he received absolutely no obedience from the air force. The real Air Minister was the Russian General Duglas."—*El comunismo y la guerra de España*, pp. 24–5. "I can state clearly that during the whole war neither the Air Force nor the Tank Corps was controlled by the Minister of National Defence, nor in consequence by the Central General Staff. The Minister and his Staff were not even aware of the quantity and types of their machines and only knew the situation of those which were used in actual operations. In the same way the Minister and his Staff were not aware of the situation, and even of the existence of a great number of unknown 'flying-fields' (aerodromes) maintained in secret by the 'friendly advisers' and certain of the Aviation Chiefs who were entirely in their confidence."—Casado, *The Last Days of Madrid*, p. 54. See also *ibid.*, pp. 55–7, and Largo Caballero, *Mis recuerdos*, p. 206.

Some idea of the friction that soon arose between Largo Caballero and Miaja as a result of the latter's virtual dependence on the Russians may be gained from a telegram sent by the War Minister to the General on November 17, 1936, reminding him that the only orders he should obey were those issued by the government, and from Miaja's reply, in which, after taking cognizance of the fact that Caballero had found it necessary to remind him of the most elementary principle of discipline and subordination, which in his long military career he had never forgotten, he asked to be relieved by someone worthy of

the marked favouritism shown to the Communists in the distribution of arms and supplies received from Russia,[58] the conspicuous role of the International Brigades under General Kleber, their superior efficiency, as well as that of the Spanish Communist units,[59] all helped to swell the influence of the Communist Party, particularly on the central front, and to attract into its orbit not only many of the less conspicuous, but also many of the more prominent military men,[60]

Caballero's confidence.—*Actas de la Junta de Defensa de Madrid*, pp. 422–3. Because of the prestige he had acquired, Miaja no doubt anticipated that Caballero would not act upon his request.

[58] See p. 224, above. Alejandro García Val, Communist Party member who was made chief of the transport section of the General Staff in November, 1936, told the author after the war that when Russian trucks reached Spain he organized with the aid of party members and sympathizers in the UGT the first three militarized motor transport battalions composed of six hundred vehicles and three thousand men.

[59] Although some left-wing Spaniards have underrated the importance of the efficiency of the International Brigades as a model for Spanish units (see, for example, Abad de Santillán, *La revolución y la guerra en España*, pp. 131–2), it has none the less received ample recognition. *Claridad*, for example, stated on November 11, 1936: "Our proletarian and peasant masses, weighed down by centuries of oppression and ignorance—the work of social castes that have demonstrated their absolute incapacity for organization—must make super-human efforts to equal these comrades from other nations. Intelligence is sharpened in school. The militiamen of the International Column have had opportunities of cultivating their intelligence during their childhood and youth. Our masses, on the other hand, have had no such opportunities. But, when we triumph, we shall have them, and our children shall have even more. For this we are fighting; for this we are dying." See also Pérez Salas, *Guerra en España*, p. 128, Zugazagoitia, *Historia de la guerra en España*, p. 195, and Eduardo de Guzmán (director of the FAI organ in Madrid, *Castilla Libre*), *Madrid, rojo y negro*, pp. 164, 200, who praises the courage, intelligence, discipline, and military skill of the International Brigades and gives full credit to the example they set to the Anarchosyndicalist militia on the Madrid front. "[Our men]," he commented, "observe them, and, with that wonderful power of adaptation the Spanish people possesses, they imitate them without loss of time." For non-Communist praise of Spanish Communist units, see, for example, *Política* (organ of the Left Republican Party), November 11, 1936, and Colonel Segismundo Casado (whom no one can accuse of being partial to the Communists), *The Last Days of Madrid*, p. 96, who says that there were "plenty of Communist units which distinguished themselves by their impetuous fighting."

[60] "An indication—and a very important one—of the effectiveness of the Communist Party's war work," wrote the correspondent in Spain of the London *Daily Worker*, "is offered by the fact that today the majority of the loyal generals, not to mention the younger loyal officers, have applied for and received membership of the Communist Party.—*Daily Worker*, November 25,

such as General Sebastián Pozas, the commander of that front,[61] and Lieutenant-Colonel Vicente Rojo, Miaja's chief of staff—a former military instructor in the Toledo Academy, whose constant and intimate association, it should be observed, with General Goriev in organizing the defence of Madrid enabled him to live down a conservative past[62] and establish himself in Russian favour.[63] Whereas a large number of officers finally joined the party, influenced as they were by the aforementioned factors, and by its moderate propaganda,[64] as well

---

1936. See also Ramos Oliveira, *Politics, Economics and Men of Modern Spain, 1808-1946*, p. 599.

[61] His Russian military adviser was General Koulik, known in Spain as Kupper.—See Castro (former member of the Central Committee of the Communist Party), *J'ai perdu la foi a Moscou*, p. 124, and Penchienati (commander of the Garibaldi Brigade), *Brigate internazionali in Spagna*, p. 34. Before the war Pozas had been Inspector General of the Civil Guard and had earned the hostility of the Army Chiefs because of the measures he had taken in various parts of the country—by no means completely successful, it is true—to ensure the loyalty of this corps to the Republic. See, for example, the official [Franco] history of the Civil War, *Historia de la Cruzada Española*, IV, pp. 381, 391; *Política*, October 23, 1936. When interviewed by the author after the war, Captain Aniceto Carbajal, son-in-law of Pozas, stated that General Franco, a few days after the February, 1936, elections, when the latter was still Chief of the General Staff, tried through his intermediacy to purchase Pozas' support for a "National Government" by offering him a sum of money deposited in a Swiss bank. At the outbreak of the war, Pozas was made Minister of the Interior in the Giral Government, and urged that the people be armed (see speech by Jerónimo Bujeda, *El Socialista*, July 19, 1937). After his appointment to the central front in October, 1936, he fell under Communist influence, and shortly afterwards, in May, 1937, when he was made commander of the so-called Eastern Army, he joined the PSUC, the Communist-controlled United Socialist Party of Catalonia.—See Pérez Salas, *Guerra en España*, pp. 141-2, Zugazagoitia, *Historia de la guerra en España*, p. 406; also Fischer, *Why Spain Fights On*, p. 39, who says he was a member of the Spanish Communist Party.

[62] Before the war he had been a member of the UME (see n. 48, pp. 236-7, above), and had been highly esteemed by the insurgent Army Chiefs, according to information given to the author by José Giral. For other details about Rojo, see Aznar, *Historia militar de la guerra de España*, pp. 200, 203, 428; Francisco Casares, *Azaña y ellos*, p. 256; *Datos complementarios para la historia de España*, pp. 327-9; Martín Blázquez, *I Helped to Build an Army*, pp. 282-3.

[63] See laudatory article by Michael Koltzov in *Pravda*, December 13, 1936. For an account of Rojo's pro-Communist work later in the war by a professional colleague, whose testimony is beyond question, see Pérez Salas, *Guerra en España*, pp. 147, 152, 169-70, 185. Caballero also confirms Rojo's support of the Communists.—*Mis recuerdos*, p. 214.

[64] "It cannot be denied," writes a professional officer with genuine Republican sympathies, "that the Communists were masters in the art of propaganda,

as by the fact that membership enabled them to secure for their units supplies of Russian war material,[65] others were drawn to it for more personal motives. "There were," writes Bruno Alonso, a moderate Socialist and chief political commissar of the Republican fleet, "few, very few professional military leaders, without party affiliation before July 18, but loyal to the Republic, who did not bow to the predominant political influence, some from inclination, others out of weakness of will, and many out of fear lest their lack of political antecedents should result in some arbitrary and irreparable act against them."[66]

If the all-pervading influence of the Communists on the central front finally told upon the patience of the War Minister, still more provoking, especially to a man of Caballero's temperament—who even in dealings with his own colleagues was obstinate and irascible, and who, according to General Asensio, his undersecretary, wished to direct and control everything personally[67]—was the importunity of his opponents. Time and again the obduracy with which he withstood

---

as a result of which they managed to deceive everybody. This propaganda consisted principally in affirming that their only aim was to defeat Franco and put into effect once again the laws of the Republic. All their leaders, especially La Pasionaria, made loud protestations of loyalty to the régime and to the Constitution, which they claimed they were endeavouring to re-establish. To achieve this end it was necessary, they said, to organize an efficient and disciplined army, which would replace the undisciplined militia of the CNT. So well did they carry out that slogan that they managed to deceive everybody. Some professional military men fell into the snare, and not a few, out of enthusiasm for Communist propaganda, thoughtlessly joined the party.

"As for myself, who had no other desire than that of winning the war, I believed that the Communists' seemingly fine aims were necessarily a step in that direction. Unfortunately, this was not so. By their propaganda they aimed only at gaining supremacy in the Army in order to use it for their own personal advantage, subordinating to the latter the war against Franco. This was the reason that impelled me to oppose them."—Pérez Salas, *Guerra en España*, pp. 146–7.

[65] According to Alejandro García Val, Communist member of the General Staff, when interviewed by the author after the war.

[66] *La flota republicana y la guerra civil de España*, p. 38. Martín Blázquez, Republican officer in the War Ministry, affirms that the Communist, Antonio Cordón, who was on the General Staff, once said to him: ". . . Let me remind you that we are living in strange times, when people are killed for nothing at all. I seriously advise you to join the Communist Party. It needs you, and you need it."—*I Helped to Build an Army*, p. 241.

[67] Quoted Gorkin, *Caníbales Políticos*, p. 217. In an article in *Francisco Largo Caballero, 1869–1946*, Federica Montseny, a Cabinet colleague, refers (p. 74) to his "unipersonal" conception of power.

the pressure to which he was constantly submitted led to fierce clashes with the Russian generals,[68] with the Soviet Ambassador, Marcel Rosenberg,[69] and especially with the two Communist ministers during debates in the Cabinet. According to Indalecio Prieto, who, as a member of the government, must be regarded as an important witness, "a situation of unbelievable tension" arose between the two ministers and the Premier. "Very violent scenes occurred during Cabinet meetings, and, in addition, Largo Caballero had tumultuous discussions with the Ambassador of the U.S.S.R., Señor Rosenberg. I cannot make out whether the attitude of Señor Rosenberg was a reflection of the anger of the Communist ministers or whether the anger of the latter was a reflection of the attitude of the Russian Ambassador. What I do know . . ·. is that the action of Russian diplomacy on the Premier, or better still, against the Premier, and the pressure of the Communist ministers were simultaneous and alike."[70]

It was in this situation of mounting conflict with the Russians and their Spanish aides that Largo Caballero, faced by the depredations on his following, by the traditional enmity of the moderate wing of his own party, and by the silent animosity of the liberal Republicans,

[68] An employee in the War Ministry who was in intimate contact with José María Aguirre, Caballero's politico-military secretary, informed the author that the relations between the Russian officers and Largo Caballero became very bad after December, 1936, and that the Russians were particularly concerned about the political orientation of the army.

[69] "More than as an Ambassador," testifies Luis Araquistain, intimate of Largo Caballero, "[Rosenberg] acted like a Russian viceroy in Spain. He paid daily visits to Largo Caballero, sometimes accompanied by Russians of high rank, military or civilian. During the visits, which lasted for hours on end, Rosenberg tried to give the head of the Spanish Government instructions as to what he should do in order to direct the war successfully. His suggestions, which were practically orders, related mainly to army officers. Such and such Generals and Colonels should be dismissed and others appointed in their place. These recommendations were based, not on the competence of the officers, but on their political affiliations and on the degree of their amenability to the Communists."—*El comunismo y la guerra de España*, p. 10. "This gentleman [Rosenberg]," writes Ginés Ganga, a left-wing Socialist Cortes deputy, "used to carry in his pocket a collection of notes couched in the following or similar terms: 'It would be expedient to dismiss X, chief of such and such a division, and replace him by Z'; 'A, employee of such and such a ministry, does not fulfil his duty. It would be advisable to replace him by B'; 'It is necessary to imprison M and bring him to trial for disloyalty,' and so on, ceaselessly."— *Hoy*, December 5, 1942.

[70] Speech in the *Centro Republicano Español*, Mexico City, March 29, 1946, as given in *Adelante*, Mexico City, April 1, 1946.

looked to the Anarchosyndicalists for support against his tenacious adversaries. The novel relationship thus established between Caballero and his former opponents of the CNT and FAI was a potent factor in disposing him to a policy of conciliation towards them. In particular, it deterred him from carrying out, at the pressing instance of the Communists, a thorough-going militarization of the Anarchosyndicalist militia on the basis of mixed brigades, as a step in the creation of the regular army, an army which he well knew was anathema to the Libertarian movement.

23

The Libertarian Movement
and the Regular Army

"WE do not want a national army," cried *Frente Libertario*, the newspaper of the Anarchosyndicalist militia on the central front. "We want the popular militia, which incarnates the will of the masses, and is the only force that can defend the liberty and the free social order of the Spanish people. As before the civil war, we now cry, 'Down with chains.' The army is enslavement, the symbol of tyranny. Away with the army."[1]

The Anarchosyndicalists could not accept a regular army without violating their anti-authoritarian principles. True, the exigencies of an implacable struggle had forced them to recognize the need in their militia units for some measure of restraint on individualism, but that was entirely different from accepting an out-and-out militarization involving the rigorous subordination of these units to government control, the restoration of rank and privilege, the appointment of officers by the War Ministry, the introduction of differential pay rates, heavy disciplinary punishments, and the compulsory salute. "When this word [militarization] is uttered—why not admit the fact?—we feel uneasy, disturbed; we shudder, because it calls to mind the constant assaults on dignity and the human personality," avowed *Nosotros*, the Anarchist organ in the region of Valencia. "Until yesterday, to militarize implied—and for many people it still implies—regimenting men in such a way as to destroy their wills by breaking their personality in the mechanism of the barracks."[2]

But if the CNT and FAI had ethical motives for their hostility to

[1] October 27, 1936. "We do not want a uniformed and disciplined militia organized into military units."—From speech by Juan López, reported by *Fragua Social*, October 18, 1936.
[2] February 11, 1937.

militarization and the regular army, they had powerful political motives as well. Two months before the outbreak of the Civil War, at a congress of the CNT, a resolution was approved to the effect that a standing army—and by this was meant any standing army organized after the overthrow of the old régime—would constitute the greatest threat to the revolution, "because under its influence a dictatorship would be forged that would necessarily deal it a mortal blow."[3] It is no wonder, therefore, that the attempt of José Giral's middle-class government in the first weeks of the war to create volunteer battalions and, later, a volunteer army under its control[4] should have been viewed with suspicion by the Libertarian movement.[5] Nor is it surprising that when, within a few weeks of his entering the War Ministry, Largo Caballero promulgated measures providing for the militarization of the militia and the creation of a regular army anxiety should have grown in the movement, an anxiety that mounted into alarm when the progress made by the Communists in penetrating the military apparatus became manifest.

In an effort to still the fears of the Libertarian youth organization, for example, as to the Communists' intentions regarding the army,

[3] As given in *Solidaridad Obrera*, May 12, 1936. The resolution was drafted by a commission composed of some of the outstanding leaders of the Libertarian movement, and went on to say that the greatest guarantee for the defence of the revolution would be the armed people. "There are thousands of workers," it added, "who have passed through the barracks and have a knowledge of modern military technique. Every commune will have its arms and [other] elements of defence, for they will not be destroyed and transformed into instruments of labour until the revolution has been finally consolidated. We urged the necessity of holding on to aeroplanes, tanks, armoured cars, machine guns, and anti-aircraft guns, because it is from the air that the real danger of foreign invasion exists. If that invasion should occur the people will mobilize themselves rapidly in order to oppose the enemy, and will return to their work as soon as they have accomplished their defensive mission."

[4] See pp. 205–6, above.

[5] *Solidaridad Obrera*, the leading CNT newspaper in Spain, declared (August 5, 1936), with regard to the first of these two measures, that even before the military rebellion had been defeated the middle classes were thinking of the régime to be established on the day of victory. But, it affirmed, the workers would not rest on their laurels and would not allow their triumph to be snatched from them. As for the volunteer army, García Pradas, director of the principal Anarchosyndicalist organ in the central zone, *CNT*, declared that no one should enlist in it, because such an army would result in the creation of a new caste, which after the victory over fascism would try to settle accounts. The people, he added, had shown that there was no need for them to join an army in order to win the war, and should therefore not allow themselves to be deceived.—Speech reported in *CNT*, September 12, 1936.

Santiago Carrillo, the general secretary of the Communist-run Unified Socialist Youth, declared: "I know . . . there are comrades of the Unified Socialist Youth who desire unity with the young Libertarians in order to win the war, but that they believe in their heart of hearts that, when the war is over and the armies return from the front, we are going to use these armies to crush, to destroy, to liquidate our brothers, the young libertarians. . . . But I tell you, comrades, that such ideas must be discarded, because they are mistaken, because when we call for unity with the young Libertarians we do so sincerely. We know that our Libertarian comrades are a force necessary to victory, and we are also convinced that after victory they will collaborate with us in building up a strong, free, and democratic Spain. That is our belief, and all we ask of them is that on their part they should abandon their sectarian prejudices, that they should not regard us as passing friends of today and enemies of tomorrow, but as friends today, tomorrow, and always."[6]

Neither the Anarchist youth organization nor the Libertarian movement as a whole, however, was under any illusions as to the nature of the threat presented by the Communists, and it was partly in the hope of parrying the danger that the CNT–FAI leaders had proposed in September, 1936, that a "war militia" be created on the basis of compulsory service and under the joint control of the CNT and UGT.[7] But neither of these two proposals had evoked a responsive echo, and the Anarchosyndicalist leaders, with the Communist threat still uppermost in their minds, had finally decided to solicit representation in the Cabinet and thus secure for the Libertarian movement some measure of influence in the military machine. This, to be sure, had meant jettisoning not only their anti-governmental creed, but also their anti-militarist principles, principles which, in the opinion of Manuel Villar, director early in the war of the CNT newspaper, *Fragua Social*, had proved inimical to the Libertarian movement; for, he contended, whereas many Anarchosyndicalists had regarded the holding of commanding posts with repugnance, the Communists had embarked on an unbridled drive to occupy all they could.[8] "Were we in a position to

[6] Speech in January, 1937, reprinted in *En marcha hacia la victoria*, p. 51.

[7] Resolution approved at a plenary meeting of representatives of the Regional Committees of the CNT, as given in *CNT*, September 17, 1936.

[8] ". . . We failed to transform as rapidly as we should have done the spontaneous columns of the first days into regularly organized units. Positions were lost by us and taken by the Communists."—Mariano Vázquez, secretary of the National Committee of the CNT speaking at an AIT Congress, reported in Supplement of *Espagne Nouvelle*, March 15, 1939.

be squeamish about doctines?" he asked. "If the CNT had allowed the levers of revolutionary action to escape from its hands, the revolution itself would have suffered from the lessening of our influence. And as the revolution was the objective, and the CNT one of its most powerful determining factors, the most revolutionary course was to take those steps that would keep us in the political, military, and economic centre of gravity."[9]

But the role that the CNT–FAI ministers were able to play in the counsels of the Cabinet, particularly in regard to military matters, fell far short of their expectations; for they found, to use the words of Juan Peiró, the Anarchosyndicalist Minister of Commerce, that they had no rights or responsibilities as far as the direction of the war was concerned.[10] Hoping to remedy this situation they proposed that a kind of inner cabinet be created to handle military affairs, in which the CNT would be given representation.[11] This proposal—supported by the Communists no doubt in the belief that the new body would enable them to subject Caballero's actions to closer scrutiny and control[12]—materialized in the decree of November 9, establishing a Higher War Council, which was empowered to "harmonize and unify everything related to the war and its direction,"[13] and was composed of Largo Caballero, the War Minister, Indalecio Prieto, the moderate Socialist leader and Minister of Air and Navy, Vicente Uribe, the Communist Minister of Agriculture, Julio Just, the Left Republican Minister of Public Works, García Oliver, the CNT–FAI Minister of Justice, and Alvarez del Vayo, the philo-Communist Minister of Foreign Affairs and General Commissar of War.[14]

In spite of its official aim this new body was condemned to futility from the outset owing to the dissensions between Largo Caballero and the Communists as well as to the rivalry between the Premier and his Navy and Air Minister, Indalecio Prieto,[15] which deprived it, not only of any unanimity, but also of the most relevant military information essential to the proper discharge of its functions. The Communists, for their part, soon had grounds for open dissatisfaction,

[9] *Internacional*, June, 1938.

[10] Speech at Valencia CNT Congress, November, 1936, reported by *Fragua Social*, November 17, 1936.

[11] *Ibid.*

[12] Indeed, this was the opinion given to the author by Gabriel García Maroto, a friend of Alvarez del Vayo, who became a member of the new body.

[13] *Gaceta de la República*, November 10, 1936.

[14] *Ibid.*

[15] The relations between the two Socialist leaders are dealt with in Chapter 26.

since the High War Council met only on rare occasions owing to the resolve of the War Minister not to relinquish to his opponents what remained of his authority,[16] while the Anarchosyndicalists, who had hoped that it would serve to augment their influence in military affairs, found that their voice had scant effect amidst the strength of their opponents.

As a result of all this, the Libertarian movement, far from being able to use its participation in the government to increase its say in the military field or even to curb the progress of the Communists, was obliged in the end to circumscribe its efforts to maintaining control of its own militia units and securing arms from the War Ministry. This was no easy task, for the latter had decided that weapons would be withheld from those militia forces which were unwilling to transform themselves into regular units with the prescribed cadres.[17] In order to circumvent this requisite, the Anarchosyndicalists decided that their units should simulate acquiescence by adopting military names, an expedient that was employed by most of the CNT–FAI units, including those on the central front, in which, to quote the director of the Anarchist *Castilla Libre*, "everything save the nomenclature remained unchanged."[18] But this stratagem did not help the Libertarian units to secure the arms they needed, and, in the long run, they were forced to yield to the concept of militarization.

[16] In a demonstration held on February 14, 1937 (see n. 48, pp. 282–3, below), the Communists in a ten-point petition presented to Caballero demanded *inter alia* that the Higher War Council should be allowed to fulfil "the mission for which it was created," and two weeks later their organ, *Frente Rojo*, urged that it "should meet methodically and as often as necessary for discussing and reaching agreement upon all questions of the war," among which it included "the appointment and control of officers, and the cleansing of the army of all hostile and incapable elements."—Quoted, *Mundo Obrero*, March 2, 1937.

[17] At the Regional Congress of the Valencia CNT, held in November, 1936, the representative of the Alcoy paperworkers declared: "There is the case of a [CNT] column organized in Alcoy with more than one thousand militiamen enlisted, which the government does not arm because it has no officers; on the other hand, the Socialists, who are less in number, have been able to organize a column and obtain the necessary arms because they conform to the government's conditions."—*Fragua Social*, November 19, 1936.

[18] Guzmán, *Madrid, rojo y negro*, p. 200. At the Regional Congress of the Valencia CNT, held in November, 1936, the delegate of the Alcoy paperworkers declared that rather than be left without arms it would be better to meet the government's demands by introducing officer rank and insignia. "But," he added meaningfully, "as far as we are concerned, a century delegate is nothing more than a century delegate."—*Fragua Social*, November 14, 1936.

It was not only the need for military supplies that finally induced the Libertarian movement to bow to the concept of militarization: it was also—and this was no doubt the most important consideration— the need to overcome the defects of the militia system.

One of the most serious of these defects is adequately illustrated by the following unpublished article written by a regular army corporal, who was posted to a CNT–FAI column on the Madrid front: "In the column we found a professional army captain . . . who secretly advised Ricardo Sanz [its Anarchosyndicalist leader] on everything he thought should be done. Sanz, who had common sense, always accepted his counsel; but every time a decision had to be taken he had to convene a general assembly of the militiamen and make the captain's advice appear as if it were his own, cleverly inculcating it into the assembly so that it would look like the fruit of debate."[19] The disadvantages of this democratic anti-militaristic procedure soon made themselves apparent. "Those in charge would order an operation," declared Federica Montseny, the Anarchist leader, at a public meeting, "and the militiamen would meet to discuss it. Five, six, and seven hours were lost in deliberation, and when the operation was finally launched the enemy had already attained his objective. Such things make one laugh, and they also make one weep."[20]

But they did something else as well: they caused the Anarchosyndicalist militia leaders, especially on the central front, where the pressure of the enemy was unremitting, to turn their backs on their

[19] See bibliography, "Unpublished Article by a Regular Army Corporal." Captain Bayo, who headed the Catalan militia invading the Balearic Islands, records the following conversation he had with the members of the Anarchist militia committee when giving them orders for the invasion of Majorca:

" 'Now, just a minute,' one of the big chiefs replied . . . , 'We only take orders from the leaders of the CNT and we cannot carry out your orders without their approval.'

" 'Nevertheless, they will have to be carried out without their knowledge,' I retorted energetically, 'because they are in Barcelona and the landing is a military secret which I cannot risk sending by cable, radio, or even by code, and it must be undertaken tomorrow morning without vacillation and without delay.'

" 'We are very sorry,' they replied, 'but we cannot participate if it is to be carried out tomorrow. We risk our men only when ordered by our leaders.' . . .

"Over and over again I held my patience; I reasoned with them, I ordered them angrily, I beseeched them. . . .

"Finally they agreed to discuss among themselves whether they would carry out the landing the next day or wait until they received orders from their central committee."—*Mi desembarco en Mallorca*, pp. 113–14.

[20] *Solidaridad Obrera*, December 1, 1936.

traditional attitude towards militarization. "It was [after the capture of Aravaca and Pozuelo outside Madrid] that all my ideas regarding discipline and militarization were shattered," Cipriano Mera, the Anarchist militia leader, confessed some months later. "The blood of my brothers shed in the struggle made me change my views. I understood that if we were not to be definitely defeated, we had to construct our own army, an army as powerful as that of the enemy, a disciplined and capable army, organized for the defence of the workers. Henceforth I did not hesitate to urge upon all combatants the necessity of submitting to new military principles."[21] Just as the CNT–FAI units on the Madrid front had, under the spur of necessity, introduced a modicum of discipline, so, under the same impulsion, they began to substitute a military for a militia structure and to urge the creation of cadres. *Frente Libertario*, the organ of the Madrid Anarchosyndicalist militia, declared that all prejudices should be laid aside and that the CNT should send to the military training academies a large number of comrades, who should begin to see in the military profession one that was as honourable and as essential as the trades that had callused their hands. "The Popular Army now in formation," it added, "requires military technicians, and this need, which is of a national character, is felt especially by our organization, which must watch over the constant development of its power."[22] True, the Madrid Anarchosyndicalist militia was influenced not only by political considerations and by the rigour of the struggle around Madrid, but also by the example of the International Brigades, whose more efficient military organization soon asserted its superiority over the militia system. Little by little, affirms the director of the Anarchist *Castilla Libre*, the change, which at first had been purely nominal, went deeper. "The International Brigades have been observed fighting, and it has been proved that, given the same heroism and expenditure of energy, organization results in greater efficiency. In our militia, cadres appear formed in accordance with the regulations of the War Ministry. The battalion leaders become majors; the century delegates become captains, the first corporals and sergeants make their appearance."[23]

That this was not altogether a titular change was clear from statements made by many of the leading figures in the Libertarian move-

[21] *CNT*, September 20, 1937. See also his proclamation to the Anarchosyndicalist militia on the Madrid front, published in *Castilla Libre*, February 17, 1937.

[22] January 14, 1937.

[23] Guzmán, *Madrid, rojo y negro*, p. 200.

ment, who, having done with their anti-authoritarian past, became assiduous promoters of militarization. Cipriano Mera, the Anarchist militia leader, for example, considered military discipline so important that he decided "to discuss matters only with generals, officers, and sergeants,"[24] and García Oliver, who before becoming Minister of Justice had been regarded as a pure Anarchist, now enjoined the students of one of the officers' training schools, with whose organization and administration he had been entrusted,[25] to bear in mind that enlisted men "should cease to be your comrades and become the cog-

[24] *CNT*, February 23, 1937. "One of the things that has done us most harm in the Army," he declared at a later date, "is the excessive familiarity between officers and men who once belonged to the militia."—*Mundo Obrero*, as given in *Fragua Social*, September 26, 1937.

[25] This assignment—requested by the CNT in the hope of preventing the Communists from gaining control of the officers' training schools and thereby impeding the graduation of officers sympathetic to the CNT and FAI (see speech by Mariano Vázquez, secretary of the National Committee of the CNT, published in *Memoria del congreso extraordinario de la confederación regional del trabajo de Cataluña celebrado en Barcelona los días 25 de febrero al 3 de marzo de 1937*, pp. 178–85)—was given to him by the Higher War Council, whose members, because of the enmity between Largo Caballero and his rivals, had been unable to agree upon any other candidate. In a speech delivered in May, 1937 (*Fragua Social*, June 1, 1937), when he was no longer a member of the Council, García Oliver affirmed that he had received the genuine collaboration of the War Minister and that the degree of confidence the latter had placed in him was due to the fact that he had not used his assignment for the benefit of his own organization. Presumably, one of the principal reasons for Caballero's support of the Anarchist leader was his desire to keep the officers' training schools out of the hands of the Communists. It is worth noting that owing to the Libertarian movement's opposition to the creation of a regular army, the Anarchosyndicalists who enrolled in the officers' training schools were in a minority.

Referring to García Oliver's assignment, Martín Blázquez, an officer in the War Ministry, stated: "In fairness to Caballero, it must be admitted that he gave Oliver his unconditional support. Cordón and I made contact with him, but all we were left to do was to carry out his instructions. Quarters, instructors, equipment, and all other requirements were immediately supplied. Oliver was indefatigable. He arranged and supervised everything himself. He went into the smallest details, and saw to it that they were properly provided for. He even took an interest in the students' timetables and the kitchen arrangements. But above all he insisted that the new officers should be trained in the strictest discipline.

"I, who do not believe in improvisation, was astonished at the organizing capacity shown by this Catalan Anarchist. Observing the ability and assurance of all his actions, I realized that he was an extraordinary man, and could not but deplore that so much talent had been wasted in destructive activity."—*I Helped to Build an Army*, p. 299.

wheels of our military machine."[26] Moreover, in the CNT press military bearing was commended[27] and Anarchosyndicalist commissars were urged by the movement to impose "condign punishment, even the heaviest and most drastic" on men guilty of offences.[28]

But it was not easy to secure general acceptance of the new rules by men who had been taught by their leaders to look upon all armies as the symbol of tyranny, who believed themselves emancipated for all time from the will of autocratic officers, and who had not only introduced the elective principle into their units, but had also lived on terms of equality with group and century delegates.[29] "I should be guilty of insincerity if I were to say that resistance did not have to be overcome," writes Miguel González Inestal, a member of the Peninsular Committee of the FAI. "In the Libertarian camp every single militant had his share of scruples to conquer, of convictions to be adapted—and why not admit it?—of illusions to be buried.[30] This was so not only because

[26] *Bulletin de la Généralité de la Catalogne* (issued by the Propaganda Department of the Catalan Government), March 30, 1937, as quoted by *Le Libertaire*, April 8, 1937. See also Maxim Llorca in *Ideas*, April 29, 1937.

[27] See, for example, *CNT*, April 28, 1937.

[28] See *ibid.*, April 10, 1937. On February 12, 1937, an editorial in *CNT* had declared that militiamen should obey the orders of their commanders on pain of death.—As given in J. García Pradas, *Antifascismo proletario*, p. 46.

[29] Referring to the statement by García Oliver that has just been quoted, a CNT-FAI member wrote: "When ideas of emancipation, when Libertarian conceptions and revolutionary thoughts are seething within us, . . . we cannot understand how our comrade ministers can express themselves in such terms." —Maximo Llorca in *Ideas*, April 29, 1937. Writing about the militarization of the militia in the Asturias, Solano Palacio, a prominent Anarchosyndicalist, avers: "What revolted the militiamen more than anything else was the fact that they were compelled to salute their officers, whom they had hitherto regarded as comrades."—*La tragedia del norte*, p. 135. As for the question of differential pay rates, the misgivings they created among the men were reflected even in an Anarchosyndicalist newspaper that accepted militarization: "Economic differences create classes, and there should not be any in the Popular Army. In this army, everyone, from the militiamen to the generals, has the same needs and the same right to satisfy them. Differences will bring about an estrangement between those who command and those who obey, and the class feelings they engender will have repercussions contrary to the interests of the people. As we are fighting against all privileges, we cannot tolerate the existence of any in the army."—*CNT*, March 1, 1937. It is noteworthy that, according to García Pradas, director of *CNT*, the officers in the Anarchosyndicalist units on the central front handed the greater part of their pay to the CNT Defence Committee of Madrid, which used the money for the benefit of the agricultural collectives.—See his letter to the author, quoted n. 36, pp. 255–6, below.

[30] In a reply to a questionnaire which the author sent to him through the

of our respect for a traditional attitude, consecrated by experience, but also because we feared, quite reasonably, that the resurrection either in part or in whole of the old army would bring about caste privileges, the deformation of youth, the resurgence of the past, the suppression of all social rights, and, above all, that it might end in that army's becoming the devourer of the revolution, the instrument of a party."[31]

It was because the CNT and FAI feared the latter contingency, no less than because they had no project, as did the Communists, for white-anting the entire military edifice, that they were determined to maintain the integrity and homogeneous character of their armed units. Thus, although they had decided to convert these units into brigades of uniform military structure and merge them into the regular army under their own commanders, they were opposed to diluting them with non-Libertarian forces by forming mixed brigades[32] under the control of officers appointed by the War Ministry, a plan that was mainly of Russian provenance[33] and of which one of the important

---

German Anarchist, Agustín Souchy, García Oliver, who organized the officers' training schools (see p. 252, above), remarks that owing to the opposition of the Libertarian movement to the organization of a regular army, the CNT–FAI members who enrolled in the schools were in a minority. (That they were in a minority is emphasized by Mariano Vázquez, secretary of the National Committee of the CNT, in a speech published in *Memoria del congreso extraordinario de la confederación regional del trabajo de Cataluña celebrado en Barcelona los días 25 de febrero al 3 de marzo de 1937*, pp. 178–85.) "This resulted in my bringing the matter up seriously before the National Committee [of the CNT]," continues García Oliver in his reply, "and in an agreement being reached and carried into practice whereby all the [CNT] Regional Committees of Defence were to pay special attention to the recruiting of students for the training schools." And, furthermore, he says: "When we sent lieutenants to assist the leaders of our CNT militia, who at that time were still opposed to militarization, they were made to dig trenches with pick and shovel in order to humiliate them. After the fall of Largo Caballero, when the CNT was no longer in the government, and when militarization was carried forward, those very comrades who had previously humiliated the lieutenants showed a very keen interest in attaining the upper ranks of the Republican army."

[31] *Cipriano Mera, revolucionario*, p. 60.

[32] For information regarding the mixed brigades, see n. 6, p. 227, above.

[33] Two Republican officers confirm this: Martín Blázquez, *I Helped to Build an Army*, p. 295, and Segismundo Casado (article in *The National Review*, July, 1939), who says: "[The government] committed the very serious initial mistake of accepting the opinion of the 'friendly Russian advisers.' " In his book, Casado, who was appointed to organize the first brigades, writes: "One Russian General and two Russian Colonels were chosen to help me in this mission by order of the Minister[Largo Caballero]."—*The Last Days of Madrid*, p. 52.

political aims was undoubtedly that of nullifying Anarchist influence in the armed forces.[34]

At this point it is worth remarking that although Caballero, for political and technical reasons, had approved the militarization of the militia on the basis of mixed brigades,[35] his present desire for easy relations with the CNT, stemming from his growing antipathy to the Communists, inhibited him from attempting seriously to enforce the measure, with the result that the Anarchosyndicalist units, while submitting to the General Staff for the purpose of military operations, remained under the exclusive control of the CNT and were composed of men and officers belonging to that organization.[36] That Caballero

[34] In this connection, Martín Blázquez, War Ministry officer, remarked to General José Asensio, the Undersecretary of War, that "as soon as we have created our mixed brigades [Anarchist] influence will vanish."—*I Helped to Build an Army*, p. 297.

[35] A short account of the military reasons for the creation of mixed brigades is given by Martín Blázquez, *I Helped to Build an Army*, pp. 293–5. For a criticism on technical grounds, see Colonel Segismundo Casado in *The National Review*, July, 1939.

[36] In a report, dated May 8, 1937, Helmut Ruediger, representative in Spain of the International Workingmen's Association, with which the CNT was affiliated, stated: "There is now in the central zone a CNT army of thirty-three thousand men perfectly armed, well-organized, and with membership cards of the CNT from the first to the last man, under the control of officers also belonging to the CNT. Furthermore, there are many comrades in mixed units, but the CNT aims at concentrating them all in CNT units." The homogeneous character of the Anarchosyndicalist units at this stage of the war has been amply confirmed to the author by some of the leading figures in the Libertarian movement, including Cardona Rosell, a member of the National Committee of the CNT, and García Pradas, director of the Anarchosyndicalist daily, *CNT*, and member of the Anarchosyndicalist Defence Committee of Madrid, which controlled the CNT–FAI armed forces on the central front. In his corroborative letter to the author, García Pradas adds: "When the militarization of the militia was decreed, our forces in the central zone agreed to it only on the condition that they maintained a certain independence, a condition that included the retention of their own commanders. The government of Largo Caballero and succeeding ones, as well as the *Junta de Defensa de Madrid*, were not willing to assent to this condition, but they were obliged to 'swallow' it, because we would have preferred rebellion to submission. As time went on, we had to admit ordinary recruits into our units. These were never compelled to become members of the CNT, but we always refused to concede to the government the absolute right to appoint commanders on its own account. In general, what happened was that the Defence Committee proposed to the Ministry of War the names of persons it considered suitable, giving the requisite information, and the Ministry, with this information in its possession, approved the recommendations and published the appointments. It was advisable to act

had assented to, and not simply connived at, this evasion of the rigorous form of militarization agreed upon with the Russians is proved by the fact that General Martínez Cabrera, the Chief of the General Staff, who enjoyed his entire confidence, authorized the Committee of War of the Anarchist Maroto column in February, 1937, to organize a brigade composed entirely of that column's members,[37] the same dispensation being granted to the Anarchist Iron Column, as will be seen in the coming chapter. Significant, too, is the fact that the following interview on the question of militarization and the mixed brigades, given by Mariano Vázquez, the secretary of the National Committee of the CNT, to *Nosotros*, the mouthpiece of the Iron Column, was published without a dissenting comment from the War Ministry:

" *Nosotros*: 'Will our columns disappear?'

" Vázquez: 'Yes, they will disappear. It is necessary that they disappear. [The National Committee has already decided] that our columns, like all the others, should be transformed into brigades. . . . Now this transformation does not imply—although it might appear otherwise—any fundamental change, because those who were previously in command of the columns will now command the brigades. This means that our comrades, who feel affection for the men in charge of operations, can be sure that they will not be compelled through capricious appointments to accept men whose ideology and, consequently, whose personal treatment they dislike. Furthermore, the political commissars, who are the real chiefs—don't let the word

---

in this way for various reasons, one of which was to obtain the high pay allowed to commanders. Our commanders in the central zone, after collecting their pay, turned over the greater part of it to the Defence Committee, which consequently had millions of pesetas at its disposal for aiding agricultural collectives. There were times when, with the acquiescence of our National Committee in Valencia or Barcelona, the government wanted to impose certain commanders on us, but neither Eduardo Val, nor Manuel Salgado, nor myself—for a long time in charge of the Defence Committee—agreed to such a thing, and thanks to our attitude it was possible for us to maintain until the very end those forces with which we were able to crush the Communist Party in March, 1939."

[37] In a report to the General Commissariat of War, dated March 12, 1937, Alberto Fernández Ballesteros, Inspector-Commissar of the Southern Front and a left-wing Socialist Cortes deputy, stated that the Committee of War of the Maroto column alleged that it possessed written instructions from the Chief of the General Staff to form a brigade out of members of the column, and that both "the commander of the Granada sector, Colonel Arellano, and Lieutenant-Colonel Salazar certify having read said orders."

frighten you—of the brigades, will be appointed by the CNT to whom they will be answerable at all times. . . .'

" *Nosotros*: 'It has been said—and this another point that worries our men—that these brigades will be mixed, that is to say that they will be composed of regular, Marxist, and CNT battalions. Is it true?'

" Vázquez: 'There is some truth in it, for that is one of the proposals in connection with the formation of the brigades. However, we have our own proposal: the future brigades, which logically it is for us to form, must be composed of comrades belonging to the CNT and FAI and also be under the control of these two organizations, although subject to orders—another word unpleasant to our ears—from the unified command, which all the forces accept voluntarily.' "[38]

Although the attenuated form of militarization accepted by the CNT–FAI leadership enabled the Anarchosyndicalist units to maintain their virtual independence, it was nevertheless stubbornly resisted by the more extreme spirits of the Libertarian movement who clung passionately to their Anarchist beliefs. No account of this dramatic struggle between principle and practice, between the rank and file and the leadership, is complete unless it includes the story of the famed *Columna de Hierro* or Iron Column.

[38] February 11, 1937.

24

The Iron Column

"THERE are some comrades who believe that militarization settles
everything, but we maintain that it settles nothing. As against
corporals, sergeants, and officers, graduated from the academies,
and completely useless in matters of war, we have our own organization, and we do not accept a military structure." Thus spoke a
delegate of the Iron Column at a CNT congress in November, 1936.[1]

No column was more thoroughly representative of the spirit of
Anarchism, no column dissented more vehemently from the Libertarian movement's inconsistencies of theory and practice, and exhibited
a more glowing enmity for the State than the Iron Column, which
occupied a sector of the Teruel front during the first seven months of
the war. "Our entire conduct must not aim at strengthening the
State; we must gradually destroy it, and render the government
absolutely useless," declared the above-quoted delegate. "We accept
nothing that runs counter to our Anarchist ideas, ideas that must
become a reality, because you cannot preach one thing and practise
another."[2] Nor, in carrying out the social revolution, did any Anarchist
militia unit inspire more fear among middle and small peasants,
among landowners, merchants, and shopkeepers. Mainly recruited
from among the more fiery elements of the Libertarian movement, its
three thousand members[3] included several hundred convicts from the
San Miguel de los Reyes Penitentiary. "[The prisoners] had to be set
free and someone had to face the responsibility of taking them to the
front," ran a report issued by the column's Committee of War. "We,
who have always held society responsible for its own defects, regarded
them as brothers. They joined us and risked their lives, fighting at our

[1] *Fragua Social*, November 14, 1936.
[2] *Ibid.*
[3] This was the figure given by an Iron Column delegate at a CNT congress,
reported in *Fragua Social*, November 14, 1936; see also Martín Blázquez, *I
Helped to Build an Army*, p. 296.

side for liberty. Imprisonment had earned them the contempt of
society, but we gave them their freedom and the opportunity of
rehabilitating themselves. We wanted them to help us, and at the same
time we wished to offer them the possibility of social regeneration."[4]
But these ex-convicts soon brought opprobrium upon the Iron
Column; for, although some of them had been moved to embrace
Anarchist ideals in the course of their internment, the immense majority
were hardened criminals, who had suffered no change of heart and
had entered the column for what they could get out of it, adopting
the Anarchist label as a camouflage.[5]

Although the notoriety that these malefactors visited upon the Iron
Column created considerable friction between its Committee of War
and the Regional Committee of the Valencia CNT,[6] it should be
stressed that a more important reason for discord lay in the fact that,
whereas the Regional Committee supported the policy adopted by
the national leaders of the CNT and FAI, the Iron Column criticized
that policy on the grounds that the entry of the Libertarian movement
into the Cabinet had helped to revive the authority of the State and
had given added weight to the government's decrees. Such censure—
which was accompanied on occasions by the threat of force if the
column's views on certain matters were not adopted[7]—was mortifying
to the Regional Committee and explains in large measure why it did
little or nothing to assist the column in securing either men or supplies.[8]

This boycott was a serious matter for the Iron Column. Although it
had been able to rely, in the early months of the war, upon its own
recruiting campaigns and upon confiscations carried out with the aid
of Anarchist-controlled committees in villages and towns behind the
lines,[9] its appeals for volunteers, owing to a decline in revolutionary

---

[4] *Nosotros*, February 16, 1937.

[5] This was admitted to the author by a Valencia Anarchosyndicalist who had
been in close contact with members of the column.

[6] In a letter to the author Federica Montseny, who was a member of the
National Committee of the CNT, emphasizes this friction and states that the
Valencia CNT demanded that the column should purge itself of the male-
factors in its ranks.

[7] This information was given to the author by a well-informed member of
the Valencia CNT.

[8] For an open criticism of the CNT by the Column's Committee of War,
see p. 261, below.

[9] ". . . During our stay in Valencia," ran a manifesto issued by the column,
"we noticed that, whereas our negotiations for the purchase of arms had failed
because of the lack of hard cash, in many shops there was a large quantity of
gold and other precious metals, and it was this consideration that induced us

fervour and to the discredit into which the column had fallen in Libertarian circles, were incapable of furnishing it with an adequate supply of fresh recruits for the relief of the men at the front. Furthermore, the committees were being supplanted by regular organs of administration, in which the more revolutionary elements were no longer the preponderating force. Even more serious was the fact that the War Ministry had not only decided to withhold arms from all militia units declining to reorganize themselves along the prescribed lines,[10] but had decreed, although in carefully selected language, that the pay of all combatants—which in the case of the militia had previously been handed to each column in a lump sum without supervision and irrespective of its structure—would henceforth be distributed through regular paymasters stationed only in battalions. As the decree made no mention of paymasters in units that had not adopted a military framework, it was clear that if the Iron Column were to hold fast to its militia structure the time would soon arrive when all pay would be suspended.[11]

---

to seize the gold, silver, and platinum in several jewellers' shops."—As given in *Cultura Proletaria*, November 7, 1936.   [10] See p. 249, above.

[11] The decree was submitted to the government by Largo Caballero, and after approval was published in the *Gaceta de la República* on December 31, 1936. Although its language was discreet, its aims were clear enough. In this connection it is worth citing the following statement, which Martín Blázquez, an officer in the War Ministry, made to General Asensio, the Undersecretary of War, when suggesting to him that such a measure be adopted: ". . . I now propose that we decree that those who decline to transform themselves from militiamen into soldiers should get no pay. If we give every battalion a paymaster who will only pay men who obey orders, and if the paymasters of every mixed brigade are subordinate to the quartermaster attached to every brigade command, the brigades, and consequently the whole army, can obviously be organized at once. At the same time it will do away with abuses such as take place in the 'Iron Column,' which numbers barely three thousand men, but receives pay for six thousand every month."—Martín Blázquez, *I Helped to Build an Army*, p. 296. In connection with these abuses, it should be remarked that according to information given to Alberto Fernández Ballesteros, left-wing Socialist Cortes deputy and Inspector-Commissar of the Southern Front, the CNT–FAI militia forces in Malaga inflated their pay rolls to such an extent that in a single fortnight they obtained four hundred thousand pesetas more than the sum to which they were entitled.—Report to the General Commissariat of War, dated February 18, 1937. It should not be supposed from the foregoing that the padding of pay rolls was limited to the CNT–FAI militia, for the Communists, who greatly exaggerated the size of their Fifth Regiment (see n. 6, p. 223, above), indulged in the same practice. This was confirmed to the author by Rodolfo Llopis, Caballero's undersecretary in the premiership.— Reply to questionnaire. See also Caballero, *La UGT y la Guerra*, pp. 10–11.

In spite of the column's earlier intransigence, the Committee of War, better informed than the rank and file of the column's plight, now realized that an uncompromising stand was no longer expedient. They knew that it could not hold out against the pressure of the government and the hostility of the CNT–FAI leadership, and that it would either have to assent to the limited form of militarization advocated by the National Committee of the CNT or be left without the material support essential to its existence. But could the column be brought to heel? Unrest and demoralization were spreading,[12] and there were already murmurings and threats among the more rebellious spirits that they would leave the front if militarization, even in the mildest form, were introduced.

It was at this crucial juncture, when dangers pressed in upon the column from every side, that the Committee of War issued, at the end of January, 1937, a significant report to its members. "[In the beginning]," so this report ran, "the State was a phantom to which nobody paid any attention. The working-class organizations of the UGT and CNT represented the only guarantee for the Spanish people, . . . [but] almost without noticing it our own dear CNT itself became a sapless and lifeless phantom, having injected into the State its own power and prestige. It is now just another appurtenance of the State and another extinguisher of the flames of the revolution.

"Once strengthened, the government began the work of reorganization, and at the moment it has at its disposal an army, like any other state army, as well as several coercive bodies of the old kind. Just as formerly, the police now take action against those workers who attempt to do anything useful from a social point of view. The people's militia has disappeared, and, in a word, the social revolution has been strangled.

"If we had had the help of the government and also of our organization—we refer to the responsible committees—we should have had more war material and more men for the relief of our comrades. But things turned our differently, and we had to allow our men to wear themselves out month after month behind their parapets. Such self-sacrifice is unknown, nor can it be expected of anyone, and every day tremendous problems arise. . . . We admit the internal problems of the column are difficult to solve, and before anything serious should occur, before demoralization and fatigue should spread and deal a

---

[12] On December 22 alone, ninety-seven men abandoned the front and were denounced as deserters by the Committee of War.—See statement published in *Nosotros*, January 2, 1937.

violent blow at what has been conquered and maintained at the cost of unparalleled sacrifice, before all this should happen, we repeat, a formula satisfactory to everyone must be found.

". . . If all the Anarchosyndicalist columns are militarized, and we stand out in opposition to the decisions of the CNT and FAI as the only column that does not accept militarization, we shall be deprived of help not only from the government, but also from our own organization. With the necessary aid our column could maintain intact the revolutionary principles that are in keeping with our character, but owing to the absence of that help we must acknowledge that our method of warfare has failed.

"We know that the overwhelming majority of our comrades will be furious with those responsible for this, but we should like to point out that their protests will be suffocated violently by the State. There is no longer any possibility of organizing anything against its wishes, for it is sufficiently strong to crush whatever stands in its way. Furthermore, these days of utmost gravity impel us to silence our indignation. Once more we must imitate Christ.

"We know the disadvantages of militarization! It conforms neither to our temperament nor to that of others who have always had a fine conception of liberty. But we are also aware of the inconveniences of remaining outside the orbit of the Ministry of War. Sad indeed it is to admit that only two courses are now open to us; the dissolution of the column, or its militarization. Any other course would be futile."[13]

At the end of the report the Committee of War had expressed the hope that the question of militarization would be discussed at an assembly of the column then in progress. But, although the matter was debated, no decision was reached. It was therefore no accident that *Nosotros*, the mouthpiece of the Iron Column, published about this time the interview with the secretary of the National Committee of the CNT, quoted in the last chapter, in which he was at pains to show that the transformation of the militia columns into mixed brigades along the lines agreed upon by the National Committee would not involve any fundamental change. But even this assurance did not modify the intractability of the more zealous opponents of militarization, who constituted the majority of the members of the column.

At the beginning of March, however, matters were suddenly jolted into a climax.

In a ministerial order, which was aimed particularly at accelerating the militarization of the Iron Column and which undoubtedly was

[13] *Nosotros*, February 16, 1937.

issued after consultation with his CNT–FAI colleagues in the Cabinet, Largo Caballero announced that the militia on the Teruel front would be made subordinate to the War Ministry as from April 1, and appointed José Benedito, commander of the Anarchosyndicalist Torres– Benedito Column, to the Organizational Section of the General Staff for the purpose of effecting the necessary changes.[14] At the same time the Iron Column was notified that the decree of December 30, providing for the distribution of pay through battalion paymasters subordinate to the Paymaster General, would be enforced.[15]

Whatever the Committee of War's private opinion may have been with regard to these developments, it was submerged by the indignation that swept the column. In a general assembly the men refused to submit to military reorganization and to the new financial regulations, and a large number of them decided to leave the front in protest.[16] Fearful lest this defiance might give the War Ministry an excuse for

[14] *Diario Oficial del Ministerio de la Guerra*, as given in *La Correspondencia de Valencia*, March 3, 1937.

[15] See Martín Blázquez, *I Helped to Build an Army*, p. 323.

[16] Of this, Martín Blázquez, a War Ministry officer who claims to have inspired the decree, writes: ". . . a part of the Anarchist 'Iron Column' before Teruel revolted against the imposition of my decree concerning the financial organization of the army. They maintained that the Government was turning into a counter-revolutionary Government and that it was organizing an army of mercenaries to deprive the people of its conquests of July, 1936, when the army and the police forces had disappeared. They demanded that the money for the whole column should be paid *en bloc* as before, and refused to submit either to the organization of battalions or to the new financial arrangements."— *I Helped to Build an Army*, p. 323.

It is worth recording that on their way to the rear several centuries of the column became embroiled in an armed struggle between Assault Guards and Anarchists in the village of Vilanesa. "When the small incident was settled," ran a report issued a few days later by the left-wing Socialist Minister of the Interior, Angel Galarza, "the police, for some inexplicable reason . . . were attacked and had to be reinforced. Without instructions from the responsible elements [of the CNT and FAI], members of a certain organization ordered a kind of general mobilization, which occurred in several villages of the province, an attempt being made to cut communications and to impede the circulation of traffic as well as the entry into the villages of the police forces."—Published in *El Pueblo*, March 13, 1937. For an account of these events by the National Committee of the CNT, see *Boletín de Información y Orientación Orgánica del Comité Peninsular de la FAI*, May 1, 1937. Although neither of these reports mentioned the role of the Iron Column in the events, its members were, as everyone knew at the time, among the principal participants. After a battle that cost both sides a number of dead and wounded more than two hundred Anarchists were taken prisoner. According to *Nosotros*, March 23, 1937, ninety-two of these were members of the Iron Column.

conscripting the members of the column for service in the regular army or lest the Valencia CNT might try to incorporate them into other units of the Libertarian movement, the Committee of War issued the following guarded notice: "The Iron Column has neither been dissolved nor does it contemplate dissolution. In accordance with the resolution approved by all its members, it has asked to be relieved so as to rest and reorganize itself. That is what is now happening. At the present moment only about three centuries remain to be relieved. When this has been effected, an assembly of the whole column will be convened, . . . wherein, with our customary seriousness and sense of responsibility, the position of the column and the road to be followed will be decided upon. Hence, until then, comrades must not enlist in other organized units . . . , for, as they belong to a column which at the present moment is resting, no one can compel them to do so."[17]

Nevertheless, the Iron Column was now in a state of virtual disintegration. The Communists would no doubt have had Largo Caballero draft its members forthwith into units of the regular army,[18] but he shunned a step that would have been regarded by the CNT–FAI leaders as a precedent dangerous to the independence of other Libertarian units. In this way, the Committee of War was given a breathing spell, in the days before the proposed assembly that was to determine the column's future, in which to win support among the men for the restricted form of militarization approved by the National Committee of the CNT. While matters were in this posture it is significant that the following article, written by a member of the column, appeared in the Anarchist newspaper, *Nosotros*,[19] the mouthpiece of the Iron Column.

"I am an escaped convict from San Miguel de los Reyes, that sinister penitentiary which the Monarchy set up in order to bury alive those who, because they weren't cowards, would never submit to the infamous laws dictated by the powerful against the oppressed. I was taken there, like so many others, to wipe out an offence; namely, for revolting against the humiliations to which an entire village had been subjected; in short, for killing a political boss.

"I was young and am still young, because I entered the penitentiary when I was twenty-three and was released, thanks to the Anarchist

---

[17] Issued March 6, 1937; published in *Nosotros*, March 9, 1937.

[18] "It is necessary to put an end to what remains of party and trade union militia and autonomous columns, and to create a single army," said a manifesto issued by the Central Committee of the Communist Party, published in *Frente Rojo*, March 19, 1937.   [19] March 12–13, 15–17, 1937.

comrades who opened the gates, when I was thirty-four. For eleven years I was subjected to the torment of not being a man, of being merely a thing, a number!

"Many prisoners, who had suffered as I had from bad treatment received since birth, were released with me. Some of them, once in the streets, went their own way; others, like myself, joined our liberators, who treated us like friends and loved us like brothers. With them we gradually formed the Iron Column, with them, at a mounting tempo, we stormed barracks and disarmed ferocious [Civil] Guards; and with them we rudely drove the fascists to the peaks of the Sierra, where they are now held. . . .

"Hardly a soul has ever bothered about us. The stupefaction of the bourgeoisie when we left the penitentiary is still being shared by everyone; and instead of our being attended to, instead of our being aided and supported, we have been treated like outlaws and accused of being uncontrollable, because we did not subordinate the rhythm of our lives, which we desired and still desire to be free, to the stupid whims of those who, occupying a seat in some ministry or on some committee, sottishly and arrogantly regarded themselves as the masters of men, and also because, after expropriating the fascists, we changed the mode of life in the villages through which we passed, annihilating the brutal political bosses who had robbed and tormented the peasants, and placing their wealth in the hands of the only ones who knew how to create it: the workers.

". . . The bourgeoisie—there are many kinds of bourgeois individuals and they are in many places—wove ceaselessly with the threads of calumny the evil slanders with which we have been regaled, because they, and they alone, have been injured and can be injured by our activities, by our rebelliousness, and by the wildly irrepressible desires we carry in our hearts to be free like the eagles on the highest mountain peaks, like the lions in the jungle.

"Even our brothers, who suffered with us in the fields and factories and were vilely exploited by the bourgeoisie, echoed the latter's terrible fears, and began to believe, because they were so informed by persons who wish to be regarded as leaders, that the men fighting in the Iron Column were merciless bandits. . . .

"On some nights, on those dark nights when armed and alert I would try to penetrate the obscurity of the fields and the mystery of things, I would rise from behind my parapet as if in a dream . . . , gripping my rifle with a frenzied desire to fire, not merely at the enemy sheltered barely a hundred yards away, but at the other concealed at my side, the one who called me comrade. . . . And I would feel a desire to laugh and to weep and to run through the fields, shouting and tearing throats open with my iron fingers, just as I had torn open the throat of that filthy political boss, and to smash this wretched world into smithereens, a world in which it is hard to find a loving hand to wipe away one's sweat and to stop the blood flowing from one's wounds on returning from the battlefield tired and wounded. . . .

"One day—a day that was mournful and overcast—the news that we must be militarized descended on the crests of the Sierra like an icy wind that penetrates the flesh. It pierced my body like a dagger. . . .

"I have lived in barracks, and there I learned to hate. I have been in the penitentiary, and it was there, strangely enough, in the midst of tears and torment, I learned to love, to love intensely. In the barracks, I was on the verge of losing my personality, so severe was the treatment and the stupid discipline they tried to impose upon me. In prison, after a great struggle, I recovered that personality, for every punishment made me more rebellious. There I learned to hate every kind of hierarchy from top to bottom; and, in the midst of the most agonizing suffering, to love my unfortunate brothers. . . .

"As a result of this experience . . . when, in the distance, I heard murmurs of the militarization order, I felt my body become limp, for I could see clearly that the guerilla fearlessness I had derived from the revolution would perish . . . and that I would fall once again into the abyss of obedience, into the animal-like stupor to which both barrack and prison discipline lead. . . .

"There was never any relief for us, and worse still there was never a kind word. Everyone, fascists and anti-fascists, and even members of our own movement—what shame we have felt!—have treated us with aversion. We have never been understood . . . [because] during the war itself, we wished to lead a life based on Libertarian principles, while others, both to their own misfortune and to ours, have remained yoked to the chariot of State. . . .

"History, which records the good and the evil that men do, will one day speak, and it will say that the Iron Column was perhaps the only column in Spain that had a clear vision of what our revolution ought to be. It will also say that of all columns, ours offered the greatest resistance to militarization, and that there were times when, because of that resistance, it was completely abandoned to its fate. . . .

"Our past opposition to militarization was founded on what we knew about officers. Our present opposition is founded on what we know about them now. . . . I have seen . . . an officer tremble with rage or disgust when I spoke to him familiarly, and I know cases today of battalions which call themselves proletarian, whose officers, having forgotten their humble origin, do not permit the militiamen on pain of terrible punishment to address them as 'thou.'[20] . . .

"We used to live happily in the trenches . . . [because] none of us was superior to the other, all of us were friends, all comrades, all guerillas of the revolution. The delegate of a group or century was not imposed upon us; he was elected by us. He did not regard himself as a lieutenant or as a captain, but as a comrade. Nor were the delegates of the committees of the column, colonels or generals; they were comrades. We used to eat, fight, laugh and swear together. . . .

"I don't know how we shall live now. I don't know whether we shall be able to accustom ourselves to abuse from corporals, from sergeants and from lieutenants. I do not know whether, after having felt ourselves to be men in the fullest sense of the word, we shall get used to being domestic animals, for that is what discipline leads to and what militarization implies. . . .

"But the hour is grave. We have been caught . . . in a trap and we must get out of it; we must escape from it as best we can. . . . The militarists, all the militarists—there are fanatical ones in our own camp —have surrounded us. Yesterday we were masters; today they are. The popular army, which has nothing popular about it except that the people form it, . . . does not belong to the people but to the government and it is the government that commands, it is the government that gives orders. . . .

"Caught as we are in the militarists' net, there are only two possible roads. The first road leads . . . to the dissolution of the Iron Column, the second to its militarization. . . .

"[But] the column, that Iron Column which caused the bourgeoisie and the fascists to tremble from Valencia to Teruel must not be dissolved; it must continue to the end. . . .

"If we were to break up the column, if we were to disband and were later drafted, we should have to march, not with those whom we choose, but with those with whom we are ordered to march. . . .

"Whatever we be called, column, battalion, or division, the revolution, our Anarchist and proletarian revolution, to which we have contributed glorious pages from the very first day, bids us not to surrender our arms and not to abandon the compact body we have constituted until now."

[20] In Spanish the second person singular is used for familiar address.

Sunday, March 21, the day fixed for the holding of the assembly that was to vote on the future of the Iron Column, was a portentous one for all its members. In the past weeks the Committee of War had been urging the acceptance of militarization as the only alternative to dissolution, and now that passions had spent their force and disintegration was upon the column, it was obvious that the proponents of militarization were certain to have their way. The arguments used by the committee during the assembly in favour of converting the column into a brigade—that the men belonged to age groups then being drafted by the government; that, even should they decide to disband, they would be inducted shortly afterwards into the regular units organized by the state; that the War Ministry had agreed to all of the four battalions of the proposed brigade being formed of members of the column and that only the artillery would be in the hands of professional officers[21]—were sufficiently powerful to ensure the favourable vote of the assembly.

A few days later, the Committee of War announced to the members of the Iron Column that the unit was to become the 83rd Brigade of the regular army.[22]

[21] See *Nosotros*, March 24, 1937.
[22] *Ibid.*, March 27, 1937.

25

Largo Caballero
Breaks with Moscow

F OR all its seriousness the episode of the Iron Column added but a
ripple to the whirlpool of discord which for weeks had been
swirling in Valencia, the seat of government.

Early in February, 1937, enmities had acquired fresh malignancy
with the fall of the strategic port of Malaga, from where the loosely
organized and inadequately equipped militia columns, divided by
dissensions and mutual suspicions, had been rolled back in precipitous
confusion for more than eighty miles along the coast by an over-
whelmingly superior enemy force composed of Spanish and Italian
units. Of this disaster—for which individual and collective responsibility was widespread[1]—the Communists made what capital they

[1] Copies of two important documents dealing with the loss of Malaga have
been preserved, which no one wishing to apportion responsibility fairly can
afford to ignore, for they form, together with the valuable data in General
Asensio's book, *El General Asensio. Su lealtad a la república*, the basis of any
serious study of this subject. One is a detailed account of the disaster given on
February 12, 1937, to members of the Higher War Council by Colonel José
Villalba, a professional officer with no party ties, in charge of the Malaga sector
of the southern front; the other is a report, dated February 18, 1937, to the
Commissariat of War by the left-wing Socialist, Alberto Fernández Ballesteros,
Inspector-Commissar of the southern front. These documents refer to the
absence of military discipline and organization on the Malaga sector, the muddle
and disorder in the rear, the irresponsibility of professional officers and militia
leaders, the struggle between the different factions to the prejudice of military
operations, the inordinate proselytizing efforts of the Communist Party, the
appointment of an excessive number of Communist political commissars by
Cayetano Bolivar, chief political commissar of the Malaga sector, the wanton
neglect of defensive works, the treachery of the two commanders in charge of
fortifications, Romero and Conejo, who deserted to the enemy, the inadequate
supplies of rifles, guns, and ammunition, the lack of assistance from the fleet
and Air Force, and, finally, the failure of the War Ministry to respond to the

could. Day after day and week after week they had been urging that the military measures adopted by the government during the first months of its existence be put into effect,[2] and now the loss of Malaga gave dramatic import to their words. Certainly the agitation upon which they throve was not without self-interest, for they saw in the rigid implementation of those measures a means, not only of bringing the war to a successful issue, but also of creating a military machine which, if harnessed to their party, would ensure their ascendancy in the affairs of State. They were therefore impatient of Caballero's indulgence towards the Anarchosyndicalist militia and particularly of his dilatoriness on the matter of conscription, the more so as voluntary recruiting had fallen off and a continuous stream of fresh men was needed to replace losses. Largely as a result of their insistence the government had already decided to mobilize the 1932 and 1933 classes,[3] but this decision had remained on paper, partly because Largo Caballero believed in the superior morale and greater combat efficiency of volunteers,[4] and partly because he knew that the Anarchosyndicalists were opposed to the enrolment of their members in government units.[5] True, when taken to task by a delegation of the Madrid Defence

reiterated appeals of Colonel Villalba and other leaders for reinforcements and supplies. One of the most unlucky figures in the disaster was Villalba himself, who was assigned to the Malaga sector after enemy forces had pierced the eastern defences at Estepona and when everything was fusing into disaster. Undoubtedly selected by the War Ministry as a scapegoat, he was later arrested and imprisoned. After more than eighteen months' internment, however, he was exculpated from any blame for the disaster and rehabilitated.—See *La Vanguardia*, November 3, 1938.

[2] See p. 227, above.

[3] *Gaceta de Madrid*, September 30, 1936.

[4] See, for example, article in *Claridad*, Caballero's newspaper, August 20, 1936, to which reference has already been made on pp. 206–7, above.

[5] Although a CNT National Congress decided to agree to the mobilization of the two classes announced by the government, it did so on the understanding that all men with Anarchosyndicalist membership cards should be drafted by the CNT for service in its own militia units. In Catalonia, the Regional Committee of the CNT stated with reference to this decision of the National Congress: "As it would be very childish to hand over our forces to the absolute control of the government . . . the National Congress has decided that all persons in the [two mobilized] classes who belong to our trade union organization should present themselves immediately to the CNT [barracks] or, in the absence thereof, to the trade union or [CNT] defence committees [of their locality], which will take note of their affiliation, their age, their employment, the class to which they belong, their address and all the necessary facts. A report will be sent to the Regional Committee of Defence, Nicolás Salmerón, 10. This committee will issue militia cards, which will be sent to the inscribed

Council, shortly after the fall of Malaga, for not enforcing the draft, he retorted that the government had neither barracks in which to house the conscripts nor money and arms with which to pay and drill them;[6] but the Communists did not regard these as valid arguments, and a few days later their representatives in the government, profiting from the Malaga disaster, compelled him, with the backing of the

---

comrades, who of course will henceforth be at the disposal of the Regional Committee, which will assign them to the column or front selected."—Quoted, Prudhommeaux, *Catalogne Libertaire*, pp. 19–20. See also statements by the delegates of Puertollano and the Madrid Printers' Union at the CNT Plenum of the Central Region reported in *CNT*, October 5, 1936.

At the beginning of March, the Regional Committee of the CNT of Aragon, taking cognizance of the government's mobilization orders, urged the workers in that region to present themselves at the recruiting depots of the CNT for enlistment in Anarchosyndicalist units.—Notice published in *Cultura y Acción*, March 3, 1937. Less open in its language, but no less clear in its purpose, was a manifesto given out by the National Committee of the CNT, the Peninsular Committee of the FAI, and the Peninsular Committee of the Libertarian Youth on March 15, 1937—the day when several classes, in accordance with orders issued by the War Ministry, were to present themselves at their induction centres (*Diario Oficial del Ministerio de la Guerra*, March 9, 1937)—urging the workers to "form themselves into brigades and place themselves at the disposal of the bodies directing the war."—Published in *Fragua Social*, March 16, 1937. In view of all this, it is hardly surprising that *Frente Rojo*, the Communist organ, should have affirmed a few weeks later that in several villages in Estremadura it had been able to prove that men who should have enlisted in the regular army in compliance with the government's mobilization orders had been urged not to do so, and were being formed into battalions of a trade union character.—April 21, 1937.

[6] Quoted by Máximo de Dios at a meeting of the Madrid Defence Council on February 19, 1937.—*Actas de la junta de defensa de Madrid*.

It is worth noting that in response to Communist demands for the enforcement of compulsory military service, Largo Caballero issued, on February 11, a statement in which he declared, in reference to the decree of October 29, 1936, rendering all able-bodied men between the ages of twenty and forty-five liable to conscription (*Gaceta de Madrid*, October 30, 1936), that compulsory military service was in force "*de jure* and *de facto*." "What the government and the War Minister demand," the statement continued, "is that organizations and unions of all kinds should impose on their members the discipline this measure requires so that when the military authorities deem it necessary to employ the services of men of military age they will encounter no obstacles. It is in this way, the Minister considers, that those who wish to co-operate in the defence of national territory against the foreign invasion should carry on their propaganda and not by making demands on the government in connection with problems that have already been made the subject of legal measures, such as the decree of October 29, 1936."—*La Correspondencia de Valencia*, February 11, 1937.

Republican and moderate Socialist ministers, not only to repeat the mobilization order covering the 1932 and 1933 conscripts, but to include in the same draft the 1934 to 1936 classes.[7]

The Communist Party was able to exploit the Malaga debacle in still another way: it demanded the purging of all command posts. This demand, directed ostensibly against members of the officer corps who were suspect or incompetent,[8] soon proved to be aimed specifically at those appointees of Largo Caballero who were opposing its permeation of the armed forces. That their chief target should have been General José Asensio is natural; for, as Undersecretary of War, he held the most important position in the War Ministry next to Caballero himself, a position to which, it will be recalled, the Minister, in a defiant gesture, had elevated him in reply to the Communists' demand that he be removed from the central front.[9] Such an impediment to their plans for hegemony had this general since become that the Russian Ambassador, Marcel Rosenberg, in one of his regular visits to Caballero, demanded that he be deprived of office. To this demand, Caballero, afire with indignation, replied by expelling the Soviet diplomat from his office.

This signal event, confirmed by several colleagues of the Premier and by Largo Caballero himself,[10] is colourfully recorded by the left-wing Socialist Cortes deputy, Ginés Ganga, who affirms that Rosenberg threatened to withdraw Soviet aid unless the demand for the removal of the Undersecretary of War were heeded. "Those of us," he writes, "who used to frequent the Ministry of War were at first struck by the daily visit, to which we finally became accustomed, of his Excellency, the Soviet Ambassador, who spent several hours every day in the office of Largo Caballero, Premier and War Minister . . . Rosenberg was usually accompanied by an interpreter, but what an interpreter! Not a secretary of the Embassy, but the Minister of Foreign Affairs of the Republic, Don Julio Alvarez del Vayo! . . .

"One morning the visit behind closed doors had already lasted two hours when suddenly 'old man' Caballero was heard shouting. The secretaries gathered around the door of the office, not venturing to

[7] *Gaceta de la República*, February 21, 1937. See also Jesús Hernández' statement to the press, published *CNT*, February 17, 1937.

[8] See, for example, Communist Party statement issued after the fall of Malaga, *Frente Rojo*, February 10, 1937; also *ibid.*, February 12, 1937.

[9] See pp. 235–6, above.

[10] Largo Caballero, *Mis recuerdos*, p. 193; Baraibar, articles in *Timón*, Buenos Aires, June, 1940, and *España Libre*, New York, January 1, 1942; Wenceslao Carrillo, open letter to Indalecio Prieto, published in *Mundo*, August, 1943.

open it out of respect. Caballero's shouting increased in intensity. Then, all of a sudden, the door opened, and the aged Premier of Spain, standing in front of his table, his arm outstretched and his shaking finger pointing to the door, was heard saying in a voice tremulous with emotion: 'Get out! Get out! You will have to learn, Señor Ambassador, that although we Spaniards are very poor and need help from abroad very much, we are too proud to let a foreign ambassador attempt to impose his will on the head of the Government of Spain! And as for you, Vayo, it would be better to remember that you are a Spaniard and Minister of Foreign Affairs of the Republic and that you should not combine with a foreign diplomat in putting pressure on your Prime Minister.' "[11]

In spite of the scene with the Russian Ambassador, which furnished such dramatic proof of Caballero's antipathy towards them, in spite of constant friction in other matters, Moscow and the Spanish Communists did not entirely despair of manipulating the Socialist leader. They still hoped that they could use his influence to facilitate the fusion of the Socialist and Communist Parties,[12] as it had facilitated the unification of the two youth movements. But, actually, although he had ardently advocated the merging of the two parties before the outbreak of the war and had since made no public criticism of Communist depredations on the Socialist movement, his recent experiences had stamped out the last spark of his enthusiasm for amalgamation. True, some months later, after he had fallen from office, Caballero gave another reason for his changed attitude towards this question. "The only thing I ask," he declared, "is that those who at one time wished to carry out this fusion should keep to our original agreement, namely, that it should be realized on the basis of a revolutionary programme.

[11] *Hoy*, December 5, 1942.

[12] "The Russian plan, passionately adhered to throughout the war, was to fuse the two parties," testifies Luis Araquistain, the left Socialist leader, whose intimate relations with Caballero invest his words with special authority. "The new party would be called the Unified Socialist Party, as in Catalonia, but in reality it would be a Communist Party, controlled and directed by the Communist International and the Soviet authorities. The name would deceive the Spanish workers, and it was hoped that it would not alarm the Western Powers. Stalin fervently desired that Largo Caballero should use his power in the government and his enormous authority in the Socialist Party to impose the absorption of the latter by the Communist Party."—*El comunismo y la guerra de España*, pp. 27-8. See also Largo Caballero, *Mis recuerdos*, pp. 225-6.

"I remember very well that when we used to speak of this question the Communist Party posed as a condition—because it had been so agreed in Moscow—that we should break relations with all the bourgeois parties.[13] Do they still maintain that condition? Do they insist now, as they once did, that we should break relations with all the bourgeois parties? No, on the contrary. The slogan they now have is that we should return to the days before July 18th."[14]

Whatever may have been the real weight of this consideration in determining Caballero's changed attitude and that of other left Socialist leaders towards the fusion of the two parties, there can be no doubt that it was not so much their dislike of the Communist Party's abandonment of its former revolutionary programme and its collaboration with the Republican parties as the fear that the Communists would finally absorb the Socialists that put the matter entirely out of court. That this was so is suggested by the following account of a conversation among a group of leading left-wing Socialists that took place in January, 1937. ". . . The conversation," recalls Rodolfo Llopis, Undersecretary to the Premier, "turned to what was, for all genuine Socialists, one of the most dramatic of subjects, namely, the disloyalty of the Communists. Someone present drew a picture that was only too familiar to all of us: the campaigns waged by the Communists at the front and in the rear; their drive to remove the Socialists from various organizations; . . . their barefaced proselytism, in which they unscrupulously employed the most reprehensible of methods; their constant disloyalty towards us. He spoke of the behaviour of the Socialist youth leaders who had gone over to the Communist Party, and of the 'conquest' that the Communists had made of the two Socialist deputies, Nelken and Montiel. . . . Meanwhile, he added, our party gave no sign of life; the Executive Committee remained silent. . . .

"Several other comrades spoke. Caballero likewise. He said just a few words, but they were clear and emphatic. 'What is this nonsense about absorption?' he asked. 'Nobody will ever absorb me. The party

[13] In a letter addressed to the Executive of the Socialist Party in March, 1936, proposing the fusion of the two parties, the Central Committee of the Communist Party posed, *inter alia*, the following conditions: "Complete independence with regard to the bourgeoisie"; "complete rupture of the social democratic bloc with the bourgeoisie"; "recognition of the need for the revolutionary overthrow of bourgeois domination and for the establishment of the dictatorship of the proletariat in the form of soviets."—As published in *Claridad*, March 12, 1936.

[14] Speech in Madrid, October 17, 1937, as reprinted in *La UGT y la guerra*, p. 41.

has a tradition as well as potentialities that cannot be thrown overboard. . . . The party cannot die. As long as I live there will be a Socialist!"[15]

No enticement laid before Caballero by members of the Politburo, not even a promise that he could head the united party,[16] could induce him to yield to their importunity. Nor did the intervention of Joseph Stalin himself, who urged Caballero, in a personal message conveyed through Marcelino Pascua, the Spanish Ambassador in Moscow, to support the fusion of the two parties, fare any better. "Largo Caballero," writes Luis Araquistain, "replied that he did not think the moment had come for unification owing to the proselytical work of the Communists, which was so troublesome to the Socialists. Pascua carried this categorical reply to Moscow."[17]

This unequivocal expression of Caballero's intractability, which came just a few days after the incident with the Soviet Ambassador, finally convinced the Russians of the futility of further attempts to knead the Socialist leader to their purpose and became the signal for the launching of a whispering campaign to destroy his prestige and authority. "Why was this campaign waged? Do you know why?" Caballero asked his audience at a public meeting some months later. "Because Largo Caballero did not want to be an agent of certain elements in our country, and because Largo Caballero defended national sovereignty in the military field, in the political field, and in the social field. And when these elements learned, very late, to be sure, that Largo Caballero could never become an agent of theirs, the line changed and the campaign against me started. [But] I can affirm that until shortly before this campaign commenced, I was offered everything that could be offered to a man with ambition and vanity: I could have been the head of the Unified Socialist Party; I could have been *the* political figure of Spain; I would have had the support of those who approached me; but only on the condition that I carried out their policy. And I replied that on no account would I do so.

"As I was saying, they got to know me very late. They should have understood from the very first moment that Largo Caballero has neither the temperament nor the substance of a traitor. I categorically

[15] *Tribuna*, March, 1949. See also Rodolfo Llopis' speech, reported in *La Correspondencia de Valencia*, August 13, 1937.

[16] See article by Ginés Ganga in *Hoy*, December 12, 1942; also Caballero's speech in Madrid in October, 1937, as given in Largo Caballero, *La UGT y la guerra*, p. 5.

[17] *El comunismo y la guerra de España*, p. 28. See also Largo Caballero, *Mis recuerdos*, p. 226.

refused [to carry out their policy], with the result that on one occasion
. . . I had a very violent scene with official representatives of a certain
country whose duty it was to be more discreet, but who did not fulfil
that duty. And I told them—in the presence of one of their agents, an
agent, however, who held a ministerial portfolio—that Largo Caballero
would not tolerate any kind of interference in the political life of our
country."[18]

Undeterred by the Soviet Ambassador's failure to secure the dismissal of Asensio from the Undersecretaryship of War, the Communists applied pressure from other directions. Without actually
naming him, *Mundo Obrero*, their Madrid daily, which enjoyed a wide
diffusion at the front, gave a brief biography that left no doubt as to
the real identity of the "organizer of defeats," who had "furnished
grounds for imposing the maximum penalty,"[19] and at a Cabinet
meeting a few days later, the Communist ministers formally demanded
Asensio's removal, a demand to which Alvarez del Vayo, the Foreign
Minister, despite his personal conviction that the general was "unquestionably one of the most capable and intelligent officers in the
Republican army"[20] gave strong support. ". . . Having decided that
the fundamental factor was not one's own personal trust in the
General," he explains, "but the suspicion which he inspired in a large
section of the troops, I was one of the Cabinet ministers who stood out
most firmly for his dismissal. . . . The fight waged by Caballero
against what he thought was an injustice done to his Undersecretary
had a certain greatness. He deeply resented the fact that I, for the first
time, took a position different from his, and from that day, to my great
regret, I ceased to be his most trusted Minister."[21] In spite of Caballero's
vehement defence of General Asensio, Caballero was defeated on this
issue by a broad opposition spanning the political spectrum from the
Anarchosyndicalist to the Left Republican ministers.[22] The next

[18] Speech in Madrid, October, 1937, as given in Largo Caballero, *La UGT
y la guerra*, pp. 5–6.
[19] February 16, 1937.
[20] *Freedom's Battle*, p. 126.   [21] *Ibid.*
[22] This was confirmed by Federica Montseny in a letter written to the author
after the war. Her honesty is particularly appreciated, because of the reluctance
of several of her former Cabinet colleagues to furnish the author with service-
able information regarding the attitude adopted by them. It is worth noting
that the stand of the Left Republican ministers during the debate was reflected
in a derogatory allusion to Asensio in large type on the front page of *Política*,
the national organ of their party, on February 21, 1937.—See n. 41, p. 280,
below.

day Asensio's resignation was published in the official gazette.[23]

If Alvarez del Vayo had done much to undermine Caballero's position in this crisis, no less so had the hostile attitude of the CNT and FAI towards the general, both in Cabinet meetings and in their press.[24] A strict disciplinarian who had employed stern measures against retreating militiamen when in command of the central front,[25] Asensio had long been distrusted in Libertarian circles, where in the early days opposition to professional officers and to militarism in all its forms had been an article of faith. Hence, the CNT and FAI had been easily sucked into the campaign against the general, and, without consciously desiring it, they thereby facilitated the workings of the Communists against Caballero.[26]

But Caballero was not to be easily divested of a collaborator in whose technical ability he had the maximum confidence, and, with the object of using him in some capacity in the War Ministry, instructed him to remain in Valencia under his direct orders.[27] At the same time, provoked by the struggle over Asensio, he took vigorous action against Communist influence in the War Ministry. He assigned Lieutenant-Colonel Antonio Cordón, a member of the Communist Party and head of the technical secretariat of the Undersecretaryship of War,[28] to the Cordova front,[29] dismissed his aide-de-camp, Lieutenant-Colonel Manuel Arredondo, on account of his sympathy for the party,[30] and posted him, along with Captain Eleuterio Díaz Tendero, the crypto-Communist chief of the vital Information and Control

[23] *Gaceta de la República*, February 21, 1937.

[24] For attacks in CNT–FAI newspapers, see *Castilla Libre*, February 19, 1937, *CNT*, February 17, 1937, *Fragua Social*, February 23, 1937, *Frente Libertario*, February 16, 1937, *Solidaridad Obrera*, February 20, 25, 27, 1937.

[25] According to Martín Blázquez (*I Helped to Build an Army*, p. 217), Asensio had once ordered the execution of several militia leaders who had refused to obey his orders to attack.

[26] It should be recorded that in her letter to the author (n. 22, p. 276, above), Federica Montseny avows that she later considered that the Libertarian movement's opposition to Asensio was a mistake, not only because of his exceptional ability, but because it helped to weaken Caballero in relation to the Communists.

[27] *Gaceta de la República*, February 21, 1937.

[28] For the importance of this post, see n. 10, pp. 228, above.

[29] *Gaceta de la República*, February 23, 1937.

[30] That he was a sympathizer was confirmed to the author by Alejandro García Val, himself a Communist Party member, and adjutant of Major Manuel Estrada, the former Chief of the General Staff. For further confirmation, see n. 32, below.

Department,[31] to the Bilbao front.[32] Furthermore, he appointed six inspectors, all of them trusted left-wing Socialists,[33] to scrutinize the work of generals, of the lesser officers and non-commissioned officers, of the top officials in the Commissariat of War,[34] and political commissars of every rank.[35]

Cowed momentarily into discretion by this vehement reaction, the Communists ventured a mild criticism only of the latter measure[36] and refrained from mentioning in their press the removal of their own men from key positions in the War Ministry, lest they exacerbate Caballero's anger still further. Nevertheless, without any risk to themselves, they contrived a means of denouncing these dismissals and, moreover, of preventing Caballero from retaining Asensio in any capacity in the War Ministry, thanks to the ingenuity of Díaz Tendero. As former head of the Information and Control Department, Díaz Tendero had been in friendly contact with all organizations, and was able—by

[31] In this department, which investigated the antecedents of every man before he could join the army, Díaz Tendero, without actually being a member of the Communist Party, did "wonderful things" for it, according to information given to the author by Margarita Nelken, left-wing Socialist Cortes deputy, who knew Tendero personally, and who became a member of the Communist Party in December, 1936.

[32] *Gaceta de la República*, February 21, 1937. Referring to the series of dismissals from the War Ministry, Martín Blázquez, who at the time was an aide of Antonio Cordón's, writes: "Whether because my services were regarded as more essential, or because I was believed to be less of a sympathizer with the Communist Party, I was not dismissed from the Ministry as so many others were. On the contrary, I had to do Cordón's work in addition to my own. Some of my colleagues, including Caballero's aide-de-camp and Díaz Tendero, were sent to the Army of the North at Bilbao. I confess I was alarmed at the prospect of being vindictively sent there myself. I was very pessimistic about the prospects on that front. I had made frequent requests for supplies for Bilbao, but they had all been rejected. 'We shall send nothing to the Army of the North,' I had been told. 'Let the Basques look after themselves! What have they got an independent Republic for?' In view of this shortsighted policy, being sent to the Army of the North obviously meant a very good chance of ending up before a Fascist firing-squad."—*I Helped to Build an Army*, p. 320.

[33] These were, according to the *Gaceta de la República*, February 23, 1937: José Díaz Alor, Luis Barrero Hernando, Mariano Muñez Sánchez, Carlos Hernández Zancajo, Manuel Arias Fernández, and Julio de Mora Martínez.

[34] Specific reference was made to the General Commissar (Alvarez del Vayo), the Secretary-General (Felipe Pretel), both secret Communist supporters (see p. 230, above), and to the Sub-Commissars of War, the chief of whom was Antonio Mije, a member of the Politburo of the Communist Party.

[35] See circular order published in the *Gaceta de la República*, February 23, 1937.

[36] See *Frente Rojo*, February 24, 1937.

virtue of the fact that his allegiance to the Communists was barely known outside the War Ministry—to turn to account the columns of *Nosotros*, the mouthpiece of the Iron Column,[37] whose dislike for Caballero was untempered by the political considerations that restrained the language of the less extreme Libertarian organs, which, in spite of their attacks on Asensio and their hostility to the Socialist leader before the war, were conscious of his present value as an ally against the Communists. Accordingly, on February 25, *Nosotros*, documented by Díaz Tendero, published under the caption "How the purging of the army is being carried out," an article containing one list of "sincere Republican officers" dismissed from their posts, and another of officers appointed in their stead, who had "never been known for their Republican sympathies" and were "either disloyal or just indifferent." The first list included the three Communist and pro-Communist officers removed from the War Ministry, and the second the name of Lieutenant-Colonel Fernández, who had succeeded Díaz Tendero in charge of the Information and Control Department, and who was, according to *Nosotros*, a great friend of Asensio's. But more interesting than all these facts, the paper affirmed, was that although the impression had been created that General Asensio had been removed he had, in reality, been relieved of all responsibility and placed behind the scenes as technical adviser to the minister and the new Undersecretary. "Moreover, his appointment has been made by a simple ministerial order, whereas assignments and appointments of generals, whatever their status, should be made by decree on the proposal of the government and with the signature of the head of the state."[38]

Although there is no corroborative evidence that such a ministerial order was ever issued by Caballero—and, indeed, it should be noted that Asensio himself has denied its existence[39]—the War Minister certainly did have in mind the idea of using the general's services, as the latter himself has conceded.[40] Nevertheless, no formal appointment was made of the kind suggested, and it may be safely assumed that the allegation was designed to forestall any attempt to revive Asensio's authority in the War Ministry.

In addition to the above-mentioned article, *Nosotros* came out with the following invective against the War Minister:

[37] This information was given to the author after the war by Carlos Contreras, chief political commissar of the Fifth Regiment.

[38] February 25, 1937.

[39] In a letter to the author.

[40] *Ibid.*

"Largo Caballero is old, too old, and does not possess the mental agility necessary for solving certain problems upon which our own lives as well as the lives and liberty of the whole people depend.

"When the newspapers, all the newspapers—with the exception of those inspired by the War Minister himself—accuse one man; when in the trenches, in the barracks, in the committees, in the streets, and in the ministries themselves, it is whispered or openly stated that General Asensio either through ineptitude or treachery has gone . . . from defeat to defeat; when it is common knowledge that on the very night that news of Malaga's fall was received, the general, now adviser to Largo Caballero, got drunk in a cabaret just like any individual who thinks only of wallowing in the mire and debasing himself, the Minister should not . . . send letters to the press and adopt tragic airs with the idea of silencing such things. . . .[41]

"With hostile eyes the people see that they are being fooled. The resignation of Asensio is a trick, because behind their backs he is extolled, having been elevated to a position of greater confidence at the side of the Minister. . . .

"The Minister of War, Comrade Largo Caballero, should bear in mind that he is old, and, what is more, that he is falling into senility, and that senile men should neither govern nor be allowed to govern."[42]

Incensed by this abusive language and by the allegation regarding Asensio's appointment—an allegation that compelled him to abandon all idea of using his services, even unofficially, in the War Ministry, lest he be accused of flouting public opinion and the will of the

[41] This is a reference to two open letters, one to Carlos Esplá, the Left Republican minister, the other to the National Executive of the Left Republican Party, protesting against the following allusion to Asensio's successor, Carlos de Baraibar, on the front page of the party organ, *Política*, of February 21: "If in the dismissals we can discern victory, do not let us encounter defeat as a result of the appointments." In the first of these letters Caballero asked Esplá whether *Política* was about to begin "a new campaign of a disruptive character such as the one that has compelled me to deprive myself of an able collaborator?" and urged him to use all his influence to stop it from developing.— *Adelante*, February 24, 1937. And in his letter to the National Executive, he declared that he was not prepared to tolerate the initiation of a campaign by an official organ of a Popular Front party that might create "disagreeable situations" for his trusted collaborators (*ibid.*). In reply, *Política* (February 25, 1937) contended that the words to which Caballero objected had been set up in type before the name of Asensio's successor was known, while the National Executive (*La Correspondencia de Valencia*, March 2, 1937) affirmed that it did not see in them any attack on Carlos de Baraibar.

[42] February 25, 1937.

Cabinet[43]—Caballero had Angel Galarza, left-wing Socialist Minister of the Interior, suspend the publication of *Nosotros*[44] and ascertain the source of its information. The truth was soon forthcoming. Two days later the minister announced—without mentioning Díaz Tendero by name—that a regular army officer suspected of inspiring several articles had been arrested and that about two hundred copies of *Nosotros* had been found in his home.[45]

This incident was the crowning indignity and injury Largo Caballero had suffered at the hands of the Communists. For months he had watched their stealthy permeation of the Socialist movement and of the armed forces, which had resulted in the loss of a substantial part of his own following, including many intimate associates; but

[43] A few months after the fall of Largo Caballero , when the Communists had strengthened their position still further, Asensio was indicted for neglecting to supply the Malaga front with the necessary arms and munitions, and was imprisoned pending trial. (The text of the indictment is given in his book, *Asensio. Su lealtad a la República*, pp. 29–62, which was written in jail in defence of his conduct.) In May, 1938, however, he was released and rehabilitated, partly because of the intervention of influential friends, including Diego Martínez Barrio, the Vice-President of the Republic, and of General Vicente Rojo, the then Chief of the General Staff, who was personally convinced of his innocence (see his letters to Asensio, *ibid.*, pp. 110–11), partly because he could have made a powerful case against his chief accusers, and partly because of the difficulty—having regard to the need at that time for avoiding as much enmity as possible between Socialists and Communists—of placing him on trial without impeaching his chief, Largo Caballero, to whose orders he was, as Undersecretary of War, directly subordinated.

[44] See *Claridad*, February 28, 1937. That *Nosotros'* attack on Caballero had been embarrassing to the national leaders of the CNT was clear when, a few days later at the Extraordinary Congress of the Catalan CNT, the secretary of the National Committee opposed, and succeeded in defeating, a motion of the Catalan organization that a protest should be made against the suspension of the paper.—See *Memoria del congreso extraordinario de la confederación regional del trabajo de Cataluña celebrado en Barcelona los días 25 de febrero al 3 de marzo de 1937,* pp. 114–17. Referring some months later to the attacks on Caballero that had appeared in some of the CNT–FAI newspapers, Helmut Ruediger, representative in Barcelona of the AIT with which the CNT was affiliated, wrote: "We all knew Caballero's past, but not all the editors of the CNT provincial papers knew that several months ago Caballero had become an opponent of Communist influence and that, consequently, to demand his removal was to do the work of the Communist Party."—Report to AIT dated May 8, 1937.

[45] *Claridad*, February 28, 1937. It is of interest to record that, according to General Asensio (letter to the author), the Communists, with the support of representatives of other organizations, had proposed Díaz Tendero as his successor in the Undersecretaryship, but that Caballero had refused to countenance this proposal.

fearing no doubt to forfeit Soviet supplies and no less fearing to reveal to the outside world—particularly to Britain and France, which he still hoped might be enticed to raise the arms embargo—the depth of Communist penetration behind the Republican façade,[46] he had been inhibited from making any public statement against his tireless adversaries.[47] However, he could no longer suppress the anger that fermented in him. Issuing from his silence he hit back with the following manifesto, in which his references to fascist agents were unmistakable allusions to the Communists:

"On Sunday, February 2, large contingents representing antifascist Spain marched through the streets of Valencia affirming their adhesion to the government and to the Republican Constitution it represents.[48] . . .

[46] As an example of Caballero's concern for foreign opinion because of Communist influence in the army, see his speech in October, 1937, *La UGT y la guerra*, p. 16.

[47] In his speech in October, 1937, he stated that he had not replied to the campaign the Communists had waged against him since the fall of his government five months previously, because he did not wish it to be said that he had made any statement which had adversely affected Spain's position at Geneva or had demoralized the soldiers at the front. "I can assure you," he added, "that one of the greatest sacrifices I have ever made in my life was to keep silent during these past five months. But I am not worried, for, although the calumniators have thrust tooth and nail into my flesh, my conscience is satisfied that my silence was in the interests of Spain and in the interests of the war."—*La UGT y la guerra*, p. 5. These considerations must no doubt have influenced him also during his incumbency.

[48] This refers to a demonstration in support of Largo Caballero organized after the fall of Malaga by the Provincial Secretariat of the Valencia UGT, which was under the control of the left-wing Socialists. In a notice sent to all the trade union, political, and cultural organizations in Valencia province, inviting them to participate, the Secretariat stated that it wanted the Government to see by the demonstration that it had the support of the working people. The Communists accepted the invitation, and, at a gathering of the leaders of the local organizations, succeeded, thanks to the propitious atmosphere created by the fall of Malaga, in securing the adoption of a proposal that a ten-point petition should be presented to Caballero on the day of the demonstration embodying, among other things, the following demands: compulsory military service and the cleansing of all responsible military posts. That the Caballero Socialists resented the petition is clear from the following lines in an editorial published in their paper the day before the demonstration: "We should not ask for compulsory military service, but should present ourselves when we are called up. . . . We should not ask for anything, but should give everything."—*Adelante*, February 13, 1937. See also Caballero's statement on compulsory military service issued a few days before the demonstration, n. 6, p. 271, above. Owing to the participation of the Communists and to the petition, with which

"While they were expressing their willingness to give the government unqualified support, and while as a result of this clamorous demonstration the position of Republican Spain and its legal government was strengthened in the eyes of the world, fascist agents redoubled their efforts to such an extent that they found in the midst of traditionally Republican and working-class organizations a certain response and even help for their aims and intrigues. Disguised among us, and favoured by our proletarian and Republican kindness, they sowed confusion, stirred up passions, and encouraged indiscipline in our ranks.

". . . The authorities know that fascist agents, with membership cards of the Republican parties, the Socialist Party, the Communist Party, and the UGT and the CNT, have been operating freely in Loyalist Spain and that their criminal acts have succeeded in disorienting many Republican soldiers and even civilians, whose clean and self-sacrificing past certify to their good faith and loyalty. . . . A section of the press and of the anti-fascist parties and organizations, responsible members of those bodies, and well-intentioned yet thoughtless people, have become involved in the enemy's dark plot and facilitate his work. So well organized is espionage among us that I affirm in all sincerity that intrigues and passions are coiled around our feet like reptiles. . . .

". . . A whole apparatus has wedged itself between the people and the government, perverting the consciences of many individuals and encouraging the darkest appetites, an apparatus which works consciously or unconsciously—in both ways I believe—against our cause, with the result, as I have already stated, that around the feet of those who should march, and are ready to march at the head of the democratic and working people, serpents of treason, disloyalty, and espionage are coiled.

"I am not prepared to tolerate this state of things an hour longer."[49]

---

great play was made, the left-wing Socialists were unable to use the demonstration, as they had intended, to bolster Caballero's authority.

[49] *Claridad*, February 27, 1937.

26

Largo Caballero Hits Back

ALTHOUGH the Communists later denounced Largo Caballero's manifesto as a mean and coarse attack upon themselves,[1] they gave it a discreet reception at the time it was made[2] and, indeed, for fear of provoking a crisis for which they were not quite ready, joined with other organizations at a meeting called by the Premier in assuring him of their support.[3] Nevertheless, they continued to press their efforts to strip the military summits of all officers who were an impediment to their plans for hegemony. In this they were greatly aided by an offensive launched on March 8 by General Franco's Italian allies on the Guadalajara sector of the Madrid front.

On the fifth day of the enemy's advance, when it seemed that nothing could arrest his triumphant progress, the Communist ministers, supported by the majority of the Cabinet, forced Largo Caballero to request the Chief of the War Ministry General Staff, General Martínez Cabrera, to resign, and demanded that the Higher War Council, which on Caballero's proposal had approved the General's appointment in December, be immediately convened to decide on his successor.[4] Although *Mundo Obrero* had urged some days earlier, with Martínez Cabrera and other officers in mind, that the Council should meet

[1] Speech by Jesús Hernández in Valencia, May 28, 1937, as given in Hernández, *El partido comunista antes, durante y después de la crisis del gobierno Largo Caballero*, p. 11.

[2] See, for example, *Mundo Obrero*, March 1, 1937.

[3] Reported, *El Día Gráfico*, February 28, 1937.

[4] For these and subsequent details about the Martínez Cabrera incident not credited to any precise source, I am indebted to the staff of the Febus news agency, which was in daily contact with persons having close relations with members of the government and the Higher War Council. After the fall of Caballero, Jesús Hernández, Communist Minister of Education, publicly declared that his party had been instrumental in removing Cabrera.—See his speech of May 28, 1937, reproduced in Hernández, *El partido comunista antes, durante y después de la crisis del gobierno Largo Caballero*, p. 24.

regularly to discuss all questions appertaining to the war such as "the appointment and control of officers and the cleansing of the army of all hostile and incompetent elements,"[5] no action had been taken by the War Minister. But now the demand of the Communist ministers could not be denied. Under the chairmanship of Caballero the Council met, and voted that Martínez Cabrera should be succeeded by José Miaja's chief of staff, Lieutenant-Colonel Vicente Rojo, whose Communist bias, it should be noted, was not generally known at this time.[6] In spite of the fact that within a few hours of this meeting a dramatic counter-offensive, which transformed the Italian advance into a confused flight, made it expedient to cancel Rojo's new assignment so that he could remain at his post on the central front,[7] Martínez Cabrera was not suffered to continue in office.[8] This victory over Caballero was swiftly followed by another; for no sooner had Cabrera been ousted than the Communist ministers and their allies in the Cabinet secured the appointment of Vicente Uribe, the Communist Minister of Agriculture, and of Alvarez del Vayo, the pro-Soviet Foreign Minister, as government representatives on the General Staff.[9]

While the Communist Party was registering triumphs in the Cabinet and in the Higher War Council, Soviet representatives in Spain were endeavouring to undermine Caballero's influence still further by winning the unconditional adhesion of Carlos de Baraibar, who had succeeded General Asensio in the Undersecretaryship of War. A left-wing Socialist belonging to Caballero's intimate circle, Baraibar had been deprived, owing to serious illness, of a first-hand knowledge of the events that had recently extinguished Caballero's enthusiasm for the unification of the Socialists and Communists—the information he had received having derived, according to his own account, solely from

[5] March 2, 1937.

[6] A short account of Rojo is given on p. 241, above.

[7] *Gaceta de la República*, March 16, 1937.

[8] For a War Ministry announcement paying tribute to Martínez Cabrera, see *El Mercantil Valenciano*, March 16, 1937. He was replaced by Colonel Alvarez Coque, a Republican, who occupied the post until Rojo was reappointed after the fall of the Largo Caballero government.

[9] "Experience has proved to us," stated *Mundo Obrero* (March 18, 1937), "that the subordination of the highest military body to the Ministry of War is insufficient. Infinitely more just is the direct representation of the government in all the deliberations of the General Staff. In this way, the officers who form the latter have at all times the help and advice of the government itself. . . . On the other hand, the arduous task of the holder of the portfolio of war requires this direct help of the two ministers. Our sincere congratulations to the government on this magnificent agreement."

pro-Communist sources[10]—and had taken up his new post inclined to work for the fusion of the two parties. ". . . I frankly avow," he writes, "that there was a moment when I, of all the left-wing Socialists, was the most influenced by the Communists—allowing for the unsurpassable exception of Alvarez del Vayo—and that I understood my resumption of work should distinguish itself by a continual and positive labour in favour of the immediate fusion of the two parties in order to rescue our own from the catastrophe into which its inefficiency was plunging it and at the same time to demonstrate the superiority of Communist methods."[11] Notwithstanding the accusations he heard from the lips of Socialist colleagues, when he was about to resume work, that "on the very fronts, even in the field hospitals, the Socialists, just because they were Socialists, were receiving disgraceful treatment, whereas the Communists were favoured in everything and even monopolized glory for themselves," and that a Socialist or an Anarchist battalion could be seen "barefooted and in tatters at the side of another battalion of the same brigade, but of Communist affiliation, which was equipped as if for a military parade,"[12] he was disposed to make

[10] Article in *Timón*, Buenos Aires, June, 1940. It is worth noting that during Baraibar's illness, Largo Caballero had confined his conversation to the former's state of health and had refrained from troubling him with political developments.—*Ibid.*

[11] *Ibid.* In another article he states that he believed that "without unity of action, as a transitional stage towards organic unity, the proletariat would never be in a position to oppose successfully the bourgeoisie and fulfil its historic mission," and that the "dynamic quality of the Communists was very congenial to me as compared with the extreme sluggishness of many Socialists."—*Vía Libre*, August 5, 1939.

[12] In another article he says: "As the control of the Quartermaster Corps was in their hands, this terrible weapon of corruption and proselytism was employed unscrupulously [in the commission of abuses ranging] from the petty fraud of giving a friend a special voucher to the enormous infamy of granting or not granting, as the case may be, food and clothing to an entire unit, depending on its political colouring or that of its commander."—*Vía Libre*, August 5, 1939. "I learned that on some fronts," records Largo Caballero, "an annoying preference was shown for the Communists; they were given shoes, clothing, tobacco, and food. The others were treated as stepchildren—that is, when they were not shot in the back. I likewise learned that in some hospitals—just as the priests and nuns had once acted towards non-communicants—non-Communists were not taken care of. They were neither treated nor fed properly; all the attention was given to Communist Party members and future prospects."—*Mis recuerdos*, p. 209. "It is a lamentable thing to have to acknowledge the fact that in order to get rope sandals a soldier must be a Communist . . . ," declared the left-wing Socialist, Carlos Rubiera (speech reported in *Fragua Social*, July 7, 1937). "In the [military] hospitals the same thing goes on as in the days of the

allowance for exaggeration.[13] But once in the Undersecretaryship of War, he changed his mind. "In that observatory . . . the impression I received was the most disagreeable of my life and shattered the dearest illusions I had cherished during my illness. I gradually discovered to what degree I had been credulous and had run the risk of letting myself be seduced by rose-coloured spectacles that were as odious as they were distorting. In the short period during which I held that post, it was necessary to change the administration of the health and transport services and prepare for changes in the Quartermaster Corps. Without any desire to offend those persons who occupied positions of maximum responsibility, I must declare that all the levers on which they relied— the exceptions are so few that they are not worth mentioning—were in the hands of Stalinists who ran the services of the Army with the utmost unscrupulousness and profited from its funds and perquisites of office, concerned only with the growth of the Communist Party, with the reinforcement of its power, and, in some cases, only with personal gain. And what happened in the departments of the Undersecretary-ship of the War Ministry also occurred in the different sections of the General Staff. By means of a fantastic web of intrigue and in spite of the honesty of many persons who held technical posts of the greatest responsibility, and who were not members of any political party, . . . the Communists cornered all the commanding positions, and,

---

nuns, when, in order to get a stew or chicken, or whatever there was, you had to wear and venerate the scapular or the cross. Now you need the hammer and sickle." For a condemnation by the moderate Socialists of the privileged position enjoyed by the Communists at the front, see *El Socialista*, February 25, 1937.

[13] "The impression I received was so shocking," he writes, "that I honestly believed that there had been considerable exaggeration in all I had heard. Furthermore, the extremely artful replies made in various speeches by Socialists, such as Vayo, who, as we learnt later, had long been in the service of the Communist Party, appeared so impregnated with revolutionary Marxist fervour, so inspired by the great ideal of unification, so ardently desirous of eradicating whatever might be true in those accusations by means of a far-reaching policy, through which the Socialists and Communists, united more closely every day, would devote themselves to winning the war, that although I no longer lived in the state of ingenuousness that I did when I was cut off from active politics, I nevertheless believed that the evil could not be as great as it appeared, so heinous did it seem to me. For this reason, I felt inclined to continue working for that broad policy of unification, together with men who were incapable of committing such injustices—injustices that conformed to a carefully prepared plan."—Article in *Timón*, Buenos Aires, June, 1940.

protected by them, waged a campaign of proselytism as barefaced as it was menacing."[14]

From the moment he entered the Undersecretaryship Baraibar was regaled by the Russians in the Hotel Metropol, Soviet headquarters in Valencia, and received regular visits from them at the War Ministry, during which they endeavoured to seduce him from his allegiance to Caballero.[15] Although he does not refer in detail to these occasions, he nevertheless reveals: "I received all manner of flattery, and was conceded the honour of being the only Socialist—next to Alvarez del Vayo, of course—capable of appreciating the urgent need . . . for the fusion of the working class. In short, I was being tenderly cultivated for the role of traitor to Largo Caballero."[16] But Baraibar refused to forsake the Socialist leader, and from the day he gave the Soviet Ambassador to understand that he would not assume the role the Russians and their Spanish aides expected of him, he ceased to be the object of their cajolery.[17] His rebuff came as a rude surprise, for his recent support of the idea of Socialist–Communist unification, particularly at a time when its lustre had begun to tarnish before the eyes of many of his own colleagues, had encouraged the Communists to believe that he would advance their interests in the War Ministry; but far from fulfilling these expectations, Baraibar became a prop for Caballero's policy, and, in the succeeding weeks, helped the War Minister to carry out his most rigorous assault on Communist positions in the armed forces. By the end of March this assault had acquired such amplitude as to elicit a public denunciation by the Politburo: ". . . The unity of all anti-fascists necessary for winning the war is being hindered by a whole series of acts, especially during the last few days, such as the transfer or removal from commanding positions of officers and commissars—just because they are Communists—who have given repeated proofs of their abilities and talents."[18]

Caballero's anger had undoubtedly been inflamed not only by the

[14] *Ibid*. "The Communist Party," declared *CNT* (June 28, 1937), "orders officers who are subject to its control to use military discipline in order to make converts, with the result that we find thousands of cases where a military commander employs his prerogatives and the military code not in order to fight fascism, but to annihilate revolutionary organizations and weaken the power of other anti-fascist bodies."

[15] For this information the author is indebted to a member of the staff of José María Aguirre, Largo Caballero's politico-military secretary.

[16] Article in *Timón*, Buenos Aires, June, 1940.

[17] *Ibid*.

[18] Published in *Frente Rojo*, March 29, 1937.

Communists' behaviour in the War Ministry and by the practices of their political commissars now being brought to his attention— practices ranging from the withholding of non-Communist newspapers from the front[19] to the coercing of soldiers to join their party[20]— but also by the information that had recently reached his ears regarding the sectarian conduct of the General Commissariat of War which, it will be remembered, had been set up in October, 1936, to regularize the appointment of commissars, and which had passed under the control of the Communists owing to the secret defection of Alvarez del Vayo and Felipe Pretel, whom the War Minister had selected because they enjoyed his highest confidence.[21] On November 25 he had issued instructions whereby all commissars were to be appointed by him on the proposal of Alvarez del Vayo, the General Commissar, whose recommendations were to be submitted for his approval through Felipe Pretel, the Secretary General.[22] Although no authority had been given to the Commissariat in these instructions to permit candidates to take up their proposed assignments before formal ratification by the War Minister, the candidates recommended by Alvarez del Vayo, as well as by Mije, the Communist head of the Sub-Commissariat of Organization, to whom the former frequently delegated his powers, had been allowed to assume their duties "provisionally," a procedure that had greatly benefited the Communist Party.[23] "One of those most responsible," writes Caballero, "was Alvarez del Vayo . . ., who until then had professed to be my trustworthy friend. He

[19] See letter sent by *Claridad*, at that time still a Caballero Socialist organ, to Francisco Antón, the secretary of the Madrid Communist Party organization and Inspector-Commissar of the Central Front, charging that the Madrid section of the Commissariat of War, which he controlled, was obstructing the distribution of that paper at the front.—Published in *Claridad*, March 1, 1937. See also *Frente Libertario*, February 20, 1937, complaining that the CNT–FAI newspapers were not reaching the front regularly owing to sabotage.

[20] At the beginning of March, Pascual Tomás, supporter of Caballero and vice-secretary of the UGT, declared that political commissars who tried to make converts "often using methods in opposition to all sense of decency," should not remain in their positions a moment longer.—Quoted, *La Correspondencia de Valencia*, March 3, 1937. See also interviews with Tomás published in *El Pueblo*, February 14, 1937, *Claridad*, February 16, 1937, and his article, *ibid.*, April 6, 1937. Even Antonio Mije, Communist head of the Sub-Commissariat of Organization, admitted, in April, 1937, that there had been some "overstepping of powers" by commissars.—See *Frente Rojo*, April 15, 1937.

[21] See p. 230, above.

[22] *Gaceta de la República*, November 26, 1936.

[23] For this information I am grateful to Gabriel García Maroto, head of the Sub-Commissariat of Propaganda.

labelled himself a Socialist, but was unconditionally in the service of the Communist Party and abetted all its manoeuvres. . . . I summoned [him]; reprimanded him for his conduct and for appointing more than two hundred Communists without my knowledge and signature. He turned pale as he listened to me and with an absolutely deadpan expression replied that the appointments were of Company commissars and that he had made them because he thought he had the authority. With the law in my hand I showed him that there were no exceptions whatsoever. . . ."[24]

Finding himself cheated in the trust he had placed in Alvarez del Vayo, the Commissar General, and realizing how very greatly he was under the spell of Communist influence, Largo Caballero decided to apprise Manuel Azaña, but although the President of the Republic authorized Alvarez del Vayo's dismissal from the Cabinet, Caballero, oddly enough, retained him in office.[25] There was undoubtedly an

[24] Largo Caballero, *Mis recuerdos*, p. 212; see also *La UGT y la guerra*, pp. 10-11. Alvarez del Vayo himself has the following to say on the question of the Commissariat: "When it was formed in Spain, the Spanish Communists . . . took a greater interest in its development and expansion than the other political parties. The latter, for whom it had no particular meaning and who looked on it at first as something rather exotic and unnecessary, contented themselves with presenting lists of candidates drawn up with no special care. The Communists, on the other hand, sent their most active members right from the day of its inception. This inequality grew during the critical period of the defence of Madrid. The situation on that front during the months of November and December, 1936, made it necessary to increase the number of commissars. Hundreds of provisional nominations were made, and these only served to increase the existing disproportion."—*Freedom's Battle*, p. 127.

[25] "One day in 1937," testifies Indalecio Prieto, the moderate Socialist minister, who was in constant and intimate communication with Azaña during the war, "the Premier—Largo Caballero—telephones from Valencia to Barcelona, asking President Azaña for an urgent interview, which is held halfway in Benicarló. Largo Caballero loses no time in declaring: 'I have asked for this conference because I must tell you, and I could not do so by telephone, that one of my ministers is betraying me.' Azaña is surprised. Largo Caballero continues: 'The Minister belongs to my own party; he is a Socialist, the Foreign Minister.' The Prime Minister then informs the President of the Republic of the disloyal conduct of Julio Alvarez del Vayo, . . . Azaña authorizes Largo Caballero to discard Alvarez del Vayo, but the Prime Minister does not use the authority granted him, just as a few weeks earlier he did not take advantage of an opportunity I gave him to get rid of that Communist puppet when, in the very midst of a Cabinet meeting, I told Alvarez del Vayo that his conduct was more befitting a Soviet official than of a Spaniard who was a Minister in the government. Annoyed by my words, Alvarez del Vayo resigned [for the latter's own account of this incident, see his book, *Freedom's*

element of inconsistency in his action, which in all likelihood derived partly from his hesitation to disrupt Alvarez del Vayo's work and diplomatic connections in the League of Nations,[26] and partly from his fear of how Russia, the sole purveyor of arms, might react to Alvarez del Vayo's removal. But his action must also have stemmed in some measure from a knowledge of the frailness of his position should the dismissal of his Foreign Minister provoke a Cabinet crisis. For, while it is certain that Caballero and his followers could rely upon the CNT in the event of a government shake-up, divided though they were by differences of principle and practice, it is no less certain that the Communists and their allies, whatever the differences between them, were united as one man in their hostility to the left Socialist leader. It was in straits like these that Caballero, rather than risk ejecting Alvarez del Vayo from the government, or even from the Commissariat of War, issued, on April 17, a sensational order curbing the powers of that influential body. Not only did he subordinate it to himself in the matter of orientation, but all nominations, removals, and promotions were henceforth to be decided directly by him, while any commissar whose appointment and rank had not been confirmed by May 15 was to consider himself dismissed from the corps of commissars.[27]

This order provoked a hurricane of protest from the Communist Party. "It is quite clear," objected *Frente Rojo*, "that the political commissar does not have everybody's sympathy and appreciation. . . . Who are those persons who are attempting to restrict his functions, and who would even suppress them, were that possible? They are men with antiquated ideas who are still among us, men who counteract the creative work of our people with the foul practices of the old school. These are the enemies of the political commissars. . . . Far from restricting the work of the commissars and giving them a one-sided orientation, it is necessary for our army that their sphere of activity be broadened and that they be given ample means, as well as the necessary stimulus, for accomplishing their tasks."[28] And the following day it asked: "Who can feel hostile to this corps of heroes? Who can feel antagonistic to the forgers of the people's army? Only the declared

---

Battle, pp. 219–20], but Largo Caballero, far from accepting his resignation, retained him in office. . . . There are some men with a reputation for firmness who are given to absurd weaknesses."—*Correo de Asturias*, July 10, 1943.

[26] Some idea of the extent to which Caballero's concern for Spain's position in the League of Nations influenced his behaviour was given in n. 47, p. 282, above.

[27] *Gaceta de la República*, April 17, 1937.

[28] April 16, 1937.

enemies of the people; only those who are irreconcilably opposed to the anti-fascist army; only the blind or the insensate who are driven by a torrent of passion to commit the worst infamies. Our commissars are the pride of our army! We must defend them as we would our own children!"[29]

"There are some persons," affirmed La Pasionaria, the Communist leader, "who want to kill the commissar's initiative by subjecting him to bureaucratic regulations that will tend to render his magnificent work ineffective and to transform him into a man without enterprise, fearful of any bold action on which the commanding officer may frown.

"But this must not be allowed. The commissar cannot on any account be deprived of his distinguishing characteristics, he cannot be placed in subjection and politically castrated without inflicting grave damage on the organization and the discipline of our people's army.

"That would nullify all the constructive work, all the cleaning up that was effected in order to create the people's army, the genuine army of the people.

"It would mean leaving our soldiers at the mercy of officers who could at a given moment disfigure the character of our army by returning to the old days of barrack discipline.

"Commissars, stick to your posts!"[30]

"The War Minister's recent order concerning the Commissariat," retorted Caballero's mouthpiece, *Adelante*, "in no way restricts its functions. On the contrary, it invigorates them and places them within the bounds of the Commissariat's aim, which is not to practise political sectarianism . . . but to create the moral atmosphere and sense of responsibility that will carry our army to victory under the supreme control of the man who, at this historic hour, is undertaking the tremendous and glorious task of directing the destinies of Spain."[31]

In its rejoinder, *Frente Rojo* declared: "The War Minister can give the Commissariat whatever orders he likes, but control must rest in the hands of the Commissariat itself. If that is not so, why was it created? For the purpose of making another department of the War Ministry? In that case the Commissariat would be superfluous."[32]

"Nobody," contended *Adelante*, "least of all the Minister of War . . .

[29] April 17, 1937.

[30] *Frente Rojo*, April 17, 1937. For criticism of the order in *Mundo Obrero*, the Madrid Communist organ, see, for example, issues for April 24, 29, 1937.

[31] April 20, 1937.

[32] April 20, 1937 (*Frente Rojo* was an evening paper).

seeks to diminish the prestige of the [Commissariat]. We have already pointed out the aim [of the order], an aim which of course will be carried out, namely, that the Commissariat of War shall not be used by any party belonging to the Popular Front governmental coalition for the purposes of propaganda. It is essential that we all act with honesty and with loyalty. On behalf of the Socialist Party, we declare that certain commissars belonging to the Communist Party have misused their posts in order to make political converts. . . . We affirm that individuals of scant ideological stability and frivolous political behaviour who should have entered the corps of commissars as Socialists, Republicans, or Anarchists have, contrary to their intimate convictions, submitted to pressure from commissars of a higher rank belonging to the Communist Party and have asked to become members of that organization. And because pressure and coercion, if these did not have the desired results, were followed by a crescendo of defamation and threats, [the Premier and War Minister] decided . . . to put an end to a state of affairs which would necessarily have led to disaster, to an unbridgeable chasm of distrust and sectarianism being created between the soldiers belonging to different political and trade union organizations."[33]

Largo Caballero's order had of course the unqualified support not only of the left-wing Socialists, but also of the Anarchosyndicalists, who had long been exercised by the activities of the Communist political commissars.[34] "The War Minister, adopting a firm and just attitude which we all praise," declared *CNT*, "has cut short the manoeuvres through which the Communist Party was planning to secure the political control of the entire People's Army, manoeuvres which included the appointment of a number of commissars utterly out of proportion to the size of its forces at the front. We all laud . . . the mission of the General Commissariat of War, but no one can allow this body, which was to guarantee the revolutionary character of our army, to bring to the battle fronts not only the same frenzied partisan-

[33] April 22, 1937. For charges by *Adelante* that Francisco Antón, Inspector-Commissar of the Central Front and secretary of the Madrid Communist Party organization, had replaced Socialist by Communist commissars, see issues of April 23–5, 1937. For *Frente Rojo's* replies, see isues of April 23, 24, 1937.

[34] On December 25, 1936, *Frente Libertario*, organ of the CNT armed forces on the Madrid front, stated that the editors had received countless letters complaining that in many units composed of members of different organizations the non-commissioned officers and commissars were devoting themselves to making political converts and were using coercive measures to this end. See also *CNT*, February 25, 1937.

ship that the Communist Party practises behind the lines, but also its intolerable plans for hegemony."[35]

The press controversy that had arisen between the Communists and left-wing Socialists over the Commissariat of War assumed every day a more rancorous character as mutual recrimination was stimulated by the presence of other barbed issues in the military field—such as the creation of reserves, which the Communists considered were being organized at too leisurely a pace,[36] the removal from the army of alleged traitors, a decree of Largo Caballero limiting the highest rank to which civilian militia leaders could rise to that of major,[37] regarded by the Communists as a hindrance to their plans to gain control of the regular army through the cadres trained in their Fifth Regiment,[38] and the designation by the Higher War Council, over Caballero's objections, of the Communist Ministers of Education and Agriculture to discharge missions of military significance in Madrid and the Basque Country[39]—issues which, though important in themselves, were

[35] April 22, 1937. For other articles approving the War Minister's order, see issues of April 23, 26, 27, 1937; also *Fragua Social*, April 27, 1937.

[36] See, for example, report by José Díaz to the Central Committee of the Communist Party, March 8, 1937, as reprinted in Díaz, *Tres años de lucha*, pp. 288–339, speech by Francisco Antón, *Mundo Obrero*, March 18, 1937, manifesto of the Central Committee of the Communist Party, *Frente Rojo*, March 19, 1937, editorials, *ibid.*, March 23, 31, April 8, 13, May 18, 1937.

[37] *Gaceta de la República*, February 17, 1937.

[38] On January 27, 1937, at a public meeting held to celebrate the formal dissolution of the Fifth Regiment, José Díaz had declared that the posts of generals and other officers whose hearts were not in the war "should be occupied by the new talents discovered in the Fifth Regiment."—Speech reprinted in Díaz, *Tres años de lucha*, pp. 253–7. Although, after the publication of the decree of February 16, the Communists frequently referred to the question of promotions and implicitly criticized Caballero's policy (see, for example, José Díaz' report to the Central Committee of the Communist Party, March 8, 1937, *ibid.*, pp. 288–339, the resolution of the Central Committee, *Mundo Obrero*, April 7, 1937, also *Frente Rojo*, April 21, 1937), there was no open criticism of the decree itself until January, 1938 (*ibid.*, January 5, 1938), when the provision restricting the promotion of civilian militia leaders was annulled.—*Gaceta de la República*, January 5, 1938.

[39] In mid-March the Higher War Council appointed Jesús Hernández, the Communist Minister of Education, and Julio Just, the Left Republican Minister of Public Works, to represent the government in Madrid with the object of establishing closer relations with the *Junta de Defensa* and of studying the needs of the central front, but when the appointments came up for ratification by the government, Largo Caballero, fearing the additional influence that the Communists might gain from the presence of one of their ministers in Madrid, took

for the most part only symptomatic of the fundamental cleavage between the two factions.

"For some time," wrote *Adelante*, "we have been consuming our reserves of patience in face of the sly insinuations and the malevolent criticisms that the newspapers and agitators of the Communist Party have been directing . . . against members of the Spanish Socialist Party and especially against the work of its most prominent figure. . . .

"The Communist organ [*Frente Rojo*] inclines towards a monstrous abuse of criticism. Everywhere it sees defects, shortcomings, and lack of foresight. The time has come to silence these irresponsible statements by asking whether or not the inspirers, who see so many motes in the eyes of others, do not have a beam in their own. And on this matter, what can be said of the activities of the Communist Party representatives in the government? The activity of the Minister of Agriculture is certainly not in all respects the most adequate to our national requirements. Nor is the behaviour of the Minister of Education, as far as the functions entrusted to him by the government are concerned, the kind circumstances demand. In the whole of Loyalist Spain the problems of agricultural production and distribution are still without a solution capable of guaranteeing the tranquillity of the rear. Thousands upon thousands of children are left without proper care by the Minister of Education.

"Reserves? . . . Thousands of young Spaniards in the barracks are integrated into the war machine. The fundamental reserves, however, are based on the regulation of agricultural production and distribution. That is the matter that lies within the competence of the Minister of Agriculture!

"Reserves? The most important reserves of the Spanish people are

---

exception to a proposal that the mission of the two ministers should be of a permanent character. Owing to disagreement, the Cabinet never defined the precise duties of the two ministers or settled the length of their stay in the capital, and when they returned temporarily to Valencia, *Adelante*, Caballero's mouthpiece, declared that their mission had terminated (quoted by *Castilla Libre*, March 31, 1937). Debate was still gyrating around this issue when the Higher War Council designated Vicente Uribe, its Communist representative, to undertake an investigation into the situation in the north, where a large-scale offensive had been opened on April 1 by General Franco's forces and his German and Italian allies, an assignment that was viewed by the War Minister with no less hostility than that of Jesús Hernández, particularly as Uribe was accompanied by the Soviet General, Goriev. For *Frente Rojo's* reply to an attack on Uribe by *Adelante*, see issue for April 21, 1937. For all details regarding Hernández and Uribe not contained in the above newspapers the author is indebted to members of the staff of the Febus news agency.

the children, the younger generation. What care are they receiving? What attention is being paid to them?

"It is advisable to remind every member of the government that he has precise functions limited to the problems affecting his ministry. It is stupid, for instance, for a Minister of Education and Fine Arts, or for a Minister of Agriculture, to attempt to solve war problems. The ministers should confine themselves to their specific tasks and not meddle in business foreign to their own departments—except at Cabinet meetings. They have enough to do solving their own problems.

". . . We are not prepared to tolerate any further attempt to disturb the rear by negative criticisms and hypocritical assertions aimed at a systematic disparagement of those who are facing the rigours of the war with that silent and modest heroism with which great deeds are accomplished.

"Enough silly talk! An end to high-sounding slogans that are not carried out and to appeals for cordiality, unity, and fraternity that are put into effect with mental reservations and with a view to personal advantage! . . . We Socialists raise above everything else the banner of the Spanish Revolution, a revolution that, thanks to the sacrifice of our martyrs and heroes and to our Spanish slogans and leaders, has been achieved in a Spanish way."[40]

"Do the comrades of *Adelante* really believe," argued *Frente Rojo*, "that the ministers are mere trade union secretaries who should concern themselves only with the 'business' of their respective unions? The Communist ministers represent their respective organizations in the government, as do the Socialist, Republican and Anarchist ministers, and are, and should be, as much concerned as anyone else about the problems and situations created by the war. Or does *Adelante* believe that the war is being waged only by the War Minister and that the question of victory or defeat affects him alone? The war and the administration of the country are conducted by the Popular Front, by all the parties and organizations comprising the Popular Front, and the men who represent them in the government have the same right and obligation to concern themselves with questions affecting the entire country as well as the lives and future of all Spaniards. From where does *Adelante* get its absolutist conceptions?

"Our ministers intervened in the North and in Madrid at a very serious moment . . . and the results of their work inspire confidence. We do not say that they alone have solved the difficulties; they have

[40] April 22, 1937.

contributed to their solution in a large degree, and their efforts, all the things they have accomplished, have the frank and full support of our party. . . .

"*Adelante* demands that Hernández organize child reserves. It is true that the children have to be prepared for life as well as for the kind of society that will stem from our victory, but first we have to equip our army with the necessary reserves for attaining that victory. . . .

"The comrades of *Adelante* should let us know whether they want a Popular Front policy or a policy based on a personal dictatorship.

"Finally, is it not strange, having regard to the fact that the whole people—Anarchists, Socialists, Communists, and Republicans—have been demanding for months and months the cleansing of the commanding army posts, that this cleansing should begin with the political commissars? How many commissars have passed over to the enemy, we should like to know? How many officers have deserted and are still deserting? Here is a concrete task for the person concerned with the fate of our army. . . .

"We do not quite understand the reiteration of the adjective 'Spanish' in *Adelante*'s article. What is it insinuating? No one is more Spanish, profoundly and fervently Spanish, than the Communist Party and its leaders, and it was precisely our party that characterized the present war as a war of national independence, as a war for the maintenance of Spanish sovereignty."[41]

"The Communist Party says it is supporting a Popular Front policy," declared *Adelante*, "but avails itself of every seasonable opportunity to pursue its own policy and to spread propaganda which must of necessity irritate non-Communists. In this way it only succeeds in achieving something quite distinct from what it brags about every day; in other words, it sows suspicion and sectarianism among the workers, rendering difficult the organic unity of the proletariat for which the Socialist Party has been fighting for so long, and especially Largo Caballero, against whom the rage of four or five petty, resentful leaders is now concentrated . . . , leaders who are incapable of understanding that a man who is all self-sacrifice and determination can work modestly for seven long months while heaps of nonsensical slogans are spread about the rear with no better result than that of creating confusion.

". . . Where are the wits of those who disparage the leader of the Spanish working class? Do they think it is such an easy matter to destroy his prestige by a blustering political campaign? Do they not

[41] April 22, 1937.

realize that Largo Caballero is not a political boss as *Frente Rojo* insinuated the night before last, nor an apprentice in dictatorship, nor even a potential dictator. He is the incarnation of a whole revolutionary movement. He is the personification of the history of the Spanish working class and the Marxist movement in Spain. He is the embodiment of forty years of exemplary conduct in our trade union and revolutionary struggles."[42]

[42] April 23, 1937.

PART V

THE COMMUNIST TRIUMPH

27

The Communist Party
Cultivates the
Moderate Socialists

THWARTED by Largo Caballero's opposition to its plans for military hegemony, especially by his threat to dismiss any political commissar whose appointment and rank he had not confirmed by May 15, by his refusal to promote the fusion of the Socialist and Communist Parties, by the mounting hostility among left-wing Socialists to its agricultural policy, the Communist Party, which for some time had been cultivating the moderate Socialists of the so-called centre faction of the Socialist Party, now turned towards them in the hope of undoing the left Socialist leader.[1]

Before the Civil War, the centre faction, which controlled the Executive Committee of the party, had been hostile to the Communists. It had viewed their campaign for the merging of the two parties with unconcealed animosity, as witnessed by the strictures of *El Socialista*, its organ, on the "fraud of unification,"[2] while the fusion of the two youth movements had been denounced by it as the "absorption of the Socialist youth by the Communist Party."[3] Indeed, with such distrust and revulsion had the centre faction regarded the Communists that it had refused even to answer a proposal which they had made to establish official relations with them: ". . . The Communist Party," wrote José Díaz, in April, 1936, "has proposed to the Socialist Party the formation of a contact committee with a programme designed to facilitate the development of the democratic revolution and

---

[1] Because of its relative political insignificance, the small right wing of the Socialist Party, led by Julián Besteiro, has not been mentioned in this volume.
[2] July 3, 1936.
[3] *Ibid.*, July 2, 1936.

to carry it to its final consequences. This proposal has been left un-
answered by the present reformist and centrist leadership. On the other
hand, it has been welcomed by the left wing. The masses of the Socialist
Party repudiate the attitude of the present reformist executive and see
in the line of Largo Caballero one that approaches most the revolutionary path, the path of the Communist Party and the Communist
International."[4]

The leading light and dominant force of the centre faction of the
Socialist Party was Indalecio Prieto, a masterful character with great
prestige among the liberal and even conservative Republicans, with
whom he had infinitely more in common than with the left-wing
Socialists.[5] Eloquent speaker and expert parliamentarian, skilled in
moves behind the scenes both in governing circles and in his own party
—moves that had helped to raise Manuel Azaña to the Presidency of
the Republic[6] and to oust Caballero from the Executive Committee
of the Socialist Party[7]—he was often cited as the most astute politician
in the Republican régime, and acknowledgments of his ability came
from opponents as well as from friends. In the critical months before
the Civil War, he had, in contrast to Caballero, his personal as well as
his political enemy, thrown all his influence on the side of moderation.
"Two positions, equally disinterested and honest," writes Julián
Zugazagoitia, himself a moderate Socialist, "confronted each other in
the Socialist Party: the majority, led by Largo Caballero, which
regarded the coalition with the Republicans as a thing of the past and
advocated the formation of a united working-class front with a view
to the total exercise of power . . .; the minority, personified by Prieto,
which took into account the realities of the Spanish scene, and which
considered, in view of the fact that the conservative parties were
fighting resolutely, that any dissociation from the Republic and the
Republicans would be extremely dangerous."[8] In the midst of the
disturbances that had convulsed the country, a movement had been

---

[4] Article in *Correspondencia Internacional*, April 17, 1936, reprinted in Díaz,
Tres años de lucha, pp. 116–25. See also Manuilski, as quoted by Santiago
Carrillo, p. 107, above.

[5] In a statement to a Valencia newspaper before the outbreak of the Civil War
(*El Mercantil Valenciano*, May 16, 1936), Prieto had declared that the dissensions
in the Socialist Party would result in a split at the next party congress.

[6] See *Historia de la cruzada española*, II, pp. 477, 488; Zugazagoitia, *Historia
de la guerra en España*, p. 3.

[7] See Morón, *Política de ayer y política de mañana*, pp. 60–3.

[8] *Historia de la guerra en España*, p. 4; see also Morón, *Política de ayer y política
de mañana*, p. 25.

set in motion—with which Prieto himself had not been unconnected—
to place him in the premiership. ". . . Around his person," records a
right-wing historian, "an atmosphere was being created—which
Miguel Maura [leader of the Conservative Republican Party] was
trying to build up and diffuse—an atmosphere favourable to placing
him in a position from which he would be able to curb as far as possible
the disorders that were taking place. Prieto was the hope not only of
the moderates of the Popular Front . . . but of many moderates of the
Right."[9] But when Azaña offered him the premiership, he dared not
accept the post, not only because of the opposition of the Executive
Committee of the UGT, controlled by Caballero,[10] but because the
parliamentary fraction of the Socialist Party, dominated by the left-
wing Socialists, had previously resolved that the party should not share
power with the Republicans. ". . . What would have been said of me
at that time," Prieto declared some years later, "if, ignoring the resolution of the parliamentary fraction, I had accepted the power Señor
Azaña offered me? I should have appeared, with a certain amount of
justification, as the only person responsible for the destruction of the
Socialist Party. Furthermore, if in parliament I had been denied the
votes of the majority of the representatives of the Socialist Party, I
should have been compelled, in order to govern parliamentarily, to
seek support among the Right, as a result of which I should have
covered myself with ignominy."[11]

In spite of the fact that at that time the Communists had been
secretly more in sympathy with Indalecio Prieto's moderation than
with Largo Caballero's revolutionism, they knew that the centre
faction of the Socialist Party represented only a small section of the
Socialist movement and that it behoved them to associate themselves
with the left wing. But the hostility that Caballero developed towards
them within a few months of the outbreak of the Civil War soon
compelled them to turn to his opponents of the centre faction.
Although collaboration with the moderate Socialists had been impossible for the Communists before the war, it now appeared practicable,

[9] Plá, *Historia de la segunda república española*, IV, p. 384. It will be recalled that
after the outbreak of the military revolt, Prieto's centre faction supported Diego
Martínez Barrio's government of conciliation.—See n. 50, p. 32, above, also
n. 58, p. 34.

[10] See statement issued by the executive, published in *El Socialista*, May 8,
1936.

[11] Speech in Mexico City, April 21, 1940, as published in *Inauguración del
círculo 'Pablo Iglesias' de México*, p. 19. See also his statement in *El Mercantil
Valenciano*, May 16, 1936.

not only because of Prieto's unexpected friendliness towards the
Soviet Ambassador, Marcel Rosenberg,[12] and towards General Duglas,
the head of the Russian air force unit in Spain, to whom he offered
every facility in his capacity as Navy and Air Minister,[13] but also
because of a statement he made to Victorio Codovilla, the Comintern
agent in Spain, assuring him of his readiness to work for the fusion of
the Socialist and Communist Parties.[14]

If in strident contradiction with his past Prieto expressed friendly
intentions, he did so undoubtedly with mental reservations, to judge
from his subsequent resistance to the Communists.[15] But for the
moment he needed the Communists, as they did him, to compass the
ruin of Caballero, with whom, it is worth remarking, his relations

[12] See Morón, *Política de ayer y política de mañana*, pp. 106-7.

[13] Hidalgo de Cisneros, the Spanish Chief of the Air Force, and, until he
attorned to the Communists, a close friend of Prieto's, told the author when
interviewed after the war: "Prieto was at first on excellent terms with the
Russians. He said that we should do everything we could to encourage them to
help us. He urged the Russians to send us war material. He made two or three
speeches to the Russian pilots, one of which he made in Albacete, thanking
them for coming to Spain and saying that their country was the only one that
had helped the Republic. He spoke like a Communist. He was on excellent
terms with Duglas and Rosenberg."

[14] This was common knowledge in Communist circles, and was confirmed
to the author by José Duque, a member during the war of the Central Committee of the Communist Party. Some months after his conversation with
Codovilla, Prieto told Louis Fischer (*Men and Politics*, p. 455) that he had once
favoured merging the two parties. In fact, he is said to have come out flatly in
favour of fusion at a meeting of the Executive Committee of the Socialist Party
in the summer of 1937 on the ground that the only help the government could
hope to receive was from Russia.—See Morón, *Política de ayer y política de
mañana*, p. 107; Alvarez del Vayo, *Freedom's Battle*, p. 67.

[15] Although this subject lies outside the scope of this volume, the following
episode that occurred after Prieto had replaced Largo Caballero in the War
Ministry is worth recording: "One night, at an unaccustomed hour," the
moderate Socialist leader recalls, "Gaisky [Gaikis, the Soviet Ambassador,
who succeeded Rosenberg], brought me some welcome news: an important
shipment of war material which I felt might be decisive was about to leave
Russian ports. The Ambassador showed pleasure at my display of satisfaction.
Two days later he came back to see me and asked me to support the fusion of
the Socialist and Communist Parties. I refused, and he repeated his demands
almost threateningly. He insisted with tenacity, hinting that he was carrying
out orders from Moscow and that I would be rewarded or punished according
to the attitude I adopted. He did not sway me. During a third visit, but without
referring in any way to our earlier conversation, Gaisky informed me that the
much-needed war material that had been offered would not be shipped. That
was the punishment I received."—*El Socialista*, Paris, November 9, 1950.

were so strained that they avoided each other as much as possible and used intermediaries to discuss affairs jointly affecting their respective ministries.[16] Moreover, like the Communists, he was animated by hostility to the left wing of the revolution[17] and by the hope that a moderate course would induce Britain and France to abandon their policy of neutrality.[18] On this latter question, however, there was a profound divergence of aim; for whereas the Comintern was concerned first and foremost with the advantages that Russia's strategic position would derive from the raising of the arms embargo,[19] Prieto—like Azaña and many other liberal Republicans who looked to the moderate Socialist politician for leadership—was interested solely in the Spanish scene. To his mind, Anglo-French aid would counteract the mounting influence of Russia, which he attributed largely to their neutrality: "The Western democracies," he declared after the war, "fearful of Communism, did not realize that this movement grew in Spain as a result of their own lack of assistance. To the extent that these countries denied us help, popular sympathy went openly to Russia when it was learnt that she was supplying us with the means of defence."[20]

Yet, because he now needed the Communists for his own purposes, and little realized that he, like Caballero, would later fall victim to them, Prieto did not allow the misgivings their growth and proselytizing methods were causing him—methods that were the subject of sharp and even violent criticism in *El Socialista*, the organ of the moderate Socialists[21]—to interfere with the close association they were establishing with the Executive Committee of the party, over which he still preserved a directing influence through its secretary, Ramón

[16] For this information I am indebted to Ignacio Hidalgo de Cisneros, the Spanish chief of the Air Force, and an intimate of Prieto's.

[17] His attitude is reflected in the editorials of *Informaciones*, his mouthpiece, and of *El Socialista*, the organ of the Socialist Party executive. See, for example, *Informaciones*, August 5, 1936, and *El Socialista*, March 2, 10, 11, 1937. The director of the latter, Julián Zugazagoitia, was Prieto's man of confidence.

[18] *El Socialista*, which expressed the viewpoint of Prieto, stated in its issue of October 4, 1936: ". . . we have to take into account the attitude of the States that surround us. . . . We still hope that the estimate of Spanish events made by certain democracies will be changed, and it would be a pity, a tragedy, to compromise these possibilities by accelerating the revolution."

[19] See p. 131, above.

[20] Speech in Mexico City, April 21, 1940, as published in *Inauguración del círculo 'Pablo Iglesias' de México*, p. 13.

[21] See, for example, articles published on January 14, February 20, 25, March 6, April 22, 23, 25, May 15, 1937; also circular letter of the Executive Committee, published in *El Socialista*, March 28, 1937.

Lamoneda, and its president, González Peña. In a statement reflecting this rapprochement between the centre faction and the Communists, as well as the breach with the left-wing Socialists, the Politburo of the Communist Party declared at the end of March:

"Having regard to the fact that the relations between the Communists and Socialists are becoming closer every day owing to a correct understanding of the policy of the Popular Front, and that the hostility to the Communist Party is not due to the opposition of the Socialist Party itself, but to a few isolated individuals who do not interpret the correct feelings of the masses, the Politburo considers it necessary to strengthen its ties with the Socialist Party. It therefore invites the Executive Committee to hold a joint meeting with a view to examining the present situation and establishing on a permanent basis closer relations than have existed until now by the setting up of contact committees of a local and national character, which will facilitate the discussion and adoption of measures leading to unity of action and AS QUICKLY AS POSSIBLE to the FUSION OF THE SOCIALIST AND COMMUNIST PARTIES into a GREAT SINGLE PARTY of the Spanish working class.

"With this aim in view, the Politburo has appointed a delegation to establish relations immediately with the leadership of the Socialist Party."[22]

As a result of the negotiations that followed this move a National Contact Committee was formed, in which Ramón Lamoneda represented the Socialist Party and José Díaz the Communist Party. Its first action was the issuance of instructions to all units of the two organizations to set up similar contact committees in their respective localities.[23] In the succeeding months the idea of fusing the two parties was extolled, both theoretically and rhetorically, with only slightly less enthusiasm by the Prieto Socialists[24] than by the Communists, but, for reasons that lie outside the scope of the present volume, it never became a reality. Nevertheless, the close relations that the Communist and Prieto Socialist leaders had now established through their National Contact Committee were destined to exercise a fateful influence on the course of events during the decisive days ahead; for, behind the public agreement to work for the fusion of the Socialist and Communist Parties, there lay a secret compact to oust Largo Caballero from the Cabinet, as developments during the next few days will eloquently testify.

[22] *Frente Rojo*, March 29, 1937. Emphasis in text.
[23] See announcement published in *Frente Rojo*, April 26, 1937.
[24] See speeches by Ramón Lamoneda, reported in *El Socialista*, July 16, 1937; *Adelante*, August 3, 1937.

28

The Overthrow
of Largo Caballero

STRENGTHENED by their secret agreement with the Prieto Socialists, the Communists now required a suitable opportunity to bring their struggle with Caballero to a climax. They did not have to wait for long.

On May 3—in circumstances that have yet to be fully analysed—an armed conflict flared up among the anti-Franco forces in Barcelona, the capital of Catalonia, followed by four days of costly fighting.[1] Exploiting this episode, the Communists demanded the suppression of the anti-Stalinist POUM,[2] a Marxist party which they held responsible for the bloodshed, and whose leaders they had long been denouncing as Trotskyists and fascist agents. Every instrument of propaganda at their disposal was immediately set in motion to force acceptance of their will, and their agitation assumed a frenzied character:

"Our principal enemies are the fascists," declared José Díaz at a public meeting on May 9. "However, these not only include the fascists themselves but also the agents who work for them. Of course, if these agents were to say, 'We are fascists and we are working among you in order to create difficulties,' we should immediately put an end to them. For this reason they have to give themselves other names. . . . Some call themselves Trotskyists, which is the name used by many disguised fascists who use revolutionary language in order to sow confusion. I therefore ask: If everyone knows this, if the government knows it, why does it not treat them like fascists and exterminate them pitilessly? . . .

[1] A detailed account of this conflict lies beyond the purview of this volume.
[2] *Partido Obrero de Unificación Marxista*. This party, which was important in Catalonia, possessed little more than a skeleton organization outside that region, and is therefore not dealt with in this volume.

"Every worker must know about the trial of the Trotskyists that has taken place in the U.S.S.R. It was Trotsky himself who directed the gang of criminals that derailed trains in the Soviet Union, carried out acts of sabotage in the large factories, and did everything possible to discover military secrets with the object of handing them over to Hitler and the Japanese imperialists. And, in view of the fact that all this was revealed during the trial and that the Trotskyists declared that they had done these things under Trotsky's direction and in complicity with Hitler and the Japanese imperialists, I must ask: Is it not perfectly clear that the Trotskyists are not a political or social organization of a definite tendency like the Anarchists, Socialists, or Republicans, but a gang of spies and *provocateurs* in the service of international fascism? The Trotskyist *provocateurs* must be swept away!

"That is why I stated in my speech at the recent plenary session of the Central Committee not only that they should be liquidated in Spain, their press suspended and their organization dissolved, but that they should be swept out of all civilized countries, that is, if we really want to get rid of these vermin. . . .

"In Spain itself, who but the Trotskyists inspired the criminal putsch in Catalonia? *La Batalla* [the POUM organ] in its May 1 edition was full of brazen incitements to revolt. . . . This paper is coming out in Catalonia. . . . Why? Because the government cannot make up its mind to seize it as every anti-fascist demands. . . .

"If, after ten months of war, a strong policy is not instituted . . . , if the government does not establish order, then I shall be forced to conclude, and I am sure every anti-fascist will be too, that another Popular Front government will have to do so."[3]

A few days later, on May 13, at a dramatic meeting of the Cabinet, Jesús Hernández and Vicente Uribe, the two Communist ministers, demanded the dissolution of the POUM in terms that left no room for compromise. But Caballero vehemently dissented from their view that this party was a fascist organization, and steadfastly refused to adopt measures that he believed were not merely unjust but could only strengthen his opponents. In the course of his acrimonious exchanges with the two ministers, he declared that he would not dissolve any party or trade union, that he had not entered the government to serve the political interests of any of the factions represented in it, and that the courts of law would decide whether or not any particular organization should be dissolved.[4]

[3] Speech reprinted in Díaz, *Tres años de lucha*, pp. 350–66.
[4] Taken from his own account of this episode in a speech in October, 1937,

Failing to receive satisfaction, the two ministers rose and left the room.⁵

"When the split in the Cabinet occurred, and Messrs. Jesús Hernández and Vicente Uribe left the room . . . ," testifies Indalecio Prieto, "Largo Caballero intended to continue the dispatch of routine matters. I was sitting next to him . . . and said: 'Look here, Caballero, something serious has happened. The ministerial coalition has been broken, because one of the parties in the government has withdrawn from it. I therefore think it is your duty, without continuing this meeting, to tell the President of the Republic what has happened and resolve the situation with him.'"⁶

"The opinion expressed by Prieto," writes Julián Zugazagoitia, himself a moderate Socialist, and Minister of the Interior in the succeeding government, "surprised Largo Caballero, who believed that the Cabinet could nevertheless continue its deliberations. . . . Prieto's viewpoint, which was perfectly constitutional, was [later] condemned as part of the manoeuvre begun by the Communists to overthrow Largo Caballero."⁷

Frustrated in his attempt to continue the meeting, the Premier notified the President of the Republic that the Communist ministers had withdrawn from the Cabinet. Apprised of the crisis, Azaña

---

reprinted in Largo Caballero, *La UGT y la guerra*, p. 8. See also Juan Peiró (CNT Minister of Industry at the time), *Problemas y cintarazos*, pp. 201–2.

⁵ Largo Caballero, *La UGT y la guerra*, p. 8.

⁶ Speech in exile, March 29, 1946, published in *Adelante*, Mexico City, April 1, 1946.

⁷ *Historia de la guerra en España*, p. 274. It was not until some years after the war that Prieto, reconciled with Caballero, attempted to correct the impression that he had acted in secret agreement with the Communists. In the speech (see previous note) from which the above-quoted passage has been taken, he declared: "Not until now that it is pertinent to do so have I bothered to rectify the erroneous belief that I had dealings with the Communists in order to oust Largo Caballero. Apart from a rule that has guided my conduct towards them ever since the first unfortunate split in our party in 1921, a rule which has always kept me at a distance from them, I am incapable, because of my moral temper, of acting disloyally towards a co-religionist and a friend, who, as Premier, was charged at that time with such delicate and complicated functions." On the other hand, Vicente Uribe, one of the two Communist ministers who precipitated the crisis, declared in a speech in exile: "Prieto participated in the plan to remove Caballero from the leadership of the government, although without revealing himself openly. . . . He wanted to take revenge on Largo Caballero, whom he had not forgiven, among other things, for frustrating his ambition to become head of the government in May, 1936 [see p. 303, above].— *Mundo Obrero*, Paris, September 25, 1947.

suggested that it be postponed until an important military offensive then being planned, had been launched.[8] "For months," writes Luis Araquistain, the left Socialist leader, "Largo Caballero had been preparing a military operation in Estremadura, in the west of Spain. Its aim was to cut the rebel army's lines of communication with the south, whence it received steady reinforcements of Italian and Moroccan troops. The success of that operation, by splitting the enemy into two unconnected parts and depriving him of the foreign troops and war material that were entering through the ports near the Strait of Gibraltar, could have changed the course of the war completely. The north would have been saved; the whole of Andalusia would have been recovered. Probably the war itself would have been won. . . . At any rate, Franco's victory would have been neither so quick nor so decisive, and at least there would have been time and favourable circumstances for negotiating a diplomatic peace.

"Everything was ready for the offensive, which was fixed for the middle of May. At the last hour some resistance in the army had to be overcome. General Miaja, who had been ordered to send some of the troops stationed in Madrid to the Estremadura sector, at first refused.[9] His disobedience was inspired by the Communists, who were then Miaja's real chiefs and who made of him—an officer of limited ability —a great international figure. In the end Miaja had to abandon his insubordination in face of the energetic attitude of Largo Caballero, and the required troops were dispatched.[10]

[8] Largo Caballero, *La UGT y la guerra*, pp. 8–9.

[9] This is confirmed by Colonel Segismundo Casado, the Chief of Operations on the War Ministry General Staff, in his book, *The Last Days of Madrid*, pp. 71–2. See also communication, dated May 1, 1937, sent to Largo Caballero by General Miaja, refusing to dispatch the troops requested owing to the situation on the Madrid front.

[10] Colonel Segismundo Casado, Chief of Operations on the War Ministry General Staff, writes: "[Miaja] realized that after the orders he had received he must proceed at once to move the forces under his command to the positions assigned to them. But during the afternoon of the same day a General, a 'friendly [Russian] adviser,' came to my office telling me that no aircraft could take part in the action against Merida [Estremadura], because it was needed on other fronts. For several days past I had realized the possibility that the Communists were trying to hold up this action, and after listening to the 'friendly adviser' I was convinced that it could not be carried out. I simply told him that it was not his duty to give me this disagreeable information, that it was a matter exclusively for the Spanish Chief of the Air Force. He smiled, and called the office of the Air Force Command, so that they should inform me on this point. They replied in writing, stating in a somewhat ambiguous way that I could not count on having the aircraft which I had anticipated."—*The Last Days of*

"But suddenly, at a Cabinet meeting, very shortly before the day scheduled for the offensive, the Ministers of Education and Agriculture, both of them Communists, resigned.[11] . . . Largo Caballero went to see President Azaña and handed him the resignation of the whole Cabinet. At the same time he told him about the operation that had been prepared, deploring the fact that the Communists had provoked a crisis at such an inopportune moment. On being informed of this very important and imminent offensive, Azaña requested Largo Caballero to continue at the head of the government until the operation had been carried out. . . .

"Two Socialist ministers [belonging to the centre faction], having heard—perhaps through Azaña himself, who used to be in constant touch with Indalecio Prieto, the Socialist Navy and Air Minister—about the President's conference with Largo Caballero, presented themselves at the latter's office a few hours later. Dr. Negrín was one of them.[12] They told Caballero that in view of the attitude adopted by the Communist ministers and bearing in mind that under the existing circumstances the Communist Party could not be dispensed with, they were resigning along with Prieto. The manoeuvre was clear. The three ministers of the centre faction . . . joined hands with the Communists in order to oust Caballero. It was essential to prevent the Estremadura offensive from being carried out, lest it prove successful. This view was expressed by Simeón Vidarte, a Socialist deputy belonging to the Prieto faction, in the following frank and criminal words: 'If Caballero should succeed in this offensive, no one will be able to throw him out of the government.' "[13]

It was because of the resignation of the moderate Socialist ministers—a resignation which had been decided by the Executive Committee of the party[14] and which could have been avoided had Prieto so desired in view of the influence he still exercised over Ramón Lamoneda, the

---

Madrid, pp. 72–3. It is noteworthy that Jesús Hernández, one of the two Communist Ministers in the Cabinet, later confirmed the opposition of the Russian advisory staff to the proposed Estremadura offensive.—*Yo fui un ministro de Stalin*, pp. 79–85.

[11] According to Rodolfo Llopis, undersecretary of the Premier, the offensive was scheduled to begin on May 18.—See his article in *Spartacus*, July 15, 1937.

[12] The other was Anastasio de Gracia.

[13] *El comunismo y la guerra de España*, pp. 13–14.

[14] At one of the sessions of the National Committee of the Socialist Party held in July, 1937, Bugeda, a Prieto Socialist, stated that the Executive Committee had taken the view that the Socialists could not remain in the government after the Communists had withdrawn their collaboration.—Report on the proceedings, as given in *El Mercantil Valenciano*, July 22, 1937.

secretary, and González Peña, the president of the Executive Committee—that the suspicion that the leader of the centre faction had acted in secret concert with the Communist ministers hardened into positive belief. Moreover, it had not been forgotten that it was Ramón Lamoneda who had carried out, at Prieto's bidding, the subtle manoeuvre that had resulted in Caballero's removal from the Socialist Party executive before the outbreak of the Civil War.[15]

When, on May 15, Largo Caballero was commissioned by President Azaña to form a new ministry, the concurrence of the Socialist executive and the Communist Party was no less patent than at the outset of the crisis. Although they made no overt objection to his being Premier, they did not conceal their desire to exclude him from the War Ministry. While the Communist Party insisted, among other things, that the Prime Minister in the new government should occupy himself exclusively with the affairs of his own office,[16] the Socialist executive demanded that Indalecio Prieto should occupy a new department known as the Ministry of National Defence,[17] a department that was to combine not only the Navy and Air Ministry, which he had held in the outgoing government, but also the Ministry of War. These demands—which were undoubtedly formulated in accordance with a prior agreement between the Communist and moderate Socialist leaders[18]—were tantamount to rejecting Caballero not only as War Minister, but also as Premier, for the Prieto Socialists and the Communists understood well the psychology of the left Socialist leader; they knew that he would voluntarily relinquish no part of his authority, that in his heart there existed an indestructible pride, and that he would

[15] See Morón, *Política de ayer y política de mañana*, pp. 60–1.

[16] See document issued by the Central Committee, stating its conditions for collaboration in the government, as given in *El Mercantil Valenciano*, May 16, 1937. One other significant condition worth mentioning was that the Commissariat of War should enjoy autonomy in all matters connected with the appointment and political direction of the commissars.

[17] See point 6 of its declaration, published in *El Socialista*, May 18, 1937; also circular letter sent to the local sections of the Socialist Party, published, *ibid.*, May 30, 1937.

[18] "Prieto was appointed Minister of National Defence by mutual agreement and on the understanding that he would correct the errors of Caballero, strengthen the unity of the people, and tighten the bonds between the Communists and the Socialists," Vicente Uribe wrote after the war. "I myself raised these matters with Prieto several times before he became Defence Minister, and he always told me that he was agreeable and would do nothing prejudicial to the unity of the Socialists and the Communists."—Article in *España Popular*, March 11, 1940.

refuse to become an ornamental figure in a Cabinet in which Prieto, his perennial adversary, would assume control of the most vital ministry. Indeed, even before they had publicly made known their views, the UGT executive, controlled by the left-wing Socialists, declared that it would give no support of any kind to a government in which both the premiership and the War Ministry were not held by Largo Caballero.[19] This statement had undoubtedly been inspired by Caballero himself, for it corresponded to his own position throughout the crisis. "You will remember," he wrote to a colleague in the Socialist Party, "that the Communists wanted to throw me out of the War Ministry and to leave me as a figurehead in the premiership. . . . I declared at the time that, as a Socialist and as a Spaniard, it was my duty to remain in the War Ministry, and that otherwise I would not accept the premiership; but I did not say that because I considered myself irreplaceable, nor anything of the kind, but because I had the firm intention of fighting it out with the Communist Party and all its accomplices; this I could do only from the War Ministry."[20]

In his efforts to retain both the War Ministry and the premiership, Caballero received the full backing of the CNT. While editorials in the Anarchosyndicalist press declared that the working class wanted him to remain in office as a guarantee for the proletarian revolution,[21] that it saw in him "the most capable and honourable person for presiding over the government that must carry us to victory,"[22] and that his presence in the premiership and War Ministry was "the most solid guarantee for the proletariat that the character of the struggle being waged against international reaction will not be distorted by anybody or anything,"[23] the National Committee declared emphatically that it would not collaborate with any government in which he was not both Premier and War Minister.[24] Yet, in spite of this support, Caballero did not even bother to consult the Anarchosyndicalists when drafting his plan for a new government and, indeed, offered them only two seats, as compared with four in the previous Cabinet.[25] This treatment was intensely galling to the CNT, and, in its reply to Caballero, it declared that although it did not aim at increasing its representation in the government it could not accept fewer portfolios than before, or

[19] *Claridad*, May 15, 1937.

[20] Letter to José Bullejos, November 20, 1939, published in ¿*Qué se puede hacer?*, pp. 20–4.   [21] *Frente Libertario*, May 17, 1937.

[22] *Fragua Social*, May 16, 1937.   [23] *Solidaridad Obrera*, May 16, 1937.

[24] *Fragua Social*, May 16, 1937.

[25] See his plan, as given in *La Correspondencia de Valencia*, May 17, 1937.

agree on any pretext to parity with the Communist Party, which had likewise been offered two seats, and which, it affirmed, had provoked the crisis, and had not collaborated in the government with the same degree of loyalty as itself.[26]

If Caballero had drafted his plan for a new government without any regard for the views of the CNT, even less did he take into account the opinion of the Communists.

Far from heeding their demand that the Premier should occupy himself exclusively with the affairs of his own office, he defiantly claimed for himself not only the control of the land forces, but also the control of the fleet and air force as well as that of arms production.[27] If he really expected that the Communists and their allies would consent to his counter-proposal, his hopes were doomed to swift disappointment, for while José Díaz replied that it did not reveal the slightest inclination to take into consideration the wishes of the Central Committee of his party, wishes which were those of the Spanish people as a whole, and that the Communists could not form part of the government on the proposed terms,[28] Ramón Lamoneda declared, in the name of the Socialist executive, that his party could not accept representation in the government, because the plan neglected to take into consideration the executive's demands, and, moreover, because the Communist Party had replied in the negative.[29] Likewise united with the Communists in its hostility to Caballero's proposed solution of the crisis was the Left Republican Party, which, in its reply, echoed the Communist demand that the Premier in the new government should concern himself solely with the affairs of his own office.[30]

For the sake of appearances, President Azaña—who shared with Indalecio Prieto the hope that a government purge of left-wing Socialists and Anarchosyndicalists would persuade Britain and France to discontinue their policy of neutrality,[31] but who, as head of the state,

---

[26] Published in *Fragua Social*, May 18, 1937.   [27] *Loc. cit.*

[28] See letter published, *Frente Rojo*, May 17, 1937.

[29] See letter to Caballero published in *El Socialista*, May 18, 1937.

[30] Reply to Caballero, as given in *Frente Rojo*, May 17, 1937.

[31] On May 17, *The Times*, London, published a dispatch from its Valencia correspondent, in which the following passage appeared: "In the main the crisis is due to an attempt to oust the Prime Minister by the Communist Party and others displeased with his policy. It is also a move for a more moderate Government . . . , one of the effects of which, it is believed, would be to attract greater friendliness for the Government cause on the part of 'democratic European Powers.' Such is understood to be the aim of President Azaña and of the Spanish Republican Party."

could not intervene openly in party politics—attempted to iron out the differences between Caballero and his opponents;[32] but as the Communists remained adamant, as was to be expected, and inasmuch as the Prieto Socialists and the Left Republicans stood behind them, Caballero was forced to abandon his attempt to form a government.[33]

Thereupon President Azaña entrusted a new man with the task of organizing a Cabinet. This was Juan Negrín, candidate of the Communists, of the moderate Socialists, and of the Left Republicans.

Easygoing and a *bon vivant*, infinitely more pliable than the austere and stubborn Caballero, and presumed to be more acceptable to the Western democracies than the left Socialist leader because of his moderate background,[34] Negrín had long been selected as Caballero's successor in the premiership by Arthur Stashevsky, the Soviet trade representative.[35] "In my conversations with Stashevsky in Barcelona in November [1936]," writes General Krivitsky, the head of Soviet Intelligence in Western Europe, "Stalin's next moves in Spain were already cropping out. Stashevsky made no secret to me of the fact that Juan Negrín would be the next head of the Madrid government. At that time, Caballero was universally regarded as the favourite of the Kremlin, but Stashevsky had already picked Negrín as his successor.[36] . . .

"Dr. Juan Negrín . . . had all the makings of a bureaucratic politician. Though a professor, he was a man of affairs with the outlook of a businessman. He was just the type to suit Stalin's needs. . . . He would impress the outside world with the 'sanity' and 'propriety' of the Spanish Republican cause; he would frighten nobody by revolutionary remarks. . . .

"Doctor Negrín, of course, saw the only salvation of his country in close co-operation with the Soviet Union. It had become obvious that active support could come only from that source. He was ready to go along with Stalin in everything, sacrificing all other considerations to secure this aid."[37]

---

[32] See report from Valencia by the Febus news agency, "Una referencia de la reunión celebrada en la República," published in *Mundo Obrero*, May 17, 1937.

[33] *Ibid.*   [34] See p. 121, above.

[35] For other details regarding Stashevsky, see pp. 122–3, above.

[36] It is worth recording that Miguel Serra Pamies, a member of the Central Committee of the Communist-controlled PSUC, informed the author after the war that in February, 1937, three months before the crisis, "Pedro," the Comintern agent in Catalonia, told him and other leaders of his party that Negrín was favoured as Caballero's successor. See also Jesús Hernández, *Yo fuí un ministro de Stalin*, p. 71.

[37] *In Stalin's Secret Service*, pp. 100–101.

Caballero had been defeated and the Communists had triumphed. Within a few months the man who had enjoyed more real influence and popularity than any other left-wing politician at the outbreak of the Civil War had to all intents and purposes been reduced to impotence. Not only had he lost control of the UGT of Catalonia and the Federation of the Spanish Socialist Party in that region, not only had he been despoiled of his authority in the Unified Socialist Youth Federation, but he had been betrayed or forsaken by some of his closest collaborators as well as by countless supporters holding commanding positions in the ÚGT and in local Socialist units. On the other hand, the Communists, through their adroit permeation of almost the entire machinery of state, had risen within that same brief period from a position of insignificance to one where they virtually controlled the destinies of the anti-Franco camp.

But this power they themselves could never have achieved without the active support, the connivance, the unsuspecting good faith, and the obtuseness of others. As "El Campesino," the former Spanish Communist, quoted earlier in this volume,[38] asks: "With few exceptions, especially during the early part of the war, how many Spanish politicians and military men were there who did not welcome the Communist agents with open arms and refuse to play their game? At least I was a convinced Communist and my attitude had some logic to it; but what logic was there in the attitude adopted by the others? Without the lack of understanding and the complicity that were almost general would it have been possible, in the course of a few months, for a party, as weak numerically as the Communist Party, to penetrate—and nearly dominate—the whole governmental apparatus? Without this lack of understanding and complicity, could it have overthrown at first a Largo Caballero, supported by two organizations as powerful as the UGT and the CNT, then an Indalecio Prieto, and raised to power a Juan Negrín, its ambitious and docile tool?

"I am not trying to excuse my mistakes, but I should like everyone else to confess his own. If we Spanish Communists were guilty of abuses and iniquities and established our rule completely or were on the point of doing so, it was because the others, with few exceptions, did not rise to the occasion. The Communist parties [of the world] are strong in proportion as the other parties and trade union organizations are weak and vacillating and play their game. That was the lesson of Spain and that, today, is the lesson of Europe and the world. If they understand this lesson, they will save themselves, but if they do not, then they are lost."[39]

[38] See n. 39, p. 144, above.   [39] *Solidaridad Obrera*, Paris, March 11, 1951.

Bibliography

I. BOOKS AND PAMPHLETS

APPROXIMATELY two thousand five hundred books and pamphlets have been consulted, but since considerations of space do not permit a complete bibliographical listing, only those sources are given which have been cited in the text or in the footnotes, or which have been most helpful to the author. Books and pamphlets published before the Spanish Civil War have not been included unless they have actually been cited in this work. All publications marked with an asterisk are in private possession, but photographic reproductions, either of the entire publication or of the pages referred to in the present work, are in the Hoover Institute and Library. All other books and pamphlets listed are in one or more of the libraries specified at the beginning of this volume, unless otherwise stated.

Abad de Santillán, Diego. *After the Revolution*. New York: Greenberg, 1937.
——. *Los anarquistas y la reacción contemporánea*. Mexico City: Ediciones del Grupo Cultural "Ricardo Flores Magon," 1925.
——. *La bancarrota del sistema económico y político del capitalismo*. Buenos Aires: Ediciones Nervio, 1932.
——. *El organismo económico de la revolución. Cómo vivimos y cómo podríamos vivir en España*. Barcelona: Editorial Tierra y Libertad, 1938.
——. *Por qué perdimos la guerra*. Buenos Aires: Ediciones Imán, 1940.
——. *La revolución y la guerra en España*. Havana: Editorial "El Libro," 1938.
Actas del congreso regional de sindicatos de Levante celebrado en Alicante, en el Teatro Verano, los días 15, 16, 17, 18 y 19 de julio de 1937. Valencia: Publicaciones de la Confederación Regional del Trabajo de Levante, 1937.
Actas del pleno regional de grupos celebrado los días 1, 2 y 3 del mes de julio de 1937 Federación regional de grupos anarquistas de Cataluña. Federación Anarquista Ibérica, Comité Peninsular Prensa y Propaganda, 1937.
La agresión italiana. Documentos ocupados a las unidades italianas en la acción de Guadalajara. Valencia: Ministerio de Estado, 1937.
Aláiz, Felipe. *Indalecio Prieto. Padrino de Negrín y campeón anticomunista*. Toulouse: Ediciones "Páginas Libres," n.d.

Alba, Luz de. *19 de julio*. Montevideo: Colección Esfuerzo, 1937.

Aldana, B. F. *Como fué la guerra en Aragón*. Barcelona: Ediciones "Como Fué," 1937.

Algarra Rafegas, Comandante Antonio. *El asedio de Huesca*. Saragossa: Talleres Editoriales "El Noticiero," 1941.

Alianza CNT-UGT. Barcelona: Editorial Tierra y Libertad, 1938.

Allison Peers, E. *The Spanish Tragedy*. New York: Oxford University Press, 1937.

Alonso, Bruno. *La flota republicana y la guerra civil de España*. Mexico City: Imprenta Grafos, 1944.

Alvarez, Basilio. *España en el crisol*. Buenos Aires: Colección Claridad, 1937.

Alvarez, Segis. *La juventud y los campesinos*. Conferencia Nacional de Juventudes, enero de 1937. Valencia: JSU de España, 1937.

——. *Nuestra organización y nuestros cuadros*. Valencia: JSU de España, 1937.

Alvarez del Vayo, Julio. *Deux discours prononcés à la 101me session de la Societé des Nations*. Paris: Services d'Information du Rassemblement Universel pour la Paix, 1938.

——. *L'Espagne accuse*. Paris: Comité Franco-Espagnol, 1936.

——. *Freedom's Battle*. New York: Alfred A. Knopf, 1940.

——. *The Last Optimist*. New York: The Viking Press, 1950.

——. *Speech at the Council of the League of Nations, May, 1938*. London: Union of Democratic Control, 1938.

Un año de las brigadas internacionales. Madrid: Ediciones del Comisariado de las Brigadas Internacionales [1937?].

Ansaldo, Juan Antonio. *¿Para qué . . .? De Alfonso XIII a Juan III*. Buenos Aires: Editorial Vasca Ekin, S.R.L., 1951.

Araceli, Gabriel. *Valencia 1936*. Saragossa: Talleres Editoriales de "El Noticiero," 1939.

*Araquistain, Luis. *El comunismo y la guerra de España*. Carmaux (Tarn): 1939.

——. *Mis tratos con los comunistas*. Ediciones de la Secretaría de Propaganda del P.S.O.E. en Francia, n.d.

——. *La verdad sobre la intervención y la no-intervención en España*. Madrid: n.d.

Arrarás, Joaquín. *Memorias íntimas de Azaña*. Con anotaciones de Joaquín Arrarás. Madrid: Ediciones Españolas, S.A., 1939.

——. *El sitio del Alcázar de Toledo*. Saragossa: Editorial Heraldo de Aragón, 1937.

Asedio de Huesca. Huesca: Ayuntamiento de Huesca [1938?].

Asensio, General. *El General Asensio. Su lealtad a la república*. Barcelona: Artes Gráficas CNT [1938?].

L'assassinat de Andres Nin. Paris: Spartacus, 1939.

Avilés, Gabriel. *Tribunales rojos*. (Vistos por un abogado defensor.) Barcelona: Ediciones Destino, 1939.

Azaña, Manuel. *Madrid*. London: Friends of Spain, 1937.

——. *Speech by His Excellency the President of the Spanish Republic.* (January 21,

1937.) London: The Press Department of the Spanish Embassy in London [1937?].

Azaña, Manuel. *La velada en Benicarló.* Buenos Aires: Editorial Losada, 1939.

——. *A Year of War in Spain.* London: The Friends of Spain, 1937.

Azaretto, Manuel. *Las pendientes resbaladizas.* (Los anarquistas en España.) Prólogo de José A. Barrionuevo. Montevideo: Editorial "Germinal," 1939.

Aznar, Manuel. *Historia militar de la guerra de España.* Madrid: Ediciones "Idea," 1940.

Bakunin, M. A. *Bog i gosudarstvo.* New York: Union of Russian Workers of the City of New York, 1918.

——. *Gosudarstvennost i anarkhiia.* Petersburg–Moscow: 1922.

Barea, Arturo. *The Forging of a Rebel.* New York: Reynal Hitchcock, 1946.

Battaglione Garibaldi. Paris: Edizioni di Coltura Sociale, 1937.

Bayo, Capitán Alberto. *Mi desembarco en Mallorca.* (De la guerra civil española.) Guadalajara: Imprenta Gráfica, 1944.

Belforte, Generale Francesco. *La guerra civile in Spagna.* I. La disintegrazione dello stato. Milan: Istituto per gli studi di politica internazionale, 1938.

——. *La guerra civile in Spagna.* II. Gli interventi stranieri nella Spagna rossa. Milan: Istituto per gli studi di politica internazionale, 1939.

——. *La guerra civile in Spagna.* III. La campagna dei volontari italiani. Milan: Istituto per gli studi di politica internazionale, 1939.

——. *La guerra civile in Spagna.* IV. La campagna dei volontari italiani e la vittoria di Franco. Milan: Istituto per gli studi di politica internazionale, 1939.

Beloff, Max. *The Foreign Policy of Soviet Russia 1929–1941.* 2 vols. London, New York, Toronto: Oxford University Press, 1947.

Bernard, Ino. *Mola martir de España.* Granada: Editorial y Librería Prieto, 1938.

Bertrán Güell, Felipe. *Caudillo, profetas y soldados.* Madrid–Barcelona: Editorial Juventud, 1939.

——. *Preparación y desarrollo del alzamiento nacional.* Valladolid: Librería Santarén, 1938.

Bessie, Alvah. *Men in Battle.* New York: Charles Scribner's Sons, 1939.

Beumelburg, Werner. *Kampf um Spanien.* Die Geschichte der Legion Condor. Oldenburg–Berlin: Gerhard Stalling Verlag, 1939.

Bley, Wulf. *Das Buch der Spanien-Flieger.* Leipzig: Hase & Koehler, 1939.

Bollati, Ambrogio and Bono, Giulio del. *La guerra di Spagna.* Torino: Giulio Einaudi, Editore, 1937.

Borkenau, Franz. *The Spanish Cockpit.* London: Faber and Faber Ltd., 1937.

Borras, T. *Checas de Madrid.* Madrid: Escelicer, S.A., 1940.

Bowers, Claude. *My Mission to Spain.* New York: Simon and Schuster, 1954.

Brenan, Gerald. *The Spanish Labyrinth.* London: Cambridge University Press, 1943.

La brigada del amanecer. Valladolid: Librería Santarén, n.d.

Brockway, Fenner. *Workers' Front.* London: Secker and Warburg, 1938.

Buckley, Henry. *Life and Death of the Spanish Republic*. London: Hamish Hamilton, 1940.

Bullejos, José. *Europa entre dos guerras. 1918–1938*. Mexico City: Ediciones Castilla, 1945.

Cabo Giorla, Luis. *Primera conferencia nacional del P.S.U.C.* Ediciones del Departamento de Agitación y Propaganda del PSUC, 1937.

El camino de la victoria. Valencia: Gráficas Genovés [1936?].

"El Campesino," General. *La vie et la mort en U.R.S.S. 1939–1949*. Paris: Les Iles d'Or, Librairie Plon, 1950.

——. *Comunista en España y antistalinista en la U.R.S.S.* Mexico: Editorial Guarania, 1952.

Campoamor, Clara. *La révolution espagnole vue par une républicaine*. Paris: Librairie Plon, 1937.

Cánovas Cervantes, S. *Apuntes históricos de "Solidaridad Obrera."* Barcelona: Ediciones C.R.T., n.d.

——. *De Franco a Negrín pasando por el partido comunista*. Historia de la revolución española. Toulouse: Colección "Páginas Libres," n.d.

——. *Durruti y Ascaso. La CNT y la revolución de julio*. Toulouse: Ediciones "Páginas Libres," n.d.

Capo, José María. *España desnuda*. Havana: Publicaciones España, 1938.

Cardona Rosell, M. *Aspectos económicos de nuestra revolución*. Barcelona: Oficinas de Propaganda CNT–FAI, 1937.

Carrascal, G. *Asturias*. 18 julio 1936–21 octubre 1937. Valladolid: Imprenta y Librería Casa Martín, 1938.

Carrillo, Santiago. *En marcha hacia la victoria*. Conferencia nacional de juventudes. [Valencia?]: 1937.

——. *La juventud, factor de la victoria*. Valencia: Ediciones del Partido Comunista de España, 1937.

——. *Somos la organización de la juventud*. Madrid: n.d.

Carrillo, Wenceslao. *El último episodio de la guerra civil española*. Toulouse: La Secretaría de Publicaciones de la J.S.E. en Francia, 1945.

Casado, Colonel S. *The Last Days of Madrid*. London: Peter Davies Ltd., 1939.

Castro, Enrique. *Balance y perspectivas de nuestra guerra*. Barcelona: Ediciones del Partido Comunista de España, Comisión Nacional de Agit-Prop, 1937.

——. *J'ai perdu la foi a Moscou*. Paris: Gallimard, 1950.

——.*Hombres made in Moscú*. Mexico City; Publications Mañana, 1960.

Cattell, David T. *Communism and the Spanish Civil War*. Berkeley: University of California, 1955.

Ceyrat, Maurice. *La trahison permanente*. Parti communiste et politique russe. Paris: Spartacus, 1948.

Checa, Pedro. *A un gran partido, una gran organización*. Ediciones del Partido Comunista de España, Comisión Nacional de Agit-Prop, 1937.

——. *Qué es y cómo funciona el partido comunista*. Ediciones del Partido Comunista de España, n.d.

Checa, Pedro. *Tareas de organización y trabajo práctico del partido.* Madrid, Barcelona: Ediciones del Partido Comunista de España, 1938.

Churchill, Winston. *Arms and the Covenant.* London: George G. Harrap and Co., 1938.

——. *The Gathering Storm.* Boston: Houghton Mifflin Co., 1948.

Clavego, Pablo. *Algunas normas para el trabajo de los comisarios políticos.* Madrid: Ediciones Europa América [1937?].

Collectivisations. L'oeuvre constructive de la révolution espagnole. Recueil de documents. Avant-propos de A. Souchy. Place of publication not indicated, n.d.

Communist International Executive Committee, *XIII Plenum IKKI. Stenograficheskii Otchet.* Moscow: 1934.

Le contrat de travail dans la république espagnole. Madrid: Ministère du Travail et de Prévoyance, Gráficas Reunidas, 1937.

Contreras, Carlos J. *Nuestro gran ejército popular.* Barcelona: Ediciones del Partido Comunista de España, Comisión Nacional de Agit-Prop, 1937.

——. *La quinta columna.* Valencia: Ediciones del Partido Comunista de España [1937?].

Dashar, M. *The Revolutionary Movement in Spain.* New York: Libertarian Publishing Society, n.d.

Datos complementarios para la historia de España. Guerra de liberación 1936–1939. Madrid: 1945. (In University of California Library, Los Angeles.)

Davies, Joseph E. *Mission to Moscow.* New York: Simon and Schuster, 1941.

Decret de collectivizacions. Barcelona: Conselleria d'Economia, Generalitat de Catalunya, 1936.

Decret sobre la collectivització i control de la industria i el comerç a Catalunya. Barcelona: Conselleria d'Economia, Catalunya, Industries Grafiques Seix i Barral Germans, S.A., 1936.

De julio a julio. Un año de lucha. Barcelona: Ediciones Tierra y Libertad, 1937.

Deutscher, Isaac. *Stalin. A Political Biography.* New York and London: Oxford University Press, 1949.

Díaz, José. *Tres años de lucha.* Por el frente popular, por la libertad, por la independencia de España. Toulouse: Ediciones "Nuestro Pueblo," 1947.

Documents and Materials Relating to the Eve of the Second World War. Vol. II, Dirksen Papers 1938–1939. Moscow: Ministry of Foreign Affairs of the U.S.S.R. Foreign Language Publishing House, 1948.

Documents on German Foreign Policy. Series D. Vol. III, Germany and the Spanish Civil War, 1936–1939. Washington: Department of State, 1950.

Dodd, Ambassador. *Ambassador Dodd's Diary.* New York: Harcourt Brace and Co., 1941.

Domingo, Marcelino. *España ante el mundo.* Mexico City: Editorial "Mexico Nuevo," 1937.

Domínguez, Edmundo. *Los vencedores de Negrín.* Mexico City: Editorial Nuestro Pueblo, 1940.

Dzelepy, E. N. *The Spanish Plot.* London: P. S. King & Son Ltd., 1937.

Epistolario, Prieto y Negrín. Paris: Imprimerie Nouvelle, 1939.

España, su lucha y sus ideales. Documentos de Ossorio y Gallardo, Federica Montseny, Juan P. Fábregas, F. Marti Ibañez, García Oliver, H. Noja Ruiz. Buenos Aires: Editorial Acento, 1937.

*Estatutos de la federación nacional de campesinos. Valencia: 1937.

Les événements survenus en France de 1933 à 1945. Témoignages et documents recueillis par la commission d'enquête parlementaire. Vol. I. Paris: Presses Universitaires de France, n.d.

Exposure of the Secret Plan to Establish a Soviet in Spain. London: Published by the Friends of National Spain, n.d.

Fabbri, Luis. *Vida y pensamiento de Malatesta.* Barcelona: Editorial Tierra y Libertad, 1938.

Fábregas, Juan P. *Los factores económicos de la revolución española.* Barcelona: Oficinas de Propaganda CNT–FAI, 1937.

Falcón, César. *Madrid.* Madrid–Barcelona: Editorial Nuestro Pueblo, 1938.

Ferrándiz Alborz, F. *La bestia contra España.* Montevideo, 1951.

Fischer, Louis. *Men and Politics.* New York: Duell, Sloan and Pierce, 1941.

——. *Why Spain Fights On.* London: The Union of Democratic Control [1937?].

Francisco Largo Caballero. 1869–1946. Toulouse: Ediciones El Socialista, 1947.

Führing, Hellmut H. *Wir funken für Franco.* Verlag C. Bertelsmann Gütersloh, 1939.

Gabriel, José. *La vida y la muerte en Aragón.* Buenos Aires: Imán, Colección Realidades Ibéricas, 1938.

Galíndez, Jesús de. *Los vascos en el Madrid sitiado.* Buenos Aires: Editorial Vasca Ekin, 1945.

García, Regina. *Yo he sido marxista.* Madrid: Editora Nacional, 1946.

García Oliver, Juan. *El fascismo internacional y la guerra antifascista española.* Barcelona: Oficinas de Propaganda CNT–FAI, 1937.

García Pradas, J. *Antifascismo proletario.* Madrid: Ediciones "Frente Libertario," n.d.

——. *Rusia y España.* Paris: Ediciones "Tierra y Libertad," 1948.

——. *La traición de Stalin.* New York: Ediciones Cultura Proletaria, 1939.

Garibaldini in Ispagna. Madrid: 1937.

Garrachón Cuesta, Antonio. *De Africa a Cádiz y de Cádiz a la España Imperial.* Cádiz: Establecimientos Cerón, 1938.

Geraud, André (Pertinax). *The Gravediggers of France.* Garden City: Doubleday Doran & Co., 1944.

Gilabert, A. G. *Durruti, un anarquista íntegro.* Barcelona: Comité Nacional de la Confederación Nacional del Trabajo, n.d.

Giral, o una historia de sangre. Spain: Ediciones Combate, n.d.

Goded, Manuel. *Un "faccioso" cien por cien.* Saragossa: Talleres Editoriales Heraldo, 1939.

Gollonet, Angel and Morales, José. *Sangre y fuego, Málaga.* Granada: Editorial Imperio, 1937.

Gómez, Sócrates. *Los jóvenes socialistas y la JSU.* Madrid: Rivadeneyra, n.d.

Gómez Bajuelo, Gil. *Málaga bajo el dominio rojo.* Cadiz: Establecimientos Cerón, 1937.

Gómez Málaga, Juan. *Estampas trágicas de Madrid.* Avila: Tip. y Enc. de Senén Martín, n.d.

González, Valentín. See "El Campesino," General.

González Inestral, Miguel. *Cipriano Mera, revolucionario.* Cuba: Editorial Atalaya, S.A., 1943.

Gorkin, Julián. *Canibales políticos.* Mexico City: Ediciones Quetzal, S.A., 1941.

Gracia, Padre Vicente, S.J. *Aragón, baluarte de España.* Saragossa: Talleres Gráficos "El Noticiero," 1938.

Graf Hoyos, Max. *Pedros y Pablos.* Munich: Verlag F. Bruckmann, 1939.

Guadalajara. Madrid: Comisariado General de Guerra (Inspección Centro) Comisión de Propaganda, 1937.

Guzmán, Alfarache de. *¡18 de julio! Historia del alzamiento glorioso de Sevilla.* Seville: Editorial F.E., 1937.

Guzmán, Eduardo de. *Madrid, rojo y negro.* Barcelona: Editorial Tierra y Libertad, 1938.

Hernández, Jesús. *A los intelectuales de España.* Ediciones del Partido Comunista de España, Comisión Nacional de Agit-Prop, 1937.

——. *¡Atrás los invasores!* Barcelona: Ediciones del Partido Comunista de España, 1938.

——. *Negro y rojo. Los anarquistas en la revolución española.* Mexico City: La España Contemporánea, 1946.

——. *El orgullo de sentirnos españoles.* Barcelona: S.G. de Publicaciones [1938?].

——. *El partido comunista antes, durante y después de la crisis del gobierno Largo Caballero.* Valencia: Ediciones del Partido Comunista de España, 1937.

——. *Todo dentro del frente popular.* Ediciones del Partido Comunista de España, Comisión Nacional de Agit-Prop, 1937.

——. *Yo fuí un ministro de Stalin.* Mexico City: Editorial America, 1953.

*Hernández Zancajo, Carlos. *Tercera etapa de octubre.* Valencia: Editorial Meabe, 1937.

Hispanicus. *Foreign Intervention in Spain.* London: United Editorial Ltd., 1938.

Historia de la cruzada española. 12 vols. Madrid: Ediciones Españolas, S.A., 1940.

Historia de la revolución nacional española. 2 vols. Paris: La Sociedad Internacional de Ediciones y de Publicidad, 1940.

Homenaje del comité peninsular de la FAI a Buenaventura Durruti (1896–1936). En el segundo aniversario de su muerte. Barcelona: 1938.

How Mussolini Provoked the Spanish Civil War. London: United Editorial Ltd. [1938?].

Ibarruri, Dolores. *Ejército popular unido, ejército de la victoria.* Madrid–Barcelona: Ediciones del Partido Comunista de España, 1938.

Ibarruri, Dolores. *Es hora ya de crear el gran partido único del proletariado.* Madrid: Stajanov, 1937.

——. *No hay más posibilidad de gobernar que a través del frente popular.* Barcelona: Ediciones del Partido Comunista de España, 1938.

——. *Un pleno histórico.* Ediciones del Partido Comunista de España, Comisión Nacional de Agit-Prop, 1937.

——. *Speeches and Articles, 1936–38.* London: Lawrence and Wishart Ltd., 1938.

——. *Unión de todos los españoles. Por la independencia de España. Por la libertad. Por la república.* Madrid–Barcelona: Ediciones del Partido Comunista de España [1938?].

Iniesta, Juan de. *Escuchad, campesino.* Madrid: Ediciones de la Comisión de Propaganda del Comité Regional del Centro, 1937.

Iribarren, José María. *Con el General Mola. Escenas y aspectos inéditos de la guerra civil.* Saragossa: Librería General, 1937.

——. *Mola.* Saragossa: Heraldo de Aragón, 1938.

The Italian Air Force in Spain. London: United Editorial Ltd., n.d.

Iturburu, Cordova. *España bajo el comando del pueblo.* Buenos Aires: Acento, 1938.

Jellinek, Frank. *The Civil War in Spain.* London: Victor Gollancz Ltd., 1938.

Jiménez de Asua, Luis. *La constitución política de la democracia española.* Santiago de Chile: Ediciones Ercilla, 1942.

Joaniquet, Aurelio. *Calvo Sotelo.* Santander: Espasa-Calpe, S.A., 1939.

Kaminski, H. E. *Ceux de Barcelone.* Paris: Les Editions Denoël, 1937.

Keding, Karl. *Feldgeistlicher bei Legion Condor.* Berlin: Ostwerk-Verlag [1938?].

Kerillis, Henri de. *Français, voici la guerre!* Paris: Bernard Grasset, 1936.

Krivitsky, W. G. *In Stalin's Secret Service.* New York: Harper & Brothers, 1939.

Kropp, Major A. *So kämpfen deutsche Soldaten.* Berlin: Wilhelm Limpert Verlag, 1939.

Lacruz, Francisco. *El alzamiento, la revolución y el terror en Barcelona.* Barcelona: Librería Arysel, 1943.

Landau, Katia. *Le stalinisme en Espagne.* Paris: Spartacus, 1938.

The Land of Socialism Today and Tomorrow. Reports and Speeches at the Eighteenth Congress of the Communist Party of the Soviet Union (Bolshevik) March 10–21, 1939. Moscow: Foreign Language Publishing House, 1939.

Langdon-Davies, John. *Behind the Spanish Barricades.* New York: Robert M. McBride & Co., 1937.

Lapeyre, Aristide. *Le problème espagnol.* Paris: Edition "Ce qu'il faut dire," 1946.

Lapeyre, Paul. *Révolution et contre-révolution en Espagne.* Paris: Spartacus, 1938.

Largo Caballero, Francisco. *Discurso pronunciado en Valencia el día 1 de febrero de 1937*. Valencia: Comisariado General de Guerra, 1937.

———. *Discursos a los trabajadores*. Madrid: Gráfica Socialista, 1934.

———. *Mis recuerdos*. (Cartas a un amigo.) Mexico: Ediciones "Alianza," 1954.

*———. *¿Qué se puede hacer?* Paris: 1940.

———. *La UGT y la guerra*. Valencia: Editorial Meabe, 1937.

Last, Jef. *The Spanish Tragedy*. London: George Routledge & Sons Ltd., 1939.

Lazareff, Pierre. *Deadline*. New York: Random House, 1942.

Lazarillo de Tormes (Benigno Bejarano). *España cuna de la libertad*. Valencia: Ediciones "Ebro" [1937?].

———. *España, tumba del fascismo*. Valencia: Ediciones del Comité Nacional de la CNT, Sección Propaganda y Prensa [1938?].

Lent, Alfred. *Wir kämpften für Spanien*. Berlin: Gerhard Stalling Verlag, 1939.

Leval, Gaston. *Le communisme*. Paris: Les Editions du Libertaire, n.d.

———. *L'indispensable révolution*. Paris: Editions du Libertaire, 1948.

———. *Né Franco né Stalin*. Istituto Editoriale Italiano, Milan, 1952.

———. *Nuestro programa de reconstrucción*. Barcelona: Oficinas de Propaganda, CNT–FAI [1937?].

———. *Social Reconstruction in Spain*. London: Spain and the World, 1938.

Lévy, Louis. *Vérités sur la France*. England: Editions Pingouin, 1941.

Liébana, M. and Orizana, G. *El movimiento nacional*. Valladolid: Imp. Cat. Francisco G. Vicente, n.d.

Le livre blanc de l'intervention italienne en Espagne. Paris: Comité Franco-Espagnol, 1937.

Lizarra, A. de. *Los vascos y la república española*. Buenos Aires: Editorial Vasca Ekin, S.R.L., 1944.

Lladó i Figueres, J. *El 19 de julio a Barcelona*. [Barcelona?]: Biblioteca política de Catalunya, 1938.

Llovera, Fernando. *La columna Uribarry*. Valencia: Gráficas Turia [1937?].

Lloyd, Lord. *The British Case*. London: Eyre & Spottiswoode Ltd., 1939.

Lojendio, Luis María de. *Operaciones militares de la guerra de España*. Barcelona: Montaner y Simón, S.A., 1940.

Londonderry, The Marquess of. *Wings of Destiny*. London: Macmillan and Co. Ltd., 1943.

Longo, Luigi (Gallo). *Un anno di guerra in Spagna*. Paris: Edizioni di Coltura Sociale, 1938.

López, Capitán Antonio. *Defensa de Madrid*. Relato histórico. Mexico City: Editorial A. P. Márquez, S.A., 1945.

López, Juan. *Concepto del federalismo en la guerra y en la revolución*. Oficinas de Propaganda CNT–FAI, n.d.

López-Muñiz, Teniente Coronel de E. M. *La batalla de Madrid*. Madrid: Editorial Gloria, 1943.

Louzon, R. *La contra-revolución en España*. Buenos Aires: Ediciones Imán, 1938.

Madariaga, Salvador de. *España.* Buenos Aires: Editorial Sudamericana, 1942.

Manuel, Frank E. *The Politics of Modern Spain.* New York: McGraw-Hill Book Co. Inc., 1938.

Martín, J. *La transformation politique et sociale de la Catalogne durant la révolution.* 19 juillet–31 décembre, 1936. Generalitat de Catalunya, n.d.

Martín Blázquez, José. *I Helped to Build an Army.* London: Secker & Warburg, 1939.

Martín Retortillo, Cirilo. *Huesca vencedora.* Huesca: Editorial V. Campo y Compañía, 1938.

Martínez Abad, Julio. ¡ *17 de julio! La guarnición de Melilla inicia la salvación de España.* Melilla: Artes Gráficas Postal Express, 1937.

Martínez Barrio, Diego. *Orígenes del frente popular español.* Buenos Aires: PHAC, 1943.

——. *Páginas para la historia del frente popular.* Madrid–Valencia: Ediciones Españolas, 1937.

Martínez Leal, Comandante. *El asedio del Alcázar de Toledo.* Toledo: Editorial Católica Toledana, 1937.

Marty, André. *En Espagne . . . ou se joue le destin de l'Europe.* Paris: Bureau d'Editions, 1937.

Mateu, Julio. *La obra de la federación campesina.* Barcelona: Ediciones del Partido Comunista de España, 1937.

Mattioli, Guido. *L'aviazione legionaria in Spagna.* Rome: Editrice "L'Aviazione," 1938.

McGovern, John. *Terror in Spain.* London: Independent Labour Party [1937?].

Melchor, Federico. *Organicemos la producción.* Valencia: JSU de España, 1937.

★*Memoria del congreso extraordinario celebrado en Madrid los días 11 al 16 de junio de 1931.* Confederación Nacional del Trabajo. Barcelona: Tipógrafo Cosmos, n.d.

★*Memoria del congreso extraordinario de la confederación regional del trabajo de Cataluña celebrado en Barcelona los días 25 de febrero al 3 de marzo de 1937.* Barcelona: Talleres Gráficos Juan, 1937.

Memoria del Peninsular de Regionales. FAI. *Celebrado en Valencia los días 4, 5, 6 y 7 de julio, 1937.* Valencia: 1937.

★*Memoria del pleno regional de grupos anarquistas de Levante celebrado en Alicante, durante los días 11, 12, 13, 14 y 15 del mes de abril de 1937.* Federación Anarquista Ibérica. Valencia: Editorial "Nosotros" [1937?].

Merin, Peter. *Spain between Death and Birth.* New York: Dodge Publishing Co., 1938.

Micaud, Charles A. *The French Right and Nazi Germany 1933–1939.* Durham, North Carolina: Duke University Press, 1943.

Mije, Antonio. *El papel de los sindicatos en los momentos actuales.* Madrid–Valencia: Ediciones del Partido Comunista de España, 1937.

——. *Por una potente industria de guerra.* Barcelona: Ediciones del Partido Comunista de España, 1937.

Montiel, Francisco Félix. *Por qué he ingresado en el partido comunista.* Barcelona: Ediciones del Partido Comunista de España, Comisión Nacional de Agit-Prop, 1937.

Montseny, Federica. *La commune de Paris y la revolución española.* Conferencia pronunciada en el Cine Coliseum de Valencia el día 14 de marzo de 1937. Oficina de Información, Propaganda y Prensa del Comité Nacional CNT-FAI [1937?].

——. *María Silva. La libertaria.* Toulouse: Ediciones "Universo," 1951.

Morón, Gabriel. *Política de ayer y política de mañana.* Mexico City: Talleres Linotipográficos "Numancia," 1942.

Morrow, Felix. *The Civil War in Spain.* New York: Pioneer Publishers, 1938.

——. *Revolution and Counter-Revolution in Spain.* New York: Pioneer Publishers, 1938.

Munis, G. *Jalones de derrota: promesa de victoria.* [España 1930–39.] Mexico City: Editorial "Lucha Obrera," 1948.

Namier, L. B. *Diplomatic Prelude. 1938–1939.* London: Macmillan & Co. Ltd., 1948.

——. *Europe in Decay. 1936–1940.* London: Macmillan & Co. Ltd., 1950.

Nazi–Soviet Relations. 1939–1941. Documents from the Archives of the German Foreign Office. Edited by Raymond James Sontag and James Stuart Beddie. Washington: Department of State, 1948.

Negre, Juan. *¿Qué es el colectivismo anarquista?* Barcelona: Agrupación Anarquista, Los de Ayer y Los de Hoy, 1937.

Nothing but Danger. Thrilling adventures of ten newspaper correspondents in the Spanish War. Edited by Frank Hanighen. New York: Robert M. McBride & Co., 1939.

Nuestra lucha por la unidad. Valencia: J.S.U. [1937?].

Nuestro programa y el de la CNT. Valencia: Ediciones del Partido Comunista de España, 1937.

Nuñez Morgado, Aurelio. *Los sucesos de España vistos por un diplomático.* Buenos Aires: Talleres Gráficos L. J. Rosso, 1941.

d'Ormesson, Wladimir. *France.* London: Longmans, Green & Co., 1939.

Orwell, George. *Homage to Catalonia.* London: Secker & Warburg, 1938.

Ossorio y Gallardo, Angel. *Discursos pronunciados los días 25 de agosto y 6 de septiembre de 1936 respectivamente.* Madrid: Socorro Rojo Internacional, 1936.

——. *Mis memorias.* Buenos Aires: Editorial Losada, 1946.

——. *Vida y sacrificio de Companys.* Buenos Aires: Editorial Losada, S.A., 1943.

Pacciardi, Randolfo. *Il battaglione garibaldi.* Lugano: Nuove Edizioni di Capolago, 1938.

Padelford, Norman J. *International Law and Diplomacy in the Spanish Civil Strife.* New York: The Macmillan Co., 1939.

Palacio, Solano. *La tragedia del norte.* Barcelona: Ediciones "Tierra y Libertad," 1938.

El partido comunista por la libertad y la independencia de España. (Llamamientos y discursos.) Valencia: Ediciones del P.C. de E. (S.E. de la I.C.), Comisión Nacional de Agitación y Propaganda, 1937.

El partido comunista y la unidad antifascista. Valencia: Ediciones de la Sección de Prensa y Propaganda del Comité Peninsular de la FAI, 1937.

Peirats, José. *La CNT en la revolución española.* Vols. I, II, III. Toulouse: Ediciones C.N.T, 1951, 1952, and 1953 respectively.

Peiró, Juan. *Perill a la reraguarda.* Pròleg de Julià Gual. Mataró: Edicions Llibertat, n.d.

——. *Problemas del sindicalismo y del anarquismo.* Toulouse: E.M.L.E., 1945.

——. *Problemas y cintarazos.* Prólogo de Domingo Torres. Rennes: Imprimeries Réunies, 1946.

Penchienati, Carlo. *Brigate internazionali in Spagna.* Delitti della "Ceka" comunista. Milan: Edizioni "Echi del Secolo," 1950.

Pérez Madrigal, Joaquín. *Augurios, estallido y episodios de la guerra civil.* Avila: Imp. y Enc. Sigirano Díaz, 1938.

Pérez Salas, Coronel Jesús, *Guerra en España.* (1936–1939.) Con un prólogo del Coronel D. Mariano Salafranca, diplomado de Estado Mayor y Abogado. Mexico City: 1947.

Pérez Solis, Oscar. *Sitio y defensa de Oviedo.* Valladolid–Palencia: Afrodisio Aguado, 1938.

La persécution religieuse en Espagne. Paris: Librairie Plon, 1937.

Plá, José. *Historia de la segunda república española.* Vol. IV. Barcelona: Destino, 1941.

Política del frente popular en agricultura. Madrid–Valencia: Ediciones Españolas, 1937.

Ponce, Anibal. *Examen de la España actual.* Montevideo: Ediciones "Mundo," 1938.

Por la revolución agraria. Madrid: Federación Española de Trabajadores de la Tierra, UGT, 1937.

Prader, Jean. *Au secours de l'Espagne socialiste.* Paris: Spartacus, 1936.

Prats, Alardo. *Vanguardia y retaguardia de Aragón.* Buenos Aires: Ediciones Perseo, 1938.

Prieto, Horacio. *El anarquismo español en la lucha política.* Paris: 1946.

——. *Marxismo y socialismo libertario.* Paris: Ediciones Madrid, n.d.

Prieto, Indalecio. *Cómo y por qué salí del ministerio de defensa nacional.* Mexico City: Impresos y Papeles, S. de R.L., 1940.

——. *Inauguración del círculo "Pablo Iglesias" de México.* Mexico City: 1940.

——. *Palabras al viento.* Mexico City: Ediciones Minerva, 1942.

Primo de Rivera, José Antonio. *Discursos frente al parlamento.* Barcelona: Ediciones F.E., 1939.

Programa de acción común para la creación del partido único del proletariado. Valencia: Ediciones del Partido Comunista de España, 1937.

Programa de unidad de acción entre UGT–CNT. Barcelona: Ediciones Españolas, 1938.

Propaganda y cultura en los frentes de guerra. Valencia: Ministerio de la Guerra, Comisariado General de Guerra, 1937.

Prudhommeaux, A. and D. *Catalogne libertaire 1936–1937. L'armement du peuple. Que sont la CNT et la FAI?* Paris: Spartacus, 1946.

Puente, Isaac. *Finalidad de la CNT. El comunismo libertario*. Barcelona: Ediciones "Tierra y Libertad," 1936.

——. *Propaganda*. Barcelona: Editorial "Tierra y Libertad," 1938.

Puig Mora, E. (El Ciudadano Desconocido). *La tragedia roja en Barcelona*. Saragossa: Librería General, 1937.

Queipo de Llano, Rosario. *De la cheka de Atadell a la prisión de Alacuas*. Valladolid: Librería Santarén, 1939.

Rabasseire, Henri. *Espagne creuset politique*. Paris: Editions Fustier, 1938.

Ramos Oliveira, Antonio. *Politics, Economics and Men of Modern Spain, 1808–1946*. London: Victor Gollancz Ltd., 1946.

Ravines, Eudocio. *La gran estafa*. Mexico City: Libros y Revistas, S.A., 1952.

Raymundo, Francisco J. de. *Cómo se inició el glorioso movimiento nacional en Valladolid y la gesta heroica del Alto del León*. Valladolid: Imprenta Católica, 1936.

La reforma agraria en España. Valencia: Instituto de Reforma Agraria, 1937.

La reforma agraria y los problemas del campo bajo la república española. Buenos Aires: Servicio Español de Información, "Prensa Hispánica" [1938?].

Regler, Gustav. *The Great Crusade*. New York: Longmans, Green & Co., 1940.

Reparaz, Capitán, y Souza, Tresgallo de. *Desde el cuartel general de Miaja, al santuario de la Virgen de la Cabeza*. Valladolid: Artes Gráficas Afrodisio Aguado, 1937.

Reynaud, Paul. *La France a sauvé l'Europe*. Vol. I. Paris: Flammarion, 1947.

Richards, V. *Lessons of the Spanish Revolution (1936–1939)*. London: Freedom Press, 1953.

Rio Tinto Company Limited. Report of the Transactions at the Sixty-Third Ordinary General Meeting. London: April 24, 1936.

Rocker, Rudolf. *Anarcho-Syndicalism*. London: Secker & Warburg, 1938.

——. *Extranjeros en España*. Buenos Aires: Colección Realidades Ibéricas, Imán, 1938.

Rodriguez de Cueto, José. *Epopeya del santurario de Santa María de la Cabeza*. San Sebastian: Editorial Española, S.A., 1939.

Rojo, General Vicente. *¡Alerta los pueblos!* Estudio político-militar del periodo final de la guerra española. Buenos Aires: Aniceto López, 1939.

Rolfe, Edwin. *The Lincoln Battalion*. New York: Random House, 1939.

Romano, Julio. *Sanjurjo*. Madrid: Imprenta de la Viuda de Juan Pueyo, 1940.

Romero, Coronel Luis. *Impresiones de un militar republicano*. Barcelona: Oficinas de Propaganda CNT–FAI [1937?].

Romero Solano, L. *Vísperas de la guerra de España.* Prólogo de Indalecio Prieto. Mexico City: El Libro Perfecto, S.A., 1947.

Romilly, Esmond. *Boadilla.* London: Hamish Hamilton, 1937.

Rosselli, Carlo. *Oggi in Spagna, domani in Italia.* Paris: Edizioni di giustizia i libertà, 1938.

Rubió i Tudurí, Mariano. *La justicia en Catalonia.* 19 de julio de 1936–19 de febrero de 1937. Paris: 1937.

Ruediger, Helmut. *Ensayo crítico sobre la revolución española.* Buenos Aires: Colección Realidades Ibéricas, Imán, 1940.

Rust, William. *Britons in Spain.* London: Lawrence and Wishart Ltd., 1939.

Sáenz, Vicente. *España en sus gloriosas jornadas de julio y agosto de 1936.* San José, Costa Rica: Imprenta "La Tribuna," 1936.

———. *España heroica.* New York: Editorial Iberoamericana, 1938.

Sánchez del Arco, Manuel. *El sur de España en la reconquista de Madrid.* Sevilla: Editorial Sevillana, 1937.

Sanz, Ricardo. *Buenaventura Durruti.* Toulouse: Ediciones "El Frente," 1945.

Schempp, Otto. *Das autoritäre Spanien.* Leipzig: Wilhelm Goldmann Verlag, 1939.

Schlayer, Felix. *Diplomat im roten Madrid.* Berlin: F. A. Herbig Verlagsbuchhandlung, 1938.

Segundo congreso del partido socialista obrero español en el exilio. Toulouse: May, 1946.

Serrano Poncela, Segundo. *La conferencia nacional de juventudes.* Valencia: JSU de España 1937.

Serrano Suñer, Ramón. *Entre Hendaya y Gibraltar.* (Frente a una leyenda.) Madrid: Ediciones y Publicaciones Españolas, S.A., Madrid, 1947.

Siete de octubre: una nueva era en el campo. Madrid: Ministerio de Agricultura, 1936.

Silva, José. *La revolución popular en el campo.* Ediciones del Partido Comunista de España [1937?].

Sommerfield, John. *Volunteer in Spain.* New York: Alfred A. Knopf, 1937.

Somoza Silva, Lázaro. *El General Miaja.* Biografía de un heroe. Mexico City: Editorial Tyris, 1944.

Souchy Bauer, Agustín. *Entre los campesinos de Aragón.* Barcelona: Ediciones Tierra y Libertad [1937?].

Los soviets en España. La lucha por el poder, por la república obrero y campesina en España. Paris: Editorial Sudam, 1935.

Stache, Rud. *Armee mit geheimen Auftrag.* Bremen: Henry Burmester Verlag, n.d.

Stackelberg, Karl-Georg von. *Legion Condor.* Deutsche Freiwillige in Spanien. Berlin: Verlag Die Heimbücherei, 1939.

Steer, G. L. *The Tree of Gernika.* London: Hodder and Stoughton Ltd., 1938.

Strong, Anna Louise. *Spain in Arms, 1937.* New York: Henry Holt & Co., 1937.

Tabouis, Genevieve. *Blackmail or War.* England: Penguin Books Ltd., 1938.

——. *Ils l'ont appelée Cassandre.* New York: Editions de la Maison Française Inc., 1942.

Tasis i Marca, Rafael. *La revolución en los ayuntamientos.* Paris: Talleres Tipográficos "Associación Hispanophile de France," 1937.

Tedeschi, Paolo. *Guadalajara.* Paris: Edizioni di Coltura Sociale, 1937.

Téry, Simone. *Front de la liberté.* Paris: Editions Sociales Internationales, 1938.

Three Years of Struggle in Spain. London: The Freedom Press, 1939.

Torriente Brau, Pablo de la. *Peleando con los milicianos.* Mexico City: Editorial "México Nuevo," 1938.

Toryho, Jacínto. *La independencia de España.* Barcelona: Editorial Tierra y Libertad, 1938.

——. *La traición del Señor Azaña.* New York: Ediciones de la Federación Libertaria, 1939.

Trautloft, Hannes. *Als Jagdflieger in Spanien.* Berlin: Albert Nauch & Co., n.d.

Trial of the Major War Criminals before the International Military Tribunal. Nuremberg. November 14, 1945–October 1, 1946. Vol. X. Nuremberg: 1947.

Tschapaiew. Das Bataillon der 21 Nationen. Madrid: Imprenta Colectiva Torrent, 1938.

Uhse, Bodo. *Die erste Schlacht.* Strasbourg: Editions Prométhée, 1938.

Urales, Federico. *La anarquía al alcance de todos.* Barcelona: Ediciones de la Revista Blanca, 1932.

Uribarry Barutell, Manuel. *Sin contestar.* Valencia: Imprenta J. Ruig, 1937.

Uribe, Vicente. *Los campesinos y la república.* Valencia: Ediciones del Partido Comunista de España, n.d.

——. *Nuestra labor en el campo.* Barcelona: Ediciones del Partido Comunista de España, 1937.

——. *Nuestros hermanos los campesinos.* Valencia: Ediciones del Partido Comunista de España, 1937.

——. *La política agraria del partido comunista.* Valencia: Ediciones del Partido Comunista de España, 1937.

La victoria exije el partido único del proletariado. Valencia: Ediciones del Partido Comunista de España, 1937.

Villanueva, Francisco. *Azaña, el gobierno.* Mexico City: Editorial Moderna, 1941.

Vita, A. de. *Battaglione garibaldi.* (Ottobre 1936–Aprile 1937.) Paris: Edizione di Coltura Sociale, 1937.

Weizsäcker, Ernst von. *Memoirs of Ernst von Weizsäcker.* Chicago: Henry Regnery Co., 1951.

Welles, Sumner. *The Time for Decision.* New York: Harper & Brothers, 1944.

Werth, Alexander. *Which Way France?* New York and London: Harper and Brothers, 1937.

Wintringham, Tom. *English Captain.* London: Faber and Faber Ltd., 1939.

Wolfe, Bertram. *Civil War in Spain*. New York: Workers' Age Publishers, 1937.

Zugazagoitia, Julián. *Historia de la guerra en España*. Buenos Aires: Editorial La Vanguardia, 1940.

II. DOCUMENTS

This list includes all items referred to in the text or in the footnotes, but does not include a large number of other important documents consulted, which are available in the Hoover Institute and Library and in the Library of Congress.

Actas de la junta de defensa de Madrid. (The Library of Congress.)

Aguirre y Lecube, José Antonio de. Report to the central government by José Antonio Aguirre, Premier of the autonomous Basque Government. (A microfilm copy of the first ninety-five pages of this report, loaned to the author by Manuel de Irujo, is in the Hoover Institute and Library.)

Barcelona Traction, Light and Power Company, Limited. Statements issued on September 3 and November 16, 1936. (Public Library of Toronto.)

Bolloten, Burnett. Dispatch from Valencia to the United Press. Extracts from Largo Caballero's unpublished statement to British Members of Parliament on December 4, 1936. (The Hoover Institute and Library.)

Duque, José. "La situación de Aragón al comienzo de la guerra." Unpublished manuscript, given to the author by José Duque. (Hoover Institute and Library.)

Fernández Ballesteros, Alberto. Reports to the General Commissariat of War, dated February 18 and March 12, 1937. (Typewritten copies of these documents, made from the originals, which were loaned to the author by Gabriel García Maroto, Sub-Commissar General of Propaganda, are in the Hoover Institute and Library.)

Irujo, Manuel de. "La guerra civil en Euzkadi antes del estatuto." (A microfilm copy of this unpublished work, loaned to the author by Manuel de Irujo, is in the Hoover Institute and Library.)

Lazarillo de Tormes (Benigno Bejarano). "Les morts ne vous pardonnent pas." (A photographic reproduction of some of the pages of this unpublished work, loaned to the author by José Peirats, are in the Hoover Institute and Library.)

Miaja, General José. Communication sent to Largo Caballero, dated May 1, 1937. (A copy of this document, signed by Miaja and by the political and military chiefs of the Central Army, is in the Library of Congress.)

Ruediger, Helmut. *Informe para el congreso extraordinario de la AIT.* (December 6, 1937.) (University of Michigan Library, Labadie Collection.)

——. Report to the AIT, dated May 8, 1937. (The Hoover Institute and Library.)

Unpublished article by a regular army corporal. (A photostatic copy of this document, loaned to the author by Jordi Arquer, is in the Hoover Institute and Library.)

Verbatim report of a meeting of political and military leaders on the Aragon front in September, 1936. (Hoover Institute and Library.)

Villalba, Colonel José. Report on the fall of Malaga to the Higher War Council, dated February 12, 1937. (A typewritten copy of this document, made from the original, which was loaned to the author by Colonel Villalba, is in the Hoover Institute and Library.)

III. NEWSPAPERS AND PERIODICALS

This list includes only those newspapers and periodicals actually cited in the text or in the footnotes.

ABC, Seville.

Acción Libertaria. Boletín Informativo sobre España, Buenos Aires.

Acción Socialista, Paris.

Acracia, Lérida.

L'Action Française, Paris.

Adelante, Marseilles.

Adelante, Mexico City.

Adelante, Valencia.

El Adelanto, Salamanca.

L'Adunata dei Refrattari, New York.

The Atlantic Monthly, Boston.

Avant, Barcelona.

La Batalla, Barcelona.

Boletín de Información CNT–FAI, Barcelona.

Boletín de Información (CNT National Committee), Valencia.

Boletín de Información y Orientación Orgánica del Comité Peninsular de la Federación Anarquista Ibérica, Barcelona.

The Canadian Forum, Toronto (Public Library of Toronto).

Castilla Libre, Madrid.

Claridad, Madrid.

CNT, Madrid.

CNT, Paris.

CNT, Toulouse.

CNT–FAI–AIT Informationsdienst, Barcelona.

Colectivismo, Valencia.

Combat, Paris.

The Communist International, London.

Correo de Asturias, Buenos Aires.

La Correspondance Internationale, Paris.

La Correspondencia de Valencia, Valencia.

La Correspondencia Internacional, Paris.

Cultura Proletaria, New York.

Cultura y Acción, Alcañiz.
Daily Herald, London.
Daily Mail, London.
Daily Telegraph, London.
Daily Worker, London.
El Debate, Madrid.
Democracia, Madrid.
Dépêche de Toulouse, Toulouse.
El Día Gráfico, Barcelona.
Dialéctica, Havana.
Diario de Burgos, Burgos.
Diari Oficial de la Generalitat de Catalunya, Barcelona.
Diario Oficial del Ministerio de la Guerra, Madrid. [Published in Valencia after November 7, 1936.]
Documentos Históricos de España, Buenos Aires.
L'Ere Nouvelle, Paris.
Espagne Antifasciste, Paris.
España Libre, New York.
España Libre, Toulouse.
Espagne Nouvelle, Montpellier.
España Popular, Mexico City.
España Republicana, Buenos Aires.
Le Forze Armate, Rome.
Fragua Social, Valencia.
Frente Libertario, Madrid.
Frente Rojo, Valencia. [Published in Barcelona in November, 1937.]
Frente y Retaguardia. [Place of publication not indicated.]
Gaceta de la República, Valencia.
Gaceta de Madrid, Madrid.
Heraldo de Aragón, Saragossa.
Hoy, Mexico City.
La Humanitat, Barcelona.
L'Humanité, Paris.
Ideas, Hospitalet.
Independent News, Paris.
Informaciones, Madrid.
Inquiétudes, Bordeaux.
Internacional, Paris.
International Press Correspondence, London.
Izvestiia, Moscow.
Le Jour, Paris.
Journal des Débats, Paris.
Juventud Libre, Madrid.
The Labour Monthly, London.

The Left News, London.
La Libertad, Madrid.
Le Libertaire, Paris.
The Listener, London.
Luz y Fuerza, Barcelona.
Manchester Guardian, Manchester.
Mar y Tierra, Altea.
El Mercantil Valenciano, Valencia.
*Milicia Popular, Madrid.
Modern Monthly, New York.
Mujeres Libres, Barcelona.
Mundo, Mexico City.
Mundo Obrero, Madrid.
Mundo Obrero, Paris.
The Nation, New York.
The National Review, London.
The New Republic, New York.
The New York Herald Tribune, New York.
The New York Times, New York.
La Noche, Barcelona.
El Norte de Castilla, Valladolid.
Nosotros, Valencia.
Las Noticias, Barcelona.
El Noticiero, Saragossa.
El Noticiero Universal, Barcelona.
La Nouvelle Espagne Antifasciste, Paris.
Nuestra Bandera, Barcelona.
Nuestra España, Havana.
El Obrero de la Tierra, Madrid.
The Observer, London.
Orientaciones Nuevas.
Pasaremos, Madrid.
El Pensamiento Navarro, Pamplona.
El Poble Català, Mexico City.
Política, Madrid.
Pravda, Moscow.
El Pueblo, Valencia.
Regeneración, Mexico City.
La République, Paris.
La Revista Blanca, Barcelona.

* This periodical is not available in any of the libraries listed at the beginning of this volume, or in any other library as far as the author knows, but
typewritten copies of the principal items, which were made from a collection
loaned to the author by Carlos Contreras, are in the Hoover Institute and
Library.

La Révolution Prolétarienne, Paris.
Il Risveglio Anarchico, Geneva.
Ruta, Barcelona.
El Socialista, Algiers.
El Socialista, Madrid.
El Socialista, Paris.
Socialist Review, New York.
El Sol, Madrid.
Solidaridad Obrera, Barcelona.
Solidaridad Obrera, Mexico City.
Solidaridad Obrera, Paris.
Die Soziale Revolution, Barcelona.
Spanish Labor Bulletin, Chicago.
Spanish Revolution, New York.
Spartacus, Alicante.
The Sunday Times, London.
Le Temps, Paris.
Tiempo, Mexico City.
Tiempos Nuevos, Barcelona.
Tierra y Libertad, Barcelona.
Tierra y Libertad, Mexico City.
The Times, London.
Timón, Barcelona.
Timón, Buenos Aires.
Treball, Barcelona.
Tribuna, Mexico City.
Ultima Hora, Barcelona.
Umanità Nova, Rome.
Umbral, Barcelona.
Unión, Seville.
El Universal, Mexico City.
Universo, Toulouse.
La Vanguardia, Barcelona.
Verdad, Valencia.
La Veu de Catalunya, Barcelona.
Vía Libre, New York.
The Volunteer for Liberty, Madrid.
La Voz Valenciana, Valencia.
Die Wehrmacht, Berlin.
Workers' Age, New York.

Acknowledgments

(See Foreword, p. 10)

Diego Abad de Santillán.
Francisco Aguilera (Library of Congress).
Marcos Alcón.
José Almudí.
Luis Araquistain.
Jordi Arquer.
General José Asensio.
Arturo Barea.
Ralph Bates.
Nicolás Bernal.
Biblioteca Universitaria de Barcelona.
Bibliothèque Nationale de Paris (Photographic Service).
Betty F. Bolloten.
The British Museum (Newspaper Library and Photographic Service).
José Bullejos.
Cambridge University Press.
Severino Campos.
Captain Aniceto Carbajal.
F. P. Carbajal.
Mariano Cardona Rosell.
Wenceslao Carrillo.
Ralph H. Carruthers (New York Public Library).
Enrique Castro.
Carlos Contreras.
James Crafts (Hoover Institute and Library).
Peter Davies Ltd.
Ricardo del Río.
Duell, Sloan & Pearce, Inc.
José Duque.
Les Editions Denoël.
Editorial La Vanguardia.

Editorial Losada, S.A.
Editorial Sudamericana, S.A.
Sylvia England.
Antonio Escribano.
X. J. Eudin.
Faber and Faber Ltd.
Febus news agency (members of the Civil War staff, Valencia).
F. Ferrándiz Alborz.
Gerritt E. Fielstra (New York Public Library).
H. H. Fisher (Hoover Institute and Library).
Jesús de Galíndez.
Gabriel García Maroto.
Juan García Oliver.
J. García Pradas.
Alejandro García Val.
Antoni Gilabert.
José Giral.
Colonel Juan Gómez.
F. González.
Charles L. Grace (Harvard College Library).
Howard Green.
Rachel and Robert Green.
Harcourt, Brace and Company Inc.
Harper & Brothers.
Hemeroteca Municipal de Madrid.
Ignacio Hidalgo de Cisneros.
Donald C. Holmes (Library of Congress).
Henry Holt and Company Inc.
Agnes Inglis (University of Michigan Library).
Andrés María de Irujo.
Manuel de Irujo.
Miguel Jiménez.
Charles F. Keyser (Library of Congress).
Alfred A. Knopf Inc.
Gaston Leval.
Lena Lever.
Ramón Liarte.
Le Libertaire.
Librairie Plon.
The Library of Congress (Division of Manuscripts).
Rodolfo Llopis.
Macmillan & Co. Ltd.
Salvador de Madariaga.
J. Martín Blázquez.

Pedro Martínez Cartón.

S. Martínez Dasi.

Robert M. McBride and Company.

McGraw-Hill Book Company Inc.

Philip T. McLean (Hoover Institute and Library).

Federica Montseny.

Constancia de la Mora.

José Muñoz López.

Margarita Nelken.

Paul North Rice (New York Public Library).

Eduardo Orozco y G. ("El Pintor").

Oxford University Press Inc.

Randolfo Paccidardi.

H. S. Parsons (Library of Congress).

Concha Patiño.

Arline B. Paul (Hoover Institute and Library).

José Peirats.

Jesús Pérez Salas.

Jacobo Prince.

Eugene B. Power.

General Sebastián Pozas.

Putnam & Co. Ltd.

A. Ramos Oliveira.

Gustav Regler.

Ludwig Renn.

Reynal & Hitchcok Inc.

Warner Rice (University of Michigan).

Miguel Robledo.

Felipe Sánchez Román.

William T. Sayre-Smith.

Manuel Schwartzmann.

Martin Secker and Warburg Ltd.

Miguel Serra Pamies.

Agustín Souchy.

Luis Suárez.

Leopoldo Suárez del Real.

Alma Tapia.

Toronto Public Library.

Manuel Vidal.

The Viking Press Inc.

Colonel José Villalba.

Antonio Villanueva.

Victor Zaragoza.

INDEX

Index

(q. = quoted, coll. = collectivization, throughout)